Persuasion and Social Movements

Fourth Edition

Persuasion and Social Movements

Fourth Edition

Charles J. Stewart
Purdue University

Craig Allen Smith
Wayne State University

Robert E. Denton, Jr.
*Virginia Polytechnic Institute
and State University*

WAVELAND
PRESS, INC.
Prospect Heights, Illinois

For information about this book, write or call:
Waveland Press, Inc.
P.O. Box 400
Prospect Heights, Illinois 60070
(847) 634-0081
www.waveland.com

Cover photo by Bjorgen of the *Minneapolis Star-Tribune*.
Permission granted by the Minnesota Historical Society.

Printed in the United States of America

7 6 5 4 3 2 1

CONTENTS

PREFACE

The history of the United States has arguably been a history of social movements. A social movement precipitated the Revolutionary War for independence in the eighteenth century. The nineteenth century witnessed movements to free the slaves, end child labor, improve the plight of industrial workers and farmers, gain rights for women, temper or abolish the use of alcoholic beverages, and improve animal welfare. The twentieth century saw the continuation of many of these movements as well as those for peace, the environment, abortion rights, changes in U.S. culture, suffrage for women, and the rights of African Americans, Native Americans, Hispanic Americans, Asian Americans, the elderly, gays and lesbians, students, and animals. The twenty-first century appears to be a continuation of these movements and the timeless struggles between those on the social, political, and religious left and right.

Regardless of the pervasiveness of social movements in U.S. history, we have only recently begun to study social movements systematically. Studies of social movements were encouraged in the field of communication as early as 1923, but the first serious discussion of how one should study the persuasive efforts of social movements did not appear until 1947 when S. Judson Crandell discussed social movement patterns developed by social psychologists and offered suggestions to the prospective rhetorical analyst. Five years later, Leland Griffin's "The Rhetoric of Historical Movements" presented a rudimentary rhetorical pattern for movement studies and a workable approach to the analysis of social movements. The 1950s and 1960s witnessed an increased interest in the persuasive dimensions of social movements, but most studies focused on biographical accounts of a few social movement leaders, such as woman's rights leader Susan B. Anthony, and attempted to demonstrate that public speaking was central in movements' persuasive efforts.

The state of affairs changed rapidly with the dawn of the 1970s, undoubtedly in part because social movements had become commonplace on college campuses and could no longer be avoided or ignored. Three publications more than any others helped us turn an intellectual corner. Herbert Simons published "Requirements, Problems, and Strategies: A Theory of Persuasion for Social Movements" in 1970. He synthesized the notions of social-psychological resources, situational tasks, and rhetorical adaptation into an emphasis on the social movement's management of its persuasive resources—a leader-centered approach to social movements. *The Rhetoric of Agitation and Control,* by John Waite Bowers and Donovan Ochs, appeared the next year. It was the first book about persuasion and social movements that was not primarily a collection of speeches and the first to focus on the methods institutions employ to counter the persuasive efforts of social movements. In 1972, Simons wrote "Persuasion in Social Conflicts: A Critique of Prevailing Conceptions and a Framework for Future Research," arguing that most previous research had reflected an establishment bias by focusing on persuasive tactics more appropriate for the drawing room than for the streets.

The contributions of these three works are evident in both the quantity and quality of social movement studies since the early 1970s and in the structure and philosophy of this book. Many communication journals have included at least one "movement" study in each issue, and in 1980 and 1991 entire issues of the *Central States Speech Journal* and *Communication Studies* were devoted to the study of persuasion and social movements. Literally hundreds of articles and book chapters during the past three decades have generated thought-provoking results, research approaches, and controversies. Many students of persuasion and social movements—whether undergraduates, graduates, or professors—have experienced difficulties in understanding and using these results and approaches and in resolving the controversies that have often appeared in brief and highly sophisticated journal articles. We first conceived this book as a solution to this state of affairs. Our purpose since the first edition in 1984 has been fourfold: to synthesize, apply, extend, and develop findings, theories, and approaches to the persuasive efforts of social movements.

Chapters 1, 2, and 3 of this fourth edition address the role of persuasion in social movements and include topics that explore the characteristics of social movements, the social movement from an interpretive systems perspective, and the persuasive functions of social movements. Chapters 4, 5, and 6 address personal needs and social movements (focusing on authoritarian and democratic personalities), the nature of leadership and how it is attained and maintained, and the typical life cycle of social movements. Chapters 7, 8, and 9 address symbolism and symbolic acts in social movements, including the strategies of identification and polarization, the use of slogans, obscenity, and ridicule, and the persuasive functions of music. Chapters 10, 11, 12, and 13 address argument in social movement persuasion, including types of political argument, argument from narrative vision, argument from transcendence, and argument from conspiracy. And chapter 14 addresses the strategies institutions and counter-movements use to resist social movements.

This fourth edition contains new chapters on identification and polarization and on argument from conspiracy. All other chapters are updated in research cited, examples, the use of the Internet that has become prevalent since the third edition, and new insights into social movement persuasion. For example, the treatment of persuasive functions that a social movement must fulfill to bring about or stifle change now includes altering self-perceptions of protestors and legitimizing the social movement. Considerable attention is devoted to recent movements such as animal rights, militias, the religious right, workers' rights in sweatshops, and the rising resistance to the globalization of the economy and production. The selected bibliography is reorganized and updated to the summer of 2000.

We have approached this book once again with five fundamental assumptions. First since persuasion is inherently practical, we can study it most profitably by examining the functions of persuasive acts. Second, even apparently irrational acts make sense to the actor; the trick is discovering the reasoning behind the act. Third, people create and comprehend their world through symbols, and it is people who create, use, ignore, or act upon these symbolic creations. Fourth, public speeches are an important form of social movement persuasion, but they are neither the most prevalent nor necessarily the most effective form. The Internet is rapidly becoming a major resource for protest activities of all sorts. And fifth, social movements are rarely mere instances of orneriness, perversion, or ignorance. Someone once wryly observed that a rebel who loses is a traitor, while a rebel who wins is a patriot and founder. These assumptions may strike some readers as heresy and still others as old-hat. We hope this revised, restructured, and updated edition strikes a useful balance.

Charles J. Stewart, Craig Allen Smith, Robert E. Denton, Jr.

THE SOCIAL MOVEMENT AS A
UNIQUE COLLECTIVE PHENOMENON

As the second millennium ended and the third commenced, histori-ans and journalists provided insightful accounts of the great strides made in technology, science, medicine, transportation, and communication dur-ing the twentieth century.[1] Hosts of game shows, creators of documenta-ries, and pundits on news shows asked participants to name the most influential invention of the twentieth century. Responses ranged from the automobile, airplane, and computer to the telephone, television, and anti-biotics. Perhaps the correct answer was "all of the above." In the short span of a single century, the world became a global village and humans walked on the moon, but bloody military conflicts and "ethnic cleansing" claimed the lives of millions and ideological struggles brought the world to the brink of nuclear annihilation.

Those who lived during the twentieth century moved rapidly from a machine age to a nuclear age, a space age, and an electronic age fueled by tiny microchips. But this century could just as easily have been called the age of the social movement. Accounts of the twentieth century have readily acknowledged the influences social movements (many carried over from the nineteenth century) had on U.S. society and a large portion of the world. African, Hispanic, Asian, and Native Americans, women, gays and lesbians, college students, prison inmates, and workers from the vineyard to the university campus struggled for constitutional and human rights, equality, justice, identity, and a share of the American dream. Some formed consciousness raising groups to share common con-cerns, to strive for equal opportunities, and to enhance self-esteem while others formed heavily armed militias to defend themselves against the encroachment of the federal government and other societal elements that threatened their world.

Social movements organized during the twentieth century to end military conflicts, to protect the environment, to prevent the construction of nuclear power plants, to limit violence and sex on television and the Internet, to end apartheid in South Africa, to gain rights for animals, to halt legalized abortion, to legalize marijuana, and to reduce the power of corporate, governmental, religious, and educational bureaucracies. The growing conflict over moral, religious, social, political, and economic values, beliefs, and attitudes fueled social movements on the left and the right. And for every movement created to bring about change, a countermovement arose to confront the dissatisfied and to sustain the social order. But just as the nineteenth century passed along unfulfilled dreams and agendas of social movements, the twentieth century has passed to the twenty-first century struggles for justice and equality, protection and prohibition, values and attitudes.

Theorists have used the label *movement* to identify all forces for and against change. This label has encompassed internal changes within established institutions and groups, protest organizations, campaigns, uprisings, acts of violence, revolutions, civil wars, trends, fads, and crazes. When theorists wanted to recognize differences among these phenomena, they sometimes attached modifiers such as social, political, religious, historical, rhetorical, reform, nationalistic, and individualistic. People who were suspicious or fearful of movements called them radical, violent, revolutionary, repressive, and fanatical. Many groups compounded this confusion by calling themselves "movements" to inflate perceptions of their size, importance, and influence.[2]

This book focuses on the persuasive efforts of a unique collective phenomenon designed to bring about or resist change. It is essential to determine if a phenomenon under investigation is a social movement or a portion of a social movement, such as a social movement organization or campaign. This chapter identifies the essential characteristics of social movements and contrasts social movements with other collective phenomena such as political parties, established institutions, advertising campaigns, lobby or special interest groups, civil wars, and revolutions.

An Organized Collectivity

A social movement is at least minimally organized. If we cannot identify leaders or spokespersons, members or followers, and organizations or coalitions, the phenomenon under investigation is a trend, fad, or unorganized protest, not a social movement.[3] A phenomenon of the early 1990s called the men's movement—in which groups of men attended weekend retreats, sweated around fires in teepees, poured out their hearts, and sought comfort in brotherhood—has never quite developed into an *organized* social movement. There are no organizations, no recognizable leaders (other than poets and writers), and no identifiable membership.[4] On the other hand, the concern over clothing made in sweatshop conditions first surfaced in the late 1990s in labor union literature, within human rights organizations, and on television talk shows. It remained beneath the consciousness of most U.S. citizens until the winter and spring of 2000. Students and faculty on college campuses around the country formed local organizations and demanded that their institutions become members of the Worker Rights Consortium (WRC), a coalition of universities, labor unions, and human rights groups created to investigate and take actions against human rights abuses. A major target was university apparel produced in sweatshops from which universities received a portion of the profits. Student-led groups brought pressure on administrations to create codes of conduct for manufacturers and to join the WRC. They employed Web sites, leaflets, symbolic actions, demonstrations, sit-ins, tent cities, and hunger strikes.[5]

Degrees of Organization

The degree of organization, visibility of leaders, and nature of membership varies from movement to movement. For instance, Martin Luther King, Jr. of the Southern Christian Leadership Conference, Roy Wilkins of the National Association for the Advancement of Colored People (NAACP), and Stokely Carmichael of the Student Nonviolent Coordinating Committee (SNCC) were highly visible leaders of the civil rights movement. Although it would be difficult for most of us to name a leader or organization of the gay rights, animal rights, or pro-choice movements, they do exist, have sizable memberships, and are essential for the continuing existence and progress of each social movement. Leaders, members, and organizations that stage frequent public demonstrations and media events—such as pro-life's National Right to Life Committee and environmentalism's Greenpeace—are more visible than ones that operate primarily through the courts, in small groups, or within the social movement community such as the Sierra Club or the Humane Society of the United States. Regardless, all must have at least minimal organization to qualify as social movements.

The mass media may create the illusion of a social movement by treating "relatively isolated, but similar, rhetorical situations throughout the nation . . . as a single, dynamic, and interrelated phenomenon."[6] For example, the "death of God theology" attracted a great deal of media coverage and attention of religious leaders in the 1970s and 1980s and appeared to be a thriving social movement when no leadership, membership, or organization existed.[7] A similar phenomenon, the "secular humanist conspiracy," attracted a great deal of attention in the 1980s and 1990s from Christian fundamentalists and political conservatives who saw it as a powerful, demonic social movement responsible for the moral decline of the United States. However, the secular changes occurring in the United States and elsewhere appear to be decades-old *trends* rather than the results of a well-organized Secular Humanist social movement.[8] There is no evidence of organizations, leaders, or demonstrations. There are no campaigns urging teenagers to have sex, athletes to use drugs, husbands and wives to divorce, women to substitute the workplace for the home place, or God-fearing people to stop attending churches, temples, and mosques. A trend indicating an alteration of norms and values is not the equivalent of a social movement.

Social Movement Campaigns

Social movements are often confused with campaigns because social movements conduct numerous campaigns to achieve specific goals. For instance, Operation Rescue has conducted campaigns to close down abortion clinics in targeted cities around the country and to clog the jails with arrested demonstrators so police will be unable to disrupt their sit-ins and blockades. Earth First! has conducted campaigns to stop the logging of redwoods in the northwest, often by sitting in the tops of giant trees, lying in front of bulldozers, driving spike nails into trees, or sabotaging equipment.[9] Although campaigns and social movements share similarities, they have significant differences.[10]

Social movements tend to be organized from the bottom up while campaigns tend to be organized from the top down.[11] A social movement leader usually rises from a protest group as it develops and sees the need for leadership. It is an evolutionary process in which an effective spokesperson who can articulate the fundamentals of the cause often emerges as a leader. On the other hand, a campaign leader is usually selected by an organization prior to the start of the campaign and then selects and organizes a staff to run the campaign. Campaigns typically have managers with assigned roles, organizational charts, chiefs of staff, schedules of operations, specific goals, budgets, and known end points such as Election Day, an anniversary celebration, or date when a fund or membership drive is to "go over the top." For instance, Native American leaders organize protests when the Atlanta Braves or Washington Redskins play in the World Series or playoffs. The demonstrators demand that these teams stop employing what they see as offensive, racist nicknames, "sham rituals and ridiculous impersonations."[12] Similarly, animal rights activists picket Macy's and other department stores that sell fur coats, particularly during the Christmas holiday season. But these protest campaigns end when the sports event or the holiday season ends. By contrast, the Native American and animal rights social movements have lasted for decades, changed as circumstances have changed, rarely maintained tight control over memberships, and altered or added goals as they have proceeded.[13] No social movement knows when or if it will achieve its ends.

Social Movement Organizations

Specific organizations are often confused with social movements. The National Organization for Women (NOW), the American Indian Movement (AIM), People for the Ethical Treatment of Animals (PETA), and White Aryan Resistance (WAR) are organizations within social movements, not social movements in themselves. Each is *one* organization striving for equality for women, Native American rights and dignity, humane treatment of wild and domestic animals, and preservation of a way of life and the so-called Aryan race. To understand fully the persuasive efforts of the animal rights movement, for example, you would need to study the messages and symbolic actions of several organizations within the movement, including Friends for Animals, the Animal Protection Institute of America, Beauty Without Cruelty International, Trans-Species Unlimited, the Animal Welfare Institute, Humans Against Rabbit Exploitation (HARE), and PETA. Thus, while one or more organizations are an essential component of social movements, a single organization is not synonymous with the whole movement.

Minimal organization is characteristic of social movements. Many never evolve to high levels of organization. Unlike campaigns, they do *not* proceed in orderly step-by-step fashion, contain one supreme leader who controls the organization, appeal to a single target audience, have carefully defined and identifiable membership, or strive to attain a single, well-defined goal through the employment of one persuasive strategy. In the late 1990s, the Promise Keepers held large rallies of men in sports stadiums promising to be strong heads of their households and good fathers and husbands, but only time will tell whether they were part of the fledgling men's movement or merely a series of rallies that ended after a few years.[14] The same is true of the "Million Man March" in Washington, D.C. on October 16, 1995.[15] There appears to be no membership or organizational commitment by those attending rallies, merely pledges to be better persons, sons, fathers, and husbands when they return home. However, personal reform has been an important element of such movements as temperance and antismoking. Similarly, only time will tell whether the "Million Mom March" in Washington, D.C. on Mother's Day, May 14, 2000 demanding "sensible gun laws" and an end to gun violence will flower into a social movement or remain a one-day protest.[16]

An Uninstitutionalized Collectivity

A social movement is an uninstitutionalized collectivity. No social movement or social movement organization is part of an established order that governs, maintains, or changes social, political, religious, or economic norms and values.[17] Movements by the Southern Baptist Convention to recommit the denomination to the inerrancy of the Bible, by members of the House of Representatives to impeach President Clinton, by banks to consolidate with other banks, by Democrats to recount the Florida 2000 presidential vote, or by the Teamster's Union to get a better contract with United Parcel Service are not social movements. Rather, they are established institutions changing themselves and striving for goals through institutionalized means and procedures. Primary impetus for change comes from within rather than from without and only recognized members have a say in the change.

To understand the persuasive efforts of complex social movements, observers have often presumed they are little different from the activities of political parties, political action committees (PACs), legislatures, legislative lobbies, religious organizations, and corporations. But an essential difference is that social movements exist and operate primarily from *outside* established institutions. Although social movements may attempt to persuade members of established institutions (legislators, governors, judges, bishops, trustees, industrialists, college presidents) to support or resist programs for change, they cease to be social movements if they become parts of institutions. For instance, the Lutheran Church was once a social movement in Germany, but it later became the official church of Germany and a recognized religious denomination around the world. The American Federation of Labor was an organization within the American labor movement until it attained the legal right to represent workers in collective bargaining and grievances and achieved institutional status.

Social Movements as Out-Groups

The *outsider* or *uninstitutionalized* status of social movements, according to Simons and others, presents leaders with "extraordinary rhetorical dilemmas" in the rhetorical requirements they must fulfill, the problems they will face, and the available strategies they may use to meet these requirements.[18] Although success is never assured in any persuasive undertaking, a comparison of the persuasive situations uninstitutionalized social movements and institutionalized organizations face suggests that social movements encounter unique requirements and handicaps.

Social movements are always *out-groups* that society views as illegitimate.[19] They are criticized for not handling conflicts and controversies through normal, proper channels and procedures, even when those channels and procedures are systematically denied them. Social movements have virtually no powers of reward and punishment beyond disruptions and personal recognition or expulsion, and expulsion may lead the exiled or disillusioned to create organizations. They have neither legislative nor enforcement powers—nor any assured means of financial support. Monetary funds are fractions of those available to established governments, churches, political parties, PACs, and corporations.

Uninstitutionalized leaders survive only as long as they perform necessary tasks well. When new tasks, abilities, or strategies are required, movement organizations may unceremoniously discard the old. Leaders have minimal control over single factions or fragile coalitions of movement organizations, and none over important institutions such as courts, investigative agencies, boards of trustees, and media. Rarely can they bring most of a social movement's resources to bear on a single event, let alone a lengthy campaign.

The mass media who must cater to viewers and readers, government agencies, advertisers, and owners devote little space or air time to social movements. News reports are rarely favorable toward movements (unless success appears near or an element is becoming institutionalized), are rarely controlled by social movements (although some movement organizations and leaders become adept at manipulating the media to attain coverage), and provide exposure only when a social movement does something spectacular or stupid. The need for media attention may drive an organization to ever more extreme proclamations and actions. Social movement organizations rarely have the money to purchase significant space or air time to present their cases directly to the people. A single presidential candidate may generate and spend more money in a few months than a social movement will in decades. Persuasion is the sole means available to most social movements to accomplish such functions as transforming perceptions of reality, attaining a modicum of legitimacy, and mobilizing the discontented. Limited funds relegate most persuasion to leaflets, pamphlets and, increasingly, the Internet.

Institutions as In-Groups

Institutionalized groups and leaders, on the other hand, are always in the *in-group*; society views them as legitimate agents for sustaining the social order. Leaders strive to maintain the appearance of dealing with conflicts and controversies through normal, proper channels. Institutions have immense powers of reward and punishment because they control the procedures that populate the agencies that enforce the law, investigate crime and misbehavior, regulate the media and commerce, create and discard laws, levy and collect taxes, conduct trials, operate the prisons, and appoint persons to lucrative positions in government, church, bureaucracy, and corporation. They may keep the disgruntled in line by enhancing or diminishing their economic well-being, threatening their membership status, amending or burying pieces of legislation, and granting or withholding contracts and licenses.

Institutional leaders may serve guaranteed terms (ranging from two years to life), enjoy the support of organized and well-financed groups, and advance within corporate, political, educational, and church hierarchies. Funding is far less of a problem for institutionalized groups and individuals. Legislatures have access to billions of tax dollars. PACs can raise millions of dollars through sophisticated computerized mailings.

Lobbies such as the National Rifle Association fund the increasingly expensive political campaigns of sympathetic legislators and executives. Large corporations such as Mobil Oil and Georgia Pacific have vast financial resources and influence to counter environmentalists.[20] Political candidates, both challengers and incumbents, generate enormous campaign chests, often collecting millions of dollars at a single fundraiser.

Institutionalized groups and leaders are newsworthy and demand media attention. They command network, cable, and front-page coverage for trivial as well as consequential speeches, press conferences, conventions, announcements, meetings of stockholders or bishops, ceremonies or events. C-SPAN channels give continuous coverage of Congress, press conferences, speeches by institutional leaders, and interviews with those who aspire to become institutional leaders. Television interview and talk shows such as *Meet the Press, Face the Nation,* and *Larry King Live* provide leaders with opportunities to defend themselves, attack others, present programs, and build their images. Few social movement leaders appear on such programs. The president's cat or dog may attract more news coverage than a social movement demonstration by thousands. The president may gain international attention by strolling through the White House rose garden, attending the annual Easter egg hunt on the south lawn, or traveling to a foreign country.

At the same time, institutions may stifle uncooperative or unfriendly media outlets by threatening not to provide their representatives with seats on campaign planes, access to leaders, entry into restricted areas, or opportunities to ask questions at press conferences. All major networks, cable channels, newspapers, and magazines are owned by institutional groups and individuals devoted, with few exceptions, to maintaining their versions of social norms and values and making a profit. Support of social movements is likely to be minimal and implicit rather than explicit. No social movement has the connections, funds, and access to the media enjoyed by institutions and institutionalized leaders.

A Large Collectivity

Social movements are large in scope in terms of geographical area, time, events, organizations, participants, goals, strategies, and critical adaptations.[21] Scope distinguishes them from pressure groups, religious cults, lobbies, PACs, campaigns, and protests that tend to be of relatively short duration, have limited goals, and restrict membership to a small number of true believers, staff, or operatives.

Although campaigns may follow rhetorical careers *similar* to social movements, it does not follow, as Donald Fishman argues, that "it is fair to conclude that whatever differences that exist between movements and campaigns may not be rhetorically significant."[22] A campaign is to a social movement as a battle is to a war. They are similar in some ways but very different in others. Conducting the battle of Gettysburg was not the same as conducting the Civil War, and understanding the battle does not fully inform us about the war. Martin Luther King, Jr., for example, discovered that conducting limited and highly focused campaigns in Montgomery, Selma, Atlanta, and Chicago was not the same as attempting to maintain attention, cohesion, commitment, control, and excitement within a large social movement over many years. He had to adjust rhetorically to temporal and societal changes, new generations of protestors, internal and external challenges, regional differences, the need for and appearance of new strategies, a rising militancy within the movement, and growing frustrations with lack of real victories and changes. Unlike campaigns, social movements are typically national or international in scope, sustain efforts for decades, select many leaders, create many organizations, conduct continuous membership drives, carry out many campaigns, expand and constrict ideologies, set and alter many goals, and employ a wide variety of strategies. It is difficult to imagine a "campaign" that would pose such rhetorical challenges to leaders and members alike.

Size

Size of membership and scope of activities are integral portions of social movement efforts to persuade others to join and give, establish their legitimacy, and to pressure institutions and adversaries to take them and their demands seriously. Social movements in the United States cannot thrive if they are perceived to be *small* because Americans tend to see small ventures as either inconsequential, and therefore to be ignored or ridiculed, or as dangerous, and therefore to be suppressed for the safety of the people and the good of the nation.

Oliver and Marwell note "One person marching for a thousand hours is not the same as a thousand people marching for one hour."[23] Institutions and their supporters went to great lengths in the 1960s and 1970s to characterize the antiwar, student rights, and black power movements as small groups of radicals, sex perverts, traitors, cowards, racists, and degenerates—people not representative of the great "silent majority" of citizens, students, and African Americans. Conservative talk show personality Rush Limbaugh has coined the epithet "feminazi" to characterize women's rights advocates as a small group of radicals out of step with the vast majority of women in the United States. Political cartoonists have portrayed militia organizations formed in the 1990s as small populations of uneducated, unintelligent, overweight, unshaven, paranoid, trailer-park residents who play soldier on the weekends and assume exalted military ranks.

The Native American movement—relatively small in number, isolated in scattered, remote regions of the country, and ideologically split between urban and reservation residents—experienced difficulty in attracting attention, maintaining media and governmental interest, and persuading audiences to take it seriously. It resorted to takeovers of Alcatraz Island in San Francisco Bay, Wounded Knee in South Dakota, and the Bureau of Indian Affairs in Washington, D.C. to gain attention for its cause. The media and the public soon grew tired of the occupations and ignored them while the *Wall Street Journal* dismissed the occupation of the Bureau of Indian Affairs as "an exercise in playacting—an effort by a relative handful of militants to speak for the broader Indian community."[24] The recent establishment of lucrative gambling casinos on reservation lands in such states as Wisconsin and New York, successful court cases to reclaim land lost a century or more ago, and a whale hunt off the west coast in 1999 have captured more media and public attention than years of protest and demonstrations.

Forces on both sides of the abortion conflict have portrayed the other as a vocal minority, little more than a handful or radicals wishing to force their will on the majority.[25] Virtually every social movement claims to be a "great grassroots movement." Whenever social movements stage "mass demonstrations," institutional and movement estimates of turnout vary drastically because each side has a stake in the size game. A survey that found only 1 percent of men considered themselves to be exclusively homosexual (contrary to the long-standing claim of 10 percent) prompted *Time* magazine to headline a report, "The Shrinking Ten Percent: A New Survey Claiming that Only 1 percent of Men Are Gay Put the Movement Off Stride."[26]

Time

Most significant changes in social structures, norms, and values take decades, if not centuries, to bring about, so institutions have time on their side. They may wait until a social, economic, or political crisis passes; a war ends; protestors graduate or become disillusioned by lack of progress; or the impact of a movement campaign lessens. For instance, in the early 1990s, the animal rights campaign against wearing fur had forced many women to stop wearing and purchasing fur and resulted in a sharp decline in sales and profits. Many furriers closed for lack of business. By 2000, however, fur was making a comeback with brisk sales and new furriers opened for business. Women no longer feared that animal rights activists might harass them nor were they deterred by thoughts of innocent animals giving their lives for stylish, expensive garments.

Institutional leadership changes occurring through normal processes such as election, retirement, resignation, or discharge may remove favorite targets of agitators. President Johnson's decision not to run for reelection in 1968 and the end of President Clinton's second term in 2001 deprived antiwar and Christian right enthusiasts of favorite nemeses. The public may become disenchanted with and intolerant of protest and dis-order, particularly if their routines such as travel, shopping, entertain-ment, and work are affected. The mass media and their audiences become bored with issues, events, and strategies (particularly boycotts and take-overs) that seem to drag on endlessly. A person may refrain for a while from buying lettuce to support the farm workers movement, or taking children to Disney World to oppose gay and lesbian rights, or crossing a picket line to avoid a confrontation with environmental protesters, but desires and convenience may overcome commitment or reluctance.

Time directly affects social movements. Changes in movement lead-ership resulting from power struggles, deaths, or assassinations may weaken social movements or lead to the dissolution of social movement organizations. Leaders and followers may grow weary of the struggle or become disillusioned by lack of real progress. A great victory for one gen-eration of protestors, such as the Montgomery bus boycott that energized the civil rights movement and brought a young Reverend Martin Luther King, Jr. to national prominence, may mean little to the next generation that wants true equality in all aspects of life.[27] If social movement leaders and followers do not tire of the struggle, they or factions may become desperate for victory and resort to extreme methods such as violence and assassination that allow institutions and countermovements to suppress or discredit them as fanatical and dangerous.

Events

A few victories, campaigns, or events do not guarantee success. Even spectacular events such as the 1963 civil rights march on Washington, D.C. that drew over 250,000 persons and ended with Martin Luther King's "I Have a Dream" speech are soon forgotten. What happened to the men's movement after the "million man" rally in Washington? Friend and foe ask "What's next?" Social movements and the media have insa-tiable appetites for "happenings," but few social movements have suffi-cient leaders, members, funds, or energy to satisfy these appetites wisely over long periods of time while fending off counterefforts of other move-ments and institutions.

The radical environmental group Earth First! employed every tactic it could copy and invent during the 1980s and 1990s to defend Mother Earth from the logging industry and those who would pollute her streams and eliminate her wildlife. Earth Firsters! used "guerrilla" the-ater, nonviolent civil disobedience, confrontations, destruction of prop-erty and machinery (called monkeywrenching, ecotage, or ecodefense), cemented themselves into roadblocks, chained themselves to trees and logging equipment, sat in the top of trees for months at a time, dropped a three-hundred-foot roll of black plastic from the top of the Glen Canyon Dam to simulate a catastrophic crack in the dam, and draped a huge banner across the face of George Washington on Mount Rushmore reading, "We The People Say No to Acid Rain."[28] Several protesters were seriously injured or killed in accidents with trucks and bulldozers during confrontations. Yet its efforts and name have largely disappeared from the media. Logging, development, and pollution in the northwest have continued. Julia Hill, a member of Earth First!, took residence on a six-by-eight foot wooden platform at the top of a 180 foot redwood tree she called Luna in December 1997. A year later her protest, largely ignored except for Pacific Lumber that wanted to cut down the tree, garnered a picture and a single column in *People* magazine.[29] This is little attention for the personal sacrifice made for the movement, but it is more than most prolonged protests get in the media. When Hill finally descended from her treetop platform in late 1999 after an agreement to save Luna and some other trees, few people took notice.

Promotes or Opposes Change in Societal Norms and Values

A social movement promotes or opposes a program for change in societal norms and values. Its rhetoric includes prescriptions for what must be done, who must do it, and how it must be done.

Basic Types of Social Movements

Three general types of social movements are distinguishable by the nature of the changes they advocate or oppose. An *innovative social movement* seeks to replace existing norms and values with *new* ones.[30] Innovative movements include women's liberation, civil rights for African Americans, socialism, gay liberation, and animal rights. A *revivalistic social movement* seeks to replace existing norms and values with ones from a *venerable, idealized past.*[31] Revivalistic social movements include the Native American, Back to Africa, pro-life, environmental, and Christian reconstruction movements. A *resistance social movement* seeks to block changes in norms and values because it perceives *nothing wrong with the status quo*, at least nothing that cannot or will not be resolved in due time through established means and institutions.[32] Resistance social movements include anti–women's liberation, anti–civil rights, antigay rights, Aryan superiority, and pro-choice movements.

Social movements tend to be both valuistic and normative because changes in values alter norms, and changes in norms alter values. For instance, movements espousing the values of equality, fairness, and justice led to normative changes through court decisions and laws. These normative changes guaranteed equal pay, benefits, and employment opportunities for African Americans, women, and senior citizens. In turn, these changes affected how Americans perceive the values of equality, fairness, and justice. They generated opposition by those who see such changes as threats to other values.

Reform and Revolutionary Movements

Many social movements have reform-oriented (demanding partial change) and revolutionary-oriented (demanding total change) elements. Their ideologies, leaders, members, and organizations develop and change over time. The student movement, for example, began in the 1950s as a reform-oriented free speech movement at U.S. universities that had traditionally restricted who could speak, to whom they could speak, when they could speak, and where they could speak on campuses. The movement evolved into demands not only for removal of strictures on speakers but the elimination of restrictions on where students could live, the hours they could stay out at night, and the clothes they could wear. Students wanted to serve on important committees that affected their educations and well-being. They argued for the creation of grievance, grade appeal, and student affairs committees that would empower them to address unfair treatment. Eventually, on some campuses, the movement became revolutionary with demands that students determine courses offered, course content, course requirements, graduation standards, appointments of administrators, and investment of endowments.[33]

Efforts to place a social movement along a reform-to-revolution continuum depend on time, perceptions, and elements ascendant within the movement. For instance, many Americans viewed Martin Luther King, Jr. as a revolutionary until Stokely Carmichael and H. Rap Brown became leaders of the Student Nonviolent Coordinating Committee and preached black power. Suddenly the Reverend King appeared to be a reformer. Some view the animal rights movement as merely a reform movement aimed at assuring the humane treatment of animals, a simple extension of the animal welfare movement of the nineteenth century from which the American Society for the Prevention of Cruelty to Animals (ASPCA) emerged. Others see this movement as a revolutionary attempt to alter the relationships between animals and humans and thus between humans and God, to restrict the rights of hunters and those who raise animals for food, to stifle lifesaving medical experimentation, or to increase the intrusion of big government into American lives.

Moderate and Radical Movements

Labeling a movement as moderate or radical may be as misleading as labeling it reform or revolutionary. While one person's moderate is another's radical, most social movements contain both radical and moderate elements. Organizations of the women's liberation movement have ranged from the National Organization for Women to the Women's International Terrorist Conspiracy from Hell (WITCH) and the Society for Cutting Up Men (SCUM). Elements within the pro-life movement include those who believe change must come about through prayer and peaceful protest and those who believe violence and assassination are essential to ending legal abortion and stopping the slaughter of the innocents. Terms such as moderate and radical best describe types of strategies and arguments rather than types of social movements, a point we will emphasize in later chapters.

Ideologies and Belief-Systems

The natures of social movement ideologies or systems of belief preclude precise classification. They tend to be strange mixtures of vagueness and precision, part of an old and part of a new system, static and ever changing, consistent and contradictory. Some social movements have one ideology for true believers and a somewhat different one for public consumption. As Hans Toch writes, "Each person joins a somewhat different social movement, often for reasons far removed from the central concerns of the movement."[34]

Elements of society, including those who join, perceive a social movement's demands, goals, strategies, and potential outcomes from their unique personal perspectives and needs. A campaign to protest the development of a large resort at the edge of a national park may attract persons wanting to save the environment, persons desiring to protect a pristine wilderness for their children or future generations, persons seeking to protect their nearby ranches or a favorite hunting area, persons opposing development by large corporations, and persons wanting the fellowship of the protest group.

The diversity, flexibility, and fluid nature of social movement belief systems or programs for change set them apart from other collectives. Most religious, political, social, and pressure groups have a single set of principles that remain relatively constant and goals that are fairly precise: convert unbelievers, elect a party's candidate, maintain subsidies for milk producers, institute prayer in the public schools, or prevent gun control legislation. In contrast, even a fairly focused social movement such as pro-life has a wide variety of organizations that espouse positions ranging from no abortions under any circumstances to some abortions in particular situations (incest, rape, danger to mother's health), strategies ranging from prayer and legal action to violence, and goals ranging from protection of the unborn to protection of the unborn, disabled, infirm, and aged.

Local issues, what Steven Goldzwig calls "critical localism," may dominate the concerns, rhetoric, and demonstrations in a community or on a college campus.[35] For example, a large tuition increase and the firing of the student editor of the campus daily newspaper for printing editorials that included expletives fueled large demonstrations, fiery rhetoric, and arrests on the Purdue University campus in the 1960s and 1970s. The press reported these as countercultural and anti–Vietnam war movement incidents even though these issues played insignificant parts in each incident. However, it is unlikely either incident would have come about without a climate conducive to protest—the result of a number of larger movements on campus. As Goldzwig and Patricia Sullivan write, "In these local discursive performances cultural history and local experience help shape beliefs and attitudes; they meld together an epistemological outlook that authorizes an additional move."[36]

Encounters Opposition in a Moral Struggle

Whether a social movement's leaders and members are striving to bring about or resist change in norms and values and whether these changes pertain to people (right to life or right to die), things (nuclear weapons or alcoholic beverages), or animals (medical experiments or fur coats), they assume the power to distinguish right from wrong, good from evil, and ethical from unethical motives, purposes, characters, choices, strategies, and actions. Each social movement believes that it alone constitutes an ethical, virtuous, principled, and righteous force with a moral obligation it cannot ignore. The movement must raise the consciousness of the people by revealing the moral, intellectual, and coercive bankruptcy of the targeted institution, its actions, and its motives.[37] Kenneth Burke and Leland Griffin conclude "all social movements are essentially moral strivings for salvation, perfection, the good."[38]

Claim to Legitimacy

The moral stance and tone of social movement rhetoric is of critical importance to claims of legitimacy as uninstitutionalized forces. Anthony Oberschall writes that a movement's legitimacy rests on an elaboration of systems of belief and moral ideas, while Herbert Simons notes that a movement establishes its legitimacy by representing its cause as one that any virtuous individual may endorse.[39] A PETA leaflet states the case for their claim to the moral high ground.

> All species fear injury and death, and all species fight for life and freedom. How can one species, ours, consider it has the right to deny others their basic interests of liberty and life? Just as we denied these rights to other human beings in the past for arbitrary reasons, such as skin color, we now deny these basic rights to others because they happen not to be of our own species.
>
> We do not need animals' fur, skin or flesh to survive. But we have come to like the feel, look and taste of these pieces of animals and we are loathe to give them up, even though to do so means a healthier existence for us all.

> What gives human beings the right to kill other animals who have
> lives of their own to live?
>
> Truly, history will judge the worth of our "civilization" less by our
> technological accomplishments than by the way we treat our fellow
> beings.[40]

As with most individuals and collectives who place themselves upon
a moral pedestal, particularly ones striving for the mantle of legitimacy,
social movement rhetoric often magnifies its righteousness. Delegates to
the 1900 American Federation of Labor convention were welcomed with
these words:

> Upon you rests the dawn of a new century, and may the record made
> here shine forth during the years to come as does now the Declaration
> of Independence. Your work is a noble and holy one, and when accom-
> plished will be but the realization of the Savior's mission on earth – the
> uplifting and elevation morally and socially of all humanity.[41]

Herbert Simons, Elizabeth Mechling, and Howard Schreier note that
"Most ideological messages" of social movements "tend to exaggerate the
strength, unity, and intellectual and moral legitimacy of the movement."[42]

Disaffection and Confrontation

As a social movement promotes or resists a program for change from
a moral perspective and lays claim to legitimacy, members become frustrated to the point of disaffection with established institutions and institutional means of change and control. They become willing to devote their
lives, and on occasion to give their lives, to attain victory in the moral
struggle between good and evil. Innovative and revivalistic social movements see institutions as unaware of, disinterested in, or openly resistant
to necessary changes to resolve moral issues. Resistance movements see
institutions as unwilling or unable to respond to grievous threats to social
norms and values and, perhaps as contemporary militias and the Christian right claim, actively compromising norms and values.

Robert Cathcart has written that social movements must create a
"drama or agonistic ritual which forces response from the establishment
commensurate with the moral evil perceived by movement members."[43]
It seldom takes long for a social movement to pose a threat that the established order can no longer ignore, and some theorists claim that a social
movement at the national level spawns immediate organized opposition.[44] Perceived threat and increasing use of confrontational strategies
produce, according to Cathcart, a "dialectical tension growing out of
moral conflict," and provokes a clash between the social movement and
the threatened institution.[45] The struggle between institutional and uninstitutional forces becomes a "true moral battle for power and for the legitimate right to define the true order."[46]

During the 1980s, students and faculty on hundreds of U.S. college campuses launched protests against the brutal apartheid policies of South Africa, a moral outrage on a massive scale. They created shantytowns on campuses that resembled those in South Africa, distributed facsimiles of passbooks blacks were required to carry in South Africa, and gave speeches emphasizing the reality of life for the black residents of South Africa. A common demand was that the university divest itself of any endowment investments in South African corporations or U.S. corporations doing business in South Africa. At first, university administrations distributed press releases explaining why they could not or would not divest, made modest changes in their investment policies, and met with protesting groups. As protestors gained media attention, began to embarrass administrations with claims to the moral high ground, and refused to stop demonstrations or remove their shantytowns at prescribed deadlines, many were arrested and shanties were destroyed. Administrators came to see the antiapartheid demonstrations as threats to their powers of moral suasion and legitimate right to enforce university rules and determine investment policies.[47] They could not cede the moral high ground to students and faculty and sometimes resorted to force and arrests to maintain their authority.

A "social conflict," Simons writes, is "a clash over incompatible interests in which one party's relative gain is another's relative loss."[48] Thus, if the Gray Panthers representing millions of senior citizens pressure legislatures into allocating more money for Social Security, Medicare, Medicaid, and long-term care facilities, younger persons and taxpayers will pay higher taxes. Social movements are always players in zero-sum games of social control and change.

Institutions often portray themselves as goaded into action by violent acts that pose dangerous, irresponsible, and unreasonable threats to legitimate—and therefore moral—social order. They counter social movements directly and indirectly through agencies, agents, and beneficiaries. *Agencies* include legislative bodies, executive and administrative groups, courts, police, armed forces, councils, task forces, regulatory bodies, tax authorities, communication media, and investigative groups. *Agents* include legislators, presidents, governors, mayors, bishops, judges, police officers, soldiers, owners of communication media, editors, reporters, commentators, and investigators such as special prosecutors. *Beneficiaries* include most of the above plus corporations, business owners and operators (including farmers and ranchers), colleges and universities, churches, patriotic and civic groups, and the "silent majority" of citizens.

Institutions, no matter how tolerant and understanding they may seem or want to be, can accept only minor challenges to norms, values, and their legitimacy. They cannot sustain a loss to uninstitutionalized forces and still maintain their authority, credibility, and control over constituencies. They must retain the moral high ground at all cost.

Persuasion Is Pervasive

Social movements must satisfy a number of requirements if they are to *become* and *remain* significant forces for change in societal norms and values. For instance, they must transform perceptions of reality, enhance the ego of protestors, attain a degree of legitimacy, prescribe and sell courses of action, mobilize the disaffected, and sustain the movement over time. Theoretically, social movements may attempt to satisfy such requirements through coercion, bargaining, and persuasion.

Coercion and Bargaining

Coercion is the "manipulation of the target group's situation in such fashion that the pursuit of any course of action other than that sought by the movement will be met with considerable cost or punishment."[49] White Citizens Councils in the South relied heavily on coercion in their efforts to counter the civil rights movement. *Bargaining* may occur when the "movement has control of some exchangeable value that the target group wants and offers some of that value in return for compliance with demands."[50] The United Farm Workers offered productive, reliable, and loyal workers to California growers in exchange for recognition and contracts.

The typical uninstitutionalized and minimally organized social movement enjoys few means of reward or punishment necessary either to coerce people to join or to remain loyal to a cause or to coerce institutions to capitulate to some or all of its demands. Institutions, with little to gain and much to lose, resist bargaining with social movements whose leaders and followers they have stigmatized as dangerous and inferior social degenerates. Michael Lipsky notes "People in power do not like to sit down with rogues."[51] Mere association with a social movement's leaders may grant an undesired degree of legitimacy to the social movement and its cause. In addition, as Lipsky writes, institutions doubt the capability of movements to bargain effectively: "Protest oriented groups, whose primary talents are in dramatizing issues, cannot credibly attempt to present data considered 'objective' or suggestions considered 'responsible' by public officials. Few can be convincing as both advocate and arbitrator at the same time."

Social movements often have little or nothing to exchange in bargaining sessions. Ralph Turner and Lewis Killian comment, for instance, that "the difficulty that constantly besets black movements is that they have nothing to offer whites in a bargaining exchange to match their disruptive potential."[52] Institutions pressure one another not to "give in" to demands of protestors. When students and faculties were protesting the apartheid policies in South Africa, the *Wall Street Journal* commented: "A surprising number of colleges have caved in to protest and announced divestment. This cowardice, too, promotes the kind of disruption going on this week on campuses across the nation, and undermines the institutions the administrations and trustees are supposed to protect."[53]

Social movements are equally loath to bargain with the "devil"; they have vilified institutions in their portrayals of reality and demands for change. They have suffered grievous mental, economic, social, and physical abuse for their beliefs and protests. Talking to, let alone compromising with, corrupt and oppressive institutions may be deemed a moral outrage by a movement's true believers. For example, Terence Powderly, the longtime leader of the Knights of Labor in the 1880s and 1890s, complained that he should be "permitted to exercise his own judgment" and "permitted to think for the Order" and not be subjected to the "demagogue's cry" that "he is selling out the labor movement" if he is seen "talking to a capitalist or entering the office of a man of wealth."[54] Thus, the constituencies of both parties are likely to perceive offers to bargain as signs of weakness, desperation, deception, and a "selling out."[55]

Social movements can satisfy only a few major requirements through bargaining and coercion. For example, bargaining may help mobilization for action by uniting disparate movement elements into coalitions, and it may exert pressure on institutions to meet with moderate collectives operating from a position of strength that are willing to discuss potential compromises. The Christian Coalition exhibited its fundraising and voter strengths in the 1990s and was able to bargain effectively with conservative elements in Congress and political candidates at the local, state, and national levels. Coercion is limited mainly to pressuring the opposition or transforming perceptions of society by goading institutions into excessive repression, thus undermining their credibility. The Ruby Ridge incident in Idaho during which an FBI agent shot and killed the wife of white separatist Randy Weaver and the Branch Davidian standoff in Waco, Texas, instigated by agents of the Bureau of Alcohol, Tobacco, and Firearms that ended with a fiery inferno that claimed the lives of David Koresh and his followers were two examples of damaged credibility. After those incidents, some people believed that the federal government blew up the Murrah Federal Building in Oklahoma City in which 168 people died (including 19 children) to provoke public outrage against militias and other groups opposing intrusive government.

Although a social movement may unmask an institution and gain some sympathy by provoking violent suppression, the public may just as easily condemn the movement and perceive the suppression as an "unfortunate but inevitable" result of dangerous radicalism.[56] Social movements often splinter into factions over the issue of employing coercion (particularly violent acts such as bombings, assassinations, destruction of property, and disruptions) to achieve their ends. Because of the many constraints under which uninstitutionalized social movements must operate, persuasion is the primary agency for satisfying requirements and meeting obstacles.

Persuasion

Social movements use the communication process of persuasion to present their case. That is, they use verbal and nonverbal symbols to affect audience perceptions and to bring about changes in thinking, feeling, and/or acting. The Christian right, for example, has employed speeches, publications, the Internet, mass mailings, local organizations, and interpersonal contacts to sell its conservative agenda across the nation.

Persuasion is pervasive in social movements. Bargaining includes elements of persuasion. For instance, a social movement attempting to bargain must *convince* both supporters and the opposition inside and outside of the movement that it is serious in desiring to bargain, that it is a worthy participant for bargaining interactions, and that it has something of value to exchange for concessions. On the other hand, persuasion may preclude bargaining as a strategy. Lipsky writes "admission to policy making councils is frequently barred because of the angry, militant rhetorical style adopted by protest leaders."[57]

Coercion also includes elements of persuasion. Turner and Killian observe "nonviolence always couples persuasive strategy to coercion."[58] For example, sit-ins, mass demonstrations, marches, hunger strikes, and disobedience of laws perceived as unjust all have persuasive elements such as language, arguments, and symbolic acts—but they also threaten institutions. Simons uses the phrase "coercive persuasion" to emphasize that "all acts of influence are rhetorical in at least some respects." He argues:

> The trouble with the persuasion-coercion dichotomy it that it cannot be applied reliably to the real world, and especially to most conflict situations. Although the criteria used to distinguish persuasion and coercion enable us to identify different elements within a given act, and although there are a great many cases of "pure" persuasion which are free of coercive elements, by these same criteria, acts conventionally labeled as "coercive" are almost never free of persuasive elements.[59]

Are any acts devoid of symbolic value and thus instances of pure coercion? The Supreme Court has ruled that coercive acts such as marches, sit-ins, boycotts, demonstrations, and articles of clothing such as armbands and uniforms constitute "symbolic speech" and are entitled to First Amendment protection. The Berrigan brothers' destruction of draft records from the Selective Service Office in Catonsville, Maryland, was a coercive and yet highly symbolic act of protest during the Vietnam War.[60] So are pro-life's "sidewalk counseling" (during which protestors scream "Don't kill your baby!" at women attempting to enter abortion clinics) and the throwing of blood or red paint by animal rights activists on women wearing fur coats. The occasional burning of an American flag by protestors is a highly symbolic act that expresses their anger, even hatred, of certain governmental actions or policies. Each burning, particularly when the appearance of protestors makes them look "radical" or different, inevitably produces outrage in many Americans and political leaders who see this as a direct attack on the nation's highest symbol and therefore on the nation itself. Legislation is immediately proposed that would amend the Constitution to make flag burning a crime and prevent the Supreme Court from declaring the legislation unconstitutional. Parke Burgess argues that persuasion is essential when social movements *threaten* to use coercive tactics: "The Victim must be convinced that dire consequences are likely, not to say certain, *before* he can feel forced to comply, just as he must become convinced of the coercer's probable capacity and intent to commit the act of violence *before* he can conclude that the act is likely to follow noncompliance."[61]

Are any acts pure bargaining and devoid of persuasion and coercion? When two antagonists sit down to bargain, they attempt to convince one another that they are sincere, have something of value to offer, are operating from a position of strength, and can and will break off negotiations (and resort to force) if all does not proceed as desired. Neither party can be or appear to be in a situation where it must accept an offer. The coercion card must be playable.

Are any acts pure persuasion and devoid of bargaining or any hint of the carrot or the stick? Malcolm X's famous persuasive speech "The Ballot or the Bullet" opens with attempts to appease the followers of Elijah Muhammad (founder of the Black Muslims), Christians, and followers of Martin Luther King, Jr.—a kind of bargaining or negotiating of differences.[62] The speech proceeds with a lengthy appeal for black capitalism, pure persuasion. And the speech ends with thinly veiled threats to resort to the bullet if the ballot is unavailable or fails to produce results, coercive persuasion. Robert Doolittle reveals that some people perceived the race riots of the 1960s as inherently symbolic, others conceded that the riots were potentially symbolic, and some viewed them as lawless and totally lacking in symbolism.[63] News reports of the 1992 riot in Los Angeles following the acquittal of the white police officers who had attacked Rodney King indicate that people interpreted this event much the same as they had the riots of the 1960s.[64] James Andrews suggests that persuasion may be most effective when institutions "accept the harsh reality that they may be coerced."[65]

Clearly, persuasion permeates the efforts of social movements to promote or resist change and is the primary agency available for satisfying essential requirements. The role of persuasion distinguishes social movements from two, often closely related, collective actions: civil wars and revolutions. In social movements, *persuasion is pervasive* while *violence is incidental* and often employed for symbolic purposes. In civil wars and revolutions, *violence is pervasive* and rarely symbolic while *persuasion is incidental*.

To say that persuasion is pervasive in social movements and that it is the primary means for satisfying major requirements and overcoming obstacles is not to suggest that persuasion *alone* can bring ultimate success to social movements. Social movements must have skilled leaders, dedicated followers, effective organizations, a social system that permits or at least tolerates protest, a climate conducive to change, and luck. Pivotal incidents such as the nuclear power accidents at Three Mile Island in Pennsylvania and Chernobyl in the Ukraine, the advent of AIDS in this country, *Brown v. Board of Education* that overturned the separate but equal court interpretations that had made separation of the races legal, the Great Depression of the 1930s, and withdrawal of U.S. troops from Vietnam were critical to the progress and dissolution of antinuclear power, civil rights, labor, and the anti–Vietnam war movements. However, such events would disappear into the pages of history if social movements did not employ persuasion to interpret them, focus media attention on them, and bring them back to audiences in demonstrations, anniversary celebrations, ceremonies, monuments, speeches, songs, and books. Persuasion grows stale without the urgency that events inject into protest.

Conclusions

A social movement, then, is an organized, uninstitutionalized, and large collectivity that emerges to promote or resist change in societal norms and values, operates primarily through persuasion, and encounters opposition in a moral struggle. This definition addresses *what* a social movement is and *how* it attempts to achieve its program for change or resistance to change. Persuasion is pervasive and is not restricted to a particular audience, purpose, requirement, strategy, or stage of a movement's life cycle. No other phenomenon called a movement or campaign shares all of these characteristics. A trend or fad, for example, is unorganized and contains no program for change. A revolution relies primarily upon violence rather than persuasion. A PAC or lobby group tends to be institutionalized (licensed and incorporated), small in size, and created for limited, pragmatic ends (get a candidate elected, maintain a subsidy for rice farmers, prevent gun legislation) rather than a moral struggle for change or maintenance of societal norms and values. A campaign is typically organized from the top down, includes managers with assigned roles, has specific and narrow goals, is relatively short in duration, and often has a known end point.

Our attempt to define the social movement as a unique collective phenomenon is designed to provide a clear focus for the chapters that follow and to inform readers of the underlying premises upon which this book is based. This definition is not designed to place rigid limitations on *movement* or *campaign* studies, and we recognize that movements occur within established institutions, describe changes in academic fields of study and voting trends, and determine our personal dress, appearance, habits, actions, and tastes. The continuing discussion about the uniqueness of *social* movements is analogous to the study of other common phenomena. For instance, researchers who analyze political, health, sales, advertising, and recruiting campaigns recognize that all campaigns share *some* common persuasive characteristics. They do not claim, however, that the sharing of some characteristics means they have no significant differences. Institutional movements share many persuasive characteristics with social movements. These shared characteristics, however, do not make them identical twins. We are using the term *social movement* to identify a specific type of movement for study and research, a unique collective phenomenon.

Endnotes

1　Peter Jennings and Todd Brewster, *The Century* (New York: Doubleday, 1998).

2　Michael C. McGee, "A Social Movement: Phenomenon or Meaning," *Central States Speech Journal* 31 (Winter 1980): 233–244.

3　Herbert W. Simons, "Requirements, Problems, and Strategies: A Theory of Persuasion for Social Movements," *Quarterly Journal of Speech* 56 (February 1970): 1–11; John Wilson, *Introduction to Social Movements* (New York: Basic Books, 1973): 156–166.

4　"Drums, Sweat, and Tears: Heeding the Call of the Drums," *Newsweek*, 24 June 1991, 46–51 and 52–53.

5　"Hunger, Tents Now Part of Sweatshop Strike," Lafayette, Indiana *Journal and Courier*, 28 March 2000, C1-C2; "Anti-Sweatshop Group, School to Meet Again," Lafayette, Indiana *Journal and Courier* 6 April 2000, A1 and A10; "Activists Visually Portray Reality of Sweatshop Labor," *The Purdue Exponent*, 4 April 2000, 3.

6　James W. Chesebro, "Cultures in Conflict: A Generic and Axiological View," *Today's Speech* 21 (Spring 1973): 12.

7　Roger W. Howe, "The Rhetoric of the Death of God Theology," *Southern Speech Communication Journal* 37 (Winter 1971): 150.

8　Paul Kirtz, ed., *Humanist Manifestos I and II* (Buffalo, NY: Prometheus Books, 1973).

9　Brant Short, "Earth First! and the Rhetoric of Moral Confrontation," *Communication Studies* 42 (Summer 1991): 172–188.

10　Herbert W. Simons, James W. Chesebro, and C. Jack Orr, "A Movement Perspective on the 1972 Presidential Campaign," *Quarterly Journal of Speech* 59 (April 1973): 168–179.

11　Herbert W. Simons, Elizabeth W. Mechling, and Howard N. Schreier, "The Functions of Human Communication in Mobilizing from the Bottom Up: The Rhetoric of Social Movements," *Handbook of Rhetorical and Communication Theory,* Carroll C. Arnold and John W. Bowers, eds. (Boston: Allyn and Bacon, 1984): 792–867; Elizabeth Jean Nelson, "'Nothing Ever Goes Well Enough': Mussolini and the Rhetoric of Perpetual Struggle," *Communication Studies* 42 (Spring 1991): 22–42.

12　Jackson B. Miller, "'Indians,' 'Braves,' and 'Redskins': A Performative Struggle for Control of an Image," *Quarterly Journal of Speech* 85 (May 1999): 189.

13　Richard Morris and Philip Wander, "Native American Rhetoric: Dancing in the Shadows of the Ghost Dance," *Quarterly Journal of Speech* 76 (May 1990): 164–191; Randall A. Lake, "Enacting Red Power: The Consummatory Function in Native American Protest Rhetoric," *Quarterly Journal of Speech* 69 (May 1983): 127–142.

14　A. Phillips, "Christian Men on the March," *Macleans*, 6 October 1997, 52–53; E. Doerr, "Promise Keepers: Who, What, and Why?" *USA Today*, March 1998, 30–32; J. W. Kennedy, "Up from the Ashes?" *Christianity Today*, 18 May 1998, 29.

15　"A New Awakening," *U.S. New & Report*, 30 October 1995, 32–34; "And Now What?" *Newsweek*, 30 October 1995, 28–36; "To the Beat of His Drum," *Time*, 23 October 1995, 34–36.

[16] "High Noon on the Hustings," *Newsweek*, 22 May 2000, 30–31.

[17] At one time labor organizations such as the United Auto Workers, Teamsters, and the AFL-CIO were movement organizations within the American labor social movement. Today, however, they are institutions that control millions of workers, bargain collectively with giant corporations, have direct roles in grievance processes, and have attained (in many situations) profit sharing for members. The Teamsters and other unions have attempted to thwart the efforts of new unions such as the United Farm Workers in California.

[18] Simons, "Problems, Requirements, and Strategies," 11.

[19] Joseph R. Gusfield, *Protest, Reform, and Revolt: A Reader in Social Movements* (New York: John Wiley & Sons, 1970): 310.

[20] See for example, Mobile Corporation, "Target: environmental excellence," *Time* 10 June 1991, 4.

[21] Carol McClurg Mueller, "Building Social Movement Theory," *Frontiers in Social Movement Theory*, Aldon D. Morris and Carol McClurg Mueller, eds. (New Haven, CT: Yale University Press, 1992): 9.

[22] Donald Fishman, "Reform Judaism and the Anti-Zionist Persuasive Campaign, 1897–1915," *Communication Quarterly* 46 (Fall 1998): 376.

[23] Pamela E. Oliver and Gerald Marwell, "Mobilizing Technologies for Collective Action," *Frontiers in Social Movement Theory*, 258.

[24] *Wall Street Journal*, 16 November 1972, 26.

[25] "Five Ways to Prevent Abortion (And One Way That Won't)," Lafayette, Indiana *Journal and Courier*, 8 September 1985, A-15; "In 1982, If You Have a Miscarriage You Could Be Charged with Murder," Lafayette, Indiana *Journal and Courier*, 26 May 1981, B-4.

[26] *Time*, 26 April 1993, 27.

[27] Charles J. Stewart, "The Evolution of a Revolution: Stokely Carmichael and the Rhetoric of Black Power," *Quarterly Journal of Speech* 83 (November 1997): 429–446.

[28] Jonathan I. Lange, "A Refusal to Compromise: The Case of Earth First!" *Western Journal of Speech Communication* 54 (Fall 1990): 473–494.

[29] *People*, 28 December 1998–4 January 1999, 145.

[30] Other names for innovative social movements are revisionary, alternative, redemptive, and transformative.

[31] Other names for revivalistic social movements are reactionary, regressive, and nationalistic.

[32] Other names for resistance social movements are conservative and counter.

[33] James R. Andrews, "Confrontation at Columbia: Study in Coercive Rhetoric," *Quarterly Journal of Speech* 55 (February 1969): 9–16; Donald E. Phillips, *Student Protest, 1860–1970: An Analysis of the Speeches and Issues* (Lanham, MD: University Press of America, 1985); James Miller, *"Democracy Is in the Street": From Port Huron to the Siege of Chicago* (New York: Simon & Schuster, 1987).

[34] Hans Toch, *The Social Psychology of Social Movements* (Indianapolis: Bobbs-Merrill, 1965): 21–26.

[35] Steven R. Goldzwig, "Multiculturalism, Rhetoric and the Twentieth-First Century," *Southern Communication Journal* 63 (1998): 276.

[36] Steven R. Goldzwig and Patricia A. Sullivan, "Reconfiguring the Rhetoric of Social Movements: Concepts and Approaches in Transition," unpublished paper presented at the 1999 annual convention of the National Communication Association.

[37] R. R. McGuire, "Speech Acts, Communicative Competence and the Paradox of Authority," *Philosophy and Rhetoric* 10 (Winter 1977): 33; Herbert W. Simons, "Persuasion in Social Conflicts: A Critique of Prevailing Concepts and a Framework for Future Research," *Speech Monographs* 39 (November 1972): 233.

[38] Leland M. Griffin, "A Dramatistic Theory of the Rhetoric of Movements," *Critical Responses to Kenneth Burke*, William Rueckert, ed. (Minneapolis: University of Minnesota Press, 1969): 456.

[39] Anthony Oberschall, *Social Conflict and Social Movements* (Englewood Cliffs, NJ: Prentice-Hall, 1973): 188; Simons, "Persuasion in Social Conflicts," 235.

[40] PETA, *Animal Rights*, n.d.

[41] William H. Higgins, "Welcoming Address," *Report of the Proceedings of the American Federation of Labor* (1900), 13.

[42] Simons, Mechling, and Schreier, "The Functions of Human Communication in Mobilizing from the Bottom Up," 797.

[43] Robert S. Cathcart, "Movements: Confrontation as Rhetorical Form," *Southern Speech Communication Journal* 43 (Spring 1978): 242.

[44] John D. McCarthy and Mark Wolfson, "Consensus Movements, Conflict Movements, and the Co-optation of Civil and State Infrastructures," *Frontiers in Social Movement Theory*, 275.

[45] Cathcart, "Movements," 242; Robert S. Cathcart, "New Approaches to the Study of Movements: Defining Movements Rhetorically," *Western Speech* 36 (Spring 1972): 87.

[46] Cathcart, "Movements," 246.

[47] "Shanty Raids," *Wall Street Journal*, 9 April 1986, 32; "PU Police Arrest 22 Anti-Apartheid Supporters," *The Purdue Exponent*, 7 April 1986, 1; "Berkeley Police Arrest 120 Protestors in Violent Campus Shantytown Dispute," *The Purdue Exponent*, 4 April 1986, 1; "Purdue Defends Apartheid Stance," Lafayette, Indiana *Journal and Courier*, 15 April 1986, 1.

[48] Herbert W. Simons, *Persuasion: Understanding, Practice and Analysis* (Reading, MA: Addison Wesley, 1976): 18.

[49] Ralph H. Turner and Lewis M. Killian, *Collective Behavior* (Englewood Cliffs, NJ: Prentice-Hall, 1972): 291.

[50] Turner and Killian, 291.

[51] Michael Lipsky, "Protest as Political Resource," *The American Political Science Review* 52 (December 1968): 1154.

[52] Turner and Killian, *Collective Behavior*, 421.

[53] *Wall Street Journal*, 9 April 1986, 32.

[54] Terence V. Powderly, "Address of the General Master Workman," *Proceedings of the General Assembly of the Knights of Labor*, October 1887, 1539.

[55] James R. Andrews, "Reflections of the National Character in American Rhetoric," *Quarterly Journal of Speech* 57 (October 1971): 316–324; Lipsky, "Protest as Political Resource," 1153–1157.

[56] Kurt W. Ritter, "Confrontation as Moral Drama: The Boston Massacre in Rhetorical Perspective," *Southern Speech Communication Journal* 42 (Winter 1977): 114–136.

[57] Lipsky, "Protest as Political Resource," 1154.

[58] Turner and Killian, *Collective Behavior*, 298.

[59] Simons, *Persuasion*, 43–44; Simons, "Persuasion in Social Conflict," 232.

[60] John H. Patton, "Rhetoric at Catonsville: Daniel Berrigan, Conscience, and Image Attraction," *Today's Speech* 23 (Winter 1975): 3–12.

[61] Parke G. Burgess, "Crisis Rhetoric: Coercion vs. Force," *Quarterly Journal of Speech* 59 (February 1973): 69.

[62] Malcolm X, "The Ballot or the Bullet," *The Sixties Papers: Documents of a Rebellious Age* (New York: Praeger, 1984): 126–132.

[63] Robert J. Doolittle, "Riots as Symbolic: Criticism and Approach," *Central States Speech Journal* 27 (Winter 1976): 310–317.

[64] "The Overture: The Fire This Time" and "Violence: Los Angeles in a Fury," *Time* 11 May 1992, 18–25 and 26–29; "Days of Rage," *U.S. News and Report*, 11 May 1992, 20–26.

[65] James R. Andrews, "The Rhetoric of Coercion and Persuasion: The Reform Bill of 1812," *Quarterly Journal of Speech* 56 (April 1970): 195.

SOCIAL MOVEMENTS AS
INTERPRETIVE SYSTEMS

Chapter 1 defined social movements and explained the importance of persuasion in efforts to bring about or resist change. This chapter provides a theoretical orientation for studying social movements from a communication perspective.

Simply put, communication is the process through which "you" and "I" become an "us" as well as the process through which "we" realize that "you" and "I" are drifting apart. It is the fundamental social process through which individuals create and sustain relationships or, some would say, relational units such as "The Stewarts" and "The Smiths" or "The Black Panthers" and "The United Autoworkers Union." It therefore stands to reason that understanding the social movement requires us to understand the communication process through which it came into being, interacted with other relational units such as institutions and countermovements, and tried to sustain itself.

Students of human communication, since Aristotle's day, have suggested a variety of models (sometimes called paradigms) to explain communication in terms of other familiar phenomena. For example, you have probably heard people talk about communication as though it were a mechanical process ("I couldn't convey my meaning to her" or "We weren't on the same wavelength" or "I need your feedback"). As communication theorists used models to explain communication, they posed interesting and important questions, such as: Is communication a matter of senders transmitting meaning to receivers, or is it a matter of receivers constructing meaning from all the stimuli in their environment? Over time the sophistication of our theorizing and our research techniques grew, and we realized that some approaches to communication work well in particular settings (such as advertising or arguing) and others are more overarching ways of understanding human communication. Perhaps the most widely accepted general perspective today is the "systems model." The late communication theorist B. Aubrey Fisher identified four characteristics of the systems view of communication: the nonsummativity of its components; the importance of structure, function, and evolution; the principle of openness; and hierarchical organization.[1] Let us begin by reviewing each of these tenets and its relevance to persuasion and social movements.

Systems Theory and Communication

Characteristic 1: Nonsummativity

Any system is comprised of interdependent components. The "principle of nonsummativity" describes the whole of this interdependence as something other than a simple sum of the individual parts. Consider the difference between a pile and a system: one item can be removed from the pile without altering the other pieces, but any change in a system's components will produce changes in other components as well as changes in the overall system. For example, the removal of a kidney requires the other kidney to work harder and a dirty fuel injector causes your car to run inefficiently and unreliably.

The interdependent relationships among components of a system serve as a catalyst that fosters the creation of a whole that behaves differently from its individual members. We may enjoy a rally against mistreatment of research animals more (or less) than we enjoy the company of individual rally members. As individuals interact they become a group, usually with its own identity such as MADD (Mothers Against Drunk Driving), the National Gay and Lesbian Task Force, and PETA (People for the Ethical Treatment of Animals). Thus, just as auto parts can be put together to form a Mercedes, a Taurus, or a Model T Ford, similar people interacting differently can create noticeably different human groups— each with its own identity, behavioral tendencies, needs, and energy for survival (synergy).

The principle of nonsummativity is important to understanding social movements because a movement collectivity is something more or less than the sum of its parts. In fact, Fisher illustrates nonsummativity by contrasting labor unions with "all left-handed people:"

> There is simply little or no consistent effect of one left-handed person on another because of their left-handedness. But the labor union does function as a whole in many significant ways. Its members go on strike as a whole. They all go to work, perform assigned jobs, and in other ways honor the labor contract as a whole. In short, the actions of one affect the actions of others.[2]

The interaction between individuals—their communication—serves as a catalyst for the creation of something other than an aggregate or heap of individuals.

Students of social movement persuasion need to pay close attention to the communication opportunities and activities that transform individuals into groups. Fisher's left-handed people constitute a heap only because they have yet to interact on the basis of their shared concerns about left-handedness. Conversely, the labor union is a system only because individual workers interacted over the years to develop a sense of "usness." In his autobiography, American Federation of Labor founder Samuel Gompers reflected upon the opportunities for interaction among his fellow cigar makers:

> It gave education in such a way as to develop personality, for in no other place were we so wholly natural. The nature of our work developed a camaraderie of the shop such as few workers enjoy. It was a world in itself—a cosmopolitan world. Shipmates came from everywhere—some had been nearly everywhere. When they told us of strange lands and peoples, we listened eagerly.[3]

Other social movement organizations come into being because of shared concerns over abortion, nuclear power plants, and the environment. Some of these interactions have developed into the consciousness-raising sessions of the women's liberation, gay rights, and fledgling men's liberation movements. In each case, individuals discover common experiences, aspirations, problems, and solutions through communication. Identification with a cause or social movement can emerge from the development of a social movement organization as a communication system.

Characteristic 2: Function-Structure-Evolution

The second axiom of systems theory is that interdependent relationships can be explained in terms of function, structure, and evolution. Human behaviors and actions are purposeful because they fulfill needs or "functions" for individuals and collectivities. When a function regularly recurs (such as seasonal greetings, monthly bill payments, and the selection of government representatives), we develop behavioral "structures" that assure their performance (in these examples Christmas cards, household budgets, and elections). Most of these structures perform the function imperfectly, and we continue to tinker to enhance the performance of the function. Sometimes we create a structure that performs the function so nicely that needs and functions previously obscured from view become apparent. At this point, we "evolve" into a new phase guided by these new functional necessities and we search for fresh behavioral structures. Thus, the interplay of functional behaviors leads to evolutionary change as the system moves from the performance of one hierarchy of functions to another.

The structure of a social movement can refer to its membership profile, its organizational structure, or its pattern of strategic efforts. The anti–Vietnam War movement needed dedicated workers during its early phases, but it needed a plurality of voters in 1968 and 1972. The American Federation of Labor organized skilled tradesmen and excluded unskilled industrial workers, a tactic that worked until the increasing industrialization of America led to the formation of the Industrial Workers of the World (IWW) and later the Congress of Industrial Organizations (CIO). David Duke's branch of the Ku Klux Klan moved from the old Klan's cross-burnings and lynchings to the recruitment of Catholic and women members and the use of television and radio talk shows. The pro-life movement began with emphasis on elections and the passage of a constitutional amendment, but turned toward direct actions such as Operation Rescue's blockades of abortion clinics and civil disobedience when elections and legislative efforts failed to stop abortions.

Chapter 3 will identify and illustrate the persuasive functions of social movements and the ways in which persuasive communication fulfills these needs. For now, the point is that social movements evolve structures to perform functions, thereby altering the pattern of functions remaining to be performed. This process is continuous—every aspect of a system has evolved from, and will evolve into, something else; hence beginnings and endings are basically punctuation marks between phases or stages. We rarely know when a social movement begins or ends, only that it has evolved.

Characteristic 3: Hierarchical Organization

The third axiom is that all systems have hierarchical organization. It is possible to locate each system (a social movement) within an encompassing "supra-system" (the society) and to ascertain "subsystems" (such as individual organizations and persons) within each system. All systems are influenced both by their subsystems and by their supra-systems. However, the precise distinction between subsystem, system, and supra-system is generally a matter of the observer's perspective (one could just as easily consider the movement as the supra-system, an organization as the system, and individuals as the subsystems). Once we have identified the hierarchical structure of systems, the level of analysis is largely a matter of choice.

This "nesting" of systems in other systems is important for understanding social movements. It is not uncommon for social movements to fail, even if they are led by major figures, enjoy institutional support, or have widespread support. Eugene V. Debs' American Railway Union won several major victories in 1893 leading to vast increases in membership. Although that may seem like a good thing, Debs lacked the communication structures necessary to control, discipline and organize these new members. The union was promptly and permanently demolished only months later in the Pullman Strike of 1894.

An energetic social movement may change the behavior of the supra-system by altering the supra-system's functional needs. The civil rights movement raised society's concerns about discrimination, poverty, and voting rights by demonstrating that all was not well in the United States. The War on Poverty, the Civil Rights Act of 1964, the Voting Rights Act of 1965, and other changes were responses to a restructured set of functional priorities derived from the movement's demands for justice and white Americans' discomfort over these demands. In the aftermath of the Kennedy assassination, the 1964 Democratic Party had little need for African-American votes to defeat Barry Goldwater and the Republicans. As a consequence the party convention voted against challenges to several segregationist delegations. But by 1988, the Democrats sorely needed Jesse Jackson and his multitude of new voters to contest the presidential election, and Jackson's historic convention address signaled the end of the civil rights movement as challengers at the convention gate. The African-American voting bloc had taken its rhetorical place alongside the labor and women's movements as institutionalized pillars of the Democratic Party.

Characteristic 4: The Degree of Openness

Fisher's fourth axiom of systems theory is that any system can be described on the basis of its "openness"—the permeability of its boundaries. We can assess a system with respect to the freedom of exchange between the system and its environment and thereby classify it as "open" or "closed." Open systems have boundaries that permit the interaction of system and environment, whereas closed systems are entirely self-contained. The degree of openness is important because open and closed systems are governed by different principles.

Closed systems are governed by the principle of equilibrium—the final state of the closed system is determined by its initial state because a self-contained system must sustain balance without any help from the outside. Thus, a closed system must eventually return to its initial starting point. Conversely, open systems are governed by the principle of "equifinality" which states that "the same final state may be reached from different initial conditions and in different ways . . . [and] different open systems with the same initial condition could well achieve different final states."[4] Put differently, you can get anywhere in an open system from anywhere else, and you can get there by a variety of paths.

The difference between the equilibrium of closed systems and the equifinality of open systems derives from the principle of entropy, an irreversible process of disintegration. Closed systems can only respond to entropy by exerting a counterforce (negentropy) to slow disintegration. But once slowed, the disintegration is not reversed. As Fisher observes, "The balanced state of homeostasis . . . does not suggest an increase in order or structure, only a slowing down or stoppage of the disintegrative process."[5] The rights of African Americans, women, gays, and animals have expanded in spite of Herculean efforts by institutions and resistance movements.

Open systems, capable of exchange with their environment, can combat entropy either by adding new information from the environment or by generating their own original or novel information. In this sense, open systems take stock of their environment and adjust to it. The net result is that open systems can increase order over the original state and grow stronger because of a more equal sharing of rights, duties, and rewards.

There are few truly closed systems, even in the natural sciences, and all human and social systems are considered open. Nevertheless, theorists have found it useful to draw upon the similarities between persons and machines to explain the process of human communication. Therefore, all systems models of communication emphasize that: the whole is more than the sum of its parts because of the interaction of persons; communication systems evolve as structures perform functions; each system is comprised of subsystems while itself constituting part of a suprasystem, both of which influence and are influenced by it; and each system is to some degree capable of exchange with its environment. Having said this, we turn to the differences between "mechanical" and "social" systems as models of human communication.

Mechanical vs. Social Systems

People employ a mechanical systems model to describe communication every time they mention transmission, reception, feedback, noise, barriers, breakdowns, leverage, being pushed around, or being on the same wavelength. They tend to think of communication as a process of mechanical adjustment. This thesis pervades works that emphasize the similarities between human communication and mechanical systems.[6] Indeed, a *closed system* does measure its environment and adjust to it. But a thermostat has only one pattern of reaction (when the temperature drops, it heats until the satisfactory temperature is reached). Unlike a person, the thermostat cannot decide to offer you a sweater, close the windows, or build a fire; it simply performs its specified function for the system. The thermostat cannot choose; it can only execute. Even the most sophisticated computer can only execute programs provided—at some point and in some form—by a human programmer.

Dennis Smith challenges the mechanical view of human communication when he notes that our study of communication is too heavily influenced by the engineering sciences. He argues that the differences between human communication and mechanical systems are more important than the similarities. Smith specifically challenges the concept of "communication breakdown" on the grounds that it teaches four fallacies about communication:

1. *The fallacy of linearity* presumes that communication is a straight line of actions from one person to another, rather than an interdependent process in which people anticipate and build upon one another's (and even outsiders') behaviors to create meaning.

2. *The fallacy of mechanism* mistakenly treats persons as machines rather than humans, thereby omitting consideration of biological, psychological, and sociological influences.

3. *The fallacy of noncommunication* presumes that communication involves purely what is said or written, and overlooks the communicative significance of interpretation.

4. *The fallacy of reification* presumes that unsatisfactory communication results from a "thing" (breakdown) that can be removed or fixed, rather than from interpretive behavior.[7]

We would add a fifth fallacy to Smith's list. *The fallacy of success* presumes that communication will be satisfactory and effective unless something goes wrong (i.e., the breakdown). Much communication is fairly difficult (e.g., asking for a grade change, complimenting a friend's unattractive outfit, interviewing for a job), and effective or satisfying communication is more often the exception than the rule. It is more productive to approach communication as a constructive, adaptive process at which people sometimes succeed and often fail. All of our conflicts are not due to "failures to communicate" or communication breakdowns; many derive from deep-seated, irreconcilable differences between subsystems. Too often references to "ineffective communication" or a "breakdown in communication" distract us from more important issues.

Smith's critique of communication breakdowns illustrates the implications of choosing inappropriate metaphoric models for explaining human communication. Like Smith and Fisher, we find mechanical models inappropriate for the explanation of human communication in general and social movement persuasion in particular because of their omission of human choice and creativity from the process. However, the concept of system need not be discarded simply because mechanical metaphors are inappropriate to social systems.

Brent D. Ruben summarizes the four propositions of a social or living systems approach as follows:

1. People, like other animals, are instances of living systems.

2. Living systems are structural and functional units (individual and social) that maintain themselves (and grow, change, and deteriorate) only through interactions with their environment.

3. Environmental interaction[s] are of two types: (a) transactions that involve the transformation of matter-energy, which may be termed

biophysical metabolism; and (b) transactions that involve the transformation of data information, which may be termed informational-metabolism or communication.

4. The functional goal [of the behavior] of all living systems is adaptation with the environment.[8]

First, Ruben differentiates living systems that grow and change only through interaction with their environments from both mechanical systems (which only deteriorate) and from closed systems (which cannot interact with their environments). Elaborating upon the characteristics of living systems, Ruben says that there are no "breakdowns" in communication because communication with the environment is constant so long as the system is alive. Indeed, silence itself is a means of adapting to the environment.

Second, Ruben observes that an organism adapts to its environment, and adapts its environment to it. It is not a question of how a persuader responds to a rhetorical situation *or* how the persuader creates the rhetorical situation through language.[9] Rather, we should search for both in the mutual adaptation of system with environment.

Third, adaptation occurs as "discrepancies between the needs and capacities of the system and those of the environment emerge, and the system, acting on the discrepancy, strives to close the gap." From a social systems perspective, the natural, healthy state of affairs involves people actively adapting to their environment by creating alternatives and choosing among them. This creative choosing leads us into new eras of human progress.

Conceptions of Human Influence

Influence in mechanical systems is highly manipulative. A persuader examines the persuasive landscape and ascertains (1) the audience's susceptibility to influence and (2) the persuader's resources for influence, so that (3) the persuader can construct or apply a formula or equation that creates the necessary and sufficient stimuli for the auditor to respond in accordance with the persuader's intent. Mechanical conceptions of influence suggest that we can structure message variables to produce consistently the desired audience behavior. The key to mechanistic persuasion is knowing the right equation for a particular target audience.

But influence in social systems is adaptive behavior. An organism can adapt to its environment in a variety of ways (the principle of equifinality): by attempting to change its environment, by attempting to change itself, or by attempting to escape from the environment through selective attention, selective perception, and selective retention. For example drivers choose to ignore or obey speed limits or road conditions, drive faster or slower, take dubious shortcuts, or to maintain the car's mechanical operation. No matter how many speed limit signs the driver sees, she or he can choose to ignore them. Some drivers choose to pay the cost of a radar detector for an additional 5 to 10 miles per hour.

Adaptive humans have often confounded mechanical systems theorists. Sensing that someone has concocted a formula to influence them, auditors can feel that their essential human ability to choose is endangered. These concerned humans may refuse to comply by imposing new conditions, misunderstanding the message, and/or reconstructing the relationship and its ground rules. While mechanistic theorists revise their equation to account for this erratic behavior, the social systems theorists recognize it as the kind of adaptive behavior that is central to communication studies.

Mechanical systems models are particularly ill-suited to the study of persuasion and social movements because movements need to be creative and unusual. Any social movement that responds predictably to institutions will not long survive, since institutions create and enforce all of the rules. Organizer Saul Alinsky recommends that:

> Radicals must be resilient, adaptable to shifting political circumstances, and sensitive enough to the process of action and reaction to avoid being trapped by their own tactics and forced to travel a road not of their own choosing. In short, radicals must have a degree of control over the flow of events.[10]

A social movement must adapt in a manner that retains its freedom and independence from institutions, and that would seem to render institutional equations for influence almost useless.

Additionally, it is very difficult to predict the effectiveness of a tactic. An assassination may end a movement or perpetuate it by creating a martyr (perhaps even removing an unpopular leader). Nonviolence worked well for Gandhi in India and Martin Luther King, Jr. in America, but it failed horribly for Jews in Nazi Germany (whether from their lack of organization or the society's lack of moral sensitivity is arguable). Human influence in social movements, then, is by necessity highly adaptive and does not conform to manipulative mechanical laws.

Conception of Human Conflict

Mechanistic systems view conflict as imbalances that should be either prevented or repaired. At best, imbalance is prevented and the system hums along, quietly disintegrating under the law of entropy. When imbalance does occur, balance can only be restored after considerable upheaval (negentropy). When a car breaks down, it is out of commission until the mechanic pronounces it "as good as new." Equilibrium is attained only through financial setback, after the upheaval of children waiting at school, the cat stranded at the vet's, and a strong sense of frustration. In systems terminology, negentropy has been introduced to restore equilibrium. Because nothing is ever *gained* in mechanical systems, we must engage in preventive maintenance of our mechanical systems lest they "break down."

But social systems see conflict as creating the opportunity for growth and progress. Discrepancies between the needs and capacities of the system and the needs and capacities of the environment challenge the organism. If the organism fails to resolve the discrepancy, it dies; but if it meets the challenge adequately, it survives and evolves into a new phase of life. As Alinsky observes, "in the politics of human life, consistency is not a virtue. To be consistent means, according to the Oxford Universal Dictionary, 'standing still or not moving.' Men [women] must change with the times or die."[11] Of course, this discrepancy simultaneously creates an opportunity for destruction that is the nature of equifinality. The important fact is that unlike the mechanical systems model, the social systems model views conflict and controversy as *potentially* constructive or creative, if somewhat troublesome. The difference is that upheaval can lead to an enhanced state of order rather than simply slowed disintegration and temporarily restored order. Let us return to the automobile.

A flat tire can only be restored to its original state, but the drivers who adapt by fixing their flats can improve themselves. They "grow" as a result of the problem and will never again be quite as awed by the prospect of a flat. Thus, while mechanical conflict is purely disruptive, social systems conflict leads to evolutionary change. Because institutions function to maintain systemic order, no study rooted in mechanical premises should ever sanction the creation of conflict. Indeed, rhetorical studies of agitation reflected this institutional bias until Herbert Simons attacked it and suggested a "dual perspective" (institution and social movement). In so doing, Simons revealed this weakness in mechanist assumptions.[12]

If human conflict is more nearly social than mechanical, then controversy and conflict are our only paths toward progress. If this is the case, then we should employ models that encourage consideration of multiple conflicting viewpoints and focus on the process of ongoing adaptation. Simons' works on social movements broke important theoretical ground in the early 1970s, but he needed to go further. No model based upon mechanical assumptions can admit the equivalence of both agitator and institutional perspectives since mechanical systems models assume that (1) no good can come from imbalance, (2) the institution is empowered to maintain balance, and (3) agitators and social movements function to create imbalance.

The subsystems of a social system attempt to close the discrepancy in various ways. Institutions usually minimize the discrepancy in favor of the prior state of affairs (in which they gained their authority), while one or more parts of the system strive to resolve it in other directions. After the U.S. Supreme Court's *Brown v. Board of Education* decision in 1954 ruled segregation unconstitutional, for example, civil rights activists highlighted for us the discrepancy between the law and our practices; southern politicians such as Ross Barnett raised the possibility that states could ignore the federal law; and the federal government wrestled with the problem of satisfying all of its constituent subsystems. The important point is that all parts work in their own ways to adjust their system with the environment. Therefore, all of their efforts deserve comparable attention. Conversely, it would be counterproductive to favor an institution's effort to maintain balance, because that effort could or would restrain the system's adaptive capabilities.

Conception of Human Relationships

The third issue is systemic maturation. Mechanical systems are at their prime when new or almost new (some require a brief "break-in" period). All mechanical systems experience friction, deterioration, and general wear. With proper maintenance, this process of deterioration (entropy) can be slowed, but it can never be reversed; even if a Rolls Royce appreciates in value with age, its mechanical system nevertheless deteriorates. Such an approach to human communication is depressing at best and frightening at worst. It implies that relationships begin at or near their peak and can only be slowed in their deterioration—a view that hardly squares with friendship or dating relationships.

But the social systems approach presumes that relationships develop from initial encounters. Whether we choose to nurture or to ignore them, past experiences influence future conversations. From this perspective, experience and practice become important. Fixing one flat tire is no guarantee that you can fix another, but you expect the experience to prove useful. Similarly, a first date may be the best, or it may simply be the start of a growing relationship, depending upon the parties' willingness and abilities to build upon their encounter for the process of mutual accommodation. The social systems view suggests that one is likely to find the more successful relationships among the longer ones, while admitting that some quickly develop and others may persist unhappily.

The mechanical systems observer of social movement persuasion is concerned with stability, while the social systems theorist is concerned with change. Because social systems (governed by equifinality) can develop from any state into any other state through any means, the study of social systems emphasizes the process by which the subsystems emerge and adapt by creating alternatives and choosing among them. Our country is very different in the twenty-first century from what it was in the eighteenth century. While not all of these changes have been improvements, neither have they all been disintegrative. These changes have been adaptive efforts by humans not yet born in 1776 to adapt to environments not yet existing in 1776. In this light, the American Revolution, the Civil War, women's suffrage, agrarianism, labor and civil rights, and environmental movements have led us into new eras of life in the United States that could not be satisfactorily explained as a return to equilibrium, because each of these movements created novel alternatives. Just as we study U.S. history developmentally, a social systems approach to social movement persuasion views the relationship between the movement and society developmentally. The frequent intransigence of some labor unions today, for example, can be better understood in terms of management's parental behavior during labor's infancy and adolescence.

While people will continue to use the jargon of mechanical systems to describe human communication, we hope they will become aware of the implications of their metaphors. To conceptualize communication mechanically is to conceive of conflict and change as disruptive, influence as manipulative, and relationships as disintegrative. It is more accurate, realistic, and therefore more productive to conceive of conflict as adaptive and evolutionary, influence as accommodative, and relationships as integrative. Toward this end, we need to formulate approaches to social movement persuasion that embody these assumptions.

Chapter 1 discussed the pervasiveness of persuasion in social movements, and this chapter has stressed the importance of thinking about human activities as growing and changing social systems. But we have yet to set forth a theoretical framework that can help us find answers to the basic questions about social movement persuasion. We will explain the interpretive systems model of political communication and then offer a framework for analyzing social movements.

The Interpretive Systems Approach to Political Communication

Our discussion of systems models has, until now, emphasized the ways that interdependent components shape communication. But systems theorists from other disciplines could well protest that we have been discussing sociological, political, or economic systems. Having said that we should study social movements as communication systems, it is time to see how communication variables are arranged into social systems. Craig Allen Smith's interpretive systems model of political communication is based on the structures that people develop and adopt to negotiate meaning and understanding.

The interpretive systems model begins with four involuntary "Personal Interpretive Processes": needing, symbolizing, reasoning, and preferencing.[13] *Needing* is the process through which individuals formulate and reformulate their needs and goals. *Symbolizing* is the process of formulating and reformulating one's semantic relationships among meanings and images. *Reasoning* is the process of formulating and reformulating explanatory accounts that "make sense" out of the needs and symbols. *Preferencing* is the process of formulating and reformulating one's personal hierarchy of values in relation to the needs, symbols, and reasons so that some become more important than others. These processes are independent. We learn new words when we need them and forget them when we do not. We sometimes reason our way to a preference, but we often muster reasons to rationalize an existing preference. We are often attracted to persons who think as we do, but we often learn to think like those persons to whom we are attracted.

Parents, teachers, clergy, and others teach and reinforce the "right" ways of needing, symbolizing, reasoning, and preferencing. Because each of us has different parents, teachers, and clergy, we develop personal ways of interpreting life. At home, in school, and through public discourse, each of us is exposed to multiple ways of interpreting life's ebb and flow. We soon discover that things that make sense to us sometimes make little sense to others.

Because we cannot isolate ourselves from other people, we need to coordinate our behavior with theirs. We do this by developing "Social Interpretive Structures" as ways to coordinate our personal needing, symbolizing, reasoning, and preferencing processes with those of others. People adopt or construct "languages" to coordinate their symbolizing, "logics" to coordinate their reasoning, "ideologies" to coordinate their preferencing, and "laws" to coordinate their need fulfillment activities. We use laws to guide our personal behavior, but few of us are students of the law and we all tend to interpret and apply society's laws in ways that are personally useful. Similarly, we use languages, logics, and ideologies to guide our daily behavior, and because few of us are professional students of language, logic, or ideology, most of us use them in ways that are personally useful.

Persons who share a Social Interpretive Structure are an "interpretive community." They are bound together, and separated from others, by their agreement to coordinate their personal interpretive behaviors. Thus, people who speak the same language are a linguistic community (such as French and English speaking Canadians); those who share rules of reasoning are a logical community (such as creationists and evolutionists); those who share ways of establishing their preferences are an ideological community (such as socialists and capitalists); and those who coordinate their needing with a set of laws are a legal community (such as lawyers and anarchists).

Each of us is born into an array of interpretive communities, and we soon learn to use their interpretive structures. Sometimes we merge multiple interpretive structures into one, perhaps by blending the economic logic of capitalism, the ideology of Christianity, and the laws of popular sovereignty. Social movements often try to separate these fused structures. As we go through life, we encounter other people and their interpretive structures. We window shop a good deal, trying on new and old needs, words, reasons, and preferences to see how they fit. Over time we change the importance of our interpretive communities, and sometimes we change communities.

Interpretive communities are not congruent, and social and political stability require some kind of interpretive coalition. Liberals and conservatives, for example, disagree about many things, but they share a commitment to institutions that distinguish them from radicals and reactionaries. Institutions, by definition, legitimize a dominant language, logic, ideology, and law (such as the Constitution). They emphasize the importance of "working within the system," "following proper procedures," and "not rocking the boat," and, indeed, that is how most changes come about.

But sooner or later some of these incongruent interpretive communities come into conflict. Language, logic, ideology, and laws are interdependent. As elections, appointments, and rulings empower interpretive communities, they also empower their languages, logics, and ideologies. The language of the interpretive community in power necessarily disadvantages members of its competing communities, as when they define words such as patriotic, right, and America. The temporarily dominant ideology frames the society's problems and solutions, such that the outgoing community's solutions often become the incoming community's problems. And the logic of the temporarily dominant interpretive community defines the rationality of policies, as when they tackle deficits by cutting taxes and spending, by increasing taxes and spending, or by increasing one and cutting the other. The establishing of one interpretive structure as legitimate necessarily disadvantages people who do not share it. Moreover, it poorly equips people who use it to coordinate their perceptions with all those people who do not use it. Thus, the people with the most severe grievances are generally least able to voice them in the ways that institutions either understand or recognize as legitimate. The movements toward and against bilingual education are examples of conflicting linguistic communities struggling over laws, while the pro-life and pro-choice movements are examples of conflicting languages, logics, and ideologies.

Politics consists of the struggle among interpretive communities to establish their own interpretive structures as legitimate so as to define social and political realities for everybody else. When an interpretive community feels that it can be effective within the system, it plays by the rules because those rules provide them with advantages. But when individuals or communities lose confidence in the responsiveness of institutions they begin to mobilize from the bottom up. They step outside existing laws, language, logic, and ideology to challenge them. They begin to become social movements. The interpretive systems model is an integrative framework that can help us to see that controversies arise because different people have incongruent needs, preferences, and verbal constructions of reality. Moreover, it helps us to see that these interpretive structures are created and learned through communication. Thus, the interpretive systems model helps us understand social movements as communication.

The interpretive systems approach to social movements enables us to see that individuals form relationships and groups on the basis of their needs, symbols, reasons, and preferences. Agitators use language to artic-ulate their potential followers' needs and to critique institutions. They frequently must avoid the dominant language and ideology because fig-ures of speech are figures of thought that can trap the protestor in the web of established modes of thinking. Later chapters will explore some of the ways in which social movements use nontraditional rhetorical forms such as music, slogans, ridicule, and obscenities to introduce new ways of thinking about persistent sources of dissatisfaction.

Studying Social Movements as Interpretive Systems: "The Question"

Those who study the persuasive efforts of social movements can use the interpretive or social systems perspective by pursuing the question, *Which individuals, conceiving themselves to be what "people" in what environ-ment, use what relational patterns and what adaptive strategies with what evolu-tionary results?* Let us examine each part of this question.[14]

Which Individuals?

Since persuasion is a human activity, we must ascertain precisely which people create the system's adaptive effort. This means locating prominent individuals, their demographic traits, and their personality or character traits. We must devote more attention to the discovery of similarities and differences among the people who come to share particular rhetorical visions or self-conceptions. Discovering that a particular social movement is largely comprised of people with a low tolerance of ambiguity, a familiar-ity with crime and violence, and/or a common regional, racial, or religious experience may help us understand better their susceptibility to one charac-terization of their environment and their aversion to others. Thus, biologi-cal, sociological, and psychological information can help us to understand the movement, the hierarchy, and their interdependence.

Information about leaders is easily found in biographies, autobiogra-phies, movement studies, journalistic accounts, histories, and sin-gle-speaker rhetorical studies. The social systems approach does not equate a leader's background or behavior with the movement, but instead seeks to understand the leadership subsystem as a means of understanding the social movement system. It helps, for example, to study the theological development of Martin Luther King, Jr. and Mal-colm X before studying their persuasion. It is also helpful to know that John Birch Society founder Robert Welch wrote a primer on salesman-ship, that socialist labor leader Eugene V. Debs originally opposed strikes, and that neighborhood organizer Saul Alinsky held a Ph.D. in psychol-ogy. Much helpful information about major movement figures and their rhetoric can be found in two reference books: *American Orators* by Bernard Duffy and Halford Ross Ryan and *Free at Last? The Civil Rights Movement and the People Who Made it* by Fred Powledge.[15]

If studying the leadership subsystem requires biographical materials, studying the membership subsystem requires social-psychological data. This kind of scientific research is rare in communication literature. One exception is J. Michael Hogan's study of the people participating in rallies for former Alabama Governor George Wallace.[16] Consequently, the social systems critic will often need to draw upon surveys and studies from other disciplines, such as political scientist Fred Grupp's survey of John Birch Society members in 1964. His data suggested that Birchers were unrepresentative of the American population in several respects, and he was able to identify four types of Birch Society members based upon their reasons for joining: the "informed" who joined for educational benefits, the "like minded" who wanted to associate with people who "thought like them," the "politically committed" who wanted an outlet for their political activities, and the "ideological" who wanted something in which to believe.[17] (Chapter 4 will explore further the role of personality in the adaptive behavior of John Birch Society members, and chapter 14 will explore the logic of conspiracy argument.)

Our first task, then, is to identify the influential leaders and their followers: who are they? What are their demographic, experiential, sociological, psychological, and political traits? This first step tells us something about the people from whom the social movement develops. With this information we can better predict and explain the leaders' and members' adaptive choices. But unfortunately, it is not enough to identify individuals' traits or tendencies since systems theory is based on the principle of nonsummativity.

Conceiving Themselves to Be What "People?"

Having ascertained who people are and what they are like, it remains for us to discover who they think they are. Michael C. McGee, Aaron Gresson, and others have described the processes by which "peoples" arise through their shared myths and pasts.[18] In the final analysis, real people, not rhetorical creations, take action. In this sense, then, we need to be concerned with the movement's and the institutional hierarchy's self-conceptions. We should ascertain who they think they are, the degree to which this self-image corresponds with our appraisal of who they really are, and the psychological/sociological reasons for their rhetorical susceptibility to these particular characterizations. For example, many segregationists thought of themselves as protecting rather than disadvantaging African Americans.

When "you" and "I" create an "us," we begin to see something beyond our individuality. This "us" is the relational system created as you and I adapt to our environments (including each other's). In an old joke, the "faithful Indian companion Tonto" exemplifies our ability to adapt self-conception to environmental discrepancy:

> Lone Ranger: Well, Tonto, the Indians have us surrounded. It looks like we're done for.
>
> Tonto: What do you mean "We," Paleface?

In this joke, Tonto adapts to his environment by transforming his relational bonds: his Native-American identity became more salient for him than his friendship with the Lone Ranger. Tonto did not physically become "more Indian," but his perceptions changed significantly. He conceived himself as "Indian" rather than as the Lone Ranger's faithful companion. Similarly, when the labor movement song asks "Which Side Are You On?" the listener faces a choice much like Tonto's.

The self-conceptions of movement leaders and members are not always consistent with the demographic or experiential profiles. Well-heeled labor leaders are often seen on television complaining about inadequate wages as they prepare to be chauffeured back to labor headquarters. Religious groups believe they serve God by throwing bombs or by enacting a mass suicide in Guyana or Waco. The interpretive or social systems analyst wants to know how these people see themselves and how they develop that self-conception (in light of their objective characteristics) through communication.

In What Environment?

"In what environment" draws our attention to the world in which the organism must survive. Just as the organism develops, so does the environment, partly in response to the organism's adaptive behavior. But the environment contains other social and mechanical systems as well as the movement, all of which mitigate an organism's ability to adapt effectively to its environment. The social systems analyst needs to pursue factual materials about, for example, labor conditions or discriminatory practices against which to compare complaints of women, African Americans, and gays.

We are not interested only in the objective environment because humans interpret their environments. We must also consider characterizations or depictions of the environment. Our experiences (both direct and vicarious) and our relationships help us construct vocabularies and logical frameworks that we use to "make sense" of the world. We interpret people and events through these frameworks whenever possible and reformulate the interpretive frameworks whenever they prove dysfunctional (see, for example the frameworks of authoritarian and democratic personalities discussed in chapter 4). For example, the discrepancies that concern people most are instances of "relative deprivation": being denied something to which they feel entitled. These deprivations may be as blatant and specific as a wage cut, denial of the right to vote, expulsion from

the armed forces for being gay, or imprisonment. The perceived deprivation may be more subtle. The important point, as sociologist John Wilson
notes, is that "the individuals involved come to feel that their expectations are reasonable" and are being denied.[19] A frequent complaint of
protestors is that they are losing their status or self-respect. In testimony
before the Senate in 1883, a machinist emphasized dehumanization and
limited horizons:

> Well, the trade has been subdivided . . . so that a man never learns the
> machinist's trade now. . . . It has a very demoralizing effect upon the
> mind . . . . When I first went to learn the trade a machinist considered
> himself more than the average workingman; in fact he did not like to
> be called a workingman. Today he recognizes that he is simply a
> laborer the same as the others.[20]

The Native-American movement addresses the lost status and
self-respect of tribes that were well-developed and established centuries
before Europeans arrived to take their lands and their lives and subject
them to meager existences on barren "reservations." Women, African
Americans, Hispanics, and gays demand status and self-respect and to be
able to rise above the "glass ceiling" that permits them to view, yet prevents them from assuming, significant leadership roles in U.S. society.

Persuasion is important to the development of a sense of relative deprivation because people must realize that they have been short-changed.
How do both the social movement and institutional hierarchy perceive
the environment? Real things do happen to real people that constitute an
objective reality (a bloodied nose, a picket line, a limit on how high they
can rise on the corporate ladder, and a wage cut are all more than perceptual "tricks of the mind"). But these "real" events are perceived, experienced, and understood in diverse ways, leading to diverse realities. Thus,
we should focus on the competing characterizations of the environment
and the discrepancies among them.

Use What Relational Patterns?

Who establishes and maintains communicative systems with whom,
and how do people connect with one another? Not all that long ago the
only alternatives people had were written messages and face-to-face communication. Aggrieved people could write petitions or print fliers, but
that limited them to people who could read and write—a real constraint
on communication with unskilled workers and people denied education
by institutions. Face-to-face communication was inefficient, as loudspeakers did not come into common use until the 1920s and, during the Depression, the expenditure of scarce resources on amplifiers was unusual.
Union organizers talked to their fellow workers on the job, at campfires,
and at impromptu meetings. But it was difficult for them to gain access to
management or, to put it differently, management could simply refuse to

meet with protestors. And if the protest meetings seemed to pose a threat, private security forces and police were on call to disperse them.

But the twentieth century was the century of technological change. Huey Long of the "Share Our Wealth" movement was the first to exploit the potential of loudspeakers by introducing the sound truck into political campaigns. Father Charles E. Coughlin of Detroit became known as "The Radio Priest" because of the widespread popularity of his sermons on social justice. Bob Dylan and other folksingers of the early 1960s used the popularity of records among young people to critique U.S. social practices. The eventual popularity of counterculture music became a potential radio market that profit-oriented programmers could not ignore, and "underground" FM radio stations quickly emerged. It is important to notice that these developments produced indirect communication. For example, you may prefer a radio station because of its music, but you also get its news reports; you may buy a CD because your friends seem to like it or because you like the singer's voice, but repeated exposure to the lyrics alters the verbal environment in which you live.

By the 1980s the growth of satellite communication, cable television, and FM radio were drastically altering the mass communication environment. Religious groups who had long criticized the moral decay in popular television began their own television networks. Reverend Pat Robertson established the Christian Broadcasting Network. Potential followers could add it to their cable menu and delete the "immoral" networks, and Robertson and his associates could present news and talk shows to an audience with common interests. As popular music broadcasting shifted from AM stations to FM stereo, AM stations switched formats to talk shows and telephone callers. Few people call radio shows because they are happy with things as they are, so these call-in shows began to provide modern day equivalents of the old face-to-face meetings. Indeed, many of these stations were small enough that groups with an antiestablishment political agenda could purchase them.

The 1990s saw the development of the Internet. Increasingly, individuals who had never met found one another through chat groups, Web sites, and e-mail. A wide variety of antiestablishment groups established home pages that carried their critiques of the establishment, links to allied organizations, means of subscribing to periodicals and ordering books. Some sites provided information about how to make bombs and how to use firearms and other weapons. Because the Internet is unregulated, because software development has made Web site development user friendly, and because search engines such as Yahoo! have made it easy to find related sites in cyberspace, it is now easier for aggrieved people to share their views than at any time in history. At the same time, it is more difficult for establishment forces to harass or destroy these cyber radicals. In short, social movements have used a variety of communication channels (the mechanistic theorist's conveyor belts for meaning).

But the more important point is how relational patterns include and exclude potential supporters and critics, foster or preclude the sense of transformation from individuals to group, and reinforce or contradict adaptive efforts. It is much less threatening for today's potential radical to surf the Web, call a talk show, or watch cable television than it was for anarchists of the 1880s to attend a rally, for an orator like Eugene V. Debs to tell his followers not to fight in World War I, or for Freedom Riders to ride buses into Birmingham in the 1960s. On the one hand, this means that aggrieved persons can interact more freely than they once could. On the other hand, these same possibilities provide fewer disincentives for irresponsible communication.

"Use what relational patterns" reminds us that not all social movement persuasion is the product of an orator on a soapbox. Relationships are important for several reasons. First, they indicate the audiences that persuaders believe to be capable of resolving the problem. Second, relational patterns suggest the persuader's conception of the auditor's importance to both the social movement (system) and to the larger society (supra-system). Third, relational choices suggest the persuader's working assumption that auditors either are, or should be, involved in the process of systemic adaptation.

Attention to relationships, then, can help us distinguish functional differences between, for example, the animal rights demonstrations at the meat packing plant (which seek to influence local implementation), those on the steps of the Capitol (which seek to influence national legislation by drawing national attention), and similar demonstrations on Main Street (which enhance solidarity and recruiting while polarizing the demonstrators from their opposition). Similarly, it should focus our attention on the hierarchy's response to acts of protest, particularly to the differences between meetings with demonstrators, meetings with representatives of demonstrators, arrests of demonstrators, and press conferences that reassure public and press that the demonstrators are "simply a handful of troublemakers."

In "The Rhetorical Situation," Lloyd Bitzer defines an audience as one or more people capable of resolving an exigence or problem. Too rarely do we take the time to ascertain the relationships between persuader and audience, or audience and exigence. Thus, relational systems and their evolution are important elements of a social systems approach to social movement persuasion that deserve careful study.

And What Adaptive Strategies?

"And what adaptive strategies" directs our attention to the ongoing, thoughtful process of adjustment as individuals and groups, perceiving a discrepancy between their experienced and preferred environments, create instrumental techniques to minimize that discrepancy. Again, we should look for links between individual characteristics, self-conceptions, relationships, and environment. Immigrant workers at the turn of the century who shared no common language marched rather than spoke; reactionary groups with a fundamentalist strain preached; while African Americans in the South expecting to be brutalized by white authorities, opted for a Gandhian approach to dramatize the system's inhumanity.

Unlike the dichotomy between a "rhetoric of agitation" and a "rhetoric of control," we should search for adaptive, evolutionary patterns in which choices reflect the attempts of individuals to adapt to the system as they try to help their system adapt to its environment.[21] This should produce a richer understanding of social movements and their strategies. "What adaptive strategies" leads us to the classic Aristotelian focus of "discovering the available means of persuasion." Rather than simply cataloguing strategies, we must view these strategies from the larger perspective of unfolding adaptations—what others have done and what they may be expected to do in response to one's own adaptive efforts.

With What Evolutionary Results?

"With what evolutionary results" is our measure of movement growth. Because the social systems approach is developmental, it disdains the notion that adaptations are permanent (the environment and other organisms are themselves constantly adapting). We can therefore look for evolutionary phases such as the typical life cycle of social movements presented in chapter 6. These evolutionary results might be changes in the movement's people or their self-conception, changes in the environment or their characterizations of it, changes in their relational patterns or their adaptive strategies. In any case, we need to know how the change facilitated the movement's adaptation with its environment. Did the system adapt effectively? Did it adapt too late to a discrepancy that was otherwise resolved? Did an attempted adaptation exacerbate the initial discrepancy? Did the organism appear to enter a new evolutionary phase? We can compare any social movement to the normative life cycle. The answers to such questions should enable us to understand more fully the rhetorical (i.e., adaptive, accommodative) functions of movements in society.

Emphasizing evolutionary results requires an examination of the system-environment fit at a minimum of two points in the adaptive process. These points are a matter of critical judgment and may be chosen in either of two ways. The more traditional of these methods identifies historic transitions in the social movement's life cycle and then investigates the role of persuasion in that transition. Although this is a reasonable historical approach, it raises the possibility that persuasive evolution and historical evolution may be "out of synch." The second approach is closer to Fisher and Hawes' approach to interpersonal and small group communication.[22] It involves the careful analysis of persuasion over time for the purpose of ascertaining shifts in recurrent patterns. This is an effective method for finding shifts in argument (such as segregationists' shift from white supremacy to states' rights), changes in audience (the Communist party's shift from workers to intellectuals), relational patterns (the John Birch Society's shift from study sessions to the Goldwater campaign and back again), self-conceptions (the emergence of the notion of Black Power and Black Is Beautiful), or exigencies (pro-life's shift from opposing the legalization of abortion to supporting an antiabortion amendment to the Constitution).

In any case, watch for signs that the social movement and its environment are entering a qualitatively different evolutionary phase. Since change is unavoidable, we are looking for empirically discernible changes in the system-environment fit, not mere changes in the movement, the hierarchy, the environment, or in rhetorical strategy. To the disappointment of many Americans, Richard Nixon's succession to the presidency after Lyndon Johnson only marginally changed the system-environment fit; despite the change in personnel, both the anti–Vietnam War movement's argument and the government's response remained essentially the same.

Many parts of our original question (Which individuals, conceiving themselves to be what "people" in what environment, use what relational patterns and what adaptive strategies with what evolutionary results?) are frequently asked in similar ways. A successful analysis de-emphasizes the parts in favor of their interrelationship. It is not sufficient to know only which people were active in a social movement or which symbols pervaded the social movement's rhetoric. We need to know why certain symbolic behaviors proved useful (or futile) for certain people in a particular environment—how all aspects of a social movement worked together to arrive at a particular stage.

Conclusions

Stemming from Aristotle's attention to speaker, audience, message, and occasion, the elements of communication have often been emphasized rather than the interdependence and interaction of these variables. In recent years, we have increasingly noticed that an understanding of the pieces fails to explain the whole of human communication. At the same time, we have seen a growth in social systems models of interpersonal communication that suggest an approach to communication as the efforts of parties in a relationship adapting to one another and their environment.

This chapter has developed an interpretive or social systems approach to the persuasive activities of social movements that provides a framework for bringing analysis of societal communication into line with our knowledge of interpersonal communication. This perspective not only permits but encourages us to examine people and events not always classified as "social movements," to incorporate insights from interpersonal and organizational communication, and to turn to individual orator and event studies.

We must find and share better ways of understanding and handling adaptation. We must understand that conflict cannot simply be avoided; it is unavoidable. Conflict is a sign of system-environment adaptation. Agitation, exhortations, and threats of violence are signs that the system is not adapting satisfactorily with its environment. We must recognize that the system-environment relationship is not a thing but a process and that restraining or retarding that process often increases the trauma of adaptation when it ultimately comes. In the final analysis, we must remember that persuasion is a process of mutual adjustment in which people and societies engage.

The social systems model presented here seeks to discover and to explain the interdependent, adaptive, growing nature of social movements. It is predicated on the notion that all of us—Black Panthers, Gray Panthers, Nazis, Klansmen, radical feminists, populists, environmentalists, gays, Democrats, Republicans, presidents, legislators, and the "Great Silent Majority"—are part of the same sociopolitical-rhetorical system. A full understanding of who we are, why we are as we are, and how we got this way requires that we take a holistic, developmental perspective.

Endnotes

[1] Unless otherwise noted, all references to the axioms of systems theory are taken from B. Aubrey Fisher, *Perspectives on Human Communication* (New York: Macmillan, 1978): 196–204.

[2] Fisher, 197–198.

[3] Samuel Gompers, *Seventy Years of Life and Labor*, vol. I (New York: Augustus M. Kelly, 1967): 69–70.

[4] Ludwig von Bertalanffy, *General Systems Theory: Foundations, Development, Applications* (New York: George Braziller, 1968): 40 cited by Fisher, 201.

[5] Fisher, 201.

[6] Norbert Wiener, *The Human Use of Human Beings: Cybernetics and Society* (Boston: Houghton Mifflin, 1954); and Claude Shannon and Warren Weaver, *The Mathematical Theory of Communication* (Urbana: University of Illinois Press, 1949).

[7] Dennis R. Smith, "The Fallacy of the Communication Breakdown," *Quarterly Journal of Speech* 56 (December 1970): 343–346.

[8] Brent D. Ruben, "Communication and Conflict: A Systems-Theoretic Perspective," *Quarterly Journal of Speech* 64 (April 1978): 205.

[9] Lloyd Bitzer argues that rhetorical acts are responses to the situation, while Richard Vatz argues that the persuader defines that situation through language. See Lloyd Bitzer, "The Rhetorical Situation," *Philosophy and Rhetoric* 1 (Winter 1968), 1–14; and Richard E. Vatz, "The Myth of the Rhetorical Situation," *Philosophy and Rhetoric* 6 (Summer 1973): 154–161.

[10] Saul D. Alinsky, *Rules for Radicals: A Practical Primer for Realistic Radicals* (New York: Vintage, 1971): 6–7.

[11] Alinsky, 21–32.

[12] Herbert W. Simons, "Persuasion in Social Conflicts: A Critique of Prevailing Conceptions and a Framework for Future Research," *Speech Monographs* 39 (November 1972): 239.

[13] This chapter is based on a significant revision of the interpretive systems model published in Craig Allen Smith and Kathy B. Smith, *The White House Speaks: Presidential Lead-*

ership as Persuasion (Westport, CT: Praeger, 1994). The model was first presented in Craig Allen Smith, *Political Communication* (San Diego: Harcourt Brace Jovanovich, 1990), 1–77. It was later used to suggest an approach to the college course in political communication and to using C-SPAN materials in the classroom, respectively, "Interpretive Communities in Conflict: A Master Syllabus for Political Communication," *Communication Education* 41 (October 1992): 415–428; and "The Interpretive Systems Approach to Teaching Political Communication," *C-SPAN in the Classroom: Theory and Applications*, Janette K. Muir, ed. (Annandale, VA: Speech Communication Association, 1992): 21–34.

14 For an example of social systems criticism see Craig Allen Smith, "An Organic Systems Analysis of John Birch Society Discourse, 1958–1966," *Southern Speech Communication Journal* 50 (Winter 1984): 155–176.

15 Bernard K. Duffy and Halford Ross Ryan (eds.), *American Orators of the Twentieth Century* (Westport, CT: Greenwood, 1987); Fred Powledge, *Free at Last? The Civil Rights Movement and the People Who Made It* (Boston: Little, Brown and Company, 1991).

16 J. Michael Hogan, "Wallace and the Wallaceites: A Reexamination," *Southern Speech Communication Journal* 50 (Fall 1984): 24–48.

17 Birchers responding to the survey were younger, better educated, and better off financially than the American norm of that period. Most were white-collar Republicans whose education was disproportionately in the natural sciences and engineering, who became politically aware during or after World War II, and lived in states with rapidly fluctuating populations. Fred W. Grupp, Jr., "The Political Perspectives of John Birch Society Members," *The American Right Wing*, Robert A. Schoenberger, ed. (Atlantic: Holt, Rinehart, and Winston, 1969): 83–118

18 Michael C. McGee, "In Search of 'The People': A Rhetorical Alternative," *Quarterly Journal of Speech* 61 (October 1975): 235–249; and Aaron D. Gresson, III, "Phenomenology and the Rhetoric of Identification: A Neglected Dimension of Communication Inquiry," *Communication Quarterly* 26 (Fall 1978): 14–23.

19 John Wilson, *Introduction to Social Movements* (New York: Basic Books, 1973), 70.

20 Testimony of John Morrison (excerpted), Leon Litwack, ed., *The American Labor Movement* (Englewood Cliffs, NJ: Prentice-Hall, 1962): 10–12.

21 John Waite Bowers, Donovan J. Ochs, and Richard J. Jensen, *The Rhetoric of Agitation and Control* (Prospect Heights, IL: Waveland Press, 1993).

22 Aubrey Fisher and Leonard C. Hawes, "An Interact System Model: Generating a Grounded Theory of Small Groups." *Quarterly Journal of Speech* 57 (1971): 444–453.

3

THE PERSUASIVE FUNCTIONS OF SOCIAL MOVEMENTS

As emphasized in previous chapters, persuasion is the primary *agency* through which social movements perform *functions* that enable them to come into existence, to satisfy requirements, to meet oppositions, and, perhaps, to succeed in bringing about or resisting change. Theorists for thirty years have identified and discussed a variety of functions or requirements—indispensable processes—that contribute to the success or maintenance of social movements.[1] Building from these theories, this chapter focuses on a scheme of six interrelated functions: transforming perceptions of reality, altering self-perceptions of protestors, legitimizing the social movement, prescribing courses of action, mobilizing for action, and sustaining the social movement.[2] Understanding how social movements perform these functions will enable us to begin our pursuit of the question central to the social systems perspective developed in chapter 2: "Which individuals, conceiving themselves to be what 'people' in what environment, use what relational patterns and what adaptive strategies with what evolutionary results?"

Several caveats are in order before explaining and illustrating each of the persuasive functions. First, although these functions are essential to the existence and success of social movements, they are not unique to social movements. As noted in chapter 1, social movements differ from institutionalized collectivities not principally in terms of the functions their persuasive efforts must perform but in terms of the constraints placed upon the fulfillment of these functions. The uninstitutionalized nature of movements greatly limits their powers and access to the mass media and hence strategic options.[3]

Second, while social movements must perform all six functions, their fundamental programs for change (innovative, revivalistic, or resistance), the degree of change desired (reform to revolutionary), the rhetorical situation, and the stage of the movement or movement organization will determine which functions assume greater prominence at a particular time. This functional scheme is not intended to be chronological or related to a series of progressive stages. No social movement will perform any function once and then proceed to another. Although some functions may dominate the persuasion of a social movement at a given time (transforming perceptions of reality during an early stage or pressuring the opposition and gaining support of legitimizers during a later stage), most functions demand attention on a continual basis.

Third, while a focus on persuasive functions encourages studies of entire social movements, we may study the persuasive efforts of a portion of a social movement, a social movement organization, or a social movement campaign. We may focus on one or more functions such as transforming perceptions of reality and altering self-perceptions of protestors. Let us turn now to a discussion and illustration of each of the six interrelated persuasive functions.

Transforming Perceptions of Reality

William Gamson contends that social movements are essentially struggles "over the definition and construction of social reality."[4] Every social movement must make a significant number of people aware that the generally accepted view of reality fostered by political, social, religious, educational, legal, literary, and mass media institutions is false and that something must be done about it. Wil Linkugel, R. Allen, and Richard Johannesen note, "A problem is not really a problem to an audience until they perceive it as such. A situation may exist, and the audience may know that it does, but in their eyes it remains nothing more than a lifeless fact until they view it as something that threatens or violates their interests and values."[5] Thus, social movement persuaders must transform how people see their environment—the past, the present, and the future—to convince them that an intolerable situation exists that warrants urgent attention and action.[6]

The Past

Social movements must transform how people perceive the past if they are to succeed in bringing about or stifling change. The past may be well known and ugly. For instance, the American Nazi Party (later known as the National Socialist White People's Party) had to address the horrors of World War II and the holocaust in which their German predecessors and hero, Adolf Hitler, killed millions of allied troops, citizens in occupied countries, and Jewish inmates in concentration camps.

The past may be more fiction than reality. The Native-American movement has had to overcome the Hollywood-inspired vision of "injuns" and "redskins" as bloodthirsty savages who killed and mutilated innocent settlers and peace-loving cavalry led by John Wayne look-alikes.[7] This version of the past has been fostered not only in film but in classrooms, history books, drama, and hallowed historical sites. Until recently, for example, visitors to the Custer Memorial at the Little Bighorn Battlefield received guided tours complete with a rousing story of how the gallant and brave General Custer made his last stand, outnumbered but defiant until the evil Sioux under Sitting Bull shot him down in cold blood.

The past may be generally unknown. Revivalistic movements such as pro-life and the evangelical religious right attempt to reveal how wonderful the past was before the immoral changes of premarital sex, divorce, homosexuality, a turning from God, and the murder of millions of unborn infants. A resistance movement such as pro-choice must reveal the horrors of back-alley and self-induced abortions that were prevalent prior to safe, legalized abortions after *Roe v. Wade* in 1973.

Social movements use a variety of persuasive tactics and channels to transform perceptions of the past. For example, the American Nazi party has produced "facts" to prove that the "alleged" holocaust in Europe was a clever creation of the Jews (through untruths, fantastic exaggerations, twisted words, confessions extracted under torture, falsified evidence, a best-seller hoax of the diary of Anne Frank, and fake photographs) to spread the world communist conspiracy.[8] In a pamphlet entitled *The Big Lie: Who Told It?*, Nazi writers identify who was responsible for spreading lies about Hitler, the German Nazi party, and events during World War II.[9] The Native-American movement has attempted to change fiction into fact through historical accounts such as Dee Brown's *Bury My Heart at Wounded Knee: An Indian History of the American West*, novels such as the Pulitzer Prize winning *House Made of Dawn* by N. Scott Momaday, and analyses of social interactions such as Vine Deloria's *Custer Died for Your Sins*.[10] Commercially produced movies such as *Little Big Man* starring Dustin Hoffman and *Dances with Wolves* starring Kevin Kostner have given millions of Americans a different view of Native-American history.

Other social movements have had to reveal a past that is generally unknown. For example, The Reverend Billy James Hargis, founder and leader of the Christian Crusade against communism, often made startling revelations in his radio addresses about President Franklin Roosevelt's deals with Stalin and how the United Nations was a creation by and for the atheistic, communist Soviet Union to further its quest for world domination.[11] Robert Welch, founder and leader of the John Birch Society, searched for explanations in an ambiguous and uncertain world for the rise of communism that threatened the United States and all that it stood for. In 1966, he presented an unbroken chain of events beginning in 1776 with the founding of the Illuminati in Bavaria and ending with the cold war in the last half of the twentieth century.[12] The National Abortion Rights Action League has produced statistics to show that abortions have existed since ancient times and that, prior to the Supreme Court decision, a million illegal and self-induced abortions took place each year in the United States in back alleys and on bathroom floors.[13]

The Present

Social movements must transform perceptions of the present. Target audiences, particularly when a movement is in its infancy, may (1) be unaware of the problem, (2) refuse to believe that it exists, (3) believe the problem is not severe or does not require drastic action, (4) believe the problem does not affect them, or (5) believe the problem should be and will be handled by appropriate institutions through normal channels and procedures. Nearly all institutions (from schools and political parties to labor unions and the mass media) foster and reinforce these perceptions. After all, a problem that appears briefly on a few evening newscasts and then disappears, occurs on the plains of South Dakota far from most Americans, is apparently sanctioned by the Bible, or is being looked at in congressional committees does not require a mass movement or impolite and inconvenient protests and boycotts.

When the antislavery movement emerged in the 1830s and 1840s, American institutions did not see slavery as a degradation of the slave but rather as the slave's salvation as a civilized, Christianized human being.[14] The Bible, according to pro-slavery clergy, supported slavery as God's wonderful and mysterious way to save the black savage-child. When the women's liberation movement emerged during the 1960s, institutions maintained the status of women as housewives and mothers who raised children and supported the careers of their husbands.[15] A woman was not to compete in a man's world (not a place for ladies and girls), and a man was not to compete in a woman's world (not a place for a real man). Demands by the gay and lesbian rights movement in the 1990s to add sexual orientation clauses to human rights ordinances and laws were countered, on the one hand, with denials that any discrimination existed and, on the other, that discrimination was necessary because homosexuality was a sin condemned by the Bible and homosexuals were responsible for AIDS, child molestation, and the destruction of the American family.[16]

Movement persuaders search for words to communicate the urgency of the problem and the need to take action. The ability to describe the relevance to the lives of listeners is a critical necessity in transforming perceptions of the present. Gary Woodward writes "We commit ourselves to different realities through the act of naming because words are devices for telling others *how they should see the world*."[17] Animal rights activists, for instance, use such words as brutality, invasion, ruthless slaughter, oppression, exploitation, and speciesism. A series of pictures in an animal rights leaflet showing a little ermine trying to gnaw its way out of a trap is accompanied by this emotion-laden caption: "Blood-spattered snow provides a nightmare setting for the terror, pain, and despair which the implacable trap elicits from its small victim—a barbaric drama of suffering which has been compared to crucifixion."[18]

Storytelling is a primary means of altering perceptions of the present. For example, former slaves such as Frederick Douglass, Henry Highland Garnet, and Sojourner Truth delivered speeches throughout the North prior to the Civil War relating the horrors they had experienced as slaves and their harrowing escapes to freedom in the North. Animal rights pamphlets and leaflets contain gruesome stories by trappers of leghold entrapments. A leaflet entitled *Say No to Torture* includes this bit of testimony: "One day, I saw a large beaver, a front paw caught in a leghold trap. The front paw was no longer covered with skin or flesh, the bone was visible, naked and white. At my approach, the beaver struggled desperately to free itself, the bone broke with a sickening sound."[19] Pro-life persuasion is replete with testimony from nurses and doctors who give heartrending accounts of aborted fetuses being bashed and smothered to death because they would not die.

Other stories are mythical but no less effective in portraying reality to sympathetic audiences. A letter from Cleveland Amory, President of The Fund for Animals, included the detailed story of a bear hunt complete with a "snarling, yapping pack" of dogs, a "terror stricken black bear," and a "hunt" that ends when a smiling "high-tech" hunter who has been tracking all of this drama through his radio "walks to the base of the tree when the bear is trapped . . . takes aim and shoots her at point blank range."[20] The imagery, emotions, and values" appealed to in fictional and nonfictional stories such as these make them a persuasive means of portraying a reality—an environment—different from the institutional version.

When feasible, social movements intensify their stories and claims with gory pictures. Animal rights literature shows animals caught in traps or being subjected to horrible scientific experiments. Pro-life publications show tiny bodies of aborted fetuses in trashcans or tiny body pieces in buckets, and a famous video entitled "The Silent Scream" purportedly shows a fetus undergoing the agony of abortion. Early pro-choice leaflets showed dead women on bathroom floors after "back-alley" or self-induced abortions. The United Farm Workers produced videos entitled "The Wrath of Grapes" that showed deformed children and children suffering from cancer, both attributed to the use of pesticides in grape vineyards.

Some movements have used the theatre to "tell it like it is." Plays by black authors such as "The Militant Preacher" and "The Job" by Ben Caldwell, "The Bronx Is Next" by Sonia Sanchez, "And We Own the Night" by Jimmy Garrett, and "The Monster" by Ronald Milner portray ministers as Uncle Toms, indict the welfare system, emphasize bad housing, show the detrimental effects of a dominant black mother on her sons and husband, and attack a black college dean who wants to be accepted by whites. Anti–Vietnam war protestors used street theatre to dramatize the horror and death of U.S. soldiers in Vietnam.

Social movement persuaders may emphasize glaring paradoxes or inconsistencies in the rhetoric and practices of institutions or social movements they oppose. John L. Lewis, founder of the United Mine Workers, pointed out in speeches that Illinois had 16 mine inspectors and 147 game wardens while Kentucky, the leading coal mining state, budgeted $220,000 for game wardens and only $37,000 for mine safety. Clearly these states valued wild game over coal miners.[21] Similarly, an advertisement placed in college newspapers by Americans for Medical Progress Educational Foundation challenged the animal rights movement's preference for animals over people. One headline entitled "How Many More Will Die Before You Say 'No!' To The Animal Rights Movement?" introduced an advertisement that read in part:

> The Cure for AIDS will come like every cure before it, through animal research. And yet, there is a growing movement of animal rights activists who oppose any use of animals in biomedical research. As one of their leaders, Ingrid Newkirk, stated: *Even if animal research resulted in a cure for AIDS . . . we'd be against it."*[22]

Both movements, one innovative and one resistance, emphasize that an institution's or movement's values are the opposite of what they should be.

The Future

Social movement persuaders portray a vision of the future that instills a sense of urgency in audiences to organize and do something *now.* Audiences, however, tend to be preoccupied with day-to-day needs and desires. If they look ahead at all, they tend to think things will work out (they always have) or that institutions will take care of the future. As Hans Toch writes:

> For a person to be led to join a social movement, he [she] must not only sense a problem, but must also (1) feel that something can be done about it and (2) want to do something about it himself [herself]. At the very least, he [she] must feel that the status quo is not inevitable, and that change is conceivable.[23]

Social movement persuaders try to transform perceptions of the future by showing it as bright and full of hope or dark and full of despair. Which future ultimately comes about, they proclaim, will depend upon the "people" and their collective actions.

A rhetoric of hope relies upon one of two appeals or a combination. *Utopian appeals* present a perfect space (often a promised land), while *millennium appeals* present a perfect time (an era when peace, love, and happiness will abound). Eugene V. Debs, a labor and socialist leader and five-time presidential candidate from the 1880s to the 1920s, often spoke of a future when socialism would triumph and life would be wonderful for everyone. In a speech in Girard, Kansas in 1908, Debs described a socialist utopia and millennium:

> Every man and every woman will then be economically free. . . . Then society will improve its institutions in proportion to the progress of invention. Whether in the city or on the farm, all things productive will be carried forward on a gigantic scale. All industry will be completely organized. Society for the first time will have a scientific foundation. Every man, by being economically free, will have some time for himself. He can then take a full and perfect breath. He can enjoy life with his wife and children, because then he will have a home. . . . We will reduce the workday, and give every man a chance. We will go to parks, and we will have music, because we will have time to play music and desire to hear it.[24]

Notice Debs' careful selection of words, concepts, and values likely to motivate his American, midwestern audience to strive for the future he is portraying: freedom, progress, invention, science, fairness, family, and home. Martin Luther King's "I Have a Dream" speech was also a careful blend of utopian and millennium appeals designed to instill hope in the future if his audience would have faith and continue to support the movement's crusade for change. The rhetoric of religious social movements includes oft-repeated descriptions of a heavenly paradise, a time and place of eternal happiness for which all must strive.

A rhetoric of dread and despair, particularly prevalent in resistance and revivalistic social movements, warns that the current state of affairs can only get worse unless the people act immediately to change the course of events. The *domino theory* predicts that one right, power, possession, place, value, or virtue will fall after another, like dominos, until all is lost. Robert Welch, founder of the John Birch Society, warned in his speech that launched the Society in Indianapolis on December 9, 1958 that:

> Unless we can reverse the forces which now seem inexorable in their movement, you have only a few more years before the country in which you live will become four separate provinces in a worldwide Communist dominion. . . . We are living, in America today, in such a fool's paradise as the people of China lived in twenty years ago, as the people of Czechoslovakia lived in a dozen years ago, as the people of North Vietnam lived in five years ago, and as the people of Iraq lived in only yesterday.[25]

Anti-animal rights forces launched a campaign with the warning, "Today fur. Tomorrow leather. Then wool. Then meat . . . "[26]

A related appeal, the *slippery slope*, claims society is sliding inexorably down a slope into oblivion. Randall Lake writes about the "moral landscape" presented in pro-life rhetoric and how it warns of a society sliding into total immorality because it no longer protects its unborn.[27] Christian fundamentalists point to the escalating results of a morally bankrupt country—premarital sex, abortion, divorce, scandals in the highest office in the land, killings in our schools, pornography on the Internet and throughout the mass media, drug use, and acceptance of homosexuality. The environmental movement warns of the greenhouse effect and the end of life as we know it if destruction of the world's rain forests, release of fluorocarbons into the atmosphere, widespread use of fossil fuels, uncontrolled toxic wastes, and water pollution continue at present levels.

Religious social movements or religious elements of movements often use *apocalyptic appeals* when resisting other movements or trying to revive the past. Persuaders warn state legislatures, city councils, and university senates considering sexual orientation clauses in human rights documents that God destroyed Sodom in ancient Palestine because of its wickedness, particularly homosexuality and perverse sexual preferences, and will destroy the United States if homosexuality is accepted as normal. Some cite the assassination of President Kennedy as the first installment of God's punishment for our sinful ways and outlawing of prayer and Bible study in the public schools. Succeeding installments include the Vietnam War, natural disasters, and the AIDS epidemic.

Inherent in many social movement messages is the notion that society is in the final battle between good and evil, Armageddon, merely *one step away* from disaster. For example, during the 1980s, the Clamshell Alliance in New England staged mock nuclear disasters on the ocean beaches a short distance from the Seabrook nuclear power plant, then under construction, to show the impossibility of evacuation and massive deaths that would result from an accident if the plant came on line. Nuclear plants, they warned, were always moments away from disasters like the one in the Ukraine: "Chernobyl has made it crystal clear that nuclear power means nuclear death."[28]

Although we can identify techniques social movements use to transform perceptions of reality, we do not know when movements are most likely to use them and how they might change over time. James Darsey has shown, for example, how "catalytic events," particularly the "scourge of AIDS," greatly altered the rhetoric of the gay rights movement from 1977 to 1990.[29] Studies indicate that revivalistic social movements tend to view the past as a paradise lost that is worth resurrecting at any cost in order to have a possible utopia or millennium in the future. Resistance movements tend to view the present as a paradise achieved and see efforts of social movements and established orders as threatening to return society to a primitive past or transport it to a future devoid of all that is sacred. Innovative movements tend to portray a defective present resulting from an intolerable past and argue that the future can be bright only if the movement is successful.

Altering Self-Perceptions of Protestors

Enhancing the self-concepts of protestors is an essential rhetorical function of social movements; protestors must have strong, healthy egos when they take on powerful institutions and entrenched cultural norms and values.[30] They must see themselves as substantive human beings with the power to change the world.

Some social movements are *self-directed* in that (1) they are created, led, and populated primarily by those who perceive themselves to be dispossessed and (2) are struggling primarily for personal freedom, equality, justice, and rights. These movements include those fighting on behalf of women, African Americans, Native Americans, Hispanic Americans, Asian Americans, and gays and lesbians.

Other movements are *other-directed* in that (1) they are created, led, and populated primarily by those who do not perceive themselves to be dispossessed and (2) are struggling for the freedom, equality, justice, and rights of others rather than selves. These movements include animal rights, pro-life, and students opposed to sweatshop and slave labor working conditions and segments of self-directed social movements such as white leaders and members of the antislavery movement, white freedom riders in the civil rights movement, and faculty in the student rights movement. The ego function of self-directed and other-directed social movements is similar but different in significant ways.

The Ego Function in Self-Directed Social Movements

The rhetoric of self-directed social movements addresses members as *innocent, blameless victims of oppression*. For example, Hispanic rhetoric claims Chicanos are "united by desire for equality and escape from oppression."[31] Richard Gregg theorizes "If one feels oppressed, he [she] implies that there is an oppressor—someone responsible for the oppression."[32] Targeted oppressors of self-directed movements include men, women, whites, Anglos, straights, the system, corporations, and industrialists. Persuaders of these movements emphasize that they are oppressed because of their sex, race, ethnic origin, sexual orientation, labor class, or student group. As innocent victims of powers beyond their control, oppressed groups are exploited as cheap labor, sex objects, servants, and tourist attractions, and they demand an end to what oppresses them: injustice, inequality, segregation, discrimination, reverse discrimination, racism, and tyranny. It is not surprising that the rhetoric of self-directed protestors exhibits a siege mentality.[33]

The rhetoric of self-directed social movements addresses *self-esteem and self-worth,*—and often precedes this theme with terms such as inferior, low, poor, negative, and fragile. Society has taught the oppressed to stay in their place and reduced them to the status of things. Victims of this oppression have often suffered from self-hatred and guilt for allowing themselves to be stripped of their dignity, degraded, humiliated, and dehumanized. An essential ingredient in self-directed rhetoric is to establish the self-hood of members and target audiences by refurbishing, repairing, restoring, and enhancing self-esteem and confidence.[34] Persuaders preach messages of self-worth, respect, dignity, and confidence. Michael Sedano writes that the poetry of the Chicano movement saw "tomorrow's transformation of identity from a quiet, polite, patronized, domesticated pet to a fiercely self-assured Chicano who is in control of his or her destiny."[35]

Ego is also enhanced in self-directed social movements through searches for *new self-identities and self-definitions* that will result in identification with groups according to sex, race, ethnic origin, age, sexual preference, and student or labor status. Individual status is affirmed through group identity that provides members with a critical sense of unity, togetherness, solidarity, and community. They often see themselves as brothers and sisters. They are no longer isolated victims standing alone to face powerful oppressors but comrades united through their unique identities and working within organizations populated with people like themselves who are part of powerful, ever-growing social movements. They have meaningful relational patterns. Self-naming is often a critical step toward self-identity and mobilizing the oppressed. They are now African Americans rather than Negroes, Native Americans rather than Indians, women rather than girls, and Hispanics or Chicanos rather than Mexicans or Mexican Americans.

The rhetoric of self-directed social movements addresses the *status of the oppressed in society*. Gregg writes that the oppressed find themselves in "symbolically defensive positions from which they must extricate themselves before they can realize positive identities."[36] Protestors must locate their proper places in the symbolic and social hierarchy if they are to overcome their oppression and realize equality and justice. They see themselves as marginalized, disenfranchised, and ignored, and claim they are stereotyped and bracketed with children and the lowest elements of society such as criminals, idiots, and the insane. Their contributions to society and accomplishments cry out for recognition and a place equal to or above others within the social hierarchy.

The Ego Function in Other-Directed Social Movements

The rhetoric of other-directed social movements is not aimed at restoring, refurbishing, or establishing the selfhood of movement members but at *affirming a positive self-esteem*. Members do not see themselves as members of oppressed or exploited groups but as saviors of the oppressed and exploited. There are no signs of despair, insecurity, or sense of inferiority. Rhetoric affirms and enhances an already exalted self-esteem by celebrating and recognizing the protestor's moral principles, commitment, compassion, humanitarianism, and victories in great moral struggles. There is no siege mentality, no fortifying of walls against attacks because of who or what they are. Persuaders are on offense rather than defense. The mentality is one of the moral, righteous crusader on a sacred quest to stop the suffering and oppression of others.

There is little evidence of seeking a higher place in the social hierarchy in the rhetoric of other-directed social movements. Activists appear to believe that they are already at the top of the social and moral hierarchy, because they are committed to a struggle for the oppressed and against evils. There is status seeking, but it is *locating a proper status within the social movement and among social movement organizations.* Members implicitly and explicitly contrast social movement organizations according to longevity, size, activities, effectiveness, and victories. Messages for members and sympathizers emphasize that they are supporting and working for excellent organizations struggling for the oppressed. People should feel pride in being part of the very best organization of like-minded crusaders.

Self-identity in the rhetoric of other-directed social movements, like societal status, comes not through identity with a sexual, ethnic, racial, or age group, but through *identity with a movement and specific social movement organization.* The emphasis is not on what or who a person is individually but on a person's collective association with an organization working for the welfare of others. A meaningful relational pattern comes through the movement.

Persuaders celebrate unification through struggle. The rhetoric of other-directed movements does not attempt to create a new self-identity or to redefine an old self-identity; self-naming and self-discovery are unnecessary. It attaches an identity to other positive self-identities, an addition rather than a transformation. Activists are now heroes as well as college students, rescuers as well as Christians. Self-identity emanates from association with moral crusades and courageous organizations at the forefront of social movements, not from identification with other brothers, sisters, Asian Americans, or senior citizens.

Victimage permeates the rhetoric of other-directed social movements, but it dwells on the oppression and exploitation of others, not selves. Typical messages portray the brutality of abortion, apartheid in South Africa, or treatment of animals and how activists are struggling in their selfless, moral crusades to end this brutality. Occasionally, rhetoric addresses movement members as victims of countermovements and/or institutions determined to maintain things as they are. This victimage enhances ego because no institution would bother with a weak or ineffective protest group. Activists are innocent victims because they are willing to sacrifice their security, dignity, and social status for other innocent victims. Ego-enhancement appears to be a major by-product, if not the aim, of such rhetoric.

Legitimizing the Social Movement

Theorists have claimed that legitimizing the social movement is the principal goal or demand of social movements, the primal challenge of movements to institutions, and the most central obstacle leaders of movements must overcome.[37] Gaston Rimlinger and Joseph Gusfield, for example, argue that for a social movement to be successful, its demands and methods must somehow become legitimate in the eyes of institutions, government, the public, and potential members.[38] A major struggle, then, is to attain positive relational patterns with the larger society. Protestors have in their favor only the somewhat mythical American tolerance of dissent, a tolerance most evident when the dissent is nonthreatening or ineffective.

Conferring and Maintaining Legitimacy

The notion of legitimacy contains two inherently rhetorical elements. The first element is the act of conferring, by one person or group to another person or group, the "right to exercise authoritative influence in a given area or to issue binding directives."[39] The second element is the act of retaining legitimacy once it is conferred. Robert Francesconi writes "Rhetoric bridges the gap between legitimacy as claimed and legitimacy as believed."[40] All societies and their institutions have prevalent ideologies that explicitly and implicitly support and are supported by the prevailing social structure. William Garrison observes that social movement persuaders

> Face a field of combat that is already occupied by a competing legitimate frame that is established and quiescent rather than emergent and action-oriented. When truly hegemonic, the legitimating frame is taken for granted. Would-be challengers face the problem of overcoming a definition of the situation that they themselves may take as a part of the natural order.[41]

When a people or social order confers such legitimacy upon a person or institution, it also confers five powers that, in combination, sustain the original grant.

The power to reward is perhaps the most important retentive power because it allows legitimate institutions to reward those who conform and obey and to coerce or punish those who strive to be different or challenge approved norms, values, and institutional arrangements.[42] Institutional leaders urge protestors and reformers to consider the consequences of their actions, typically the granting or denial of tangible benefits and rewards such as diplomas, jobs, advancements, incomes, research and development grants, and tax exemptions. If the disaffected refuse to take the carrot, an institution may resort to the stick to maintain compliance and justify its use of coercive persuasion in the name of God, the founding fathers, the people, the Constitution, or the law.

The power of control allows legitimate institutions to regulate the flow of information and persuasion to members of organizations and the populace. Thus, they determine if, how, when, where, under what circumstances, and with whom communication will occur. Frances Piven and Richard Cloward contend "The ideology of democratic political rights, by emphasizing the availability of legitimate avenues for the redress of grievances, delegitimizes protest; and the dense relationships generated by electoral politics also divert people from protest."[43] Institutional leaders often brand reformers and agitators as well-meaning but ignorant of the facts that are well known only to established authorities. In the information age, control of information and information flow may be more important than military and police forces. The global availability of the Internet is seriously challenging institutional control.

The power of identification accrues to institutions because they are the keepers, protectors, and proselytizers of the sacred symbols, emblems, places, offices, documents, codes, values, and myths of the social order. Institutions and their leaders are seen as the legitimate heirs or successors of the order's founding fathers, patriots, revered leaders, prophets, and martyrs. Identification with the sacred is easy and frequent as is seen in the courts, legislatures, and schools and at religious and national observances and sporting events. As Anthony Oberschall writes, their positions allow institutional leaders to provide "elaborate systems of beliefs and moral ideas upon which legitimacy rests."[44]

The power of terministic control allows institutions to control language and thereby the "legitimated meanings for such politically sensitive terms as order, violence, repression, deviance, protest, persuasion, coercion, and symbolic speech."[45] Thus institutional violence is the legitimate maintenance of law and order, never terrorism. Overzealous supporters of the social order are patriots, never fanatics. "National security" justifies withholding information, infiltration of protest groups, spying on citizens, and amassing secret files on social movement organizations, leaders, members, and sympathizers.

The power of moral suasion allows institutions to exert control by operating in the realms of attitudes and emotional attachments. R. R. McGuire claims that people often come to see obedience or deference to legitimate authority as a moral obligation.[46] Thus, institutions persuade people that they have a duty to honor institutional decisions even when those decisions have "unpleasant consequences."[47] Louis Kriesberg, for example, contends that "people learn rules and if they accept them they may become so internalized that violation would be shunned in order to avoid the feelings of guilt or shame which would follow violation."[48]

Thus, when uninstitutional forces collide with institutional forces, the rhetorical deck is heavily stacked in favor of the legitimate institutions and their leaders. People tend to maintain the faith even in the face of massive economic and social breakdowns. How, then, can social movements use persuasion to establish legitimate relational patterns? A rhetoric of legitimation must be a combination of coactive and confrontational strategies.[49] *Coactive or common ground strategies* emphasize similarities, shared experiences, and a common cause with target audiences. *Confrontational or conflict strategies* emphasize dissimilarities, diverse experiences, and conflict with target audiences.

Legitimacy through Coactive Strategies

If, as Francesconi claims, "an implicit requirement" of legitimacy is a "rationality of good reasons," then social movements must identify with fundamental societal norms and values if they are to transport themselves from the margins of society to the centers where legitimacy resides.[50] They must access the sources institutions claim as their rightful domains.

Social movements may identify with what Max Weber refers to as the "sanctity of immemorial traditions."[51] Molefi Asante and John Wilson note that social movements usually link themselves with the traditional rights and values of equality, justice, and dignity. Irving Zaretsky and Mark Leone claim that nonlegitimacy of religious social movements is a function of appearing to threaten deeply held secular values.[52] While most Americans saw Malcolm X as a dangerous radical, a cursory review of his speeches reveals that he appealed continually to the fundamental American values of a virtuous life dedicated to family, community, religious beliefs, hard work, ingenuity, and the free enterprise system—hardly radical or revolutionary beliefs. Movements are wise to identify with the moral symbols, sacred emblems, heroes, founding fathers, and revered documents of society rather than to attack or disparage them.

Social movements may rework the pieces of tradition into new stories that befit their ideologies. Thus, to avoid being stigmatized as a mere fad, a "people going crazy together," or an evil force in society, protestors may emphasize the hallowed tradition of protest in American history, showing for instance what our founding fathers really were—revolutionaries.[53] Carl Oglesby, president of the SDS (Students for a Democratic Society), asked an audience during the antiwar march in Washington on October 27, 1965 what would happen if Thomas Jefferson and Thomas Paine were to sit down with President Johnson to discuss the war in Vietnam:

> They might say: "What fools and bandits, sirs, you make then of us? Outside help? Do you remember Lafayette? Or the 3,000 British freighters the French navy sank for our side? Or the arms and men we got from France and Spain? And what's this about terror? Did you never hear what we did to our own loyalists? Or about the thousands of rich American Tories who fled for their lives to Canada? And as for popular support, do you not know that we had less than one-third of our people with us? That, in fact, the colony of New York recruited more troops for the British than for the revolution? Should we give it all back?"[54]

Reconstructing history can alter perceptions of social reality and show the social movement as more legitimate than institutions because it alone is telling it like it really is.

Social movements may strive to establish their actions as those of legitimate organizations. They can achieve this in part by incorporating into legal organizations and operating openly to avoid fears of secretive societies. They may identify with the legal status of protest in America by conforming to rules and accepted procedures the populace perceives to be formally correct and by avoiding direct attacks on basic institutions and authorities. Most movements emphasize the importance of the ballot box rather than violence or coercion in bringing about or resisting change. Endorsements of a social movement by legitimate organizations may produce a "rub-off" effect because social movements, like individuals in society, are judged by their associations. They strive to attract legitimizers— organizations, speakers, writers, senators, clergy, entertainers, scientists, military leaders, war veterans, ex-presidents, and medical professionals— who are respectable, safe, and beyond reproach.

Social movements may employ a strategy of transcendence by identifying themselves with what is large, good, important, and of the highest order in society. *The Gray Panther Manual* relates how the Panthers grew rapidly into a powerful, national organization:

> Throughout 1973 the Gray Panthers grew tenfold again. . . . The ABC-TV network did a documentary entitled: "Gray Panthers," with nationwide viewing. Local Gray Panther Networks were convening in Philadelphia, Tucson, Dayton, D.C., Chicago, Los Angeles, San Francisco, Charlotte, New York, Denver, Decatur, Kansas City, Portland, and Baltimore. Panthers were on the prowl all over.[55]

Oberschall notes that visible signs of large-scale disaffection may shake confidence in institutions and thus undermine the legitimacy of institutional leaders.[56] Social movements, particularly religious ones, stress a sense of mission and claim to operate in accordance with a predetermined divine plan. They identify with the belief that divine plans transcend the temporal ones of human institutions, argue that "expressive" values (symbols, reflections, meanings) rather than "instrumental" values (means, instruments, tools) are the truly universal ones, and try to locate the movement within what Zaretsky and Leone call a "sacred cosmos."[57] Moral obligations to the state, agitators claim, are limited by moral obligations to humanity and a higher authority.

A coactive rhetoric is essential, then, for a social movement in its struggle for legitimacy because it chips away at three powers enjoyed by institutions: identification, terministic control, and moral suasion. Coactive rhetoric obviously serves more than the "managerial" and "reinforcement" functions ascribed to it, for it demonstrates that a social movement deserves legitimacy by *worth and right*.[58] With worth and right established, institutions can no longer call into question the fundamental legitimacy of a social movement but, as Rhodri Jeffreys-Jones explains, must attack its tactics instead.[59] Bowers, Ochs, and Jensen address the importance of a coactive rhetorical approach in establishing legitimacy when they argue that the early employment of a strategy of "petition" (asking authorities to address an urgent concern) is crucial because:

> If the establishment can show that the petition stage was not attempted by the dissenters, it can discredit the agitators as irresponsible firebrands who reject normal decision-making processes in favor of disturbances and disruption. Unless they first attempt petition, activists are unlikely to win support through more drastic strategies.[60]

Thus, coactive strategies tend to dominate the rhetoric of social movements during the early stages of protest when persuaders are attempting to make the people and institutions aware of an urgent, unaddressed problem and to gain entry to the playing field where such problems are debated and resolved They are essential for establishing legitimate relational patterns.

A coactive rhetoric by itself, however, cannot attain legitimacy for a social movement because it merely establishes the movement as *similar* to the social order in important ways—legal, law-abiding, supporter of traditions, moral—and therefore worthy of a degree of legitimacy. There is always the danger that some people may see the social movement as so similar to the social order that there is no need to join, while others may become estranged from the movement because it fails to differentiate itself significantly from evil or impotent institutions. Thus, a coactive rhetoric may produce at best a rhetorical stalemate between institutional and uninstitutional forces that leaves institutions with their powers diminished or shared but intact.

Legitimacy through Confrontational Strategies

A confrontational rhetoric is necessary to break the rhetorical stalemate by bringing institutional legitimacy into question and allowing the social movement to transcend the social order in perceived legitimacy. If a confrontational rhetoric is to raise the social movement to a transcendent position in society, it must make a significant number of people see the social order as illegitimate or at least less legitimate than the social movement. As Carol Jablonski argues, a "rhetoric of discontinuity" is necessary to "establish the legitimacy of the collective's grievances as well as the need to induce changes from the outside."[61]

Movements employ a variety of confrontational strategies to show that institutional leaders and organizations systematically distort communication, create barriers to will formation, and constrain and distort an alleged "reciprocal accountability." McGuire writes that social movements hope to demonstrate that the order is "irrational and hence illegitimate—involving no moral obligation."[62] The goal is to raise doubts in the minds of the people about their relationships with institutions.

Activists try to exploit societal restrictions on institutional actions. The civil rights, farm worker, Hispanic, gay rights, animal rights, and pro-life movements, for example, have employed strategies of nonviolent resistance and civil disobedience, including strikes, boycotts, sit-ins, demonstrations, symbolic acts, and violations of ordinances and laws to reveal the inconsistency (and therefore illegitimacy) of values and established procedures, customs, and laws. Social movements take advantage of outdated laws or quasi-legal practices of authorities by demanding that authorities stick to the letter of the law—actions that might make authorities look ridiculous, unfair, or heavyhanded. Saul Alinsky, in his book *Rules for Radicals*, urges would-be radicals to *"Make the enemy live up to their own book of rules.* You can kill them with this, for they can no more obey their own rules than the Christian church can live up to Christianity."[63] If an institution represses peaceful, nonviolent dissent and refuses to enforce or obey the laws, it may seriously undermine its legitimacy in the eyes of the people and other institutions.

Militant confrontational strategies (disruptions, verbal violence, and assaults on property, symbols, and the police) are designed to provoke institutions into overreactions and violent suppression, for, as Robert Cathcart claims, "The establishment, when confronted, must respond not to the particular enactment but to the challenge to its legitimacy."[64] If an institution "responds with full fury and might to crush the confronters, it violates the mystery and reveals the secret that it maintains power, not through moral righteousness but through it's power to kill." Activists have learned the value of mass arrests and real or apparent police brutality, particularly when television and video cameras are present. Televised images of police dragging men and women, some of them members of the clergy, to police vans may outrage significant numbers of an institution's constituency and be counterproductive to control efforts. Police have shown remarkable restraint in recent years when handling sit-ins, demonstrations, and efforts to penetrate police lines. They have learned protest management.

Activists charge that the "civility and decorum" of authorities "serve as masks for the preservation of injustice" and constitute a thin veneer that hides a vicious, repressive social order.[65] Robert Scott and Donald Smith write that social movements prod institutions to "show us how ugly you really are."[66] And Cathcart writes that a "Confrontational rhetoric shouts 'Stop!' at the system, saying, 'You cannot go on assuming you are the true and correct order; you must see yourself as the evil thing you are.'"[67] Authorities often discredit and humiliate themselves when they lose control and thereby become collaborators with protestors determined to strip them of legitimacy. Recent violent acts against white supremacists at Ruby Ridge in Idaho, a religious cult in Waco, Texas, and those protesting the World Trade Organization (WTO) in Seattle and Washington, D.C. were viewed on television by millions of Americans and aided the efforts of uninstitutionalized groups to reveal the ugly sides of institutions.

There may be two significant by-products of ugly and sometimes violent confrontations between protestors and social orders. First, violent suppression allows the social movement to claim that it acted in self-defense—a noble and legal act cherished in American society—to institutional force and violence that was both unwarranted and against the sacred principles and traditions of the nation. Second, verbal and nonverbal violence by institutions and militant elements of movements may confer legitimacy upon moderate leaders and organizations because they appear to be rational and safe in comparison.[68]

A confrontational rhetoric is essential for a social movement to gain legitimacy because it chips away at four powers institutions enjoy: reward, control, identification, and moral suasion. A confrontational rhetoric breaks the rhetorical stalemate between institutional and noninstitutional forces by demonstrating that the institution deserves neither its claim of legitimacy nor its high place in the social hierarchy. It challenges the normal relational patterns of society while offering new ones.

Although a confrontational rhetoric is essential for a social movement in its struggle for legitimacy, it alone cannot attain legitimacy for the movement. Destruction or reduction of Order A's legitimacy does not automatically bestow legitimacy on Order B, even when Order B was instrumental in revealing the evil and unworthiness of Order A. Social movements must effectively present themselves as the *innocent victims* of institutions out of control. This is why nonviolent civil disobedience as taught by Gandhi in India and Martin Luther King, Jr. in this country can be effective if institutions resort to violence and lawlessness that shatters relational bonds.

Prescribing Courses of Action

Prescribing courses of action constitutes selling the social movement's ideology. According to John Wilson, ideology "is the generic name given to those beliefs which mobilize people into action in social movements;" an ideology is "a set of beliefs about the social world and how it operates, containing statements about the rightness of certain social arrangements and what action should be taken in the light of these statements."[69] This set of beliefs addresses what must be done, who must do it, and how it must be done.

The What

In explaining *what* must be done, a social movement presents demands and solutions that will alleviate a grave condition, prevent catastrophic changes, or bring on the utopia or millennium. It is a course of action designed to produce positive evolutionary results. Each movement must explain, defend, and sell its program or product. Kenneth Dolbeare and Patricia Dolbeare write "each ideology is attached to some values, such as equality or justice, in preference to others. The crucial questions are *the way in which such values are understood or defined* by the ideology, and *how they are ranked in priority* when they conflict with each other."[70] For example, when environmentalists strive to protect wetlands from commercial development or the spotted owl from extinction if forests are cut in the northwest, they place values of preservation over progress, free enterprise, and property rights. Steve Goldzwig notes "a value or set of values *denied* helps to determine what is valued. Thus, a negative reaction to a rhetorical effort is just as clear a mirror of a culture's values as the approval of an act."[71]

Michael McGee claims that *ideographs* link rhetoric and ideology, "one-term sums of an orientation, the species of 'God' or 'Ultimate' term that will be used to symbolize the line of argument" an "individual would pursue."[72] Thus, we should be able to detect a social movement's ideology by identifying key words and phrases in its rhetoric because they are "the basic structural elements, the building blocks, of ideology." Words such as freedom, equality, justice, liberty, progress, private property, free enterprise, free speech, right of privacy, right to vote, and right to life have dominated U.S. social movements and distinguished one from another for more than two centuries.

Problems develop not only when institutions say no to demands and solutions but also when organizations within social movements prescribe diverse and perhaps conflicting demands and solutions. In the civil rights movement, for example, Martin Luther King, Jr. saw integration as the way to achieve freedom and equal rights while Malcolm X advocated black nationalism and black capitalism. In the temperance movement, some desired to limit the use of alcoholic beverages and some would settle for nothing less than banning the sale of all alcoholic beverages. In today's pro-life movement, there are those who would allow abortions under a few circumstances such as saving a woman's life and those who will settle for nothing less than the elimination of all abortions, including birth control methods that prevent conception. Intramovement conflicts seem inevitable because each organization comes into existence because it claims to have created the *perfect* doctrine and set of principles, and there can be no compromise with perfection.

Changing social situations, efforts of institutions to negate or to co-opt a movement's demands and solutions, and the necessity to address a variety of target audiences require adaptive strategies. Adaptations can include additions or deletions of ideographs, alterations in the content of demands and solutions, and changes in explanations. As John Wilson writes, "When new sensitivities are created by social events and collectives, ideologies, to be accepted, must cater to these new sensitivities."[73] Efforts to adapt to new sensitivities and events, however, always expose social movement leaders and organizations to charges of revisionism by movement purists, the true believers who will brook no changes in sacred doctrine. Bruce Cameron notes "Sometimes the zeal for 'purity' produces isolation from the general public, or even schisms within the movement."[74] Leaders face charges of going too fast or too slow, of being too rigid or too flexible. If situations seem no better or worse as time passes and crises occur, "Illusions are often offered as solutions, to *solve* problems by predicting a rapid transition to a better world." "The person, faced with an intolerable situation," Hans Toch observes, "searches for and finds a miracle."[75]

The Who

Social movements must prescribe *who* must to do the job. Their answer, seemingly without exception, is *the people*, a *great grassroots* movement for change or resistance to change. All serious social movement adherents understand, however, that the movement needs organization and leaders of some sort. First, they must convince enough people that only an *uninstitutional collectivity* is both willing and able to bring about or resist change; all others are a part or a cause of the problem. Struggles develop within social movements over how far the movement must distance itself from established institutions. Some elements within the women's liberation movement, for instance, wanted to use the system (Congress, courts, state legislators) to achieve changes. Others argued the only way women could achieve their true identities and power was to break all ties with men, male-dominated organizations, and male tactics.

Second, social movements must espouse specific types of organization and leadership or specific organizations and leaders best suited to solving urgent problems. This leads inevitably to a striving for perfection that splinters the movement into competing factions and organizations. Fred Powledge, in his book entitled *Free at Last? The Civil Rights Movement and the People Who Made It*, provides extensive documentation of the competition, jealousy, and hostility among the leaders and organizations of the civil rights movement—the National Association for the Advancement of Colored People (NAACP), the Southern Christian Leadership Conference (SCLC), the Student Nonviolent Coordinating Committee (SNCC), and the Congress on Racial Equality (CORE)—that often hampered campaigns and movement progress.[76]

One movement faction may declare open warfare against another faction it deems ideologically deviant or inferior in organizational structure and strategies. For instance, in the early labor movement, the American Federation of Labor and the competing Knights of Labor each claimed to be the perfect labor organization based on a perfect set of principles that made it the historical, natural, and moral leader of the movement and cited the other as an unnatural, unscientific, immoral, and obsolete failure that should either be abandoned or absorbed into the one true union.[77] The struggle ended when the Knights ceased to exist. Thus, persuasion may create *we-they* distinctions within a social movement as sharp as those between a social movement and an established order as elements within struggle to determine what people they are or want to be.

And third, social movements may establish membership limitations to create elites capable of dealing with unsolvable conditions and the omnipotent forces that produced them. The Ku Klux Klan restricted membership to white, Anglo-Saxon Protestants; some African-American groups restricted membership to African Americans; some women's groups restricted membership to females; some student rights groups restricted membership to people under thirty; and the American Federation of Labor restricted membership to workers from skilled trades, excluding unskilled laborers and factory workers. Chapter 4 reveals how the John Birch Society used an authoritarian rhetoric that effectively limited its membership to an elite deemed capable of defeating the communist conspiracy in the United States. While some movements limit membership to those who can truly understand the plight of the victims, others do so because they see the excluded as the enemy. The Manifesto for New York Radical Feminists declared:

> As radical feminists we recognize that we are engaged in a power struggle with men, and that the agent for our oppression is man insofar as he identifies with and carries out the supremacy privileges of the male role. For while we realize that the liberation of women will ultimately mean the liberation of men from their destructive role as oppressor, we have no illusion that men will welcome this liberation without a struggle.[78]

Other social movements freely admit anyone who espouses their causes, believing that success can come only from mass movements able to exert pressure on institutions.

The How

Social movements must determine how the job must be done and the adaptive strategies most appropriate and effective for their causes. A revolutionary, innovative movement organization may have a wide range of tactical choices (boycotts, strikes, symbolic takeovers) because that is what a revolutionary group is expected to do. The range of available channels may be limited to leaflets and the Internet because the group is considered too radical for radio and television. A reform-oriented revivalistic organization may have access to many channels (including radio and/or television talk shows and features in magazines) but a narrow range of moderate, socially acceptable tactics because it does not want to offend its many target audiences. A resistance movement may have ready access to institutions and channels because institutional leaders favor or use it when opposing a social movement but must abide by rules, expectations, and decorum of institutions to maintain these advantages.

No social movement can rely upon the same means of change for long. Movement followers, the general public, and the mass media become bored with them, and institutions learn how to deal with specific strategies and tactics rather quickly. Alinsky advises would-be social movement persuaders, *"Wherever possible go outside of the experience of the enemy.* Here you want to cause confusion, fear, and retreat." He also advises that "A tactic that drags on too long becomes a drag. Man [woman] can sustain militant interest in any issue for only a limited time, after which it becomes a ritualistic commitment like going to church on Sunday mornings."[79] Social movements must search continually for new and different strategies to keep the movement fresh, alive, and moving forward and institutions off balance.

Social movements often splinter into factions over differing views on how the job must be done, and some movement members may be more committed to means than to ends. Nearly all movements have radical and moderate factions, and the differences are often more pronounced in strategies than ideologies. This is readily apparent in the current militia movement in which basic beliefs are similar but tactics range from information campaigns and military-like maneuvers to violent acts. Roxanne Dunbar, a leader of the Southern Female Rights Union, reported that her original group had seriously considered assassinating a man to make their presence known but decided the victim "would become such an important person because we'd chosen him over all these other guys."[80] This plan and one in which they would "get shotguns and go to the Boston Common to deal with the men who ogle the secretaries" seemed to "horrify" moderate members. The environmental movement has moderate elements such as the Sierra Club that believes in working through the system and radical groups such as Dave Foreman's Earth First! (eco-guerrillas) that sabotage machinery, equipment, and power lines when they are not conducting blockades and chaining themselves to cranes and trees. Organizations and leaders of the civil rights movement disagreed strongly over strategies. The NAACP advocated working through the courts. The SCLC under Martin Luther King, Jr. advocated nonviolent civil disobedience. Malcolm X advocated "black nationalism" and "action." In a speech in Detroit, he attacked the sit-in tactics of SNCC and SCLC:

> As long as you have a sit-down philosophy, you'll have a sit-down-thought pattern. And as long as you think that old sit-down thought, you'll be in some kind of sit-down action. They'll have you sittin' in everywhere. It's not so good to refer to what you're going to do as a sit-in. That right there castrates you. Right there it brings you

down. . . . Think of the image of someone sitting. An old woman can sit; an old man can sit; a chump can sit; a coward can sit.[81]

Social movements must continually search for new tactics and adapt strategies to keep the movement alive and progressing, but each new selection or change can lead to conflicts within and between organizations.

Mobilizing for Action

Persuaders must convince large numbers of people to join in the cause, to organize into effective groups, and to unify through coalitions to carry the movement's message to target audiences to bring about desired evolutionary results. Ralph Smith and Russell Windes contend that "The presence of mobilizational exigencies distinguishes, and assists in defining, the rhetorical situation of movements. The rhetorical situation of a movement," its environment, "requires discourse to organize support for united action to reach a shared goal of social change."[82]

Organizing and Uniting the Discontented

Social movements expend great persuasive effort trying to educate audiences about the cause and to convince them of the urgency to *join together* to bring about or to resist change. Mailings, newsletters, newspapers, pamphlets, leaflets, books, videos, the Internet, interpersonal contacts, and speeches are only a few channels devoted to organizing and uniting the discontented. Fund-raising appeals, often with coupons that list activities and committees for active involvement, are integral parts of most printed persuasive efforts because social movements have few other means to finance leaders, organizations, publications, phone banks, mailings, Web sites, demonstrations, and legal challenges.

Getting Americans to join and unite in uninstitutional organizations is no easy task. Traditions of rugged individualism, belief in the capacity and determination of U.S. institutions to deal with problems effectively once they are identified, and suspicion of movements and agitators prevent most Americans from protesting, let alone joining and becoming active in what they see as strange organizations.

Social movements must persuade significant numbers of people that only collective action by uninstitutionalized groups using unconventional methods can bring about or resist change. They must create a collective identity, a people, so individuals come to identify themselves as a group through "shared views of the social environment, shared goals, and shared opinions about the possibilities and limits of collective action."[83]

Even the largest and most successful social movements manage to organize only a fraction of victims and socially conscious citizens. Very few women, African Americans, Hispanic Americans, gays, workers, and supporters of the environment ever contribute to or join movements. And once people join a social movement, they may splinter into numerous organizations because of differences over tactics, ideology, leaders, personalities, organizational structures, and real or imagined grievances. An institution may aid this splintering by seeming to favor one organization or leader over another, playing the game of divide and conquer.

Pressuring the Opposition

Although all social movements are to a greater or lesser degree self-change oriented (believing that followers must purify themselves before they can change others), they all engage the opposition in symbolic combat. The weapons may be verbal, such as mass mailings, name-calling, ridicule, obscenity, and threats; or nonverbal, such as mass demonstrations, sit-ins, walk-outs, boycotts, strikes, and disruptions. They may attempt to gain control of agencies of influence such as the courts, executive offices, boards of trustees, and school boards by voting officials in or out of office, purchasing or creating mass media, or gaining control of corporations through stock proxies. Malcolm X urged audiences to use the ballot effectively to take control of their neighborhoods and lives; the bullet was a last resort for self-defense.

Movements often pressure opponents to gain recognition, concessions, compromises, or capitulations. A first step may be to make an institution admit there is a serious problem. For example, in the 1980s thousands of farm owners descended upon Washington, D.C. to protest government policies they believed kept crop prices too low and were causing many of them to lose their farms. Hundreds drove tractors or transported farm machinery to demonstrations near the Capitol, and a few burned obsolete equipment to demonstrate their frustrations and to pressure members of Congress. Tactics designed to pressure the opposition may produce negative results.

When Native Americans put on war paint and took over Wounded Knee, South Dakota and Alcatraz Island in San Francisco Bay and held off federal marshals for weeks, they succeeded in pressuring institutions and gaining national attention. Unfortunately, their symbolic actions reinforced the stereotype of the painted savage Hollywood had portrayed for decades, an image they were trying to erase.

Social movements should confine persuasive efforts to symbols and symbolic actions that are lawful or protected by the Constitution. As Bowers, Ochs, and Jensen write, violent acts void of symbolism, or that appear to be so, are likely to cost the movement the support of sympathizers and legitimizers and invite outright suppression under the rubrics of law and order, public safety, and national security.[84] Violent acts may negate much that has been gained through years of persuasive efforts. For example, radical elements of the pro-life movement who have bombed, burned, fired bullets into abortion clinics, and assassinated physicians to pressure the opposition have compromised their claims of being pro-life.

Gaining Sympathy and Support of Legitimizers

Social movement members differ markedly in their commitment to the movement and its cause. Wilson illustrates this commitment as the rings of an onion.[85] At the center are a small number of full-time, paid professionals who are totally committed to the cause and willing to sacrifice everything. The first ring around this center consists of full-time, nonpaid professionals who can be counted on to populate the front lines in marches and demonstrations and remain committed when the movement is under attack or struggling to bring about meaningful change. The second ring consists of the rank and file where total commitment is rare because the movement plays a small role in their lives. The third ring consists of sympathizers and legitimizers who are neither fully inside nor fully outside the movement.

Legitimizers are social opinion leaders such as judges, politicians, business executives, clergy, sports figures, and entertainers who can help legitimize a movement in the eyes of the public by appearing at rallies, marching in demonstrations, speaking in favor of the cause, donating money, and so on. The environmental, women's liberation, gay-rights, pro-choice, pro-life, and other contemporary movements have capitalized on the support of actors such as Robert Redford and Alan Alda; actresses such as Jane Fonda, Joanne Woodward, and Barbra Streisand; singers such as John Denver and Michael Jackson; Vice Presidents Dan Quayle and Albert Gore; Senators such as Ted Kennedy and Orrin Hatch; and clergy such as Jerry Falwell and Jesse Jackson. Some legitimizers offer more than their names, presence, and money. For example, pro-life sympathizers Ronald Reagan and George Bush supported the movement not only by speaking in its favor and advocating legal and constitutional changes but by outlawing abortion counseling at federally funded clinics, research on fetal tissue, abortions at military hospitals, funding for international population control programs, and the import of the French abortion pill RU-486. Pro-choice sympathizer Bill Clinton overturned the first three actions of the former presidents within two days of his inauguration and announced reconsideration of the fourth. RU-486 was approved for sale in the U.S. in 2000. He infuriated pro-life forces when he opposed laws that would prohibit so-called "partial birth" abortions.

Movements often attempt to provoke institutions or other movements into excessive or repressive acts that reveal the ugliness of the opposition and gain sympathy and legitimizers for the victims and their demands. Seventy-five thousand pro-lifers marched in Washington in response to President Clinton's "proabortion" actions, and, in the days that followed, thousands of Operation Rescue members were arrested as they blockaded abortion clinics around the country in an attempt to clog the jails and provoke police officers into harming protestors so television viewers would be sympathetic to their cause and treatment by institutions.

A social movement's ability to mobilize forces into action may be hindered by its relational patterns with institutions. It may be partially equal to (equal on some grounds and not on others), dependent upon (for communication channels, legitimacy, legal protection, permits to demonstrate), or subjugated (completely dominated and controlled) by institutions. We know little about how social movements adapt persuasive efforts to various and changing relationships. How, for instance, did pro-life forces adapt to a hostile presidential administration under Clinton after years of friendly administrations under Reagan and Bush?

Sustaining the Social Movement

Since social movements usually last for years and experience changing environments, they use persuasion to sustain their crusades.

Justifying Setbacks and Delays

Every movement attempts to establish we-they distinctions (relational patterns), to instill strong convictions about accomplishing goals (evolutionary results), and to preach or imply that its ends justify any means necessary (adaptive strategies) to bring about or to resist change. Inevitably, these convictions, distinctions, and ends lead to impatience with moderate leadership, strategies, and slow progress toward goals and to suggestions that radical leadership and actions are necessary. Malcolm X exclaimed that speeches, sit-ins, singing "We Shall Overcome," the 1963 march on Washington, and integration had failed to bring about real change. It was time for the ballot or the bullet, a time to "stop singing and start swinging."[86] Demands for results and effective strategies may result in leadership changes or violent acts such as assassinations and bombings that discredit the movement.

Leaders use persuasion to maintain order and discipline and to respond to actions that embarrass the movement and threaten its support inside and outside the movement. They offer believable explanations for setbacks or the lack of meaningful gains or victories. They explain why agreements with institutions remain unfulfilled or ineffective, and they justify why target dates have come and gone without results. The many audiences social movements address may perceive progress, victories, agreements, and priority of goals quite differently. For instance, while some members see all change as too little too late, others become too satisfied with achievements made. Internal and external opposition may capitalize on delays and setbacks to undermine leadership and organizations and to proclaim superiority.

Whatever its goals, a social movement needs years of untiring efforts from significant numbers of people to gain or to prevent change. It must convince followers that victory is near or inevitable if all is done correctly and members remain steadfast in their commitment and true to sacred principles. Leaders attempt to create and sustain Eric Hoffer's "extravagant hope."[87]

Maintaining Viability of the Movement

Social movements wage continual battles to remain viable. More rhetorical energy may be expended on fund raising, membership drives, acquisition of materials and property, and maintenance of movement communication than on selling ideologies to target audiences and pressuring the opposition. Reinforcing the commitment of members limits a movement's ability to perform other functions. Annual meetings are devoted more to internal squabbles, ferreting out traitors and internal conspiracies, and defending movement administrations than to planning offensive campaigns and attacking external foes.

Ironically, a social movement may become either too successful or successful too soon. When African Americans, Hispanics, women, and gays achieved some rights and when environmentalists and animal rights advocates helped to forge some laws, each movement lost membership and drive because the need seemed less urgent. Growth in membership and geographical sphere of influence and creeping institutionalization may seriously reduce the informality of structure and feeling of crisis that initially attracted people to the movement. Thus, a serious decline in membership and commitment may occur when success seems near. To counteract declines in membership and commitment, movements may turn to memories (past campaigns, victories, heroes, martyrs) to keep the struggle alive. They may strive to create new heroes to breathe life into the aging cause. New, more vibrant organizations may arise to challenge or to replace older, established ones. Leaflets, mailings, speeches, and songs contain personal statements of commitment, sometimes commitment like the persuader's parents had to the movement. Audiences are continually assured, even when an organization or movement is in rapid free fall, that it is growing stronger every day and victory is near or inevitable.

Maintaining Visibility of the Movement

Social movements are haunted by the old adage: out of sight, out of mind. Social movement members, the media, and target audiences have insatiable appetites for persuasive happenings, but few movements have adequate leadership, membership, energy, and funds to satisfy these appetites over long periods while fending off opposition. They try to remain visible through every means imaginable: billboards, bumper stickers, stickerettes, buttons, tee shirts, jewelry, uniforms and items of clothing, famous women paper dolls, playing cards, Christmas cards, dial-a-message, and coloring books. They may select new symbols. They may create newspapers, journals, or Internet Web sites to communicate directly with members because commercial media ignore the movement or are perceived to treat it unfairly. Old events, actions, and things receive less attention and produce serious drains on movement resources.

Social movements use rhetorical events and happenings such as ceremonies, annual conventions, and anniversary or birthday celebrations to remain visible and to stoke the agitational fire. Often with the help of institutional sympathizers, movements create memorials to former leaders. They may turn plots of ground where historical events occurred into hallowed ground and buildings into museums. Bernard Armada writes, for example, that the National Civil Rights Museum in the former Lorraine Motel in Memphis where Martin Luther King, Jr. was assassinated, "teaches about the black American struggle for equality while also inviting visitors to identify themselves as sympathizers for that cause; visitors are invited to join a community of civil rights sympathizers and activists."[88] He claims that the design of the museum not only invites visitors to join a community but "attempts to forge a subculture of civil rights advocates equipped with the disposition needed to carry their political power beyond the institutionalized walls of the museum." Memorials are a key means of sustaining a movement.

Conclusions

Social movements rely on persuasion as the primary agency through which they attempt to perform critical persuasive functions that enable them to come into existence, satisfy requirements, grow in size and influence, meet opposition from within and without, and effectively bring about or resist change. These essential functions are closely related to the several parts of the social systems question posed in chapter 2. Functions include transforming perceptions of reality (the environment in which they must operate), altering self-perceptions of protestors (which individuals conceiving themselves to be what people), attaining legitimacy (using what relational patterns), prescribing courses of action and mobilizing the discontented (with what adaptive strategies), and sustaining the movement until victory is achieved (with what evolutionary results).

Unfortunately for social movements, their uninstitutional status greatly limits their powers, options, and legitimacy and, therefore, their abilities to perform these persuasive functions effectively on a continual basis over long periods. They compete with other movements, countermovements, and institutions that are attempting to enable individuals to see themselves as a particular people, interpret the environment, further or assign relational patterns, adapt strategies to changing circumstances, and produce evolutionary results that make the future different from today.

Endnotes

1. This definition is from a discussion of the meaning of the term in Robert K. Merton, *Social Theory and Social Structure* (Glencoe, IL: Free Press, 1957): 19–25.

2. See for example, Herbert W. Simons, Elizabeth W. Mechling, and Howard N. Schreier, "The Functions of Human Communication in Mobilizing for Action from the Bottom Up: The Rhetoric of Social Movements," *Handbook of Rhetorical and Communication Theory*, Carroll C. Arnold and John W. Bowers, eds. (Boston: Allyn and Bacon, 1984): 807–808; Bruce E. Gronbeck, "The Rhetoric of Social-Institutional Change: Black Action at Michigan," *Explorations in Rhetorical Criticism*, Gerald Mohrmann, Charles Stewart, and Donovan Ochs, eds. (University Park, PA: Pennsylvania State University Press, 1973): 96–113; Charles J. Stewart, "A Functional Approach to the Rhetoric of Social Movements," *Central States Speech Journal* 31 (Winter 1980): 298–305; Charles J. Stewart, "A Functional Perspective on the Study of Social Movements," *Central States Speech Journal* 34 (Spring 1983): 77–80.

3. Michael Lipsky, "Protest as a Political Resource," *The American Political Science Review* 52 (1968): 1144–1148; James Q. Wilson, "The Strategy of Protest: Problems of Negro Civic Action," *Journal of Conflict Resolution* 3 (1961): 291–303.

4. William A. Gamson, "The Social Psychology of Collective Action," *Frontiers in Social Movement Theory*, Aldon D. Morris and Carol McClurg Mueller, eds. (New Haven, CT: Yale University Press, 1992): 71.

5. Wil A. Linkugel, R. R. Allen, and Richard L. Johannesen, *Contemporary American Speeches*, 5th ed. (Dubuque, IA: Kendall/Hunt, 1982): 208; Richard L. Johannesen, "The Jeremiad and Jenkin Lloyd Jones," *Communication Monographs* 52 (June 1985): 164.

6. See Ernest G. Bormann, "Fantasy and Rhetorical Vision: The Rhetorical Criticism of Social Reality," *Quarterly Journal of Speech* 58 (December 1972): 396–407; Richard B. Gregg, "A Phenomenologically Oriented Approach to Rhetorical Criticism," *Central States Speech Journal* 17 (May 1966): 83–90.

7. Haig A. Bosmajian, "Defining the 'American Indian': A Case Study in the Language of Oppression," *Speech Teacher* 22 (March 1973): 89–99.

8. *Historical Fact No. 1. Did Six Million Really Die? The Truth at Last* (Chapel Ascote, Ladbroke, Southam, Warks: Historical Review Press, n.d.); Austin J. App, *Holocaust: Sneak Attack on Christianity* (Chicago: National Socialist White People's Party, n.d.).

9. *The Big Lie: Who Really Told It?* (Arlington, VA: National Socialist White People's Party, n.d.).

10. "The Angry American Indian: Starting Down the Protest Trail," *Time*, 9 February 1970, 14–20.

11. From tapes of radio addresses by Billy James Hargis on March 11 and 12, 1963 and others that are undated.

12. Robert Welch, "The Truth in Time," *The New American*, 17 August 1987, 25–33 (reprinted from *American Opinion*, November 1966).

13. *Do You Want to Return to the Butchery of Back-Alley Abortion?* (New York: NARAL, n. d.); *Abortion Fact Sheet* (New York: NARAL, n.d.); *Twelve Abortion Facts* (Washington, DC: NARAL, n.d.).

14. Philip C. Wander, "The Savage Child: The Image of the Negro in the Pro-Slavery Movement," *Southern Speech Communication Journal* 37 (Summer 1972): 335–360.

15. Marie J. Rosenwasser, "Rhetoric and the Progress of the Women's Liberation Movement," *Today's Speech* 20 (Summer 1972): 45–56; Karlyn Kohrs Campbell, "The Rhetoric of Women's Liberation: An Oxymoron," *Quarterly Journal of Speech* 59 (February 1973): 74–86.

[16] "Local Anti-Gay Seminar to Continue: Varied Viewpoints Clash Over Issue," *The Purdue Exponent*, 1 December 1992, 1; "Gays Under Fire," *Newsweek* 14 September 1992, 35–40.

[17] Gary C. Woodward, "Mystifications in the Rhetoric of Cultural Dominance and Colonial Control," *Central States Speech Journal* 26 (Winter 1975): 301.

[18] *Say No to Torture* (Washington, DC: Animal Welfare Institute, n.d.).

[19] *Say No to Torture.*

[20] Letter from Cleveland Amory, Fund for Animals, February 1995.

[21] Mary Brigid Gallagher, "John L. Lewis: The Oratory of Pity and Indignation," *Today's Speech* 9 (September 1961): 15–16.

[22] *The Purdue Exponent*, 31 March 1992, 7.

[23] Hans Toch, *The Social Psychology of Social Movements* (New York: Bobbs-Merrill, 1965):11.

[24] Eugene V. Debs, "The Issue," *Debs: His Life, Writings and Speeches* (Chicago: Charles H. Keff, 1908): 489.

[25] Robert Welch, *The Blue Book of the John Birch Society* (Boston: Western Islands Publishers, 1961): 1.

[26] Mary Ellen Barrett, "Fur Fight," *USA Weekend*, 9–11 February 1990, 4.

[27] Randall A. Lake, "Order and Disorder in Anti-Abortion Rhetoric: A Logological View," *Quarterly Journal of Speech* 70 (November 1984): 425–443.

[28] *Seabook Alert*, 1981; *Seabrook Clamshell* letter, May 1986; *Seabook Clamshell* letter, August 1986.

[29] James Darsey, "From 'Gay Is Good' to the Scourge of AIDS: The Evolution of Gay Liberation Rhetoric, 1977–1990," *Communication Studies* 42 (Spring 1991): 43–66.

[30] Unless otherwise noted, this treatment of the ego function of protest rhetoric is taken from Charles J. Stewart, "Championing the Rights of Others and Challenging Evil: The Ego Function in the Rhetoric of Other-Directed Social Movements," *Southern Communication Journal* 64 (Winter 1999): 91–105.

[31] Fernando Pedro Delgado, "Chicano Movement Rhetoric: An Ideographic Interpretation," *Communication Quarterly* 43 (Fall 1995): 451.

[32] Richard B. Gregg, "The Ego-Function of the Rhetoric of Protest," *Philosophy and Rhetoric* 4 (Spring 1971): 79.

[33] Darsey, 55; Charles J. Stewart, "The Ego Function of Protest Songs: An Application of Gregg's Theory of Protest Rhetoric," *Communication Studies* 42 (Fall 1991): 251.

[34] Gregg, 74.

[35] Michael Victor Sedano, "Chicanismo: A Rhetorical Analysis of Themes and Images of Selected Poetry from the Chicano Movement," *Western Journal of Speech Communication* 44 (Summer 1980): 179.

[36] Gregg, 81.

[37] Joseph R. Gusfield, *Protest, Reform, and Revolt: A Reader in Social Movements* (New York: John Wiley & Sons, 1970): 310; Arthur L. Smith (Molefi Asante), *A Rhetoric of Black Revolution* (Boston: Allyn and Bacon, 1969): 1; John W. Bowers, Donovan J. Ochs, and Richard J. Jensen, *The Rhetoric of Agitation and Control*, 2/E (Prospect Heights, IL: Waveland Press, 1993): 13.

[38] Gaston V. Rimlinger, "The Legitimation of Protest: A Comparative Study in Labor History," in Gusfield, *Protest, Reform, and Revolt*, 363.

[39] Herbert W. Simons, *Persuasion: Understanding, Practice and Analysis* (Reading, MA: Addison-Wesley, 1976): 234.

[40] Robert A. Francesconi, "James Hunt, The Wilmington 10, and Institutional Legitimacy," *Quarterly Journal of Speech* 68 (February 1982): 49.

[41] William A. Garrison, "The Social Psychology of Collective Action," *Frontiers in Social Movement Theory*, Aldon D. Morris and Carol McClurg Mueller, eds. (New Haven, CT: Yale University Press, 1992): 68.

[42] Herbert W. Simons, "The Carrot and the Stick as Handmaidens of Persuasion in Conflict Situations," *Perspectives on Communication in Social Conflict*, Gerald R. Miller and Herbert W. Simons, eds. (Englewood Cliffs, NJ: Prentice-Hall, 1974): 196; Simons, Mechling, and Schreier, 820.

[43] Frances Fox Piven and Richard A. Cloward, "Normalizing Collective Protest," *Frontiers in Social Movement Theory,* 303.

[44] Anthony Oberschall, *Social Conflict and Social Movements* (Englewood Cliffs, NJ: Prentice-Hall, 1973): 188.

[45] Simons, Mechling, and Schreier, 810.

[46] R. R. McGuire, "Speech Acts, Communicative Competence and the Paradox of Authority," *Philosophy and Rhetoric* 10 (Winter 1977): 31 and 33.

[47] William A. Gamson, *Power and Discontent* (Homewood, IL: Dorsey Press, 1968): 127.

[48] Louis Kriesberg, *The Sociology of Social Conflicts* (Englewood Cliffs, NJ: Prentice-Hall, 1973): 111.

[49] Simons, "Persuasion in Social Conflicts," 239–247.

[50] Francesconi, 50.

[51] Max Weber, *The Theory of Social and Economic Organization,* A.M. Henderson and Talcott Parsons, trans. (New York: The Free Press, 1964): 328.

[52] Smith, 1; Irving I. Zaretsky and Mark P. Leone, *Religious Movements in Contemporary America* (Princeton, NJ: University of Princeton Press, 1974): 10 and 26.

[53] Gusfield, 310; Zaretsky and Leone, 500; Richard L. Johannesen, "The Jeremiad and Jenkin Lloyd Jones," *Communication Monographs* 52 (June 1985): 156–172.

[54] Contained in a collection of SDS papers compiled by James F. Walsh.

[55] *The Gray Panther Manual* (Philadelphia: The Gray Panthers, 1978): 8.

[56] Oberschall, 308.

[57] Zaretsky and Leone, 500 and 510.

[58] Robert S. Cathcart, "Movements: Confrontation as Rhetorical Form," *Southern Speech Communication Journal* 43 (Spring 1978): 237; Simons, "Persuasion in Social Conflicts," 236.

[59] Rhodri Jeffreys-Jones, *Violence and Reform in American History* (New York: New Viewpoints, 1978): 16, 30, and 38.

[60] Bowers, Ochs, Jensen, 20.

[61] Carol J. Jablonski, "Promoting Radical Change in the Roman Catholic Church: Rhetorical Requirements, Problems, and Strategies of the American Bishops," *Central States Speech Journal* 31 (Winter 1980): 289.

[62] McGuire, 44.

[63] Saul Alinsky, *Rules for Radicals: A Pragmatic Primer for Realistic Radicals* (New York: Vintage Books, 1971): 128.

[64] Cathcart, 246.

[65] Simons, "Persuasion in Social Conflicts," 243; Robert L. Scott and Donald K. Smith, "The Rhetoric of Confrontation," *Quarterly Journal of Speech* 55 (February 1969): 8.

[66] Scott and Smith, 8.

[67] Cathcart, 243.

[68] Simons, Mechling, and Schreier, 829; Theodore Otto Windt, "The Diatribe: Last Resort for Protest," *Quarterly Journal of Speech* 58 (February 1972): 14.

[69] John Wilson, *Introduction to Social Movements* (New York: Basic Books, 1969): 71.

[70] Kenneth M. Dolbeare and Patricia M. Dolbeare, *American Ideologies: The Competing Political Beliefs of the 1970s* (Prospect Heights, IL: Waveland Press, 1971): 3, as cited in Steve Goldzwig, "James Watt's Subversion of Values: An Analysis of Rhetorical Failure," *The Southern Speech Communication Journal* 50 (Summer 1985): 307.

[71] Goldzwig, 323.

[72] Michael C. McGee, "The 'Ideograph': A Link between Rhetoric and Ideology," *Quarterly Journal of Speech* 66 (February 1980): 7.

[73] Wilson, 91–97.

[74] Bruce Cameron, *Modern Social Movements* (New York: Random House, 1966):15.

[75] Toch, 30.

[76] Fred Powledge, *Free at Last? The Civil Rights Movement and the People Who Made It* (Boston: Little, Brown and Company, 1991).

[77] Charles J. Stewart, "The Knights of Labor vs. the American Federation of Labor: A Rhet-

oric Rotten with Perfection," unpublished paper presented at the annual convention of the National Communication Association, 1992; Samuel Gompers, "Address to the Machinist Convention," *American Federationist* 8 (1901), 251.

78   "Manifesto of the New York Radical Feminists," unpublished paper, n.d.

79   Alinsky, 127–128.

80   Roxanne Dunbar, "Women's Liberation: Where the Movement Is Today and Where It's Going," *Handbook of Women's Liberation*, Joan Robbins, ed. (Los Angeles: NOW Library Press, 1970), as reprinted in Charles J. Stewart, *On Speech Communication* (New York: Holt, Rinehart and Winston, 1972): 312–313.

81   Malcolm X, "The Ballot Or the Bullet," Detroit 1964, from an audio recording.

82   Ralph R. Smith and Russel R. Windes, "The Rhetoric of Mobilization: Implications for the Study of Movements," *The Southern Speech Communication Journal* 42 (Fall 1976), 1.

83   Klandermans, 81; Verta Taylor and Nancy Whittier, "Collective Identity in Social Movement Communities," *Frontiers in Social Movement Theory*, 105.

84   Bowers, Ochs, and Jensen, 77–78.

85   Wilson, *Introduction to Social Movements*, 306.

86   Malcolm X.

87   Hoffer, 18.

88   Bernard J. Armada, "Memorial Agon: An Interpretive Tour of the National Civil Rights Museum," *Southern Communication Journal* 63 (Spring 1998): 236.

PERSONAL NEEDS AND
SOCIAL MOVEMENTS
JOHN BIRCHERS AND GRAY PANTHERS

Social movements are characterized by minimal organization, but they are collectives of individuals. Like universities, corporations, and political campaigns they are always engaged in recruitment and consolidation. Without recruitment there are no members, and without consolidation the individuals do not constitute a group or a movement.[1] But all potential members are not equally attractive to recruiters—different parts of different universities, for instance, recruit seven-foot rebounders, concert violinists, and National Merit Scholars—and different recruits will find life in the organization differentially appealing.

The systems approach to persuasion presented in chapter 2 discussed the relationships among personal needs, preferences, symbols and reasoning and their social counterparts: laws, ideologies, languages, and logics. This chapter extends that discussion to demonstrate how John Birch Society and Gray Panther rhetoric spoke to potential recruits in ways that appealed to the kinds of people they could most easily consolidate while alienating those who would not fit in. They did this by providing people with gratifications that were primarily psychological rather than political, social, or philosophical. More specifically, John Birch Society materials spoke directly to the needs of a classic authoritarian character structure and Gray Panther materials spoke to the democratic character structure.

Authoritarian and Democratic Personalities

The Hitler phenomenon spurred social psychologists to explore the sources of his appeal. One of the earliest hypotheses centered on the notion of an authoritarian personality type. Early studies of the authoritarian character structure were based on clinical observation until 1950 when Theodor Adorno and his colleagues presented their California F-Scale for the measurement of Fascist tendencies. These early works were directed at understanding rightist authoritarianism, and they concentrated on the study of followers' beliefs about authority and those who exercise it. In the 1960s, Milton Rokeach steered psychological research toward the study of "topic free" open- and closed-mindedness, and interest in ideological authoritarianism waned.[2]

One of the early studies of authoritarian personality remains especially helpful for understanding how messages provide audiences with psychological gratifications. That study is Abraham Maslow's 1943 essay on "The Authoritarian Character Structure."[3] We do not ordinarily recommend framing rhetorical analyses with sixty-year-old studies from other disciplines, but Maslow's is no ordinary essay. It is useful to students of persuasion because it predates psychologists' preoccupation with pencil-and-paper scales and instead synthesizes clinical observations of people's verbal expressions—an approach that lends itself to analyzing other verbal expressions. Moreover, it describes two archetypal personality structures that have social, political, and rhetorical implications: authoritarian and democratic character structures.

Maslow's Authoritarian Character Structure

For Maslow's authoritarian character structure, everything revolves around authority. The three major premises of the authoritarian worldview are that (a) the world is a jungle that requires both (b) strict hierarchical organization and (c) the glorification of dominance and submission. The fundamental premise of the authoritarian worldview is that life is essentially threatening. Maslow explained that:

> Like other psychologically insecure people, the authoritarian person lives in a world which may be conceived to be pictured by him as a sort of jungle in which every man's [woman's] hand is necessarily against every other man's [woman's], in which the whole world is conceived of as dangerous, threatening, or at least challenging, and in which humans are conceived of as primarily selfish or evil or stupid. . . . This jungle is peopled with animals who either eat or are eaten, who are either feared or despised. One's safety lies in one's own strength, and this strength consists primarily in the power to dominate. If one is not strong enough the only alternative is to find a strong protector.[4]

Within this jungle, the protector-protected relationship must predominate. Because danger is all around, the protector demands total obedience; and because the protected must sustain relationships with the protector, submission is willing and even ecstatic.

The authoritarian's worldview makes sense when the world resembles a jungle. It is foolish to wander off from a safari to play with lions and tigers, but to fear entering a grocery store without an armed guide is probably paranoid. Most life experiences fall somewhere between these extremes, but the authoritarian character structure treats them all as dangerous. Authoritarians, therefore, express only contempt for those who fail to recognize the world as a dangerous place. Because jungle creatures compete relentlessly and unmercifully for the means of survival, every approaching creature must quickly be categorized either as superior—and thus to be feared, resented, bootlicked, and admired—or as inferior and therefore to be scorned, humiliated, and dominated. Everyone must be quickly and easily ranked in a hierarchy from strongest to weakest. The authoritarian can therefore tolerate neither diverse goals nor diverse means, because unity is essential for survival. All people, achievements, and events must be measured on one scale, the scale of survival. Different authoritarians may stress different scales—such as strength, speed, or cunning—but no authoritarian character can value diversity or tolerance because multiple scales confound superior-inferior ranking and thus compound the danger to all. The person judged superior on that one scale is judged *universally superior*, and inferiors are judged *universally inferior*.

For the authoritarian characters in their jungles, these judgments of superiority must be made quickly; but because they can identify overall superiority or inferiority from any one characteristic and generalize to others, the authoritarian character judges by externals. These externals may include titles, physical stature and grooming, wealth, family name, race, gender, age, or behavior. Externals are useful to authoritarians precisely because they are inclined to believe that a superior person is always superior and that an inferior is always inferior. The authoritarian can note external characteristics and measure them against the single vertical scale to ascertain the person's superior-inferior ranking.

Given the foregoing context for the leader-follower relationship the authoritarian character structure naturally regards any leader's kindness as weakness. Maslow explained [in the language common to the 1940s] that:

> If he [she] is in dominance status, he [she] will tend to be cruel; if he [she] is in subordinate status, he [she] will tend to be masochistic. But because of the tendencies in himself [herself], he [she] will understand, and deep down within himself [herself] will agree with the cruelty of the superior person, even if he himself [she herself] is the object of the cruelty. He [she] will understand the bootlicker and the slave even if he himself [she herself] is not the bootlicker or the slave. The same principles explain both the leader and the follower in an authoritarian group, both the slave owner and the slave.[5]

Significantly, authoritarian followers glory in their subservience to the leader. Among authoritarians there can be no negotiation of control because neither party finds such negotiations either valid or productive.

Both realize that the worthless inferior is fortunate to have the dominating protector, and both realize that the protector feels little but contempt for the inferior followers.

Because the authoritarian character structure regards people as fundamentally selfish, evil, stupid, and dependent, the superior can use inferiors as the superior sees fit. Non-leaders may even be seen as subhuman, characterized as "tools" or "pawns on a chessboard." This sadomasochistic tendency contributes to an authoritarian value system in which brutality, cruelty, selfishness, and hardness are exalted and in which sympathy, kindness, and generosity are reviled by leaders and followers alike.

Maslow lists several other characteristics of authoritarianism that deserve attention. These include an "abyss between men and women" (men purportedly being able to survive better through strength), the soldier ideal, the importance of humiliation as a mechanism for establishing superiority, antagonism toward the education of inferiors, avoidance of responsibility for one's own fate, and the pursuit of security through order, discipline, and a variety of behaviors generally regarded as obsessive-compulsive. Pervading all of these characteristics is the impossibility of satisfaction. The best one can hope for in the jungle is temporary relief from constant danger, but one must be most careful when the jungle seems safest.

Maslow's Democratic Character Structure

Maslow's democratic character sees the world as a basically friendly and supportive place, more greenhouse than jungle. Because there is little danger, there is little need for protection and, therefore, little need for submission, discipline, or obedience. Whereas the authoritarian character sees all differences between people in terms of superiority-inferiority, the democratic character views differences between people as largely independent of superiority and inferiority. When superiority-inferiority judgments must be made, the democratic character judges individuals in specific functional terms by appraising specific personal capabilities, functions, and performances. The democratic personality prefers to judge others, if judge they must, on the basis of performance. As Maslow explained, the democratic character "customarily gives his [her] permanent respect only to people who are worthy of respect for functional reasons. He [she] doesn't give his [her] respect automatically simply because he [she] is supposed to, or because everybody else respects this person."[6] The democratic character examines functional characteristics, adjudicates them (as necessary) according to diverse values, and creates a leader-follower relationship (when necessary) for the attainment of some specific goal.

The democratic character views humans as colleagues or partners rather than rivals. The democratic structure does not use or manipulate people. It exhibits no tendency comparable to the sadomasochism of authoritarians. There is room for both selfishness and generosity, for hardness and compassion since different people value differently in different circumstances at different times. Democratic character types can be happier for longer time periods because their basic needs have been satisfied. Danger is unusual, rather than normal, in everyday life.

Maslow observes that the authoritarian and democratic character types are constructions of internally consistent beliefs or tendencies, all of which revolve around the premise that the world is (or is not) an extremely threatening and dangerous place. They are frameworks for interpreting one's environment. Individuals need to interpret their worlds in ways that fit their psychological needs and enable them to coordinate their lives with others. The psychological makeup of the both character structures suggests a tendency to try to find or create like-minded people. Theoretically, authoritarian leaders should be telling people about dangers, and authoritarian followers should be listening for good protectors. Democratic leaders ought to be trying to empower people, and democratic followers ought to be developing functional relationships to work on problems. We find just such tendencies in the discourse of the John Birch Society and the Gray Panthers.

Two Social Movement Organizations

The John Birch Society and the Gray Panthers were begun by people who had found personal, professional, and financial satisfaction through institutions. Both organizations were comprised mostly of people worried about trends they saw in U.S. society, but they engaged in very different kinds of rhetoric and attracted very different followers.

The John Birch Society

The John Birch Society was founded in 1958 as a secret, activist, anticommunist organization by Robert H. W. Welch, a retired candy company executive and former official of the National Association of Manufacturers.[7] Welch wanted a cadre of dedicated and disciplined patriots who would help him *take America back* from the communists. He did not want a large organization because large organizations are difficult to discipline. Welch's central concern was the threat of communism; but while other conservatives watched the Kremlin and opposed communist expansion with foreign aid and military assistance, Welch maintained that most nations (including the United States) were ruled secretly by communists who had infiltrated and subverted their governments. He opposed the expensive military programs that most anticommunists supported, characterizing them as efforts to wreck the U.S. economy and to distract patriotic Americans from the "real" danger—communist subversion. For many years, he published an annual rating of the percentage of communist control over every nation in the world.

The Birch Society was active and especially visible during the early 1960s with their efforts to impeach Chief Justice Earl Warren, prevent fluoridation of water supplies, and "Get US out of the UN." Conventional wisdom holds that the John Birch Society disintegrated in the mid-1960s as a consequence of two phenomena. The first of these was the Goldwater presidential campaign in 1964—a campaign in which the Birch Society was highly active and visible. The second was the belief dilemma posed for Birchers by the antiwar protests of the 1960s: Birchers opposed both the Vietnam war (as an effort by American communists to squander our national resources) and protestors of virtually all political stripes (as communist-inspired troublemakers).[8] As the Birch Society's visibility diminished, the public and scholars alike inferred that the Society had become insignificant.

But the John Birch Society did not disband in the mid-1960s, it simply evolved into a new phase. This was evident in the circulation of its two publications: *The John Birch Society Bulletin* (a monthly publication for members) and *American Opinion* (later changed to *The New American*). The circulation of each periodical was virtually the same in 1979–1981 as it had been during the 1963–1965 "peak." Indeed, the mailed circulation of the members only *Bulletin* was 50 percent greater in 1981 than any known estimate of the Society's "peak" membership.[9]

The John Birch Society might better have been called the Robert Welch Society, for Welch was its founder and autocratic leader until his death in 1985. The group's ideology was set forth in its manual, *The Blue Book of the John Birch Society*, which consisted of a series of lectures Welch delivered at the organization's founding in Indianapolis in 1958.[10] The continuing influence of Welch's initial analysis are evident in two ways. The *Blue Book* is prominently featured on the Society's Web site (*http://www.jbs.org*), where it can be ordered with the click of a mouse. Moreover, Welch's picture and his writings are predominant more than fifteen years after his death and 43 years after his historic Indianapolis session. There is no official indication of the Society's current leadership structure, but a quotation in the closing paragraph of an article about the group's history is attributed to President John F. McManus (*http://www.thenewamerican.com/tna/1998/vo14no25/vo14no25_jb.htm*).

The Gray Panthers

The group that would become known as the Gray Panthers began in March of 1970 at a New York City luncheon of six women approaching forced retirement from careers of public service. The luncheon was called by Margaret Kuhn, Coordinator of Programs in the United Presbyterian Church, Division of Church and Race, and Associate Secretary in the Office of Church and Society. Others included Eleanore French (Director of the Student Division of the YWCA), Helen Smith (Director of the Division of the Laity of the United Church of Christ), Polly Cuthberson

(Director of the American Friends Service Committee College Program), Ann Bennett (a religious educator and member of the Student Christian Peace Movement), and Helen Baker (a former editor of *Churchwomen* and a United Nations reporter). They decided that they would not let forced retirement keep them from improving social conditions.[11]

The women continued to meet, and each used her large network of personal and professional acquaintances to find new members. Although their primary concern was ageism (discrimination on the basis of chronological age), their goals and priorities expanded to include "justice, freedom, and dignity for and with the oppressed" and "alternative lifestyles and opportunities for older and younger people which will eliminate paternalism, discrimination, segregation and oppression."[12] Their specific short-term goals included guaranteed employment for everyone wanting to work, a guaranteed annual income, greater participation in national decision making, radical tax reform to plug loopholes, and a drastic cut in military spending. Today the Gray Panthers Web site (*http:// www.graypanthers.org*) indicates that they are active in health care reform and discrimination on the basis of age, race, and gender.

Maggie Kuhn emerged as the Gray Panthers' most visible leader until her death in 1995 but, unlike Robert Welch, she was far from autocratic. The Gray Panthers developed networks of local groups that stressed local autonomy and independent actions. Both their ideology and their organizational style were democratic rather than authoritarian.

The Authoritarian Character of John Birch Society Persuasion

The central arguments of the John Birch Society addressed all of the psychological needs of the authoritarian character while alienating those of the democratic character. These central arguments are found in *The Blue Book of the John Birch Society*, the transcription of Welch's address at the Society's founding in 1958 that remains its formal ideological statement.[13] By analyzing this core ideology for evidence of authoritarianism and democratic character, we can see how the Society was built around its leader. This enabled Welch, as the protector, to reconcile belief dilemmas for his followers and to increase their dependence on him.

The Birch World as Jungle

The theme of the *Blue Book* was the danger of subversive communism. If people were not aroused to that danger, said Welch, "in a few short years we shall all be hanging from the same lamp posts while Communist terror reigns all around us (p. x)." He told his readers that:

the truth I bring you is simple, incontrovertible and deadly. It is that, unless we can reverse forces which now seem inexorable in their movement, you have only a few more years before the country in which you live will become separate provinces in a world-wide Communist dominion ruled by police-state methods from the Kremlin. (p. 1)

But unlike most other anticommunists, Welch regarded the danger as neither Soviet aggression nor nuclear war, but subversion. Lenin's strategy, he said:

is taking us over by a process so gradual and insidious that Soviet rule is slipped over so far on the American people, before they ever realize it is happening, that they can no longer resist the Communist conspiracy as free citizens (p. 19). This subversion comes from a gigantic conspiracy to enslave mankind; an increasingly successful conspiracy controlled by determined, cunning, and utterly ruthless gangsters, willing to go to any means to achieve its end. (p. 21)

These conspirators were "like an octopus so large that its tentacles now reach into all of the legislative halls, all of the union labor meetings, a majority of the religious gatherings, and most of the schools of the whole world" (p. 60). Indeed, Welch warned that: "The human race has never before faced any such monster of power which has determined to enslave it. There is certainly no reason for underrating its size, its efficiency, its determination, its power, or its menace" (p. 61). The John Birch Society's world was not a friendly place.

The worldview of the John Birch Society stressed constant, imminent, hidden, ruthless danger. It is difficult to read much of their material without experiencing a sense of duress. But each of us adapts to such duress differently. The prototypical democratic character rejects the argument's central premise, perhaps rejecting valid arguments along with the invalid ones. But the authoritarian character structure is inclined to recognize the fundamental theme and read on. Having accepted the premise that an illusive, dangerous conspiracy is afoot, an authoritarian character must find a protector.

The Birch Tendency toward Autocracy

The authoritarian character of the John Birch Society's argument becomes more evident when we examine Welch's alternative to communist enslavement. The democratic character type would want to fight communist enslavement with a cooperative effort based upon functional abilities, while the authoritarian would look for leadership and protection. Welch dismissed democracy as "merely a deceptive phrase, a weapon of demagoguery, and a perennial fraud" (p. 147). He observed that a republican form of government had "many attractions and advantages, under certain favorable circumstances . . . but it lends itself too readily to infiltration, distortion and disruption" (p. 146). That left autocracy: "The John

Birch Society is to be a monolithic body [which] will operate under completely authoritative control at all levels" (pp. 146–147). This autocratic structure was necessary because "no collection of debating societies is ever going to stop the Communist conspiracy from taking us over" (p. 147).

Welch's autocratic structure did not tolerate negotiations over control. The Society, he said, "cannot stop for parliamentary procedures or a lot of arguments among ourselves" because "we are now being more and more divided and deceived, by accepting within our walls more and more Trojan horses" (p. 147). Therefore, "we are not going to have factions developing on the two-sides-to-every-question theme" (p. 149). Thus, Welch offered his readers the prototypical authoritarian solution for danger: a strict autocratic relationship.

But the Society's hierarchy was not simply Welch above the membership. He explained that the Society "will function almost entirely through small local chapters, usually of from ten to twenty dedicated patriots. . . . Each will have a Chapter Leader appointed by headquarters . . . or appointed by officers in the field who have themselves been duly appointed by headquarters" (p. 51). Welch's description of the John Birch Society's organizational structure emphasized the danger of the world, a need for a clearly ordered hierarchy in which all authority would flow down from the Belmont, Massachusetts headquarters to the local chapters, and intolerance for dissension and democratic procedures. Even if a person with a democratic character structure wanted to heed Welch's alarm, such a person would be psychologically repelled from the Society by its rigid, monolithic, autocratic structure. But an alarmed authoritarian would seek precisely Welch's sort of autocracy for protection. Welch's organizational plan, therefore, meshed neatly with his alarm to persuade authoritarians and to repel democrats.

A second manifestation of the authoritarian tendency toward hierarchy was the Society's generalization of superiority from external characteristics. The reader of the *Blue Book* is introduced to all 26 members of the Council positionally: a "Boston surgeon," a "worthy son of a famous 'free enterpriser' in the Northwest lumber industry," a "well-known and highly successful Texas businessman" and several corporate, religious, and military figures (p. 172). Not only did Welch fail to indicate the specific, functional relevance of their impressive credentials to an understanding of communism or conspiracies for the benefit of any democratic characters in his audience, but he stated explicitly that the primary purpose of the Council was "to show [potential members] the stature and standing of the leadership of the Society" (p. 172). Stature and standing are important to the authoritarian, but not to the democratic character structure. Again, the rhetorical depiction of the Council could attract authoritarians but not democrats.

In addition to stature, the John Birch Society tended to generalize superiority based on one's willingness to acknowledge the danger and the solution (in this case, Birchism). Others were judged by their agreement or disagreement with Robert Welch. Historian Oswald Spengler's work fit "the known facts of history" while Arnold Toynbee was a "meretricious hack . . . who is one of the worst charlatans that ever lived" (p. 34). Presidents Roosevelt, Truman, and Eisenhower were all judged to have helped communism because Welch disagreed with them.[14] Among prominent conservatives of the time, Barry Goldwater and Ronald Reagan were applauded because they understood, while William F. Buckley and Russell Kirk were chastised because they did not.[15] Such pronouncements isolated members from the kind of two-sides-to-every-question controversy that Welch disdained. Metaphorically, those who failed to follow the safari leader endangered the whole safari. Yet the democratic character who feared communism might have found something of value in the thoughts of anticommunist conservatives such as Buckley or Kirk. Welch stressed safety through autocracy rather than safety through conservatism. Let us turn our attention, then, to the nature of the autocratic relationship that he prescribed.

Birchist Sadomasochism

The *Blue Book* is replete with references to communists' sadistic treatment of their followers. We are told of the communists' "police state features" that imposed "brutal rule" and "slavery" upon "party members who are wholly subservient" (pp. 20, 17, 28, 60). This was important because communism "has been imposed and must always be imposed, from the top down, by trickery and terror; and then it must be maintained by terror" (p. 61). This terror was directed not only at the slaves but at recalcitrant party members themselves who "are shot in some dark alley or pushed off a subway platform in front of a moving train" (p. 162). Given this alarming picture of sadistic communist rule, the democratic character type might reasonably have expected Welch to offer an alternative of kindness rather than brutality, of cooperation rather than slavery, of participation rather than subservience, and of bottom-up rather than top-down organization.

But Welch's alternative to sadistic communist domination was the Birch Society's organizational structure that mirrored the communist monolith. The Society is ordered from the top down, with members obeying official directives and subject to removal for noncompliance. Indeed, Welch observed that:

> the biggest of all organizational mistakes is to set up a local group for some continuing purpose, exhort them to do a good job, and then leave them alone to do it. It is the leadership that is most demanding, most exacting of its followers, not the one which asks the least and is afraid to ask more, that achieves really dedicated support. (p. 72)

Contrast conservative-authoritarian Welch's organizational philosophy with that of conservative-democratic Ronald Reagan, who once said:

"Surround yourself with the best people you can find, delegate authority, and don't interfere as long as the policy you've decided upon is being carried out."[16] The difference between Welch and Reagan stemmed less from differences in their conservatism than from their differing conceptions of authority. In true sadomasochistic fashion, Welch stressed (a) the leader's responsibility to push his selfish, lazy, and stupid followers to their limits, (b) the followers' ecstatic submission to that direction, and (c) his ability to understand and to empathize with followers pushed to their limits, even though "he himself is not the bootlicker." It is important that Welch argued not only that such leadership was effective but that it encouraged "really dedicated support" rather than defection or mutiny. These tendencies are unlike anything in the democratic character structure.

Thus, the *Blue Book* suggested supplanting communist domination with Welch's domination until the quantity of government could be drastically reduced and a largely anarchistic polity created in which strength and protection would determine survival.[17] This program functioned psychologically for those of authoritarian character and was dysfunctional for democratic character types, who preferred partnerships. The important point is that Welch's program paralleled the psychological continuum of authoritarianism rather than the political continuum running from freedom to control.

A second manifestation of the Birch Society's sadomasochism was the pattern of gratifications it afforded members for following Welch. Whereas democratic character types look for functional, practical benefits, the authoritarian character type seeks submission to a protector. In this regard, Welch announced that:

> The men [women] who join the John Birch Society during the next few months or few years are going to be doing so primarily because they believe in me and in what I am doing. . . . And we are going to use that [personal loyalty], like every other resource, to the fullest advantage that we can. (p. 149)

Even the criterion for continued membership was loyal submission: "those members who cease to feel the necessary degree of loyalty can either resign or will be put out before they can build up any splintering following of their own inside the Society" (p. 149).

But on what basis was the potential Bircher expected to develop this deep personal loyalty to Welch? He explained his credentials as follows:

> With all my shortcomings, there wasn't anybody else on the horizon willing to give their whole lives to the job, with the determination and dedication I would put into it. . . . . Whatever I have in me, of faith, dedication, energy, I intend to offer that leadership to all who are willing to help me. (pp. 114–115)

Put simply, others might have had better functional credentials for fighting communists, but one should attach oneself to Robert Welch (and only to him) because he alone was obsessed with this mission. The quantity of work and the obsessive-compulsive drive to spend himself thoroughly were regarded as more important than either the kind or quality of work, or the efficiency or prudence of the effort.

Welch's demand for personal loyalty on the basis of his obsession is all the more startling when we recognize that his practical, functional credentials were quite impressive. But the reader of the *Blue Book* learned neither that Welch had studied at the University of North Carolina, the U.S. Naval Academy, and Harvard Law School nor that he had written a primer on salesmanship and served in various official capacities for the National Association of Manufacturers. These seemingly pertinent facts were not divulged until a short postscript to the second printing of the *Blue Book*. The point is that Welch, a master salesman, could have sold his leadership to democratic characters by stressing his functional expertise. Instead, he emphasized (whether intentionally or not) his energy, his commitment, his constant reading of communist materials, and his willingness to exercise authority, dominance, and control—a package highly attractive to authoritarian character types.

Maslow explained that authoritarians revel in superior-inferior relationships. Inferiors know that they deserve to be controlled, while superiors find temporary satisfaction in the exercise of control. This theme pervaded *The Blue Book of the John Birch Society* as Welch condemned communist control and offered only his own control as the alternative. He sold the necessity for "dynamic, personal leadership" and personal loyalty based primarily on his compulsive-obsessive efforts and his readiness to punish those of dubious loyalty rather than on the basis of his notable, and apparently relevant, credentials. Potential members were asked to join the John Birch Society not because it would succeed, not because its tactics were well conceived, not because they could participate in it or shape its direction, but because they wanted to be personally loyal to Robert Welch.

In summary, *The Blue Book of the John Birch Society* depicted a dangerous, threatening world in which ruthless conspirators were everywhere. It suggested a monolithic, autocratic organization built around members' personal loyalty to one man on the basis of his dedication and energy. But this organization to combat totalitarianism would itself tolerate neither discussion nor parliamentary procedure, and anyone quibbling with its leader would be summarily expelled. Thus, the John Birch Society exemplified all three major characteristics of the authoritarian character structure: a view of the world as a threatening place, a tendency toward hierarchy, and a sadomasochistic tendency.

The Democratic Character of Gray Panther Persuasion

As the ideology of the John Birch Society spoke to the needs of the authoritarian character structure, the ideology of the Gray Panthers spoke to the needs of the democratic character structure. Gray Panthers viewed the world not as a jungle but as an environment that people had created and could reshape if they tried. They advocated not a strict vertical hierarchy but a nearly flat organizational structure that valued local autonomy and independent action. Finally, the Gray Panthers opposed dominance and submission, which they regarded as paternalistic. Instead, their goal was to empower persons of all ages.[18]

The Gray Panthers' World as Rational but Misguided

The world described by Gray Panthers was not an especially threatening place, but it was misguided. After all, potential members had lived in the world for six decades or more, and most of them had prospered sufficiently to devote their retirement years to social activism. The group had developed in response to forced retirement:

> At this magic age of 65, the "golden ager," alias senior citizen, is expected to settle down into a benign twilight of small deeds and trivial sentiments, unhampered by any interests more profound than crocheting, trout fishing, and bingo games. . . . [The Gray Panthers were organized by six professional women, of whom none] was the least bit impressed by crocheting, trout fishing, or bingo. Their lives had been too active for them to willingly fade away. Each devoted the whole of her adult life to social service and social change; concern and commitment was part of them. (p. 3)

These women were not people who had lived in fear or under the protective custody of autocratic leaders. Instead, the women who founded the Gray Panthers had lived professional lives that had accustomed them to altering prevailing social conditions. Had they regarded the world as a jungle, they would have sought ways to lessen the dangers so that citizens could lead their lives without fear or shame. They viewed dangers and problems as challenges to be addressed, not as permanent environmental conditions to be feared.

Nevertheless, the world perceived by the Gray Panthers was far from perfect. Panthers were concerned most by the "societal illness" of ageism: "an arbitrary discrimination on the basis of chronological age, [that] permeates Western culture and our institutions. Such discrimination is harmful to all age groups" (p. 16). Because of ageism, older people had been made to feel ashamed of their appearance and the breadth of their experiences, and they were made to feel powerless and socially useless. Gray

Panthers identified with other people who perceived themselves as powerless and sought to empower them all.

The world of the Gray Panthers also differed markedly from the world of the John Birchers because they regarded the world as amenable to change. Their 146-page *Manual* devoted nearly 70 pages to methods for effecting social change. Section V of the *Manual* explained how to organize a Gray Panther network with tips on building a constituency, planning the first meeting, holding the first meeting, selecting local officers, developing leadership, fund-raising, projects, and programs. Section VI covered "organizing issues" with suggestions on setting an objective, identifying goals, examples of successes, and even a "social action checklist." Section VII explained organizational strategies, tools for action, and resources. It covered planning for action, legislative advocacy, lobbying, advocacy with respect to administrative agencies, litigation, public hearings, and public relations. All of these suggestions presumed that the legal and administrative system could be made to work more democratically. This was most apparent in the section that explained to local Gray Panthers how to secure funding from foundations, community development block grants, and such federal programs as revenue sharing. These suggestions implied a world very different from that of the John Birch Society.

The Gray Panthers' Tendency toward Egalitarianism

Whereas Robert Welch stressed the need for a vertical organizational hierarchy, the Gray Panthers prescribed an egalitarian network of autonomous local groups. Contrast Welch's monolithic organization (local chapters with no room for debate and leaders appointed by him) with the following statement from the Gray Panther *Manual:*

> An organization is shaped and nurtured by knowledgeable and experienced, politically sophisticated, creative and concerned people . . . .
> We need a powerful and effective national organization. But to build it, we need pieces to put together, local pieces. These local pieces are the Networks, the grass roots Gray Panther groups and individuals around the country (p. 1). . . . All individual Gray Panthers and Gray Panther networks are not created from the same mold, nor are we forced to follow a strict format or role. Variation is the spice of life and we encourage local autonomy. Variations within the movement is an exciting and energizing force which we value. (pp. 15–16)

This passage valued many of the things that worried Welch. No authoritarian character type could be attracted to a group that talked about avoiding a strict format or mold because authoritarians *want* strict formats and roles. A true authoritarian personality would not want to be seen reading a manual that said, "Variation is the spice of life" (because variation is dangerous), "we encourage local autonomy" (because individual autonomy on a safari is reckless and suicidal), or that variation "is an exciting and energizing force" (because authoritarian character types perceive variation as a dangerous and debilitating force).

Another point of contrast can be found in the Gray Panthers' description of their organization. Did Maggie Kuhn appoint local leaders? Did they have stringent standards for membership? Did they dictate policy from national headquarters? The *Manual* was almost apologetic about the organization's decision to adopt Articles of Agreement in 1975, saying that "Our hope was to develop minimal structure without violating the spirit of the movement" (p. 9). The *Manual* had this to say about becoming a member under the Articles:

> Our structure is still fairly loose and flexible. A person or a group may affiliate with the National Gray Panthers by stating in writing their agreement with and willingness to work toward the goals. However, we . . . encourage and support local network autonomy in choosing those issues of importance in their own communities. (pp. 15–16)

The Panthers' seriousness about local autonomy was perhaps most evident in their discussion of networks reporting to national headquarters. "Conveners can keep the national office informed in a number of ways," it said, including an Annual Report, press clippings, Task Force reports, local news letters and, for funding proposals, notification of the Project Fund" (pp. 32–33). Nowhere did the *Manual* suggest that the national office had any power to reject, amend, or review these reports. They were simply ways for the autonomous local networks to keep the national office and other local networks informed of their activities.

The Gray Panthers' Desire to Empower

Maslow said that the democratic character structure had no tendency comparable to the authoritarian character's sadomasochism, but he might have been impressed by the Gray Panthers' desire to empower people. Where authoritarians such as the Birchers demanded obedience and rejoiced in submission to their leader, the Gray Panthers tried to advance the frontiers of democracy by fighting against paternalism and by helping people overcome feelings of powerlessness.

The theme of empowerment pervaded the 1978 *Manual*. Their movement "reflects the new mood of outrage and protest against injustices felt by increasing numbers of powerless people" (p. 15). They fought ageism with an "intergenerational coalition" of persons who shared "our concern for the larger issues of social justice and empowerment" (p. 17). They saw themselves as a Liberation Movement: "We identify with these other liberation groups and collectively reflect the widespread nature of the status disadvantaged and call for a massive redistribution of opportunities and privileges as well as major ideological changes" (p. 18). The Gray Panthers' struggle against ageism helped them see that "Many of the institutions and organizations that purport to serve people are afflicted with a deep, insidious paternalism, offering little or no voice to the recipients" (p. 18). Clearly, the Gray Panthers were committed to improving the quality of life for "those who consider themselves powerless" (p. 22).

The democratic character of the Gray Panthers was also evident in the *Manual's* section on "Developing Leadership." The authoritarian character is unconcerned about developing leaders because real leaders are people high on the survival scale. But democratic leadership entails facilitation rather than command, and its skills can and should be learned by everyone as a means of empowerment. The Gray Panther leader's role was "to inspire the group" and "to point the way" (p. 42). A good leader, the *Manual* said, is interested, personal, encouraging, enthusiastic, sharing, supportive, praising, dependable, willing to assume responsibility, willing to work hard, able to grow, and has a sense of humor (pp. 42–47). The *Manual* failed to mention the qualities of toughness and exactness that were so important to Welch, just as Welch had put little stock in being encouraging, sharing, supportive, praising, or having a sense of humor. Different personalities require different styles of leadership and followership, and the differences between the democratic Gray Panthers and the autocratic John Birchers are stark.

In summary, the Gray Panther *Manual* exhibited all of the characteristics of the democratic character structure. They saw the world as a misguided but relatively unthreatening place. They were quite egalitarian and they constructed a flat organizational structure that maximized local autonomy. They identified with people who were made to feel powerless and they sought to combat paternalistic practices in society, whether they affected older people or others. Their leaders were taught to be supportive facilitators who empowered their members.

Conclusions

This analysis of the ideological statements of the John Birch Society and the Gray Panthers suggests four conclusions. The first is that the John Birch Society's *Blue Book* depicted a threatening world and stressed the need for ecstatic submission to a dynamic, personal leader within an autocratic hierarchy—a depiction congruent with the archetypal authoritarian character structure and incompatible with the democratic character structure. In one rhetorical stroke Robert Welch (a) recruited the ardent, dedicated followers he needed and wanted, (b) alienated potentially troublesome democratic character types who valued variety and discussion, and (c) consolidated his recruits into a band of loyalists who (d) became more, not less, reliant on him during times of ideological dissonance.

On the other hand, *The Gray Panther Manual* depicted a paternalistic world and stressed the need to empower individuals and groups who perceived themselves as passive and powerless—a depiction congruent with the archetypal democratic character structure and incompatible with the authoritarian character structure. Through this coincidence, the Panthers in one rhetorical stroke (a) recruited the diverse talented people they needed, (b) alienated potentially troublesome authoritarian character types, (c) consolidated a vast array of autonomous local protests into one national movement, that (d) became less, not more, dependent on particular national leaders who faced all of the risks and dangers of advancing age.

Second, the psychological gratifications Welch provided for authoritarian characters allowed him to present contradictory arguments: the protection of freedom through dictatorial leadership, the protection of capitalism through noncompetitive organization, and strength through submission. By creating a strong protector-protected relationship with protector-hungry followers, Welch reserved for himself the ability to resolve belief dilemmas. Indeed, belief dilemmas might well have led to ideological defections without a leader such as Robert Welch to resolve them.

On the other hand, the psychological gratifications Gray Panthers provided to democratic character types enabled them to avoid the passivity they disliked. By grounding their fight against ageism in the struggle of oppressed peoples against paternalism, they invited the support of democratic personalities of all ages. And by empowering their members with local autonomy, they maximized their members' freedom to use their personal skills in the ways that they found most meaningful and rewarding.

These two cases demonstrate that it is possible for social movements to provide psychological, as well as political or philosophical, reasons for membership. Each organization discouraged from membership those persons most likely to disrupt it, while providing gratifications for those most able to advance its work. The arguments worked for members so members would work for the organizations.

Third, this chapter has demonstrated that persuasive functions do not necessarily bear a linear relationship to social movement messages. It is possible for a movement to recruit, confront, and consolidate, all in one message. Not all members of the John Birch Society fit precisely the description of the authoritarian character structure, but its message spoke to the authoritarian tendencies in each of us. It created for its members an organization which was probably more authoritarian than most of its individual members because they were bound together by shared mistrust of the world and their need for protection against it. In contrast, the Gray Panthers created a movement that was probably more democratic in character than most of its members because it allowed its individual and collective affiliates to do as they pleased without the review or approval of either the national headquarters or other locals. They were able to combat ageism with an ideology that made membership attractive to democratic personality types of all ages.

Fourth, the persuasive discourse of the John Birch Society and the Gray Panthers provided psychological gratifications that were truthful and straightforward. Welch delivered what he promised: an authoritarian, anticommunist organization under his personal control. Never did he claim to offer anything else that might have broadened his appeal. Likewise, the Gray Panthers provided local autonomy and minimal oversight. Some social movement organizations are less straightforward.

Endnotes

[1] In addition to the chapter on functions see Bruce E. Gronbeck, "The Rhetoric of Social-Institutional Change: Black Action at Michigan," *Explorations in Rhetorical Criticism*, G. P. Mohrmann, C. J. Stewart, and D. J. Ochs, eds. (University Park: Pennsylvania State University Press, 1973): 96–123; Herbert W. Simons, "Requirements, Problems, and Strategies: A Theory of Persuasion for Social Movements," *Quarterly Journal of Speech* 56 (February 1970): 1–11; and Charles J. Stewart, "A Functional Approach to the Rhetoric of Social Movements," *Central States Speech Journal* 31 (Winter 1980): 298–305.

[2] For further information on authoritarianism and dogmatism, see T. W. Adorno, Else Frenkel Brunswik, Daniel J. Levinson, and R. Nevitt Sanford, *The Authoritarian Personality* (New York: Harper, 1950); Erich Fromm, *Escape from Freedom* (New York: Avon Library, 1965); and Milton Rokeach, *The Open- and Closed-Mind* (New York: Basic Books, 1960): 39–51.

[3] Abraham Maslow, "The Authoritarian Character Structure," *Journal of Social Psychology* 18 (1943): 401–411.

[4] Maslow, 402–403.

[5] Maslow, 408.

[6] Maslow, 406.

[7] Several sources (including *Who's Who*) have reported that Robert Welch served in important capacities with the National Association of Manufacturers during the 1950s. The N.A.M. disputes this contention, insisting that Mr. Welch was only one of some two hundred honorary officials and that he never held a position of responsibility in their organization. Personal correspondence with Dr. Jane Work, Department of Legislative Planning, National Association of Manufacturers, April 15, 1983.

[8] Stephen Earl Bennett, "Modes of Resolution of a 'Belief Dilemma' in the Ideology of the John Birch Society," *Journal of Politics* 33 (1971): 735–772.

[9] Circulation data are published in accordance with federal statutes in the December issues of these publications. Circulation is the best index of Society membership, since their rolls remain secret and their primary activities are educative. The dearth of published materials about the Society since 1971 reassures us that the data are not inflated by subscriptions from researchers.

[10] For background on the John Birch Society, see J. Allen Broyles, *The John Birch Society: Anatomy of a Protest* (Boston: Beacon Press, 1966); Gerald Schomp, *Birchism Was My Business* (New York: Macmillan, 1970); and two reports by the Anti-Defamation League of B'nai B'rith: Benjamin R. Epstein and Arnold Forster, *Report on the John Birch Society, 1966* (New York: Random House, 1966), and *The Radical Right: Report on the John Birch Society and Its Allies* (New York: Random House, 1967). Welch's account of Birch's life is presented in *The Life of John Birch* (Chicago: Henry Regnery, 1954). A more dispassionate and informative treatment is James Hefley and Marti Hefley, *The Secret File on John Birch* (Wheaton, IL: Tyndale House, 1980). By either account, Birch was a fundamentalist Baptist missionary in China who became involved in American intelligence operations during World War II. Despite his compatriots' efforts to restrain him, Birch seems to have displayed too much bravado in an encounter with a Chinese officer. Welch regards Birch as the first casualty in the final struggle against communism. A survey of 1965 members indicates that 62 percent joined for "ideological reasons (only 21 percent found such sat-

isfaction), 18 percent "to associate with like-minded people" (19 percent found it), 11 percent to become informed (16 percent found it), and 8 percent for political commitment (36 percent found this); see Fred W. Grupp, "Personal Satisfaction Derived from membership in the John Birch Society," *Western Political Quarterly* 24 (1971): 79–83; and "The Political Perspectives of Birch Society Members," *The American Right Wing*, Robert A. Schoenberger, ed. (Atlanta: Holt, Rinehart, and Winston, 1969): 83–118.

[11] *The Gray Panther Manual*, Harriet L. Perretz, Compiler (Philadelphia: The Gray Panthers, 1978), 3–4.

[12] Perretz, 22.

[13] Unless otherwise noted, all references to Welch or the John Birch Society's persuasion refer to Robert H. W. Welch, Jr., *The Blue Book of the John Birch Society* (Belmont, MA: Western Islands, 1961).

[14] Robert Welch, *The Politician* (Belmont, MA: Belmont Publishing, 1963): see esp. 279.

[15] Welch strongly supported the Goldwater candidacy as early as the 1958 organizational session (see 109). But Welch believed that the conspiracy had the political process rigged so as to prevent Goldwater's election. For his part, Goldwater was not a Welch supporter. After reading *The Politician*, Goldwater "urged him not to print it. I said I couldn't accept his theory that Ike was either a dunce and a dupe or a conscious sympathizer. Most of the John Birchers are patriotic, concerned, law-abiding, hardworking and productive. There are a few whom I call Robert Welchers, and these are the fanatics who regard everyone who doesn't totally agree with them as communist sympathizers." Barry Goldwater, *With No Apologies* (New York: William Morrow, 1979): 119.

[16] Ann Reilly Dowd, "What Managers Can Learn from Manager Reagan," *Fortune* 15 September 1986, 33–41. The same management philosophy was expressed during the first debate between Reagan and Mondale published in *The Weekly Compilation of Presidential Documents* 20 (October 7, 1984): 1446.

[17] Welch's utopia is a highly individualistic society epitomized by his slogan, "Less Government and More Responsibility" (p. 117). The problem with government, he says, is neither its form nor its quality, but its quantity: "the increasing quantity of government in all nations has constituted the greatest tragedy of the twentieth century" (p. 123). If the authoritarian conceives of life as taking place in a jungle, then government represents civilization, which distorts the natural order of survival.

[18] Unless otherwise indicated, all references to the ideology of the Gray Panthers or their manual refer to *The Gray Panther Manual*.

LEADERSHIP IN SOCIAL MOVEMENTS

As discussed in previous chapters, perceptions of social movements and their leaders are often molded by mass media reports and interpretations, few of which are favorable. Most often both movement and leader are portrayed as disruptive, radical, dangerous, or laughable. For example, nearly all stories on Malcolm X refer to his prison record. An ABC 20/20 report on Operation Rescue of the pro-life movement noted that its founder and leader, Randall Terry, was a former used car salesman. Media, particularly television, rarely report social movement activities unless they are action-oriented (marches, sit-ins, boycotts, strikes, and large gatherings) or violent (bombings, vandalism, arson, and shootings), and such reports have profound effects on how the public views social movements and their leaders.

The American public's view of leadership in social movements is also heavily influenced by its faith in *individualism*, in the *sanctity* and perfection of U.S. institutions, and the ability of both individuals and institutions to cope with *real* or *serious* problems. Roberta Ash writes "Only in America is the belief that individualism and collectivism are necessarily in conflict so widely held."[1] After decades of persuasive efforts to organize factory workers, farmers, farm workers, women, African Americans, Hispanic Americans, gays and lesbians, and Asian Americans, only small percentages of each ever became active members of organizations created to resolve their plights. John Wilson discovered that during the farm income decline of the 1950s, "Most farmers had come to feel that the American public was paying too little for its food or else the middle man was taking too large a slice of the cake, and hence believed there was something drastically wrong with the marketing system."[2] Despite this widespread belief, only 6 percent of farmers actually joined the National Farmers Organization (NFO).

Institutions are able to sustain themselves even in times of massive economic breakdowns and unsettling changes. During the Great Depression of the 1930s, voters chose Franklin Roosevelt and the Democratic party to return the nation to economic prosperity and stability rather than the Socialist or Communist parties. They turned to the established party out of power rather than to one connected to a social movement. Reform parties inevitably arise when there is growing concern about the political, social, economic, or moral state of the nation, but their electoral successes are usually minimal. Even former president Theodore Roosevelt could not get elected on the Bull Moose Party ticket. An occasional victory such as former pro wrestler Jesse Ventura's election as governor of Minnesota in 1999 is an anomaly.

Public opinion polls reveal a persistent confidence in U.S. institutions during periods of disturbing change, uncertainty, and alleged unhappiness with established orders. A Gallup poll conducted in the 1990s asked respondents how much confidence they had in several institutions to serve public needs, and the combined percentages of a great deal, quite a lot, and some were as follows:[3]

Military	90%	Supreme Court	78%
Churches	82%	Labor unions	67%
Newspapers	81%	Congress	67%
Public schools	79%	Big business	65%

When asked to look ahead to the year 2000, 82 percent said they were very or somewhat optimistic. Such levels of support for institutions and general optimism about the status quo reveal why it is difficult for social movement leaders to sell their uninstitutionalized collectives and goals for urgent change or resistance to Americans. However, the remainder percentages representing "little" or "no confidence" (ranging from 10 percent to 35 percent) show that the legitimacy of institutions is vulnerable to rhetorical assaults by social movements. Institutions, most notably political parties, cannot take public support for granted or ignore the challenges social movements pose.

Public Perceptions of Social Movement Leaders

People who claim an urgent problem is being ignored, hidden, or promoted by cherished institutions are likely to be branded as irrational agitators, malcontents, losers, misfits, degenerates, outcasts, extremists, social schemers, or rabble-rousers.[4] A new epithet became popular in the electronic age of the 1990s, social engineer. If these perverse, un-American "troublemakers" or "do-gooders" persist, organize, and generate mass protests, the public (often with the aid of the mass media and institutional agencies and agents) may attach new labels suitable for social destroyers: demagogues, communists, fascists, terrorists, anarchists, fanatics, or zealots.

Strange-looking and strange-acting movement members may reinforce such characterizations when they appear to be "foreign," under the spell of sinister forces such as demagogues, revolutionaries, the devil, or socialists or under the influence of drugs or alcohol. Examples include the hippies and yippies of the counterculture movement of the 1960s; the Moonies and Symbionese Liberation Army of the 1970s; the leathermen and drag queens of the gay rights movement; and zealous religious cult members of the 1980s and 1990s. Americans are likely, with minimal assistance from institutions, to see Dave Foreman's Earth First! and its self-styled eco-guerrillas as both outrageous and dangerous.[5]

Institutions such as government agencies and agents, schools and teachers, churches and clergy, labor unions and officers, corporations and executives, and social theorists reinforce the public's attitudes toward social movement leaders. Not many U.S. students learn about social movement leaders in their history and social studies classes. Martin Luther King, Jr., a rare exception, remains controversial in many locales. Eric Hoffer, the self-made social philosopher, claims in his book *The True Believer* that social movement leaders desire to divest themselves of an "unwanted self." "The revulsion from an unwanted self, and the impulse to forget it, mask it, slough it off, and lose it," Hoffer writes, "produce both a readiness to sacrifice the self and a willingness to dissolve it by losing one's individual distinctness in a compact collective whole."[6] Comments such as these led Herbert Simons to counter that "rhetoricians and other scholars have tended to assume that methods of influence appropriate for drawing room controversies are also effective for social conflicts, including struggles against established authorities."[7]

Simons also claims that scholars "have failed to suggest viable strategies for those engaged in rough-and-tumble conflicts, and some of them have dismissed militant protestors as pathological." A number of studies by Crane Brinton (the American, French, English, and Russian revolutions), Ming T. Lee (the Communist revolution in China), and Seymour Lipset (the socialist movement in Saskatchewan) provide substantial evidence that social movement leaders (and members) do not come from the marginal areas or "lunatic fringe" of society but from the higher strata of groups and subcultures: teachers, students, editors, farmers, civil servants, businessmen, clergy, and lawyers.[8] They are more affluent, better educated, and less anxious and disoriented than their nonactivist counterparts. Writing about the leaders of the French and American revolutions, Brinton notes that they "were not in general afflicted with anything the psychiatrist could be called about. They were certainly not riffraff, scoundrels, scum of the earth."[9] Myra Ferree concludes her study of U.S. social movement organizations with the comment, "Social movement participants are as rational as those who study them."[10]

"The six who dared" to found the Gray Panthers in 1970 certainly did not fit the stereotypes of bewhiskered, disillusioned, radical revolutionaries. Maggie Kuhn instigated the first meeting, not because she and others wanted to divest themselves of an unwanted self or to fulfill a need for psychological refurbishing, but because they all faced—upon turning 65 years of age—loss of their jobs, income, contacts with associates, and opportunities to continue social commitments and active participation in their communities.[11] Neither do leaders of the Christian right such as Jerry Falwell, Pat Robertson, and Ralph Reed fit common social movement leader stereotypes.

Institutions and the public often dismiss or stigmatize social movement leaders as "demagogues" who lie, oversimplify, exaggerate, and make false accusations; who purposely misuse facts, offer insufficient evidence, and employ logical fallacies; who resort to invective, name-calling, and ridicule; and who rely on emotional appeals. The demagogue will use any means to attain personal power and gain. As Steven Goldzwig points out, "the use of the term 'demagogue' generally denotes a rhetor who employs highly suspect means in the pursuit of equally suspect ends."[12] There is no evidence, however, that the typical social movement leader lies, cheats, misuses facts, and makes false accusations intentionally or to a greater degree than institutional leaders. Similarly, no evidence exists that leaders join the movement for personal gain and power, even though the FBI and other government agencies tried desperately to prove otherwise during the 1950s, 1960s, and 1970s.[13] Most leaders could attain greater powers and material wealth through institutional means than by operating through noninstitutional organizations. Social movement leaders are guilty of using emotional appeals, invective, oversimplification, exaggeration, and insufficient evidence, but so are political, religious, business, educational, charity, and legal leaders—not to mention advertisers and sales representatives. The negative label "demagogue" accurately describes few social movement leaders.

The mass media, institutional authorities, and the public too often assume that any person who appears to *act* in behalf of a social movement or cause or *looks like* a movement member (African American, Native American, Hispanic American, woman, student, elderly person, worker) is a movement *leader*. In his study of the Watts Riot that occurred in Los Angeles in 1965 (not unlike the riot of 1992 following the Rodney King verdict), Oberschall notes that those who assaulted police, threw rocks, set fire to buildings, and harangued crowds "were neither leaders prior to these incidents nor do they subsequently play a leader role in other incidents."[14] This distinction, however, escaped the media, resistance forces, and many civil rights movement sympathizers and legitimizers. Social movements are often blamed or stigmatized by the words and actions of persons who are at best bystanders or true misfits who see opportunities to act under the guise of the movement.

Anthony Oberschall and Herbert Simons recommend that students of social movements look at the rhetorical-social situation leaders face rather than at pathological traits or early childhood experiences. Simons observes that "unless it is understood that the leader is subjected to incompatible demands, a great many of his [her] rhetorical acts must seem counterproductive."[15] The typical leader of a typical social movement has no sanctioned position, no sanctioned authority to implement decisions, no regular salary, no orderly personal or family life, and no job security. At the same time, the leader often encounters threats, harassment, denial of access to the mass media, persecution, arrest, jail terms, exile, the necessity of going into hiding, or death. "Put any ordinary, stable individual into a similar position," Oberschall concludes, "and he [she], too, would probably exhibit what some observers consider confused or arbitrary behavior as a result of the pressures and dilemmas that one is continually faced with as a leader in an uninstitutionalized and emergent organizational setting."[16]

This chapter goes beyond the public and institutional views of social movement leadership and the simplistic typologies many social theorists have developed during the past half-century. It examines the *nature* of leadership in social movements and how it is *attained* and *maintained* as social movements evolve to adapt to an ever-changing environment.

The Nature of Leadership in Social Movements

Theorists generally agree with John Wilson that "the typical pattern of domination in the typical social movement is subsumed under neither the concept of power nor that of authority."[17] Leadership in social movements, Wilson notes, tends to be more structured than a naked power relationship and less structured than an authority relationship associated with an organizational position. Simons claims the leader, at best, "controls an organized core of the movement (frequently mistaken for the movement itself) but exerts relatively little influence over a relatively larger number of sympathizers on its periphery,"[18] somewhat like the onion ring of membership described by Wilson in chapter 3. Essentially, the leader gains the right (the legitimacy) to exercise specific skills within a specific social movement organization or coalition through leadership traits, insights into a problem and means of action, bravery, and communication skills. These skills are often learned through costly trial and error as the social movement evolves.

Leaders as Organizers

Leaders must have organizational skills, particularly the ability to attract individuals to the notion of collective action and to draw people together into meaningful relationships and organizations. For example, Maggie Kuhn, the instigator behind the "six who dared" to form the Gray Panthers, was instrumental in attracting people from all ages and many fields of endeavor to join in a movement that would primarily benefit elderly Americans. She and her colleagues began with contacts among friends and former associates, attracted many young people who were also fighting for basic rights and recognition, and then organized all ages to form effective coalitions. Maggie Kuhn became known as the leader of the gray power movement after emerging from the bottom up through personal contacts and networking. According to the *Gray Panther Manual* "The group was built on the network principle, involving individuals and groups: a network of human relationships each of them has stockpiled."[19]

Saul Alinsky, a lifelong social activist and creator of a training institute for would-be activists, identified a number of essential attributes for successful organizers in his book *Rules for Radicals: A Pragmatic Primer for Realistic Radicals.*[20] For example, he claimed that an organizer must have *curiosity* that becomes contagious. Maggie Kuhn of the Gray Panthers, Frank Kameny of the gay rights movement, and Betty Freidan of the women's liberation movement questioned traditional norms, values, and ways of doing things. They asked Why? and Why not? questions that agitated both victims and victimizers.

An organizer must be *irreverent.* Malcolm X of the Black Muslims, Stokely Carmichael of SNCC, and Eldridge Cleaver of the Black Panthers detested accepted dogma, defied finite definitions of morality, and challenged and insulted both established institutions and established social movement organizations and tactics in their efforts to gain freedom, equality, and justice for black Americans. The counterculture and student movements of the 1960s and 1970s seemed to take delight in rejecting all that older generations held sacred. Women became sick and tired of "staying in their place" as wives and mothers. The Christian Right rejected all aspects of what they considered to be liberal dogma forced on God-fearing, Christian Americans since the time of President Franklin Roosevelt.

An organizer must have *imagination* to create new ideas, tactics, and organizational structures adapted to an ever-changing environment. Martin Luther King, Jr. decided that action, such as the historic Montgomery bus boycott and marches, needed to replace the slow, behind-the-scenes court actions the NAACP had pursued for decades. Black student leaders in North Carolina were the first to stage sit-ins at lunch counters. The imagination of each leader or group of leaders changed the movement forever. Maggie Kuhn's group began as the Consultation of Older and Younger Adults, a rather unimaginative title. It took the name Gray Panthers and a unique panther logo at the suggestion of a television talk show producer following a very lively and controversial appearance by Kuhn and a group of young people. They adopted it as a "fun name" and more expressive of the group's "quick minds, ready humor, radical and action orientation that characterized the members."[21] Ralph Reed of the Christian Coalition understood early on the potential power of the Internet and databases to disseminate information, raise funds, and pressure institutional leaders.

An organizer must have a *sense of humor* to relieve tensions within the movement, to allay fears members may have over imminent nonviolent actions, and to make fun of the opposition through satire and ridicule. For instance, organizers of pro-life's Operation Rescue campaigns joked at training sessions about which religious groups were better at kneeling and crawling when confronting police lines at abortion clinics and laughed at the oddity of their nonviolent tactics. During its first campaign against abortion clinics in Atlanta, its leader Randall Terry answered his cellular phone, "Maxwell Smart," an allusion to the classic television comedy "Get Smart."[22] Stokely Carmichael's young college audiences cheered, shouted, and laughed when, for instance, he would imitate "the sound of horses' hoofs, straddling an imaginary steed, bouncing up and down in a simulated gallop" to recreate the scene of historic conflicts between red men and white men."[23]

An organizer must have an *organized personality* to maintain order and structure within the movement organization and to deal with the uncertainties and disorder movements inevitably encounter when confronting institutions. When all else seems irrational, the effective organizer must remain rational and in control. Alinsky writes that "The organizer recognizes that each person or bloc has a hierarchy of values" and is able to work out coalitions in which all blocs or organizations gain something and maintain critical beliefs, attitudes, and values.[24] One of Martin Luther King, Jr.'s most important leadership traits was his ability to bring disparate civil rights organizations together for specific campaigns.[25]

An organizer must also have a *strong ego* but not egotism. Leaders must have a healthy belief in themselves and their abilities to achieve goals if they are to instill confidence and belief in others. At the same time, they must have a realistic notion of the odds against them to be able to accept minimal gains or failures, to make the best of each, and to know when it is time to draw back or retire from the field of battle. The Reverend Jerry Falwell sensed it was time to disband the Moral Majority in 1986 and return to his pulpit, leaving the political fight to others in the Christian right. In many movements, such as those attempting to protect the unborn, animal rights, and the environment, moderate elements and leaders seem more capable than radical elements of deciding when it is time to back off and when a tactic may be getting out of hand.

Leaders as Decision Makers

The social movement leader is also a *decision maker* but rarely has the powers of reward and punishment or the claim to legitimacy of an established authority. Joseph Gusfield notes that although the leader is the head of a decision-making hierarchy within a social movement organization, the leader operates within an environment of clients, enemies, adherents, and potential recruits in which he or she has no authority but merely represents the movement.[26] This environment is fraught with repressive uncertainty, complex conditions, conflicting demands, pressures from inside and outside the movement, power struggles among movement elements and organizations, disagreements over philosophies and strategies, financial crises, and competition among aspiring leaders.

Herbert Simons summarizes perceptively the plight of most social movement leaders:

> Shorn of the controls that characterize formal organizations, yet required to perform the same internal functions, harassed from without, yet obligated to adapt to the external system, the leader of a social movement must constantly balance inherently conflicting demands on his [her] position and on the movement he [she] represents.[27]

A reading of the annual *Proceedings of the General Assembly of the Knights of Labor* supports Simons' observations. Leaders of the Knights spent most of their time fending off charges from members, attacking "traitors" who had left the organization but were continuing efforts to undermine it or to start competing organizations, answering negative reports in the media, denying associations with anarchists and socialists, explaining strains or ruptures in relationships with other labor movement organizations, reporting on conflicts with institutions such as the Catholic Church, explaining failed actions such as strikes or boycotts, and attacking or negotiating with employers.[28]

The many difficulties social movement leaders encounter and the severe limitations placed upon them are exemplified in the civil rights movement. Our most common images of Martin Luther King, Jr. come from memories and pictures shown on the national holiday honoring him on the third Monday of January. We see him delivering his famous "I Have a Dream" speech on the steps of the Lincoln Memorial, walking arm-in-arm with other civil rights leaders through southern towns, and meeting with the press. These are, however, mere highlights of a social movement leader in action. Most of King's time was spent trying to keep or to make peace among fellow clergymen with giant-sized egos or among competing civil rights organizations such as the NAACP, CORE, SNCC, and his own SCLC. He preferred to be on the front lines of the movement, particularly during major campaigns such as Selma, Montgomery, and Birmingham, but frequently he was in New York or Washington trying to raise the funds necessary to keep campaigns alive. Bail for hundreds of protestors arrested during demonstrations and fines levied for breaking local and state ordinances represented a mere fraction of the expenses incurred in the operations of an enormous organization and movement. Only Martin Luther King, Jr. could perform these essential fund-raising activities effectively, but friends of the movement often grumbled about his absence at critical moments in the streets of the South. Enemies accused him of cowardice, of running away when things got rough, of accepting bail while others remained in jail. Friends and enemies alike resented the fame and adulation King achieved nationally and internationally.

Leaders as Symbols

Although social movement leaders typically do not have the powers and legitimacy of institutional authorities, they are able to lead because their skills enable them to function as the symbols of their movements. Leaders tend to become totally identified with the cause, and the cause may become totally identified with them. There would not be a United Farm Workers movement without the persistence and organizing skills of Cesar Chavez, a man's liberation movement without the poetry and writings of Robert Bly, or a Native-American movement without Russell Means who was willing to demonstrate, picket, shout, lobby, go to jail, and sacrifice his life if necessary. Successful leaders inspire absolute devotion, love, trust, and dependence in members.

Eugene V. Debs serves as an illustration from the early labor movement. In April 1894, he led his American Railway Union in a victorious strike against the powerful James J. Hill and his Great Northern Railroad, a remarkable victory for a union that was barely two years old. As Debs left by train from St. Paul, Minnesota to return to his home in Terre Haute, Indiana, railroad workers lined both sides of the tracks with their hats in their hands in homage to their leader.[29] Some social movements actually take on their leaders' names: Martin Luther (the Lutheran Church), John Wesley (the Wesleyan movement among British and American protestants), Francis Townsend (the Townsend movement of the 1930s for old age pensions), and Karl Marx (the Marxist-communist movement that began in Europe and spread around the world), to name a few.

The leader is the "face" of the social movement for members, the public, and the mass media. "It is with leadership that the public identifies in describing and judging a movement," Joseph Gusfield writes, "the leader personifies the movement in cartoon, picture, story, and legend. For much of the public, the leader becomes synonymous with the movement and its adherents."[30] For instance, more than one generation of Americans viewed the labor movement among coal miners as synonymous with John L. Lewis. The fiery, bushy eyebrowed founder and leader of the United Mine Workers was seen frequently during newsreels in theaters, on front pages of newspapers and magazines, and in numerous cartoons on editorial pages.

As we become an increasingly visual society through television, the Internet, videotapes, laser discs, and pictorials, visual depictions of leaders and their activities are likely to dominate our visions of social movements. Pat Robertson's "Family Channel" on cable television with his "700 Club" provides a continual visual link to the religious right movement. The militias use Web pages on the Internet to communicate with members and sympathizers. Appearances on talk shows are becoming a means for social movement leaders to reach mass audiences.

Herbert Simons concludes his treatment of social movement leadership with the comment that "The primary rhetorical test of the leader and, indirectly, of the strategies he [she] employs is his [her] capacity to fulfill the requirements of his [her] movement by resolving or reducing rhetorical problems."[31] In a very real sense, then, the leader is a rhetorical leader of a social movement who enables individuals to see themselves as a people, establish lasting relational patterns, and adapt strategies to an evolving social movement.

How Leadership Is Attained in Social Movements

A leadership position is attained in a social movement when members perceive a person to possess two or more of three attributes: charisma, prophecy, and pragmatism.[32]

Charisma

The charismatic leader's source of legitimacy lies in his or her apparent access to a higher source or divine inspiration. An "awe-inspiring" personality, William Cameron writes, leads social movement members to see "truth" in the charismatic leader's utterances.[33] The charismatic leader tends to be a showperson with a sense of timing and the rhetorical skills necessary to articulate what "others can as yet only feel, strive towards, and imagine but cannot put into words or translate explicitly into action."[34] For instance, Jose Angel Gutierrez of the Hispanic movement "argued that Chicanos had a history of dissent, were not inferior due to their color, had not lost their heritage, and possessed a significant history."[35] Chicanos were a people with a proud heritage. On the other hand, he applied negative terms to the Anglo, the devil to Chicanos, including bigoted, racist, exploiter, barbarian, and white supremist; while instilling self-respect, dignity, and unity among fellow Chicanos. Such rhetoric leads J. Michael Hogan and Glen Williams to approach "charisma not as a product of personality traits nor of sociological conditions, but rather as a *textual* creation—a phenomenon manifested in *rhetorical* artifacts."[36]

The person with charisma leads followers in direct actions that stir things up. Leaders supply vigor to social movements and make people believe in the impossible.[37] Examples include Randall Terry (leader of Operation Rescue for the pro-life movement in the 1980s and 1990s), Phyllis Schlafly (president of the Eagle Forum that resisted the women's liberation movement, the alleged secular humanist movement, and the decline of morals during the 1970s, 1980s, and 1990s), Martin Luther King, Jr. (leader of the civil rights movement of the 1950s and 1960s), Samuel Gompers (a founder and leader of the American Federation of Labor from 1886–1924), Susan B. Anthony (a leader of the woman's rights and suffrage movements from 1848 to 1906), and Frederick Douglass (an escaped slave who became an internationally known leader of the antislavery movement). Susan B. Anthony coined the slogan "failure is impossible" for the woman's rights movement.

The charismatic leader feels a duty, not merely an obligation or opportunity, to lead the movement and may exhibit exceptional heroism, bravery, and endurance to the point of martyrdom for the cause. The civil rights movement included famous martyrs (Medgar Evers, Martin Luther King, Jr., Malcolm X) and little-known martyrs, both black and white (James Chaney, Michael Schwerner, and Andrew Goodman murdered in Mississippi, and a Detroit homemaker named Viola Liuzzo who was shot and killed while ferrying Selma-to-Montgomery marchers in Alabama). The intense, unwavering support of followers (even when the charismatic leader blunders in selecting targets, strategies, and times to act) maintains unity within the movement and prevents a shifting of the power structure so common within minimally organized social movement organizations.

Perhaps there is no better example of a charismatic leader than Mahatma Gandhi who, for over thirty years, led India's fight for independence from Great Britain.[38] His philosophy and program called satyagraha (literally "truth-force") embodied a method of persuasion that used moral means to achieve moral ends. Gandhi understood the need for showmanship when leading a mass movement and refined actions that gained international attention, identified himself with the Indian people, and required few resources. He dressed in simple sandals and a loincloth that represented the daily attire of male laborers in India. As a protest against British textile laws, Gandhi learned to weave his own simple clothing and made the spinning wheel a major symbol of independence from British rule and influence. He underwent fifteen fasts, his "fiery weapon," to protest low wages and poor working conditions, to restore peace after riots had erupted during a visit by British royalty, to end violence (particularly among Hindus and Muslims), to protest his own imprisonment, and to pressure several British Prime Ministers into altering actions and decisions.

Gandhi spent nearly a third of his life as a social movement leader conducting walking propaganda tours that often covered hundreds of miles and lasted for months. Each walk took him among the people most sympathetic with the movement and gained attention and followers. As "sacred pilgrimages," these walks identified Gandhi and the movement with the religious traditions of India. He literally became a "holy man" for millions of Indians. Allen Merriam writes "The primacy of symbolic behavior in extending Gandhi's influence corresponded to the traditional pattern of Indian gurus, who are identified more by their lifestyle than by their pronouncements."[39] Gandhi understood the need to create strategies adapted to the environment that would bring about evolutionary results for the movement.

Prophecy

The prophet's source of legitimacy lies in his or her apparent proximity to the writings of the social movement, its ideology. The person may have written all or important segments of the movement's doctrine, may be considered the most knowledgeable authority on the doctrine, or may be seen as nearest in spirit to the doctrine. As a spokesperson for the movement's god—capitalism, socialism, freedom, equality, fundamental religious truths, the American way of life—the leader with the gift of prophecy elaborates, justifies, and explains the movement's values, myths, and beliefs.

The prophet knows the "truth" and sets a moral tone for the social movement. The Reverend Jerry Falwell was such a leader of the Moral Majority as he crusaded against liberals, secular humanism, and those who would compromise the great truths of the Bible and the Constitution and threaten our national security. The prophet alone has the ability to perceive the true nature of the urgent problem, its causes, and its solution. Because the prophet is a person of vision, has a psychological commitment to principles, and perceives the writings of the movement to be sacred, he or she is unlikely to be a reconciler between movement factions or between movement and institutions.[40] The truth cannot be compromised. When Dr. Robert Parker, pastor of the Kosmosdale Baptist Church in Louisville accepted the position of State Chairman of the Moral Majority in Kentucky, he and other leaders had no desire

> To mix "politics and the pulpit", but sensed that many of our national and state problems are due to our moral default and failure to unite under God's standards. They have accepted their burden of awakening the republic to our national sin, and have joined together to call this nation to a real moral referendum, turning America around toward the path of morality.[41]

The prophet judges the legitimacy of decisions by reference to ideology—to truth, not by ends achieved.

When Robert Welch called eleven men together for a two-day meeting in Indianapolis on December 8 and 9, 1958 to found the John Birch Society, he launched his effort to become the undisputed prophet for the anticommunist resistance movement in the United States. Welch opened his two-day speech to these eleven like-minded businessmen by establishing his qualifications to lead the movement:

> I personally have been studying the problem increasingly for about nine years, and practically full-time for the past three years. And entirely without pride, but in simple thankfulness, let me point out that a lifetime of business experience should have made it easier for me to see the falsity of the economic theories upon which Communism is supposedly based, more readily, than might some scholar coming into that study from the academic cloisters; while a lifetime of

interest in things academic, especially world history, should have given me an advantage over many businessmen, in more readily seeing the sophistries in dialectical materialism.[42]

Welch's two-day speech became *The Blue Book of the John Birch Society*, the organization's bible, and the new anticommunist crusading force was to be named after the first American martyr in the struggle, John Birch, an American army officer apparently killed by communist troops in China shortly before communist forces took over. Sunday supplements in major conservative newspapers such as *The Chicago Tribune* and *The Arizona Republic* introduced the John Birch Society to millions of Americans in the fall of 1964. An item entitled "He Has Stirred the Slumbering Spirit" presented Robert Welch as a person of vision, wisdom, and commitment in the struggle against the communist menace, a person whose words were gaining scores of converts:

> Mr. Welch's writings have created widespread comment—some critical. Few were ready to believe him when he warned of the impending Communist takeovers by Castro in Cuba, Ben Bella in Algeria, and Sukarno in Indonesia. But with events proving him correct again and again, his writings are now closely scrutinized by all serious students of anti-Communism.[43]

Welch created a monthly periodical for the movement entitled *American Opinion* and remained its editor and frequent contributor until his death in 1985. In an open letter to readers in the October 1978 issue, Welch wrote of the periodical's reason for being:

> You were to read *American Opinion* in order to learn the truth; the plain unmistakable truth about what was really happening. We set out twenty-two [sic] years ago to make this monthly compendium the most accurate, most penetrating, and most widely accepted authority in the world on the nature and the menace of the revolutionary cabal that was steadily undermining our whole civilization.[44]

Welch was never a reconciler in the struggle between good and evil that was a matter of life and death for the American way of life. As a prophet for the anticommunist movement, he structured the Society to build a "rededication to God, to family, to country, and to strong moral principles."[45]

Pragmatism

The pragmatist's source of legitimacy lies in his or her apparent organizational expertise, efficiency, and tact. As a person who believes that the social movement must have a secure and stable foundation for growth, the pragmatic leader brings common sense and a healthy skepticism to the movement, seeks to reconcile diverse interests, desires communication rather than excommunication, and replaces unattainable goals with diffuse goals and a broader range of targets. The pragmatist believes that ideals and principles are useless without organization and implementation.

The pragmatic leader seeks to make the social movement inclusive rather than exclusive by making it more acceptable to outsiders (including important legitimizers from the established order) and devotes energies to fund raising, recruitment, and organization. The pragmatist typically takes an inclusive stance regarding the people that movement members perceive themselves to be and on their relational patterns. This leader is more likely to compromise the sacredness of the movement's writings than the integrity of the organization and may come to see maintenance of the organization as an end in itself—without the organization, there can be no movement. Leaders such as Maggie Kuhn, Martin Luther King, Jr., Ralph Reed, Russell Means, and Robert Welch see clearly that successful short-term campaigns and long-term social movements require organization, planning, training, discipline, funds, and guidance.

Samuel Gompers who led, with the exception of one year, the American Federation of Labor from its founding in 1886 to his death in 1924, was primarily a pragmatist. He was keenly aware of the labor movement's history, of labor organizations that had blossomed and wilted, of U.S. opposition to labor radicals, and of the needs and desires of workers, specifically among the skilled trades. Above all, he understood the need for a strong organization with a central focus (trade unionism) and a sound financial base.[46] Although Gompers was sympathetic with all elements of the labor movement, he refused, for example, to aid the Knights of Labor when it became embroiled in the aftermath of the Haymarket Riot in Chicago and the trial of the accused anarchists. The so-called Haymarket Riot occurred on May 4, 1886 during a labor protest rally. The purpose of the rally was to protest the deaths of two workers the previous day by police in a confrontation between locked-out union members and the workers who replaced them at the McCormick factory. That confrontation "was one of many outbreaks of violence at the time due to labor and class tensions. Central among labor's demands was the eight-hour workday."[47] Seven police officers dispersing the crowd in Haymarket Square died from wounds suffered when a bomb was thrown and in the subsequent hail of bullets; sixty-eight civilians were wounded. Eight members of the anarchist movement were convicted, and four were hanged. The AFL was too young, could not afford to become identified with the Knights of Labor or the anarchists, and was, after all, in direct competition with the industrial unionism (open to all workers regardless of skill) the Knights championed. Gompers saw the trade union as "the historic and natural form of working class organization," one based on scientific principles, and shed no tears when the Knights of Labor declined rapidly after the Haymarket affair.[48] Speaking to the Machinists' Convention in 1901, he remarked:

> Those of us who have gone through the movement of the Knights of
> Labor, which is now happily removed from the path of progress;

those who have studied the previous effervescent movements of that character, know the danger with which such movements are always confronted.[49]

Gompers understood the U.S. value system and the inherent conservatism of most workers and industrialists. He struggled to make the AFL the accepted umbrella organization for all trade unions. While he tried to avoid unnecessary confrontations within the movement, Gompers was not reluctant to attack elements that posed dangers to his beloved organization. At the AFL convention in 1903, Gompers attacked socialist members head-on:

And I want to say that I am entirely at variance with your philosophy. I declare it to you. I am not only at variance with your doctrines, but with your philosophy. Economically, you are unsound; socially, you are wrong; industrially, you are an impossibility.[50]

Gompers succeeded in building and maintaining a social movement organization that withstood the onslaught of industrialists, competing labor organizations, economic depressions, and world wars to become an institutionalized force in U.S. society.

How Leadership Is Maintained in Social Movements

Social movement leaders maintain their positions as long as they hold the confidence of followers, seem to have solutions to problems, meet the exigencies of new and unexpected situations, and perform rhetorical functions necessary for the stage the movement is in at the moment. William Cameron writes that all leaders "do something exceedingly well" and "when they stop doing it well, they often cease to lead."[51]

A Mix of Leadership Attributes

Theorists agree that every successful social movement leader must display two or more of the three essential leadership attributes—charisma, prophecy, and pragmatism, though not necessarily in the same context. Joseph Gusfield, for example, argues that leadership can be conceived as a set of simultaneous roles. As mobilizer, the leader must "breathe the fire and brimstone of enthusiastic mission," and as articulator, the leader "pours the oil of bargaining, compromise, and common culture."[52] John Wilson claims that leaders gain the esteem of fellow movement members because of the peculiar mix of their rhetorical abilities.[53] Anthony Oberschall concludes, "Leaders, in sum, are the architects of organization, ideology, and mobilization for the movement."[54]

While single-dimensional institutional leaders can function and survive because they have a multitude of institutional resources at their disposal, social movement leaders rarely have such resources. Unfortunately for social movements, a great many of their leaders tend to be one-dimensional. Randall Terry is effective in organizing and leading Operation Rescue blockades of abortion clinics throughout the United States, partly because he organizes such limited actions well and partly because of his personal bravery and commitment. He has been arrested dozens of times but returns to the action as soon as he is released. It is doubtful, however, that he could lead a large national organization, be content with behind-the-scenes organizing and fund raising, or sit down with other social movement organizations or institutions to reach compromises.

Few spokespersons for black rights during the 1960s were more charismatic, particularly among young black Americans who were becoming disillusioned with the civil rights movement, than Stokely Carmichael, Chairman of SNCC (the Student Nonviolent Coordinating Committee). He was attractive, intelligent, articulate, and understood the importance of timing and showmanship. During the famous Meredith March in Mississippi in June 1966, Carmichael cooperated with the leaders of the NAACP and SCLC until the march reached Greenwood, SNCC territory, and Martin Luther King, Jr. left for meetings in Chicago. The sheriff arrested Carmichael and others briefly on June 16 for pitching tents in a school yard. Carmichael used the occasion to escalate his confrontational rhetoric at an evening rally, declaring: "This is the 27th time I've been arrested, I ain't gonna be arrested no more. . . . Every courthouse in Mississippi should be burnt down tomorrow so we can get rid of the dirt."[55] The next evening Stokely Carmichael delivered more of the same confrontational message and then, on cue, Willie Ricks shouted, "What do you want?" Carmichael responded, "Black power!" and the crowd was soon enthusiastically echoing this new battle cry. He had seized the moment beautifully, and, during the next several months, traveled throughout the country both explaining and extolling "Black Power." Charles Stewart writes:

> The civil rights movement would never be the same in tone, demands, tactics, and relationships. A new generation of activists, goaded by frustration with the lack of progress for black Americans in the rural south and the urban north and the perceived failure of established movement organizations and leaders to bring about real and lasting changes, was taking center stage and challenging the heart and soul of the movement.[56]

While Carmichael became a hero among the growing number of young black nationalists within the movement, his much misunderstood and maligned theme of black power and confrontational rhetorical style shattered the fragile coalition of black rights organizations and polarized white liberal legitimizers and blacks.[57] He lacked the attributes both of the prophet, in failing to develop a clear doctrine of black power meaningful to all elements of the movement, and of the pragmatist, by attacking other leaders in his speeches to black audiences. For instance, in Detroit on July 30, 1966, Carmichael remarked:

> I'm very concerned, because you see we have a lot of Negro leaders, and I want to make it clear I'm no leader. I represent the Student Nonviolent Coordinating Committee. That's the sole source of my power, and that's Black Power. I'm no Negro leader, but I think we have to speak out about the war in Vietnam.[58]

By 1968 Carmichael had left SNCC, reestablished his relationship with Martin Luther King, Jr., and formed a new organization called the Black United Front, an organization that experienced a brief lifespan. He remained an eloquent spokesperson for black power, pride, and independence, but he failed as a leader. William Cameron undoubtedly had one-dimensional movement leaders such as Randall Terry and Stokely Carmichael in mind when he wrote, "many a stirring evangelist makes a poor pastor."[59]

Handling Diverse, Conflicting Roles

Few social movement leaders, even multi-dimensional ones, are capable of handling the diverse and often conflicting roles thrust upon them and the rhetorical dilemmas social movements encounter daily. The leader (1) must adapt to different audiences at once but not appear to be a political chameleon, (2) produce short-run victories but not preclude meaningful evolutionary results, (3) use militant tactics to gain visibility for the movement but use moderate tactics to gain entry into decision-making centers, (4) foster strong convictions in the movement's principles but control the implication that their attainment justifies any necessary means, (5) strive for organizational efficiency without dampening the enthusiasm and spontaneity generated during the early, less-structured days of the movement, (6) understand that militants are effective with power-vulnerables such as elected and appointed officials and moderates are more effective with power-invulnerables such as judges, business owners, and much of the "silent majority," (7) vilify established orders but be willing and able to work with them when it is to the movement's advantage, and (8) grasp at opportunities to deal with an institution on its own turf without appearing to be selling out or going soft.[60] The difficulty of meeting and adapting to role demands that require different rhetorical skills and tactics typically results in a proliferation of leaders that cause conflict within and among movement organizations and results in fragmentation of structure and persuasive efforts.

The civil rights movement of the 1950s and 1960s produced a variety of leaders who performed specific roles skillfully but could not meet all rhetorical demands of the movement. Roy Wilkins of the NAACP, for instance, believed in working through the system (particularly through the courts) to bring about change, and he feared both the tactics and the results of direct actions such as sit-ins, marches, and demonstrations. Andrew Young was highly successful as a conciliator and diplomat within SCLC, particularly among its younger members and elements. However, his soft-spoken style and devotion to Martin Luther King, Jr. prevented him from speaking out on his views and becoming visible beyond the SCLC. Ralph Abernathy was highly visible but usually silent during the movement (seemingly always at King's side in marches, jails, meetings, and press conferences). His loyalty, dedication, and bravery were not sufficient to prepare him to take over the leadership of the SCLC in 1968 following King's assassination. Fred Shuttlesworth founded the Alabama Christian Movement for Human Rights in 1956 and later allied this group with the SCLC. He was highly respected within the movement and feared by the southern establishment for his reckless courage and ability to organize and lead demonstrations, but his efforts to become a major leader were plagued by autocratic, egocentric, and tactless personality traits.

Changing as the Movement Changes

Perhaps the greatest obstacle for leadership tenure in social movements is the necessity for movements to change. As movements evolve, leaders and followers must evolve. Wars, economic depressions, the resignation or replacement of institutional leaders, inventions, and political, religious, and social trends may greatly affect the nature and progress of social movements. For example, if the abortion pill RU-486 attains widespread use in the United States and recent advances in surgical procedures prove effective, women could prevent or terminate pregnancies without going to abortion clinics or finding physicians to perform abortions or they could have an abortion within weeks instead of months following conception, long before an identifiable human being is present. Both of these possibilities are currently primary targets of pro-life pressures and demonstrations. RU-486 would deprive the movement of data, stories, and pictures showing the extent and barbarism of abortions. New surgical techniques would preclude the powerful, emotional argument against late-term abortions, what the movement labels partial-birth abortions. Joseph Gusfield writes that, "The disjuncture between ideology and the adaptive problems of the movement constantly raises the issue of too much or too little accommodation; of renunciation of the mission or overrighteous inflexibility."[61]

Jerry Rubin was an archetypal leader of the student, anti–Vietnam War, and counterculture movements of the 1960s and 1970s. He was intelligent, articulate, imaginative, brave and, above all, outrageous in manner, actions, and dress. He effectively organized civil disobedience at Berkeley, demonstrations against trains carrying troops to fight in Vietnam, the October 1967 march on the Pentagon, and of the Yippies that created chaos at the Chicago convention of the Democratic party in 1968. He was brilliant at manipulating the media and creating put-ons (such as threatening to levitate the Pentagon) that led to both humorous and violent reactions from the establishment, especially police agencies who confronted the Yippies in the trenches. He helped to polarize society along age lines with the slogan, "Don't trust anyone over thirty." As one of the famous Chicago Seven, he stood trial for five-and-a-half months charged with conspiracy for actions during the Democratic convention.

By the early 1970s, however, Jerry Rubin knew "the movement," as he and others called it, was rapidly dwindling in numbers and fervor, society was changing, old methods would no longer be effective, and ironically most leaders (including himself) were nearing or had passed their thirtieth birthdays. Many members of the movement, particularly younger ones, resisted change and both loved and hated Rubin as a symbol of the '60s. They longed for another 1968-style confrontation during the 1972 Republican and Democratic conventions and called Rubin a "sellout" because he stayed in a hotel instead of a park like the old days. On July 14, Rubin's 34th birthday, a group calling themselves Zippies ("put zip back into yip") marched on his hotel in Miami armed with a cake to throw in his face to celebrate his retirement from the movement. Later in the year, a band of Zippies "trashed" Rubin's car in New York to demonstrate their independence from older Yippies. Rubin came to realize that "changes cannot be made on the political level alone, or that society we are changing will be repeated. We must examine our own process."[62] These were not words the movement and its younger members wanted to hear. A number of leaders of the antiwar and counterculture movements committed suicide because they either could not accept or could not adapt to the new social realities.

Adapting to Events

Events may thrust the social movement and its leaders in new directions, and leaders may appear to be mere puppets controlled by events or the whims of some members.[63] For example, Jane Addams, characterized as the "Grand Lady of Social Reforms" for her leadership in the woman's suffrage movement and for causes such as child labor, prison reform, and world peace, became increasingly concerned about the war in Europe in 1915 and the likelihood that the United States would become involved. On July 9 of that year, Addams delivered a speech in Carnegie Hall in which she questioned the morality of war, the desire of soldiers to fight in the war, military censorship of news about the war, the controlling forces that were encouraging the war, and nationalism that fueled the passions of nations and made war possible.[64] Her speech not only incurred the wrath of those supporting the military and the war in Europe but it greatly reduced her credibility with the American public and split the suffrage movement between pacifists and supporters of military preparedness.

Leaders must appear to be in the forefront of necessary change and wise adaptation, while not appearing to abandon major norms, beliefs, attitudes, and values of their movements in order to meet situational exigencies. Terence Powderly became General Master Workman (president) of the Order of the Knights of Labor in 1880 and helped make it the largest and most powerful labor union in the history of the United States, reaching over 700,000 members in 1886.[65] But 1886 was to be a fateful year for the Knights. Strikes by the eight-hour movement and newly enrolled members of the Order proved disastrous, and both Powderly and the Order were blamed although they authorized no strikes or involvement of Knights in them. Although the Knights and the Anarchists were bitter enemies in the struggle for labor and the Order had played no role in the Haymarket Square rally, the government, newspapers, clergy, and the public identified the Knights of Labor with the anarchists and blamed it for the bloody bombing that made Haymarket Square famous. Membership and influence plummeted year after year in spite of Powderly's charisma, persuasive skills, and considerable organizational abilities. In 1893 with the country in the midst of a terrible depression, Powderly decided that only the most drastic of actions could save the Knights and perhaps all of organized labor, so he approached Samuel Gompers with the notion of merging with the AFL, its major competitor. Other Knights were incensed at his willingness, regardless of his honorable intentions, to compromise the Order's "fundamental and vital" principle of industrial unionism open to the "laboring masses" by merging with a "mere trade union" limited to a few skilled workers and headed by archenemy Samuel Gompers. Powderly and his lieutenants were "retired from office," and new General Master Workman, James R. Sovereign, declared to the assembled Knights at the 1894 convention that "any action by members of this Order inimical to or in contravention to this principle [industrial unionism] and this policy is *treason* to the Order and the best interests of labor."[66] Powderly was expelled from the Order as a traitor and never forgiven for his "treachery."

Leading by Not Getting Too Far Ahead or Behind

Bruce Cameron writes: "The leader must seem to lead. In order to lead, he must be a little ahead of his followers, a little wiser, a little more informed. But if he gets too far ahead, contact is broken, and he may be a 'leader' without followers."[67] In a study of Malcolm X's autobiography, Thomas Benson focuses on the final year of Malcolm X's life in which he broke with Elijah Muhammad (founder of the Black Muslims). Following a trip to Africa and Mecca during which he had seen blond-haired, blue-eyed Muslims, Malcolm X realized he could call whites brothers. He shifted positions on integration and participation in civil rights demonstrations, no longer saw Uncle Toms and whites as devils, and exacerbated his break with Elijah Muhammed.[68] Many of Malcolm X's supporters and enemies viewed these changes as signs of weakness, inconsistency, softening of commitment, or evidence of the hustler element resurfacing. Yusuf Shah, a former chief assistant to Malcolm X, commented on Malcolm X's conflict with the Nation of Islam and changes during 1964 and 1965 in a CBS news program on Malcolm X. Shah concluded that if you create a Frankenstein, you have to live with it.[69]

Benson argues that a careful reading of *The Autobiography* of Malcolm X, published a few months after his assassination, reveals that Malcolm X "contained a principle of change within himself," that his changes can be "seen as consistent steps forward rather than as random and untrustworthy conversions by faith," and that his growing "sense of brotherhood with all men is not the weakening of militancy or a softening of commitment, but an extension of potency."[70] In the months before his assassination when he was facing growing opposition and harassment, Malcolm X opposed "straitjacketed thinking, and strait-jacketed societies."[71]

While some leaders streak ahead of their movements and lose contact, others lag behind or are unwilling or incapable of adapting to new circumstances or new stages in their social movements' life cycles. A person with strong attributes of charisma and prophecy, for instance, may be unable to abandon unattainable goals or to reconcile diverse elements for the harmony of the larger movement. On the other hand, events may revitalize a social movement that has settled into a comfortable bureaucratic state with a pragmatist who is task oriented, has administrative skills, and thrives on the routine and mundane. This skilled bureaucrat, unable to instill vigor, set a moral tone, and make followers believe in the impossible, is likely to be thrust aside by a charismatic leader with strong traits of the prophet who can put into words and actions what others can only feel or imagine.

Joseph Gusfield's study of the Women's Christian Temperance Union (WCTU) leadership following repeal of the prohibition of alcoholic beverages amendment in 1933 illustrates a leader who refused to move with the movement.[72] The president of the WCTU was determined to uphold the centrality of total abstinence even though the American public, many Protestant churches, a significant number of members, and other movement organizations such as Alcoholics Anonymous (AA) argued for lesser restrictions on drinking. In her annual report to the WCTU in 1952, Mrs. Z declared:

> In order not to be considered narrow or unable to see both sides some
> of the Drys have allowed themselves to be maneuvered into accepting
> the idea that [total abstinence and prohibition] is an old fashioned
> approach. . . . Between right and wrong there is only one ground and
> that is a battleground.[73]

Mrs. Z's refusal to modify her stance on principle brought ridicule upon the organization and herself. Movement members and the press described her as being "too rigid," a "one-woman drought," a "fire-eating leader," and a "diehard." When Mrs. A assumed the presidency of the WCTU in the 1960s, she emphasized the necessity of finding common ground and common goals within the WCTU and between the WCTU and other temperance organizations. Mrs. A was chosen because she was astride of the movement instead of lagging behind in defense of a principle no longer accepted by much of society and the temperance movement.

Conclusions

Social movement leaders face a daunting social environment. The U.S. public tends to view them as foreign, radical, dangerous, disruptive, and inimical to the individualism, traditions, and institutions they cherish. Confidence in the ability and determination of institutions to handle crises and issues ranging from race relations to the environment has remained persistent for two centuries. The mass media that focus primarily on social movement actions, particularly violent ones, reinforce the public's attitudes that collective action is unnecessary and dangerous.

Contrary to common impressions, social movement leaders tend to be much like the rest of us rather than fire-breathing misfits, demagogues, fanatics, or perverts. Unlike many of us, however, they become committed to a cause and are willing to devote their lives to achieving this end. As is the case with all collectives, social movements attract their share of losers, extremists, and the pathological. The public, institutions, and the media too often assume that every person involved in a social movement's activities is a leader, regardless of the person's involvement, commitment, or leadership position.

This chapter has focused on the nature of leadership in social movements and how it is attained and maintained. Typical leaders of typical social movements are organizers who must foster and maintain unity within specific organizations and coalitions, or at least cooperation, among competing organizations each of which has its own beliefs about what must be done, who must do it, and how it must be done. They are decision-makers with limited legitimacy and powers to reward and punish while constantly facing conflicting demands on their positions and movements from within and without. And they are the symbols, the faces, of their movements in the eyes of members, sympathizers, legitimizers, countermovements, and institutions.

Leaders are able to lead because they possess one or more of three critical attributes—charisma, prophecy, and pragmatism. Charisma allows leaders to inspire by leading followers to see the truth, imagine what might be, see themselves as a people, and dare to demand change in the face of real danger. Prophecy allows leaders to lead by their closeness to the writings of the movement, knowledge of truths, and ability to set a moral tone. Pragmatism allows a leader to lead through organizational expertise, efficiency, and tact. Effective social movement leaders possess two or more of these critical attributes through which they enable followers to see themselves not as individuals but as a people, form relational patterns, employ adaptive strategies, and achieve evolutionary results.

Attaining leadership positions within social movements is easier than maintaining positions in an ever-changing environment. Leaders must sustain an appropriate blend of the three critical attributes (charisma, prophecy, and pragmatism), handle diverse and conflicting roles, change as the movement changes, adapt to events, and lead without getting too far ahead or too far behind their followers. Although a few leaders such as Samuel Gompers, Cesar Chavez, and Robert Welch have led social movement organizations for decades, most, such as Malcolm X, Stokely Carmichael, Jerry Rubin, and Randall Terry, lead for a few years and then fade away because they cannot sustain organizations over time or adapt to changes demanded by both the movement and environment.

Endnotes

[1] Roberta Ash, *Social Movements in America* (Chicago: Markham, 1972): 40.

[2] John Wilson, *Introduction to Social Movements* (New York: Basic Books, 1973):78.

[3] George Gallup, Jr., *The Gallup Poll: Public Opinion 1990* (Wilmington, DE: Scholarly Resources, 1991): 1, 100–103.

[4] Eric Hoffer, *The True Believer* (New York: Mentor, 1951): 119–138; Sherry R. Shepler and Anne F. Mattina, "'Revolt Against War': Jane Addams' Rhetorical Challenge to the Patriarchy," *Communication Quarterly* 47 (Spring 1999): 151–165.

[5] "Trying to Take Back the Planet," *Newsweek*, 5 February 1990, 24.

[6] Hoffer, 58.

[7] Herbert W. Simons, "Persuasion in Social Conflicts: A Critique of Prevailing Conceptions and a Framework for Future Research," *Speech Monographs* 39 (November 1972): 236.

[8] Crane Brinton, *The Anatomy of Revolution* (New York: Vintage Books, 1952): 107; Ming T. Lee, "The Founders of the Chinese Communist Party," *Civilisations* 18 (1968): 115; Seymour Lipset, "Leadership and New Social Movements," *Studies in Leadership*, Alvin Gouldner, ed. (New York: Harper and Row, 1950): 360.

[9] Brinton, 127.

[10] Myra Marx Ferree, "The Political Context of Reality: Rational Choice Theory and Resource Mobilization," *Frontiers in Social Movement Theory*, Aldon D. Morris and Carol McClurg Mueller, eds. (New Haven, CT: Yale University Press, 1992): 48.

[11] The Gray Panther Manual (Philadelphia: The Gray Panthers, 1978): 3–4; Dieter Hessel, ed., *Maggie Kuhn on Aging* (Philadelphia: Westminster Press, 1977): 9–12.

[12] Steven R. Goldzwig, "A Social Movement Perspective on Demagoguery: Achieving Symbolic Realignment," *Communication Studies* 40 (Fall 1989): 202–228.

[13] Fred Powledge, *Free at Last? The Civil Rights Movement and the People Who Made It* (Boston: Little, Brown and Company, 1991): 222, 412–413, 558–559, and 610–612;. Kirkpatrick Sale, *SDS* (New York: Vintage Books, 1974): 499–500, 541–544, 551–557, and 643–645; "Congressmen Laugh at Zany CIA Devices," Lafayette, Indiana *Journal and Courier*, 21 September 1977, D–7; "Documents Tell of Army 'Spy' in Peace Group," Lafayette, Indiana *Journal and Courier*, 4 October 1975, C–6; "FBI Documents Show '60s Campus Capers," Lafayette, Indiana *Journal and Courier*, 25 June 1975, B–7.

[14] Anthony Oberschall, "The Los Angeles Riot," *Social Problems* 15 (Winter 1965): 324–326.

[15] Herbert W. Simons, "Requirements, Problems, and Strategies: A Theory of Persuasion for Social Movements," *Quarterly Journal of Speech* 56 (February 1970): 4.

[16] Anthony Oberschall, *Social Conflict and Social Movements* (Englewood Cliffs, NJ: Prentice-Hall, 1973): 148–149. See also William A. Gamson, "The Social Psychology of Collective Action," *Frontiers in Social Movement Theory*, 53–60; Ferree, 38–43.

[17] Wilson, 198.

[18] Simons (1970), 4.

[19] *The Gray Panther Manual*, 5.

[20] Saul D. Alinsky, *Rules for Radicals: A Pragmatic Primer for Realistic Radicals* (New York: Vintage Books, 1972): 72–79.

[21] *The Gray Panther Manual*, 6.

[22] "Operation Rescue," on ABC's *20/20*.

[23] Pat Jefferson, "The Magnificent barbarian at Nashville," *Southern Speech Journal* 33 (Winter 1967): 81; Dencil R. Taylor, "Carmichael in Tallahassee," *Southern Speech Journal* 33 (Winter 1967): 92.

[24] Alinsky, 76.

[25] Adam Fairclough, *To Redeem the Soul of America: The Southern Christian Leadership Conference and Martin Luther King, Jr.* (Athens, GA: University of Georgia Press, 1987).

[26] Joseph R. Gusfield, "Functional Areas of Leadership in Social Movements," *Sociological Quarterly* 7 (1966): 137.

[27] Simons (1970), 4.

[28] Charles J. Stewart, "The Internal Rhetoric of the Knights Of Labor," *Communication Studies* 42 (Spring 1991): 67–82.

[29] Ray Ginger, *The Bending Cross* (New Brunswick, NJ: Rutgers University Press, 1949): 106.

[30] Gusfield (1966), 141.

[31] Simons (1970), 2–3.

[32] Max Weber, *The Theory of Social and Economic Organizations*, A.M. Henderson and Talcott Parsons, trans. (New York: Free Press, 1964): 328–329; Wilson, 201.

[33] William Bruce Cameron, *Modern Social Movements* (New York: Random House, 1966): 73.

[34] Kenelm Burridge, *New Heaven New Earth: A Study of Millenarian Activities* (Oxford: Basil Blackwell, 1969):155.

[35] Richard J. Jensen and John C. Hammerback, "Radical Nationalism Among Chicanos: The Rhetoric of Jose Angel Gutierrez," *Western Journal of Speech Communication* 44 (Summer 1980): 202.

[36] J. Michael Hogan and Glen Williams, "Republican Charisma and the American Revolution: The Textual Persona of Thomas Paine's *Common Sense*," *Quarterly Journal of Speech* 86 (February 2000): 2.

[37] J. P. Roche and S. Sachs, "The Bureaucrat and the Enthusiast: An Exploration of the Leadership of Social Movements," *Western Political Quarterly* 8 (1955): 257.

[38] Allen H. Merriam, "Symbolic Action in India: Gandhi's Nonverbal Persuasion," *Quarterly Journal of Speech* 61 (October 1975): 290–306.

[39] Merriam, 305.

[40] Roche and Sachs, 250–251.

[41] *Moral Majority of Kentucky Fighting For a Moral America In the Decade of Destiny* (Louisville, KY: Moral Majority of Kentucky, n.d.): n.p.

[42] *The Blue Book of the John Birch Society* (Belmont, MA: Western Islands, 1961): xiv–xv.

[43] "The John Birch Society: A Report," *The Arizona Republic*, advertising supplement, 25 October 1964, 6.

[44] *American Opinion*, October, 1978, 56.

[45] "The John Birch Society: A Report," *Chicago Tribune*, advertising supplement, 15 November 1964, 16.

[46] Walter B. Emery, "Samuel Gompers," *A History and Criticism of American Public Address*, Vol. II, William Norwood Brigance, ed. (New York: Russell and Russell, 1960): 557–559.

[47] www.chicagohistory.org/dramas.

[48] Samuel Gompers, "President's Report," 13 December 1887, *Report of the Proceedings: American Federation of Labor*, 1888, 8.

[49] Samuel Gompers, "Address to the Machinists' Convention," *American Federationist* 8 (July 1901): 251.

[50] Samuel Gompers, *American Federation of Labor Proceedings*, 1903, 198.

[51] Cameron, 164.

[52] Gusfield (1966), 139 and 141.

[53] Wilson, 198 and 201.

[54] Oberschall, 146.

[55] Fairclough, 316.

[56] Charles J. Stewart, "The Evolution of a Revolution: Stokely Carmichael and the Rhetoric of Black Power," *Quarterly Journal of Speech* 83 (November 1997): 434.

[57] Robert L. Scott and Wayne Brockriede, *The Rhetoric of Black Power* (New York: Harper and Row, 1969): 1–9.

[58] From an audio recording and Scott and Brockriede, 88–89.

[59] Cameron, 93.

[60] Simons (1970), 1–11.

[61] Gusfield (1966), 152.

[62] Jerry Rubin, "Growing Up Again," *Human Behavior*, March, 1976, 17–23.

[63] Garth E. Pauley, "John Lewis's 'Serious Revolution': Rhetoric, Resistance, and Revision at the March on Washington," *Quarterly Journal of Speech* 84 (August 1998): 320–340.

[64] Shepler and Mattina, 151–165.

[65] Charles J. Stewart, "Labor Agitation in America: 1865–1915," *America In controversy: History of American Public Address*, DeWitte T. Holland, ed. (Dubuque, IA: W.C. Brown, 1973): 153–169.

[66] James R. Sovereign, "Annual Address of the General Master Workman," *Proceedings of the General Assembly: Knights of Labor*, 1894, 71.

[67] Cameron, 107.

[68] Thomas W. Benson, "Rhetoric and Autobiography: The Case of Malcolm X," *Quarterly Journal of Speech* 60 (February 1974): 1–13.

[69] "The Real Malcolm X," CBS Video, 1992.

[70] Benson, 7, 9, 10. See also Robert E. Terrill, "Colonizing the Borderlands: Shifting Circumference in the Rhetoric of Malcolm X," *Quarterly Journal of Speech* 86 (February 2000): 67–85.

[71] Benson, 12.

[72] Gusfield (1966), 142–145.

[73] *Annual Report of the National Women's Christian Temperance Union*, 1952, 85.

THE LIFE CYCLE OF
SOCIAL MOVEMENTS

Social movements are intricate social dramas involving multiple scenes, acts, agents, agencies, and purposes.[1] They include heroes and heroines, victims and villains, evil and good, successes and failures, hope and disillusionment.

William Cameron writes that each "social movement is determined by so many variables that its success or failure, the speed of its growth or decline, the consistency or inconsistency of its operations will not fit any a priori formula."[2] Social movements (such as women's rights, protection of the environment, and animal welfare) and social movement organizations (such as the Ku Klux Klan, the Moral Majority, and labor unions) appear, disappear, and reappear with altered purposes, ideologies, leaders, structures, and persuasive strategies. Any effort to prescribe a life cycle suitable to all social movements is fraught with dangers. Social movements differ, change, develop to varying degrees of sophistication, and proceed at varying speeds—rushing forward at times, stalling for long periods at particular stages, retrenching to earlier stages, dying premature deaths before completing all stages, or reappearing after years of absence.[3] Rarely, if ever, do social movements follow a neat, linear pattern from birth to death.

To understand complex communicative events, it is useful to try to detect cycles and phases of human interactions. For example, people studying interpersonal communication have discovered phases of conflict in small group development, interaction stages within relationships, and "how communication functions at each stage" of human relationships "to contribute to the building or dissolution of a relational culture."[4] Most closely related to our concerns is the theory of Richard Crable and Steven Vibbert that issues pass through five status levels in their life cycles: potential status, imminent status, current status, critical status, and dormant status.[5]

We can better understand a social movement by looking at the communication process through which it came into being, interacted with other elements such as institutions and countermovements, and tried to sustain itself. Attempts to portray each stage in the life cycle of *typical* social movements can help us understand the ever-changing persuasive requirements, problems, and functions of social movements and the interaction of social-psychological, political-institutional, philosophical-ideological, and rhetorical forces.[6]

The life cycle outlined in this chapter consists of five stages: genesis, social unrest, enthusiastic mobilization, maintenance, and termination.[7] It enables us to search for adaptive, evolutionary patterns in which choices reflect the attempts of individuals and organizations to adapt to the ever-changing environment and understand more fully who the "people" of the movement are, why they are as they are, and how they got that way.

Stage 1: Genesis

We rarely know when a social movement begins—only that it has evolved in particular ways. It usually begins during relatively quiet times, quiet at least with respect to the issue that the new movement will address. The "people" and established institutions are unaware of the problem or perceive it as insignificant or of low priority.[8] Other elements of the environment—economic, political, social, military, or religious—dominate the attention of the people, their leaders and institutions, and the mass media. Individuals, often scattered geographically and unknown to one another at first, perceive an "imperfection" in the existing order.[9] The imperfection may be institutional or individual corruption, abuse of power, inequality (in rights, status, power, income, opportunities, possessions, recognition), threats to one' status, an identity crisis, unfilled "legitimate" expectations (all expectations *perceived* to be legitimate), or a threat to the social order, values, or environment. Lisa Gring-Pemble labels this a "pre-genesis process wherein lies the birth, growth and affirmation of consciousness."[10] She claims, for instance, that the 1848 convention at Seneca Falls, New York that brought woman's rights advocates together for the first time "necessarily indicates an antecedent 'pre-genesis' phase, a transitional phase between private and public expression."[11]

Whether this period is labeled pre-genesis or early genesis, it is clear that restless individuals view an imperfection as a serious problem that is likely to grow more severe unless appropriate institutions address it quickly and earnestly. For instance, in the 1960s growing numbers of clergy became alarmed at the decline in public morals resulting from the anti–Vietnam War and counterculture movements. They felt something needed to be done to reverse the frightening increase in premarital sex, divorce, drug use, alcoholism, and pornography. Warnings of a dangerous moral decline emanated from pulpits and in leaflets and books. In the 1990s, legislation, laws, government actions, and taxation viewed as little different from the causes of the American Revolution frightened thousands of Americans. As James Johnson, leader of the Ohio Unorganized Militia and founder of several other militias, testified before Senate Judiciary Committee hearings in June 1995 following the Oklahoma City bombing, "the only thing standing between legislation being contemplated and armed conflict is time," time for citizens to get involved before it is too late.[12]

A social movement's early leaders—sometimes called intellectuals or prophets—strive for salvation, perfection, and the good in society. Although they see through an institution or state of affairs and strive to expose the institution's leaders or the status quo, they meet little opposition in the genesis stage because few people take them seriously. These prophets and intellectuals produce essays, editorials, songs, poems, pamphlets, books, sermons, lectures, and Web sites designed to transform perceptions of reality (the environment) and self (what people). Above all, the social movement's initial leaders believe, often with remarkable naivete, that appropriate institutions will act if the movement can make institutional leaders and followers aware of the urgent problem and its solution. The early leader is more of an educator than a rabble rouser, agitator, or fanatic. Thus, as Eric Hoffer informs us, "imperceptibly the man [woman] of words undermines established institutions, discredits those in power, weakens prevailing beliefs and loyalties, and sets the stage for the rise of the mass movement—by intention or by accident."[13]

In Lloyd Bitzer's words, the prophet not only apprehends an exigence ("an imperfection marked by some degree of urgency... a problem or defect, something other than it should be") but attempts to create interest within an audience for perceiving and solving the problem. The prophet, however, often differs little from Bitzer's "man alone in a boat and adrift at sea" who "shouts for help although he knows his words will be unheard." But prophets persist because they believe that "interest will increase insofar as the factual condition" becomes "known directly and sensibly, or through vivid representation."[14] David Snow and Robert Benford call these representations "collective action frames" and contend that they "serve as accenting devices that either underscore and embellish the seriousness and injustice of a social condition or redefine as unjust and immoral what was previously seen as unfortunate but perhaps tolerable."[15]

The genesis stage may last for months, years, or decades. Harold Mixon studied the sermons delivered from 1672 to 1774 on the first Monday in June at the election and installation of new officers into the Ancient and Honorable Artillery Company of Boston. He concluded that "decades before the agitation for independence developed," these artillery election sermons "were, perhaps quite without notice, additional parts of a large stream of discourse promoting patterns of thought which prepared the colonies for the ideas of the revolutionists" resulting in the Declaration of Independence in 1776.[16] Folk songs by Bob Dylan and others addressed war and peace a year before the Gulf of Tonkin incident thrust the United States into the Vietnam conflict in the 1960s.

If comparable social movements are active, a fledgling social movement may take shape rapidly. For example, students involved in the black civil rights movement created the student free-speech movement. The editor of the *Crimson* wrote to fellow Harvard students, many fresh from freedom rides in the south, "But the realization that lies just around the corner is that we too are an oppressed people. Any radical movement at Harvard should base itself on our own needs—the needs of the oppressed student class."[17] Students then created the peace movement that opposed the war in Vietnam, and finally the counter-culture movement that rejected most of the American value structure. Female members of these movements, who became painfully aware of their second-class status in organizations fighting for the rights of others, were instrumental in establishing the women's liberation movement. And the women's liberation movement has served as the model and inspiration for movements striving for the rights of Hispanics, Asian Americans, Native Americans, and the elderly.

The genesis stage, Leland Griffin's "period of inception," is a "time when the roots of pre-existing sentiment, nourished by interested rhetoricians, begins to flower into public notice."[18] A triggering incident is usually necessary to move the generally unorganized, ideologically uncertain, and barely visible social movement from the genesis stage to the social unrest stage. The triggering event may be a Supreme Court decision, a nuclear power plant accident, an insensitive reaction or statement by an institutional agent, a new law, an economic recession, a military or police action, the appearance of a movement-oriented book on the best-seller list, or a violent act. For instance, the comment by a North Dakota legislator to a farm delegation in 1915, "Go home and slop your hogs," infuriated farmers and gave rise to the Nonpartisan League in the Midwest.[19] Betty Freidan's *The Feminine Mystique* helped to launch the women's liberation movement, and Rachel Carson's *The Silent Spring* served as the impetus for the environmental movement. J. Michael Hogan and Glen Williams note that "prior to the publication of" Thomas Paine's pamphlet entitled *Common Sense* in early 1776, "few in the colonies talked of separating from England. . . . Within a matter of months, however, a virtual consensus had been achieved."[20]

A violent act often jars people into action, many of whom seem unlikely social movement activists. For example, a peace movement began in violence-ridden Northern Ireland on August 10, 1976 when an

I.R.A. (Irish Republican Army) getaway car, its driver killed by a British soldier, jumped a curb in West Belfast and killed three of Ann Corrigan's children aged six weeks, two, and eight. Their aunt Mairead Corrigan, a Catholic, went on television and condemned the I.R.A, something no Catholic had dared to do. At the same time, Betty Williams, who had witnessed the accident, went house to house asking Catholic and Protestant residents to sign a petition for peace and take part in a rally that Saturday. The two outraged women, one a secretary and one a mother and homemaker, joined forces and were soon holding rallies throughout Northern Ireland with numbers ranging from hundreds to 20,000.[21] They won the Nobel Peace Prize for 1976. The initial result of a triggering or catalytic event may be the first real signs of organization with titles that begin Citizens for . . ., Concerned Parents Against . . ., Workers United to . . ., or Americans Dedicated to. . . . For instance, Williams and Corrigan formed the Community of Peace People to carry on the fledgling peace movement in Northern Ireland.

Some social movements have difficulty advancing without an event or impetus. After more than a decade, the men's movement appears to remain in the genesis stage at the turn of the twenty-first century awaiting some event, person, or organization to propel it into the next stage. The movement began in the 1980s with small groups of men (similar to the consciousness-raising groups during the early stage of the women's liberation movement) meeting to share their pains, hurts, and frustrations that resulted from experiences with drunken fathers, emasculating bosses, stifling jobs, divorce laws, child custody fights, or advertisements and television programs that portray men as fools.[22] It received national attention in 1990 with a Bill Moyers-narrated PBS special entitled "A Gathering of Men," a documentary on poet Robert Bly and his book *Iron John: A Book About Men*. Hundreds of men's groups sprang up around the country, many conducting weekend retreats during which men looked inward and experienced a rebirth through sharing their painful stories and by acting out primitive masculinity through drum beating and sweating around mounds of steaming rocks in teepees. These were strivings to discover what people they were to be. This embryonic movement has created no ideology spotlighting how men are abused and oppressed, but it has gained attention from American intellectuals. A 1993 issue of the *Chronicle of Higher Education* listed 28 books published since 1990 with titles such as *The Adventurous Male, American Manhood, Running Scared, The First Sexual Revolution,* and *The Inward Gaze.*[23] In spite of large rallies of men organized by the Promise Keepers and the Million Man March on Washington, D.C., the movement seems stalled. Most intellectuals appear reluctant to associate with the "mythopoetic" men's movement because they see Bly's *Iron John* and Sam Keen's *Fire in the Belly: On Being a Man* primarily as a backlash against the feminist movement and as an effort to reclaim turf. R. W. Connell, a sociologist at the University of California at

Santa Cruz, writes that "In the final analysis, *Iron John* and the "mythopo-etic men's movement" are a massive evasion of reality. Bly is selling sim-plified fantasy solutions to real problems. In the process, he distorts men's lives and distracts men from practical work on gender inequalities."[24] Some critics have laid this charge on the Promise Keepers. No organiza-tion has yet emerged to bring together a significant number of men for purposes other than consciousness raising, so the movement continues in the genesis stage with writings and occasional rallys. If this movement develops into a full-fledged social movement, it would fit the pattern of trying to capture an idealized past and enhancing an endangered ego.

The most important contributions of the genesis stage are the appre-hension of an exigence and the cultivation of interest in the exigence within an audience. Without a genesis stage, there will be no movement. However, if the movement cannot go forward, it will eventually wither and die. Snow and Benford contend that the "failure of mass mobilization" to occur when the time seems ripe "may be accounted for in part by the absence of a resonant master frame"—an altered vision of reality centered on objects, situations, events, experiences, actions, and relationships.[25]

Stage 2: Social Unrest

As growing numbers of people rise up and express their concerns and frustrations over an issue, the social movement evolves from the gen-esis to the social unrest stage and may become visible in the media for the first time as a "movement." The prophets and intellectuals of the genesis stage turn into, or join, agitators—literally ones who stir things up. Together they begin to organize the disparate elements of the movement and take it beyond living rooms, talk shows, study groups, churches, and lecture halls. An initial act may be the calling of a convention or confer-ence of like-minded people to form an organization. Robert Welch called respected and trusted businessmen together in Indianapolis in 1958 to form the John Birch Society to expose and fight the world communist con-spiracy. The Reverend Jerry Falwell founded the Moral Majority in 1979 to unite those "who are deeply concerned about the moral decline of our nation, and who are sick and tired of the way many amoral and secular humanists and other liberals are destroying the traditional family and moral values on which our nation was built."[26] This was the beginning of the organized Christian right movement in the United States.

An important purpose of gatherings to form organizations is the framing of a manifesto, proclamation, or declaration. For instance, student leaders from a wide variety of organizations (Students for a Democratic Society, National Student Christian Federation, National Student Associa-tion, the Young Democrats, Student Peace Union, and SNCC) met in June 1963 at Michigan's AFL-CIO camp at Port Huron, Michigan to work out a manifesto. The product of these deliberations, the *Port Huron Statement,* served as the essential statement of principles for the student movement and later the Anti–Vietnam War and counterculture movements.[27]

A manifesto or body of writings sets forth the social movement's ideology, an "elaboration of rationalizations and stereotypes into a consistent pattern."[28] It serves four essential functions: (1) to describe an exigence, (2) to identify the devils, scapegoats, and faulty principles that have caused and sustained the exigence, (3) to list principles, beliefs, and stands on critical issues, and (4) to prescribe the solution and the gods, principles, and procedures that will bring it about. The ideology identifies the social movement with *the people,* a great grassroots movement in the mainstream of American society. For example, Ken Adams of the Michigan Militia told those at Senate hearings on terrorism that militia members were "everyday Americans," a "cross-section of Americans" who represented all professions.[29]

Ideologies also identify movements with established norms and values. The effort is to identify with what is good and holy in the United States and to disassociate from all that is evil. The *Port Huron Statement* begins with these words:

> We are people of this generation, bred in at least modest comfort, housed now in universities, looking uncomfortably to the world we inherit. When we were kids the United States was the wealthiest and strongest country in the world; the only one with the atom bomb, the least scarred by modern war, an initiator of the United Nations that we thought would distribute Western influence throughout the world. Freedom and equality for each individual, government of, by, and for the people—these American values we found good, principles by which we could live as men. Many of us began maturing in complacency.[30]

The next paragraph begins "As we grew, however, our comfort was penetrated by events too troubling to dismiss," and introduces a litany of problems and disillusionments with society: racial bigotry, the Cold War, the common peril of "the Bomb," politics, the economy, the military-industrial complex, poverty, and communism. This sentence summarizes the concerns of the students at Port Huron: "Not only did tarnish appear on our image of American virtue, not only did disillusion occur when the hypocrisy of American ideals was discovered, but we began to sense that what we had originally seen as the American Golden Age was actually the decline of an era."[31]

Theorists note that a social movement's ideology is "considerably more potent" and "strikes a responsive chord" if it identifies successfully with "extant beliefs, myths, folk tales, and the like."[32] The Moral Majority's "stands on today's vital issues" clearly linked it with the conservative Catholics, Protestants, Jews, Mormons, and Fundamentalists it wished to activate. These stands included "We believe in the separation of church and state;" "We are pro-life," "We are pro-traditional family," "We oppose pornography," and "We support the state of Israel and Jewish people everywhere."[33] An ideology contains a set of devil terms such as liberalism, segregation, wage slavery, commercial development, conformity, and welfare state and a corresponding set of god terms such as conservativism, integration, employee-owned cooperatives, natural environment, individualism, and free enterprise.

An overarching principle or slogan unifies the movement, such as "An injury to one is an injury to all" (Knights of Labor), "Never to laugh or love" (pro-life), "Keep abortion legal" (pro-choice), "All power to the people" (Black Power and new left), "Building a Better Tomorrow" (Liberty Federation), and "That Freedom Shall Not Perish" (John Birch Society). For the first time, there is a feeling of standing together, as concerned individuals are now members of the Knights of Labor, Greenpeace, The Clamshell Alliance (against nuclear power plants), People for the Ethical Treatment of Animals, The Moral Majority, or the Texas Constitutional Militia.

The act of joining or forming an organization sets members apart from nonmembers and established institutions and fosters a we-they division that becomes more pronounced as the social movement enters succeeding stages. Members increasingly see themselves as an elite with a mission, and they devise strategies for fulfilling the moral crusade. Movement persuaders attempt to instill new feelings of self-identity, self-respect, and power within members that was absent when they were mere individuals. Members now begin to experience an ego boost as Asian Americans, Hispanic Americans, evangelical Christians, gays and lesbians, crusaders for animal rights or pro-life, and militia members in the tradition of America's Revolutionary War heroes. As a "people" they now have new, meaningful relational patterns.

Although the social movement pays increasing attention to transforming perceptions of society by creating we-they distinctions and to prescribing courses of action (listing beliefs, citing demands, prescribing solutions, and identifying who must bring about or stifle change and through which strategies), the major persuasive effort is aimed at transforming perceptions of reality, the environment. Persuaders continue to believe that if they can raise the consciousness of institutional leaders and followers (make them aware of the facts through words, pictures, exposés, symbolic acts, and theatre), institutions will take appropriate actions to resolve the exigence. Faith in progress through the social chain-of-command remains strong. Thus, gay rights advocates portray how they are discriminated against in U.S. society; antiwar advocates portray the horrors of war; animal rights advocates portray the horrors of leghold traps and raising animals for fur, food, and experimentation; and the Christian right portrays the moral decadence of society. Movements expend most of their rhetorical energies during the social unrest stage in petitioning courts, city councils, university boards of trustees, corporate boards of directors, state legislatures, Congress, the President of the United States, scientific organizations, and religious synods and hierarchies.[34]

Spokespersons for institutions may openly deny the severity or existence of the problem (exigence) and, often for the first time, take official notice of the fledgling social movement. They may stigmatize the so-called movement as naive, ill informed, or laughable The opposition's strategy is to stall the social movement by ignoring or discrediting it in hopes that it will succumb to ridicule or inattention—that it will simply go away. The mass media may note with interest, amusement, or mild foreboding the claims or overtures of the infant social movement. When protestors on college campuses constructed shantytowns to make people aware of conditions of blacks in South Africa under apartheid, the *Wall Street Journal* ridiculed these activities as "the latest fad" in an article entitled "Shanty Raids," a play on words referring to panty raids common on college campuses decades earlier. "In spring a young student's fancy turns to political protest," the *Wall Street Journal* remarked. "This year's fashion is shantytowns, and from Yale to North Carolina to Purdue to Michigan to Wisconsin to Berkeley police are confronting student demonstrators."[35] Cartoonists have portrayed members of militias as dimwitted, overweight, unshaven, heavily-armed weekend warriors who work as gas station attendants and live in run-down mobile homes.

The duration of the social unrest stage depends upon the numbers of people who are attracted to the movement, reactions of institutional agents, and new triggering or catalytic events that may greatly exacerbate the social situation or exigence. The nuclear power plant accidents at Three Mile Island (Pennsylvania) and Chernobyl (Ukraine) and the arrest of Rosa Parks in Montgomery, Alabama because she would not surrender her seat on a city bus to a white male passenger boosted the antinuclear and civil rights movements from the social unrest stage to the enthusiastic mobilization stage. The first showed the real dangers of nuclear power that words and symbolic actions could not, and the second led to the Montgomery bus boycott that catapulted a young, relatively unknown local minister, Martin Luther King, Jr., to national prominence and leadership of the movement. Triggering events, such as the loss of an election, failure of Congress to pass legislation, or reluctance of the courts and law enforcement agencies to enforce laws, cause significant numbers of people to lose faith both in the ability and willingness of institutions to solve exigencies and the effectiveness of normal persuasive means to bring about or to resist change.[36]

Members and sympathizers may begin to see the institution as the problem or as part of a conspiracy to sustain power and to defeat all legitimate and reasonable efforts to bring about urgently needed actions. Members of the Moral Majority, for instance, came to see the "liberalized" mainline Protestant denominations (Methodists, Presbyterians, Lutherans, Episcopalians) as part of the problem rather than as part of the solution. When frustration leads to *disaffection* with institutions and their ability or desire to resolve problems, the social movement enters the stage of enthusiastic mobilization. The growth of social unrest culminates in the development of a dominant exigence, an audience, and constraints.[37]

Stage 3: Enthusiastic Mobilization

The social movement in the enthusiastic mobilization stage is populated with true believers who have experienced conversion to the cause. They have grown "tired of being sick and tired."[38] Gone is the old naivete that institutions—churches, legislatures, universities, corporations—will act if they are made aware of the problem through rational appeals. The converted see the social movement as the only way to bring about urgently needed change and believe firmly that the movement's time has come. Optimism is rampant. Important legitimizers such as entertainers, senators, clergy, physicians, labor leaders, scientists, and educators lend an air of excitement and inevitability to the cause.

Institutions and resistance movements are keenly aware of the movement's growth, change in attitude, altered persuasive strategies, perceived legitimation, and potential for success. For the first time, they see the movement as a clear and present danger to institutional power and authority. They, too, mobilize during the enthusiastic mobilization stage. The greater the threat from a social movement, particularly if it is perceived to seek revolutionary changes, the greater are the counterefforts by institutional agents, agencies, and surrogates. Institutions may encourage the creation of countermovements and provide them with resources and an aura of legitimacy. The aim is to stifle the social movement through actions of "the people" or the "silent majority," often persons the movement claims it is fighting for, and thus avoid the appearance of institutional involvement. If these actions fail and institutions come to see the movement as a radical, revolutionary force, it may unleash police forces to suppress the perceived threat to society.

As social movements expand, evolve, and confront serious opposition from institutional forces and surrogates, they may abandon judicial and legislative chambers for the streets, marketplaces, forests, vineyards, and the open seas. They have lost faith in both institutions and institutional means to bring about or resist change. Mass meetings, marches, demonstrations, hunger strikes, and symbolic actions replace sedate conventions, conferences, and testimony at hearings.

Coercive persuasion may replace the rhetoric of speeches, leaflets, pamphlets, and newsletters. Protestors burn tractors in front of the Capitol to protest farm prices, bury school buses to protest forced busing to integrate schools, burn flags to protest military actions, blockade clinics to stop abortions, shadow police on their rounds to let them know they are being watched, and appear in public with handguns and rifles to pressure police officers and courts. They boycott table grapes, corporations doing business with South Africa, department stores selling furs, and hospitals and clinics where abortions might be performed. They set up picket lines, declare strikes, defy laws and court injunctions, and welcome mass arrests that attract television cameras and news coverage and clog the jails. They stage sit-ins, sit-downs, sleep-ins, and die-ins.

Protestors harass institutional agents and persons who do not comply with their demands. Threats work. For example, a woman who fears that wearing a fur coat in public will provoke a protestor to yell at her, throw red paint on her coat, or cut it with a sharp knife, will not buy a fur coat or wear one she purchased earlier.[39] Protestors have learned that picketing the homes of the mayor, a physician who performs abortions, the owner of a video rental store that rents x-rated videos, or the manager of a supermarket that sells table grapes boycotted by the movement is more effective than picketing city hall, clinics, video rental stores, or supermarkets. Targets sense greater threats to their persons and families—not to mention reactions of irate neighbors who do not want "radicals" in their neighborhoods.

New organizations arise to compete with or overshadow earlier organizations. When the Reverend Jerry Falwell decided in 1986 to step back from his political activities, he created the Liberty Federation to take on a broader political agenda, but others were ready to join the Christian right movement. Other competing organizations in the Christian right movement include James Dobson's Focus on the Family, Citizens for Excellence in Education, Traditional Values Coalition, Free Congress Foundation/ National Empowerment Television, American Family Association, and Concerned Women of America.

Charismatic leaders, adept at countering and taking advantage of growing opposition to the movement, replace intellectuals and prophets, though they may pay homage to both. They control the movement by forming strong organizations and coalitions. They stir up great excitement within the membership, stage symbolic actions, and confront institutions and resistance movements. Increasingly, leaders such as Thomas Metzger (founder of White Aryan Resistance) are adept at using technology to raise money, attract followers through databases, reach out to thousands through sophisticated Web sites, and generate mailings to members of Congress and state legislatures urging them to vote for or against legislation. Leaders and followers may become literal or figurative martyrs for the cause by suffering physical injury, imprisonment, banishment, or death. They not only accept but may readily seek suffering because the cause has become the true believer's reason for being.

The persuasive goal of the enthusiastic mobilization stage is to raise the consciousness level of the people so significant numbers will pressure institutions. The movement presents simplified *if-only* images of social processes, problems, and solutions: if women are given the right to vote, women will achieve equal rights; if abortion is outlawed, there will be no abortions; if sexual orientation clauses are added to human rights ordinances, there will be no discrimination against homosexuals; if we stop using animals for medical experiments, we will find cures faster through high technology; if we have prayer and Bible reading in the public schools, student achievement will rise, violence will end, and the decline in morals will be reversed.

Leaders during the enthusiastic mobilization stage face severe persuasive crises both inside and outside the social movement. Externally, persuaders must employ harsh rhetoric and stage symbolic acts designed to pressure institutions into capitulation or compromise, to polarize the movement and its opposition (all who are not actively supporting the movement), and to provoke repressive acts that reveal the true ugliness of institutions and their counterefforts. Persuasion during this stage is replete with name-calling against the devils and conspirators who have perpetrated and prolonged the evil the social movement alone has the will and strength to fight. James Johnson of the Ohio Unorganized Militia claims that alarmed Americans "began to form themselves in units for their own self-defense and self-preservation" when they realized that, as individuals, they could do nothing to stem the tide of government actions that were undermining the republic.[40]

If leaders are inept at adapting and changing persuasive strategies and judging how far to push for positive results and images, they may provoke institutional and public outrage—and suppression of the movement. At the very least, the movement may lose essential support and sympathy from the public, media, and legitimizers. A few violent acts such as the bombing of a University of Wisconsin building in which Army research was conducted, the killing of physicians who perform abortions, firebombing meat wholesaler trucks, and sabotaging logging equipment may doom years of protest, even if the acts are by fanatical, minuscule, splinter groups such as the Weathermen, Army of God, Earth First! and the U.S. Animal Liberation Front. The public and institutions do not make fine distinctions: an act *in the name of* the social movement and its cause is *an act by* the movement.

Internally, movement persuaders must deal with competing and often antagonistic organizations, each with its own leaders, followers, and strategies. For instance, prior to World War I, the suffrage movement "saw a distinct split between pacifists and supporters of preparedness and eventually war." The AFL refused to allow suffragist and antiwar advocate Jane Addams to speak because its leadership was concerned "with the 'sinister influences' behind the peace movement."[41] The rise of fanatical elements who propose violence instead of symbolism or who make demands unacceptable to either the movement at large or to institutions splinter the movement and drain persuasive resources from the cause. Militia leaders, for instance, have tried to distance the movement's mainstream from dangerous "fringe elements" to attain legitimacy and credibility among the public.

Leaders may decide that alterations in ideology or persuasive strategies are necessary to keep the movement fresh, to counter resistance forces, or to meet changing circumstances. They must sell each change to movement factions or face devastating charges of *revisionism* and selling out. A movement's goals may expand or contract with changes in membership and/or situations. For example, the pro-life movement came into existence to make abortion illegal. As it progressed, it widened its focus to include all human life—the aged, infirm, mentally retarded, and minorities as well as the unborn.

When confrontations between the social movement and resistance forces become severe, persuaders draw sharp and often bitter *we-they* distinctions. Persons who do not join the movement and former members are labeled traitors. Leaders may look within and decide that some members (whites, males, nonskilled workers, religious liberals) are incapable of true understanding or involvement in the cause, so they purge memberships to purify their movements to prepare for final struggles with the evil forces arrayed against them. Leaders must explain and justify the new elites and relational patterns to internal and external audiences.

Social movements may achieve notable goals and victories during the enthusiastic mobilization stage, but earlier visions of sweeping and meaningful changes—the evolutionary results central to movement dreams—usually remain unfulfilled. Instant success is elusive. Leaders are unable to satisfy the insatiable appetites of members and the mass media for new and more spectacular events and achievements. New leaders and members ridicule what were once viewed as imaginative and potent persuasive strategies or revolutionary victories, such as the Montgomery bus boycott and civil rights legislation. John Wilson notes "It is easier for the disgruntled to agree on what is wrong with the old than on what is right with the new."[42] Leaders devote increasing amounts of persuasion to explaining and justifying setbacks, delays, lack of meaningful gains, and failures of old successes to fulfill exaggerated expectations. The extravagant hopes and unrealistic dreams that once energized the movement begin to fade and with them the enthusiasm of the movement.

In some movements, frustration may build within a new generation of activists who become increasingly disaffected with the social movement establishment preaching an uninstitutionalized version of patience and gradualism—the rhetorical staple of the institutional establishment they loathe. A revolution within a revolution awaits events and a leader who can "address members' frustrations, recreate and redefine social reality, offer new dreams, and identify with a new generation of true believers."[43] Stokely Carmichael played this role in the civil rights movement with his "black power" rhetoric that criticized the aging leaders of the movement, rejected the philosophy of integration, and opposed the strategy of passive, nonviolent, civil disobedience that had produced little change and a great deal of suffering. He denied that he was a "Negro leader" and charged that the old generation of leaders "had nothing to offer that they [audiences] could see, except to go out and be beaten again."[44] Carmichael identified with the younger generation of civil rights activists in age, appearance, dress, speaking style, and militant message. He appealed to cultural pride and heritage, attacked the war in Vietnam, and created a symbolic realignment by replacing words such as Negro, ghetto, segregation, and integration with black, colony, colonialism, and liberation. For a time, Carmichael's rhetoric of black power gave the civil rights movement a renewed vigor and purpose and involved a new generation of activists who cheered, shouted, laughed, clapped, and danced during his rousing and animated speeches. But then he organized the All African People Revolutionary Party in 1967 and moved to the People's Republic of Guinea in 1968. Without Carmichael's rousing oratory and presence, the black power phase ended, and the civil rights movement proceeded on to the maintenance stage.

Neither social movement members nor those in the larger society can accept harsh rhetoric and confrontation for long. Fatigue, fears of anarchy, and boredom inevitably set in. The persuasive efforts necessary for mobilizing the social movement may carry the seeds of its own destruction—both within and without—so that when the boiling point is reached, the movement must essentially revert to an earlier posture to sustain its existence. The movement enters the maintenance stage.

Stage 4: Maintenance

The maturing social movement needs new leadership and a less impassioned and strident rhetoric as it enters the maintenance stage. The loss of a charismatic leader such as Martin Luther King, Jr., Malcolm X, and American Nazi leader George Lincoln Rockwell to assassins may hasten the movement into the maintenance stage because no one else is capable of sustaining mobilization or re-energizing the movement. The remnants of the old enthusiasm may die with the movement's martyr.

The onset of the maintenance stage is a critical turning point for a social movement because one direction is toward ultimate victory of some sort and the other is toward oblivion. Unfortunately, the odds are against victory for, as John Wilson writes, "frustration is the fate of all social movements."[45] The movement undergoes change that is inevitable in all organizations. Lloyd Bitzer notes "a situation deteriorates when any constituent or relation changes in ways that make modification of the exigence significantly more difficult."[46]

The social movement returns to more quiet times during the maintenance stage as institutions, media, and public turn to other, more pressing concerns. Both movement and society are ready for a respite from unnerving, disruptive, and often destructive confrontations. Movement persuasion once again emanates from the pen, computer, and printer and from legislative, judicial, conference, convention, and lecture halls. It is time to retain what has been gained and to consolidate movement organization for the duration. Radical organizations such as WITCH (Women's International Terrorist Conspiracy from Hell), SCUM (Society for Cutting Up Men), and Earth First! disappear and original, more conservative groups such as NOW (National Organization for Women), Planned Parenthood, and the Sierra Club remain to carry the movement forward.

The agitator has no place in the maintenance stage, which requires a statesman or administrator. A pragmatist who can appeal to disparate elements, maintain organizations, and deal more directly and rationally with institutional leaders is essential in this stage. The agitator is a superb street fighter but a poor bureaucrat unsuited for diplomatic and administrative roles. The harsh and uncompromising rhetoric of polarization and confrontation creates too many enemies within and without.

The pragmatist, a pastor of sorts, must perfect organization, sustain the movement's forward progress as it emerges from its trial by fire, and work with established institutions. Herbert Simons notes that the militant strategies of the agitator may make the moderate strategies of the pragmatist more acceptable to institutions.[47]

While leaders continue efforts to transform perceptions of reality and society, prescribe courses of action, and mobilize believers and sympathizers, the primary persuasive function is to sustain the social movement. Both membership and commitment decline during the maintenance stage, so leaders must recruit new members and reinforce belief in the movement's ideology and potential for ultimate rather than immediate success. They must sustain or resuscitate hope and optimism. Unfortunately, leaders become more distant from members during the maintenance stage because there are fewer opportunities to see, hear, and talk with them. Dominant communication channels are newsletters, journals, movement newspapers, and the Internet rather than interpersonal exchanges and speeches before live audiences.

Incessant fund-raising is necessary to support organizations, property, and publications. Any maintenance task—fund-raising, recruiting, mailings, publications, Web pages—may become an end in itself, and the leader becomes more of an entrepreneur than a reformer or revolutionary. Routinization of dues, meetings, leadership, decision-making, and rituals is essential to maintain a highly structured and disciplined movement organization that will survive to carry the cause forward. These bureaucratic necessities, however, siphon off much of the old spontaneity, excitement, and *esprit de corps* that made the movement vibrant and attractive and set it apart from institutions. What was improvised during an emergency or passionate moment in an earlier, exciting stage now becomes a sacred precedent and wisdom of the past. While spontaneous deviation from expected behavior may be glorified as sacred precedent, such spontaneity is unacceptable in the maintenance stage because rigid adherence to organization is the norm.

Lack of visibility becomes a major preoccupation. The movement is rarely newsworthy during the maintenance stage, and the mass media begin to address the social movement and its leaders in editorials and columns that begin with phrases such as "What ever happened to" and "Where is . . . now?" The adage "out of sight, out of mind" haunts leaders, but their persuasive options are few. Paradoxically, neither members nor the public will support mass demonstrations at this stage, yet quiet behavior suggests satisfaction with things as they are. There are no charismatic leaders to fire up the membership, and there are too few active members to be fired up. The Ku Klux Klan, for instance, continues efforts to arrange mass gatherings and cross burnings in cities throughout the United States, but the fewer than fifty members who usually show up are far outnumbered by police, reporters, the curious, and counterdemonstrators. The Klan is embarrassed more than energized.

Institutions may not tolerate (or may have learned how to deal quietly with) persuasive tactics such as sit-ins, civil disobedience, boycotts, and hunger strikes. Worst of all, institutions may simply ignore outdated symbolic acts and revolutionary rhetoric. Rhetoric is increasingly internal—directed toward maintenance functions—rather than external—directed toward pressuring the opposition and gaining legitimizers. Leaders resort to ceremonies, rituals, annual meetings, and anniversary celebrations during which martyrs, tragedies, events, and victories are recounted and memorialized, but the rhetoric is more melancholy than energizing. In June 1999, Rosa Parks, "the mother of the civil rights movement," received from President Clinton the nation's highest honor, the Congressional Gold Medal. The ceremony in the Capitol Rotunda made possible by a House vote of 424–1 and a Senate vote of 86–0 and a celebration in her honor a few days later in Indianapolis included religious and civil rights songs and tributes from the governor, clergy, members of congress, and the mayor of Indianapolis. For a few days at least, the civil rights movement was once again front-page news, and the actions of its eighty-six-year-old heroine were recalled and honored for their significance. President Clinton commented "In so many ways, Rosa Parks brought America home. We should all remember the power of this one citizen."[48] Then it was back to defending the movement's hard-fought gains and new battles for freedom, equality, and justice.

The social movement looks desperately for a triggering event to return the cause to the enthusiastic mobilization stage, make the struggle fun and exciting again, and to counteract the gradual hardening of the arteries that aging movement organizations experience. As opposed to a rejuvenative triggering event, the movement may just as likely suffer a severe blow from a debilitating or disintegrating event. For instance, the coming on line of the Seabrook nuclear power plant in New Hampshire and the economic-based decision to stop construction on Marble Hill plant in Indiana were devastating events for the antinuclear power movement. They failed in their prolonged efforts to stop the first and lost a primary target in the second. The issue no longer seemed urgent. The onset of AIDS significantly affected the gay rights movement":

> AIDS became the obsessive concern of gay rights activists, coloring all activity concerning the welfare of gay men and lesbians in the United States. AIDS presented the gay community with not only a public health crisis, but crises in the social, legal, and psychological spheres as well. AIDS catalyzed a shift in the rhetoric of the gay movement.[49]

The hoped-for rebirth eludes most social movements or arrives too late. For example, when the ideals of women's rights, industrial unionism, social security, and temperance were once again high on the public agenda, original leaders and organizations were history. NOW (National Organization for Women), the CIO (Congress of Industrial Organizations), the Democratic Party, and MADD (Mothers Against Drunk Driving) arose to champion the causes.

As the movement shrinks or faces a long stalemate, it may focus its rhetorical energies on a single issue or solution. Movements claim all will be well once people get the right to vote, a prohibition amendment, the eight-hour day, equal rights legislation, integration of public places, an antiabortion amendment, or prayer in the public schools. The single goal is attractive because it is simple and more attainable than a panacea of hopes and dreams. The shrunken movement can focus its limited persuasive energies on a single less divisive target. Both movement and institutions have grown weary of confrontations, and legitimizers are more likely to support a non-radical goal that is handled through normal means and channels.

The social movement is on the threshold of the final stage, termination, during which it will cease to be a social movement. The only question is whether it will die or become another form of collectivity.

Stage 5: Termination

If a social movement is successful, it may celebrate its victory and disband. The antislavery movement did just that in 1865 after passage of the Thirteenth Amendment to the Constitution: "Neither Slavery nor involuntary servitude, except as a punishment for crime whereof the party shall have been duly convicted, shall exist within the United States, or any place subject to their jurisdiction."[50] The movement no longer had a cause for which to fight. The anti–Vietnam war movement gradually dissolved as U.S. involvement in the war came to an end. Total disbandment of a social movement is unlikely, however, because elements of every social movement make the cause their reason for being and their liveli-hood, and they will trust no one else with its principles or their jobs. Also, the social movement's ideology may be so broad or idealistic, such as the end of all prejudice in society, that all of its tasks are rarely fulfilled.

If a social movement maintains an effective organization and its prin-ciples come to match current mores, it may become the new order—as communist and Nazi movements did in Russia and Germany and the democratic-independence movements did in much of eastern Europe in the 1990s. The movement may become a new institution such as the Luth-eran Church in Germany, the Methodist Church in the United States, and the American Federation of Labor.

Leaders of transformed social movements face new and old persua-sive challenges. They must strive for obedience among the membership and the people, bring an end to tensions, and establish a perfecting myth in which the social movement organization is believed to have reached a state of absolute perfection and morality. Leaders must purge elements that will not accept the transformation of the social movement or who pose threats to the leadership's attempts to achieve peace and harmony among societal elements.

Rhetorical confrontations do not end with the transformation of a social movement into an institution. As Elizabeth Nelson points out in her study of Mussolini's rise to power in Italy, former social movements may have to continue their "perpetual struggles" to sustain their new positions and the support of followers.[51] The reformers and revolutionar-ies of movement days become the priests of the new order or institution and must be able to perform pastoral functions. Inevitably, the move-ment-turned-institution will face a new generation of reformers and revo-lutionaries who become disaffected with the new order.

Few social movements are totally successful, however. Some shrink into pressure groups (Ralph Nader's consumer-protection organizations), philanthropic associations (the Salvation Army), political parties (the Socialist party), lobbying groups (for milk, rice, or tobacco producers), or social watchdog roles (the Women's Christian Temperance Union). Oth-ers are absorbed or co-opted by established institutions such as political parties, religious denominations, and labor unions. Many principles espoused by populists, progressives, and socialists such as banking regu-lations, voting rights and reforms, social security, and unemployment insurance have been adopted into the U.S. system with no recognition of the social movements that championed them for years. Occasionally, an institution will crush a social movement organization such as the Black Panther party, the Communist party or the Weathermen if the institution and a significant portion of the public comes to view it as a grave danger to society. Many movements merely fade away.

Social movements shrink and die for many reasons. Leaders and members may despair of ever changing anything or of achieving permanent and meaningful goals equal to the sacrifices made. They may become overwhelmed by the magnitude or multiplicity of the problems they must solve, or they may lose faith in society's capacity for reform. For others, the social movement becomes merely a job, or the new lifestyle becomes boring and meaningless as years pass. Leaders and followers experience fatigue because they cannot continue to endure the dangers, thrills, and privations movements demand. Violent actions by radical groups may frighten movement members, institutions, and the public into seeking normalcy.

During the termination stage, leaders and followers may become as disaffected with social movements as they once were with established institutions. They may opt for military rather than symbolic warfare and wage a civil war or revolution to achieve change. More likely, however, members and sympathizers drop back into the institutions from which they came.[52] Some leaders such as Eldridge Cleaver, a founder and officer of the Black Panther party, have conversion experiences and become born-again Christians, capitalists, or government bureaucrats. They may or may not continue to work for change. Sam Riddle, a former Michigan State University rebel, became an oil company lawyer and remarked, "I can do a lot more with a base of capital than with a pocketful of rhetoric. I'm no longer interested in standing on my soapbox and shouting into the wind. Now I'm more interested in producing the soapboxes."[53] Other movement disciples turn inward, toward "privatism," in an effort to protect or to change themselves or their inner circles of family and friends.[54]

Conclusions

Social movements are intricate and evolving social dramas; each stage is marked by changes in acts, scenes, agents, agencies, and purposes. Social movements evolve structures to perform persuasive functions—a continuous process in which every aspect of a system evolves from and into something else. Thus, each stage (genesis, social unrest, enthusiastic mobilization, maintenance, and termination) requires certain persuasive skills and personalities. Genesis, for instance, demands an intellectual or prophet who excels at defining and visualizing, at using words. Social unrest needs an agitator who can initiate organization, help formulate an ideology, and transform perceptions of the past, present, and future. Enthusiastic mobilization requires a charismatic agitator who confronts and polarizes, excites and insults, unites and fragments. Maintenance requires a pragmatic diplomat who is capable of healing, sustaining, administering, and bargaining. Termination needs a leader who can bring the movement to an end, transform it successfully into an institution, help it evolve into a pressure group, or enable its principles to become part of the institutional beliefs, attitudes, and values. Although we may not be able to determine when a social movement begins or ends until we have time to observe the flow of history, we can discover why and how it evolved.

Each stage poses unique dilemmas and requires persuasion to serve one or more functions. For example, transforming perceptions of reality dominates the genesis stage—a critical function and stage if the movement is to evolve into something other than individual expressions of concern and isolated events. Transforming perceptions of reality, enhancing the egos of protestors, and prescribing courses of action dominate the social unrest stage as the movement becomes publicly visible. Transforming perceptions of the other and self, legitimizing the movement, and mobilizing for action dominate the enthusiastic mobilization stage as the movement, institutions, and countermovements struggle to bring about or stifle change. Sustaining dominates the maintenance stage when the movement settles in for a long struggle and hopes for a new awakening.

For social movements that reach the final stage, termination, the results are usually disappointing and disillusioning. Early goals, even when partially reached, rarely bring about the perfection creators of the movement envisioned. Some members condemn society, institutions, and human beings as incapable of reform, unable to attain perfection. Others see the means (social movements, persuasion, coercive persuasion) as impotent tools for achieving meaningful and lasting change. Ultimately, all social movements come to an end or experience frustration, such as when hard-fought gains for gay rights or affirmative action are dismantled in whole or in part. But this does not mean that social movements have little effect or that their causes die with them. As Leland Griffin writes, "And if the wheel forever turns, it is man [woman] who does the turning—forever striving, in an 'imperfect world,' for a world of perfection. And hence man [woman], the rhetorical animal, is saved: for salvation lies in the striving, the struggle itself."[55]

The study of the typical life cycle of a social movement is important because it emphasizes the evolutionary nature of social movements and that they are more than the sum of their parts. While it is important to study parts—campaigns, leaders, events, functions, messages, or strategies, true understanding of a movement requires an eventual holistic study to allow us to see conflict as adaptive and evolutionary, influence as accommodative, and relationships as integrative.

Endnotes

[1] Leland M. Griffin, "A Dramatistic Theory of the Rhetoric of Movements," *Critical Responses to Kenneth Burke*, William Rueckert, ed. (Minneapolis: University of Minnesota Press, 1969): 456–478; Kenneth Burke, *A Grammar of Motives* (Englewood Cliffs, NJ: Prentice-Hall, 1950).

[2] William Bruce Cameron, *Modern Social Movements* (New York: Random House, 1966): 27–29.

3   Herbert W. Simons, Elizabeth W. Mechling, and Howard N. Schreier, "The Functions of Human Communication in Mobilizing for Action from the Bottom Up: The Rhetoric of Social Movements," *Handbook of Rhetorical and Communication Theory,* Carroll C. Arnold and John Waite Bowers, eds. (Boston: Allyn and Bacon, 1984): 804–809.

4   Donald G. Ellis and B. Aubrey Fisher, "Phases of Conflict in Small Group Development: A Markov Analysis," *Human Communication Research* 1 (Spring 1975): 195–212; Mark L. Knapp, *Interpersonal Communication and Human Relationships* (Boston: Allyn and Bacon, 1984): 32–54; Julia T. Wood, "Communication and Relational Culture: Bases for the Study of Human Relationships," *Communication Quarterly* 30 (Spring 1982): 75–84.

5   Richard E. Crable and Steven L. Vibbert, "Managing Issues and Influencing Public Policy," *Public Relations Review* 11(1985): 6–7.

6   Bruce E. Gronbeck, "The Rhetoric of Social-Institutional Change: Black Action at Michigan," *Explorations in Rhetorical Criticism,* Gerald Mohrmann, Charles Stewart, Donovan Ochs, eds. (University Park, PA: Pennsylvania State University Press, 1973): 98–101.

7   This life cycle is based on discussions by Carl A. Dawson and Warner E. Gettys, *An Introduction to Sociology* (New York: Ronald, 1935); John Wilson, *An Introduction to Social Movements* (New York: Basic Books, 1973); and Griffin (1969): 462–472.

8   For a theoretical discussion of the concept of "the people," see Michael C. McGee, "In Search of 'The People': A Rhetorical Alternative," *Quarterly Journal of Speech* 61 (October 1975): 235–249.

9   Griffin (1969), 457–462; Eric Hoffer, *The True Believer* (New York: Harper and Row, 1951): 120–121.

10 Lisa Gring-Pemble, "Writing Themselves into Consciousness: Creating a Rhetorical Bridge Between the Public and Private Spheres," *Quarterly Journal of Speech* 84 (February 1998): 42.

11 Gring-Pemble, 43–44.

12 James Johnson, Public Affairs Video Archives of the C-SPAN Networks, June 15, 1995. Referred to hereafter as Senate Hearings.

13 Hoffer, 20.

14 Lloyd F. Bitzer, "Functional Communication: A Situational Perspective," *Rhetoric in Transition: Studies in the Nature and Uses of Rhetoric,* Eugene E. White, ed. (University Park, PA: Pennsylvania State University, 1980): 23, 26–29, and 32.

15 David A. Snow and Robert D. Benford, "Master Frames and Cycles of Protest," *Frontiers in Social Movement Theory* (New Haven, CT: Yale University Press, 1992): 137.

16 Harold D. Mixon, "Boston's Artillery Election Sermons and the American Revolution," *Speech Monographs* 34 (March 1967): 43 and 50.

17 Richard B. Gregg, "The Ego-Function of the Rhetoric of Protest," *Philosophy and Rhetoric* 4 (Spring 1971): 79.

18 Leland M. Griffin, "The Rhetoric of Historical Movements," *Quarterly Journal of Speech* 38 (April 1952): 186.

19 Leslie G. Rude, "The Rhetoric of Farmer-Labor Agitators," *Central States Speech Journal* 20 (Winter 1969): 281.

20 J. Michael Hogan and Glen Williams. "Republican Charisma and the American Revolution: The Textual Persona of Thomas Paine's *Common Sense," Quarterly Journal of Speech* 86 (February 2000): 5–6.

21 "We Want Peace, Just Peace," *New York Times Magazine,* 19 December 1976, 29–31, 64–70, 76–78.

22 "Drum, Sweat and Tears," *Newsweek,* 24 June 1991, 46–51.

23 "Scholars Debunk the Marlboro Man: Examining Stereotypes of Masculinity," *The Chronicle of Higher Education,* 3 February 1993, A6B.

24 "Scholars Debunk the Marlboro Man," A8.

25 Snow and Benford, 143–144.

26 *What Is the MORAL MAJORITY?* (Washington, DC: Moral Majority Incorporated, n.d.): n.p.

27 James Miller, *Democracy in the Streets: From Port Huron to the Siege of Chicago* (New York: Simon & Schuster, 1987): 102–125.

[28] S. Judson Crandell, "The Beginnings of a Methodology for Social Control Studies," *Quarterly Journal of Speech* 33 (February 1947): 37; Griffin (1969), 462–463.

[29] Senate Hearings.

[30] Miller, 329.

[31] Miller, 330.

[32] Snow and Benford, 141.

[33] *What Is the MORAL MAJORITY?*

[34] John W. Bowers, Donovan J. Ochs, and Richard J. Jensen, *The Rhetoric of Agitation and Control*, 2/E (Prospect Heights, IL: Waveland Press, 1993): 20.

[35] *The Wall Street Journal*, 9 April 1986, 32.

[36] James Darsey, "From 'Gay Is Good' to the Scourge of AIDS: The Evolution of Gay Liberation Rhetoric, 1977–1990," *Communication Studies* 42 (Spring 1991): 43–66. Darsey argues that "catalytic events" are essential for moving social movements from stage to stage.

[37] Bitzer, 18.

[38] Wilson, 89–90.

[39] "The Fur Flies: The Cold War Over Animal Rights," *New York*, 15 January 1990, 27–33.

[40] Senate Hearings.

[41] Sherry R. Shepler and Anne F. Mattina, "'The Revolt Against War': Jane Addams' Rhetorical Challenge to the Patriarchy," *Communication Quarterly* 47 (Spring 1999): 155.

[42] Wilson, 109–110.

[43] Charles J. Stewart, "The Evolution of a Revolution: Stokely Carmichael and the Rhetoric of Black Power," *Quarterly Journal of Speech* 83 (November 1997): 430.

[44] Stewart, 440.

[45] Wilson, 360.

[46] Bitzer, 35.

[47] Herbert W. Simons, "Requirements, Problems, and Strategies: A Theory of Persuasion for Social Movements," *Quarterly Journal of Speech* 56 (February 1970): 10–11.

[48] Press release, "NEWS from CONGRESSWOMAN JULIA CARSON," June 15, 1999.

[49] James Darsey, "From 'Gay Is Good' to the Scourge of AIDS: The Evolution of Gay Liberation Rhetoric, 1977–1990," *Communication Studies* 42 (Spring 1991): 55.

[50] Thomas James Norton, *The Constitution of the United States: Its Sources and Its Application* (New York: America's Future, 1949): 232.

[51] Elizabeth Jean Nelson, "'Nothing Ever Goes Well Enough': Mussolini and the Rhetoric of Perpetual Struggle," *Communication Studies* 42 (Spring 1991): 22–42.

[52] Peter Goldman and Gerald Lubenow, "Where the Flowers Have Gone," *Newsweek*, 5 September 1977, 24–30; Margie Casady, "Where Have the Radicals Gone," *Psychology Today*, October, 1975, 63–64, 92; "Yesterday's Activists: Still Marching to a Different Drummer?" *Notre Dame Magazine*, October, 1975, 10–21.

[53] "Yesterday's Radicals Put on Gray Flannel," *U.S. News and World Report*, 19 January 1981, 41.

[54] Jerry LaBlanc, "Unplug the World, We Want to Get off," Indianapolis *Star Magazine*, 28 July 1974, 7–8.

[55] Griffin (1969), 472.

7

IDENTIFICATION AND POLARIZATION IN SOCIAL MOVEMENTS

As noted in previous chapters, social movements are complex, dynamic, evolving, and synergistic entities with persuasive communication as their lifeblood. On the one hand, each social movement operates in a moral arena while striving for perfection, a striving that necessarily creates a dialectical tension with institutions that results in confrontation.[1] Theorists agree that such confrontation is essential for establishing relationships and attaining the legitimacy necessary to challenge institutions.[2] It establishes a "we" and "they" relationship. On the other hand, the social movement must operate as an interpretive community that conceives of itself as a "people" operating in an environment of demands and relational patterns. Establishing a people is essential for uniting individuals and groups into a cohesive force to bring about or stifle change and to attain the legitimacy necessary to attract followers and legitimizers. Conceiving themselves to be a people transforms the "you and I" into an "us."

This chapter focuses on how social movements strive to accomplish the apparently paradoxical ends of creating "we and they" and "us" relationships simultaneously. In doing so, it addresses the question at the heart of the social systems approach developed in chapter 2: "Which individuals, conceiving themselves to be what 'people' in what environment, use what relational patterns and what adaptive strategies with what evolutionary results?"

Symbolic Interaction

As the human vehicle for action and change, language involves individual selection, choice, and judgment. Rachel Holloway writes that language is symbolic action that reflects, selects, and deflects reality. "The

151

words people choose to express their perceptions betray and display their particular worldviews. They state what for them is reality and act on the basis of that reality."[3] Jacqueline Bacon has studied the trope of signifying, "a uniquely African-American rhetorical form that draws on the ambiguity and indeterminacy of language" and enables the oppressed to "gain rhetorical power by appropriating the discourse of the oppressor."[4]

In whatever reality humans select and reflect to create or modify relationships they have a basic need to identify with others in similar circumstances. Language creates this sense of interpersonal identification. Robert Cathcart, for example, contends that "movements are carried forward through language, both verbal and nonverbal, in strategic ways that bring about identification of the individual with the movement."[5]

Holloway and Cathcart base their notions of the role of language on Kenneth Burke's philosophy of human communication, which is particularly applicable to the study of social movements. According to Burke, "the use of language is a symbolic means of inducing cooperation in beings that by nature respond to symbols."[6] For Burke, society is a process of symbolic interaction because social life is a product of establishing and re-establishing mutual relations with others. Because the human condition is one of imperfect communication, we solve our problems in society through "recalcitrant and mystifying" symbols.[7] It is not surprising, then, that symbols cause a great many intentional and unintentional problems among people. "But, however remote and strange the mystery of another may become," Burke writes, "there must be some way of transcending this separateness if social order is to be achieved."[8] Social movements strive eventually to transcend separateness, but while the struggle lasts, they must employ the rhetorical strategies of identification and polarization to create seemingly contradictory "us" and "we and they" relationships. Let us turn first to a rhetoric of identification.

A Rhetoric of Identification

Division or separateness permeates our society and the social movements that would change or sustain the status quo, but communication can help societal elements articulate differences and relate to one another. Through communication we may "transcend" to higher plains of meaning that enable us to overcome differences. In communicating with one another, we seek similarity or common references, what Burke calls "identification."[9] All people are different, but we have common factors in which we are "consubstantially" or substantially the same—not identical but sharing important aspects of nature and substance.[10] The process of identification reduces ambiguity and, hopefully, encourages cooperation.

There is a very close relationship between *identification* and *persuasion*. Burke claims, for instance, that "You persuade a man [woman] only insofar as you can talk his [her] language by speech, gesture, tonality, order, image, attitude, idea, *identifying* your ways with his [hers]."[11] He notes that "we might well keep in mind that a speaker persuades an audience by the use of stylistic identifications; his [her] act of persuasion may be for the purpose of causing the audience to identify itself with the speaker's interests; and the speaker draws on identification of interests to establish rapport between himself [herself] and his [her] audience."[12]

Identification, however, is more than merely relating to others; it is an instrument of transformation. At some level, reality, an event, or a group makes sense (is rational) even though one person's rationalization is a second person's factuality. Our responses and conclusions are the results of the process of transformation that originates from our awareness of division. In the *Rhetoric of Motives*, Burke argues that "the statement of the thing's nature before and after the change is an *identifying* of it."[13]

While persuaders may strive for a substantial sameness or similarity with audiences, division is ever present. For instance, Gregory Stephens writes about how Frederick Douglass' "multiracial abolitionism" infuriated the white Garrisonian and black nationalist elements of the antislavery movement. Douglas attempted to stake out the middle ground and work with other elements through a rhetoric of "antagonistic cooperation" and "redeemable ideals."[14] Like Douglass, we seek to balance our needs for "personal coherence" and "social coordination." The need for personal coherence underscores division from those who are different; the need for social coordination underscores identification, as those with whom we identify index realities for us.

Burke writes that "one need not scrutinize the concept of *identification* very sharply to see, implied in it at every turn, the ironic counterpart: division."[15] "Identification is affirmed with earnestness precisely because there is division," Burke writes. "Identification is compensatory to division. If men were not apart from one another, there would be no need for the rhetorician to proclaim their unity."[16] In response to such division, which is constant and certain, we seek transformation resulting in identification—a level of understanding if not harmony. Transformation occurs at various levels from the most obvious to the most subtle. Thus, when you "put identification and division ambiguously together, so that you cannot know for certain just where one ends and the other begins, you have the characteristic invitation to rhetoric."[17]

Common Ground

There are many levels of identification, with the most obvious being a persuader's attempt to establish common ground with an audience. Simple common ground may result from groups identifying according to gender, age, race, ethnic background, or sexual orientation. Women identify with other women, Chicanos with Chicanos, African Americans with

African Americans, gays and lesbians with gays and lesbians, and senior citizens with senior citizens. Protestors may feel common ground because of their work, educational, religious, or social status. This happens, for instance, when a United Farm Worker organizer proclaims a farm worker and Mexican background, attends Roman Catholic services, and advocates programs that will benefit farm workers. Coal miners, college students, religious fundamentalists, welfare recipients, and so-called rednecks have organized to bring about or resist change because of perceived similarities. The early labor movement united around specific trades such as machinists, ironworkers, cigar makers, and masons and also around trades within trades such as locomotive engineers, firemen, brakemen, and conductors. Ironically, these rather superficial similarities may be all that participants have in common.

Nearly all movement persuaders use the notion of "a people" to unify and identify otherwise disparate groups. They claim to speak in the name of the people, for the will of the people, and in the "soul and spirit" of the people.[18] Movements portray themselves as majority movements, great people's or citizen's movements, and the largest of grass roots movements. The movement and the people become one. Richard Nixon's conjuring up the "great silent majority" was a clever and effective way of countering those who claimed to speak for "the people." Thus, the "people" share common interests, needs, values, and wisdom—common ground.

Protestors, then, seek common ground through associations with groups and beliefs; physical, gender, racial, or ethnic similarities; a shared notion of people; and work, religious, or social status. But for Burke, identification is a more encompassing notion than the simple expressions of common ground. Through interaction and identification, we can become involved in many groups, causes, or movements; formulate or change allegiances; and vicariously share in the role of leader or spokesperson. There are many ways social movements may enhance or create a sense of identification with audiences.

The Implied "We"

The implied "we" is a subtle means of establishing a feeling of commonality or common ground. Persuaders use plural pronouns to imply identification and a common purpose and struggle. The following example taken from the White Aryan Resistance (W.A.R) Web site (www.resist.com) illustrates the use of the implied we to establish common ground (emphasis added): "W.A.R. and Tom Metzger were probably the first to coin *our* ideological struggle, as White Separatism. Even though *our* economic determinist enemies continue to simplistically label *us* as White Supremacists, *our* message is slowly getting through."[19] In an address to The Rockford Pro-Life Breakfast for Clergy and Lay Leaders entitled "Twenty-Five Years Into the Culture of Death," Allan Carlson included these statements in his closing remarks: "We are beginning to win the contest for family renewal," "I believe that the Holy Spirit is moving in our time toward some great end," "If we but open our eyes and ears, there are portents or signs all about us that a new Great Awakening is at work in this land," and "As always, our task now as Christians is to open our hearts to God."[20]

A barrage of simple plural pronouns such as we, our, and us in place of leader-centered and individualistic pronouns such as I, me, and mine invites a feeling of common ground—a common bond. Audiences sense active involvement *together* in a great moral struggle. Plural pronouns imply that change is coming from the bottom up, from all those who believe, rather than from the top down. It is not a struggle orchestrated by leaders and a small elite while others play the roles of bystanders. Instead, it is a united effort of like-minded activists. Plural pronouns may create a sense of identification with a cause and a feeling of "usness" when less subtle and more elaborate rhetorical means fail.

Groups and Group Actions

When people become involved with groups or participate in group actions, they may become more tolerant, if not sympathetic, to the views of other persuaders or groups. Students on college campuses are becoming aware that women and children in third world countries making starvation wages make many of the university logo embossed garments sold on campus. As they take part in university-formed committees and student-led protests demanding action by administrations, they not only become more aware of the problem but become more committed to the cause. As they become more committed to the cause, they become committed to and identified with specific organizations created to further it. They may identify with local organizations such as Purdue Students Against Sweatshops and national organizations such as the Workers Rights Consortium (WRC).[21] When students at Purdue University began a hunger strike in the spring of 2000 to pressure the administration into joining the WRC, sympathetic student members from other campuses such as the University of Michigan, Indiana University, Western Michigan University, and Miami University traveled to Purdue to lend their support to the strike.[22] Similarly, animal rights activists belong to local, national, and international organizations, express intense pride in being members of PETA, Trans-Species Unlimited, or Friends of Animals, and come to the aid of those leading protests in many areas of the country.

Individuals who are usually separated by loyalties to competing groups or organizations may unite around a cause. The athletic rivalry between Indiana University and Purdue University is legendary, but students from both campuses united in the winter of 2000 to stage protests against the selling of furs at Lazarus department stores. Matt Stamps, president of Indiana University's Speak Out for Animals organization, stated to reporters that "There is no room for any kind of rivalry" between Indiana and Purdue on animal rights.[23] In the 1880s, several trade unions united under the banner of the American Federation of Labor to present a united front in their individual struggles for better wages and working conditions. It was not until 1955, however, that the organization for unskilled factory workers (the Congress of Industrial Organizations) and the American Federation of Labor merged into the AFL-CIO, a single organization with which most union members could identify.

Appearance

Social movement members and sympathizers may share significant aspects of appearance. United Farm Worker organizers tend to dress like farm workers while those of far right religious and political organizations such as the Christian Coalition and the John Birch society are likely to dress in suits and ties. In footage of civil rights protests of the 1960s, members of SNCC stood out not only because they were younger but because they often wore denim to identify with the working class black American.

Dorothy Mansfield studied the 1960s ministry of the Reverend Arthur Blessitt to the so-called hippies. In appearance "his hair was trimmed well below his ears; his vestments were a brightly printed, full-sleeved shirt, leather vest, bell-bottom hip-hugger trousers, and boots."[24] Hippies themselves, while decrying societal pressures to impose stultifying conformity on one and all, adhered to an identifying code of dress and appearance that included granny glasses, long hair, beards, old clothing, bandannas, and sandals. The group most noted for its opposition to the hippies and support of the war in Vietnam, construction workers, were clearly identifiable with their crew cut hair style, clean shaven faces, work clothes, and hard hats.

Language

Persuaders and movements may achieve identification by adapting language to audiences. Two of Stokely Carmichael's (the young leader of SNCC) mid-1960s speeches on "Black Power" illustrate this method of identification.[25] Carmichael gave one speech to a predominantly black audience in Detroit on July 30, 1966 and a second to a predominantly white, university audience in Whitewater, Wisconsin on February 6, 1967. The addresses were surprisingly similar in content and examples, but they differed greatly in style and persuasive appeals. For the black audience, Carmichael personified the ideology he was advancing—in delivery, style, and attitude, while for the white audience, he dwelt mainly on an explanation of ideology and sounded very scholarly for his academic audience. For the black audience, he interpreted the notion of black power in terms of pride, self-identity, and political mobilization, while for the white audience he interpreted the slogan in terms of mainstream

American ideals, using such phrases as "social and political integration" and "pluralistic society." He advocated violent resistance in the Detroit speech, but in the Whitewater speech he used milder references to violence and addressed them in a context of self-defense. The Detroit address contained more slang than the Whitewater address. Carmichael's delivery of his language to the black audience was "cool and very hip," while his delivery to the white audience was that of an intellectual or "politically enlightened leader." Clearly, Carmichael *identified* with each audience by carefully selecting and presenting language to match each.

Content Adaptation

Protestors may identify with audiences through content adaptation. For example, they may use examples that listeners and readers easily understand to emphasize similarity between persuader and audience. Frederick Douglass, a free slave speaking before a white audience commemorating the Fourth of July in 1852, illustrated the similarity between "slaves" and "masters" in terms of abilities, jobs, and domestic roles:

> Is it not astonishing that, while we are plowing, planting, and reaping, using all kinds of mechanical tools, erecting houses, constructing bridges, building ships, working in metals of brass, iron, copper, silver, and gold; that, while we are reading, writing, and ciphering, acting as clerks, merchants, and secretaries, having among us lawyers, doctors, ministers, poets, authors, editors, orators, and teachers; that while we are engaged in all manner of enterprises common to other men, digging gold in California, capturing the whale in the Pacific, feeding sheep and cattle on the hillside, living, moving, acting, thinking, planning, living in families as husbands, wives, and children, and above all, confessing and worshipping the Christian's God, and looking hopefully for life and immortality beyond the grave, we are called upon to prove that we are men![26]

Martin Luther King, Jr. was equally adept at selecting audience-appropriate examples and illustrations. While most Americans are familiar with the closing portion of his "I Have a Dream" speech delivered from the steps of the Lincoln Memorial in 1963, a segment that the media repeat over and over on the national holiday in his honor, few are aware of the simple but effective banking metaphor he used early in this speech. All but the youngest members of his audience could relate to this metaphor. King proclaimed:

> When the architects of our great Republic wrote the magnificent words of the Constitution and the Declaration of Independence, they were signing a promissory note to which every American was to fall heir. This note was a promise that all men—yes, black men as well as white men—would be guaranteed the unalienable rights of life, liberty, and the pursuit of happiness.

> It is obvious today that America has defaulted on this promissory note insofar as her citizens of color are concerned. Instead of honoring this sacred obligation, America has given the Negro people a bad check, a check which has come back marked "insufficient funds." But we refuse to believe that the bank of justice is bankrupt. We refuse to believe that there are insufficient funds in the great vaults of opportunity of this nation. So we've come to cash this check—a check that will give us on demand the riches of freedom and the security of justice.[27]

King's audience could easily identify with this metaphor; it placed the famous leader and orator on the same level as his listeners. They were both anxious to deposit a long overdue check.

Richard Jensen and John Hammerback have analyzed how civil rights leader Robert Parris Moses organized a full-time staff and volunteers in Mississippi in the 1960s to achieve equal rights and reverse the emigration of African Americans from that state. Moses emphasized that persuaders and organizers must first become immersed in the local communities so they could stress local issues, then teach and listen skillfully to build close relationships with audiences. The goal was "to achieve identification with immediate audiences" by appearing to be one of them, not above them as were traditional preachers.[28]

Values, Beliefs, and Attitudes

Persuaders reflect the audience's values, beliefs, and attitudes by identifying with the moral symbols and revered documents of society rather than attacking or disparaging them. Bert Klandermans argues that "attempts to persuade will be more or less successful depending on the degree to which movements can anchor their views with existing beliefs or identities."[29] The "Women's Declaration of Independence" adopted at the Seneca Falls convention in 1848 was modeled closely after the Declaration of Independence with such modifications as "We hold these truths to be self-evident, that all men *and women* are created equal." The National Labor Union used the same identification strategy when it adopted its "Platform of Principles" in 1868: "We hold these truths to be self-evident, that all *people* are created equal." Movements for and against slavery, women's rights, and temperance have employed the Bible as their central source of ideological beliefs and evidence.

Sacred emblems are prominent in movements striving to espouse and sustain traditional values, beliefs, and attitudes. American, Confederate, and Aztec Flags, Christian crosses and crucifixes, Jewish Stars of David, and Nazi swastikas are worn on clothing, portrayed on banners, and carried in demonstrations. The United Farm Workers carry red flags emblazoned with the black Aztec eagle to identify the movement with a rich historical heritage and system of beliefs shared by farm workers and other immigrants of Mexican descent.

Social movements also identify with the values, beliefs, and attitudes of audiences by identifying with heroes and founders. For example, at a gathering of modern women's rights leaders in the 1960s, a large portrait of an earlier generation of women's rights leaders—Susan B. Anthony, Lucretia Mott, Elizabeth Cady Stanton, Lucy Stone, and Anna Howard Shaw—hung in front of each leader seated on a platform. The leaders and members of the contemporary women's liberation movement wanted to show they were the heirs of the societal norms, values, beliefs, traditions, and struggles of the founders of the women's rights struggle begun more than a century before. Images of Martin Luther King, Jr., are ever present at celebrations on the national holiday in his honor and meetings of organizations striving to achieve the rights and changes for which he struggled and died. Both social movements and institutions lay claim to the nation's Founding Fathers in such conflicts as abortion, gun control, prayer in the schools, equal rights, and the environment.

Visual Symbols

Many movements achieve identification through the use of visual symbols. It is not unusual for leaders, members, sympathizers, and legitimizers to display a movement's symbol on placards, buttons, lapel pins, articles of clothing, and armbands to identify with one another and the cause. The symbol for women, gray panther, black panther, red rose (pro-life), and rusty clothes hanger (pro-choice) have become prominent in contemporary movements. In recent years, those wishing to indicate their concern for the AIDS epidemic (including some members of Congress) have worn red ribbons, a symbolic gesture that also communicates sympathy and perhaps agreement with the gay rights movement.

Protest groups may create and employ symbolic gestures that communicate similarity of feelings, experiences, or attitudes. The peace movement of the 1960s and 1970s used the V sign formed by the index and forefinger to signify unity and commitment in their opposition to the war in Vietnam. The militant phase of the civil rights movement in the 1960s introduced the clenched fist sign to signify unity and power. Other movements—women's rights, antiwar, student rights, Native-American rights—quickly adopted this sign for similar purposes.

Naming Names

A persuader may create identification by referring to individuals unrelated to the movement but whom the audience honors and respects. The announcer for the Christian Crusade radio broadcasts of the Reverend Billy James Hargis always introduced him with these words: "Now speaking for Christ and against Communism—Dr. Billy James Hargis."[30] The Nation of Islam leader Louis Farrakhan addressed his controversial status in a speech in Los Angeles by associating himself with Jesus Christ and Moses:

Farrakhan has become a very controversial figure. But to be controversial is not a bad thing. In fact, because of the controversy swirling
around Louis Farrakhan, I want the black leadership to know and the
black people to know I feel very privileged to be so controversial
because I'm walking in good shoes. Jesus appeared in the Roman
empire and his message was controversial. Moses appeared in Egypt
and his message was controversial. Whenever a man speaks against
the popular version of the truth, then he is considered controversial.
That I am.[31]

Other persuaders refer to organizations that the audience approves,
honors, or respects. For example, Vice President Hubert Humphrey, a
well-known advocate of black rights, used the naming tactic several times
in an address before the annual convention of the National Association
for the Advancement of Colored People on July 6, 1966. He declared:

I am proud to be back among my friends of the NAACP who have led
this march for 57 years . . . the road to freedom is stained with tears
and the blood of many Americans—including men such as Medgar
Evers—men already counted among authentic American heroes. . . .
And through the years the NAACP has played a role second to none
in terms of dedication and determination of sacrifice and courage.[32]

Movements attempt to link themselves with other social movements
active at the time that have already gained a degree of respect. Thus, the
civil rights movement helped to legitimize the Native-American,
women's liberation, and gay rights movements in the United States, the
Free Quebecois movement in French-speaking Canada, and the Roman
Catholic civil rights movement in Northern Ireland.

At the heart of the notion of identification, then, is the belief that symbols unite people. Language, as symbols, consists of vocabulary, rules,
and enactment or presentation. It reveals the persuader's attitude about
an issue or group, and the persuader can induce cooperation, or at least
insure a fair hearing under most circumstances, by demonstrating similarities with the audience. Sometimes persuaders, such as Stokely Carmichael's black power rhetoric and use of obscenity in the counterculture
and anti–Vietnam War movements of the 1960s and 1970s, identify and
unite by violating the rules of language.

But there is competition. To *unite* with one group, cause, or movement is to *separate* from some other group, cause, or social movement. As
Burke claims, if there were no divisions, there would be no need for rhetoric. Perfect identification would require no further communication.
Burke relates that, "Since identification implies division, we found rhetoric involving us in matters of socialization and faction."[33] And since identification and unity inevitably result in separation and division, social
movements must also employ a rhetoric of polarization.

A Rhetoric of Polarization

Andrew King and Floyd Anderson define polarization as "the process by which an extremely diversified public is coalesced into two or more highly contrasting, mutually exclusive groups sharing a high degree of internal solidarity in those beliefs which the persuader considers salient."[34] Social movements utilize a rhetoric of polarization to transform relationships by creating clear distinctions between the evil other and the virtuous self, a we-they dichotomy. Richard Lanigan, for example, notes that "polarization creates a lived perspective of reality based on values divisions that characterize one individual as 'good, right, lawful, rational, and the like,' while his neighbor becomes 'evil, wrong, unlawful, irrational, and so on.'"[35]

King and Anderson claim that persuaders create polarization—Lanigan's lived perspective of reality—through two primary strategies: affirmation and subversion: "A strategy of affirmation is concerned with a judicious selection of those images that will promote a strong sense of group identity. A strategy of subversion is concerned with a careful selection of those images that will undermine the *ethos* of competing groups, ideologies, or institutions."[36] These strategies contrast "us" with "them." The first represents the highest of values in a moral struggle; the second opposes all that is worthy of respect, admiration, and following. John Bowers, Donovan Ochs, and Richard Jensen identify "the exploitation of *flag issues* and *flag individuals* as the two major tactics protestors use to polarize. "These are issues and individuals," they write, "who for one reason or another, are especially susceptible to the charges made against the establishment by the agitator's ideology. Attacking such individuals also helps the agitating group receive media attention."[37] Persuaders employing these tactics seek issues institutions cannot defend easily to broader publics—sweatshops, inhumane treatment of animals in research, late-term abortions, cancer-causing pesticides—and individuals publics find it easy to dislike or suspect of wrongdoing—police and other enforcement officers, college administrators, bureaucrats, politicians, the wealthy, bankers.

A rhetoric of polarization, then, is meant to divide in order to unite those who support a cause and to force commitment from those attempting to remain uncommitted. Lanigan claims that "The ideological presumption is that a confrontation of power blocs will force the uncommitted middle to rally to the 'just' side—theirs!"[38] The polar opposite for social movements includes all individuals and groups who do not openly support the social movement and thus are responsible directly through actions or indirectly through indifference or fear for allowing an intolerable situation to come into existence and to worsen day by day. Persuaders hold firmly to the adage that "if you are not with us, you are against us." There is no middle ground, no neutrals, in the struggle between good and evil. *We* include all the righteous, moral, self-sacrificing individuals and groups—the true believers—who are willing to stand up and say NO! to evil conditions, forces, and trends. *They* include institutions, the so-called silent majority, the mass media, countermovements, competing social movements, competing organizations within social movements, and those for whom the movement is fighting even though they have yet to join or support the movement. Klandermans writes that "when two movements are pitted against each other. Reality will provide plenty of temptations to see the opposition as evil incarnate."[39]

Identifying Devils

Burke claims "Men [women] who can unite on nothing else can unite on the basis of a common foe shared by all."[40] He presents the ancient notion of a scapegoat, "the 'representative' or 'vessel' of certain unwanted evils, the sacrificial animal upon whose back the burden of these evils is ritualistically loaded."[41] The scapegoat, he writes, "is the 'essence' of evil."[42] And so it is with social movements that inevitably identify one or more *devils* or scapegoats.

A devil may be as ambiguous as "They"—the opposite of the implied "we." For example, when Louis Farrakhan began addressing a large audience at the Los Angeles Forum in 1985, the audience shouted they could not hear him. He shouted back, "You cannot hear me?" and remained silent while his aides adjusted the microphone closer to his face. Then Farrakhan proclaimed, "I'm not surprised that they don't want you to hear what I have to say."[43] "They" or "them" may refer to different mysterious and somewhat ambiguous people or groups at different times. Richard Raum and James Measell, in their research on how Alabama's Governor George Wallace expressed his opposition to all "liberal" movements such as the civil rights movement in his third-party campaign for the Presidency, explain how he used the vague "they" in polarizing society:

> In Wallace's speeches, "they" remain nebulous and ill-defined. "They" seem to be different people at different times. "They" may be judges, legislators, bureaucrats, professors, students, national party leaders, or anarchists, but one thing is clear: "They" are "anybody who is not 'us.'" Thus, the we/they distinction both underscores the in-group *vs.* out-group dichotomy and promotes in-group solidarity as the auditors respond favorably to the distinction.[44]

A movement's devils may be more specific than "they" but as ill-defined as the rich, capitalists, bankers, foreigners, men, polluters, animal trappers and hunters, secular humanists, and internationalists. At times devils are as specific as individuals such as Henry Ford during the labor struggles of the 1920s and 1930s, President Johnson during the Vietnam War, Martin Luther King, Jr. for the anti–civil rights forces during the 1950s and 1960s, and Ralph Nader for anticonsumerism movements. The devils may be *things* such as demon rum, nuclear power plants, cruise missiles, commercial developments, acid rain, pesticides, leghold traps, and guns.

The ideal devil according to Eric Hoffer is one, omnipotent, omnipresent foreigner.[45] A *single* devil provides a clear rhetorical target for the social movement. An *omnipotent*, all-powerful devil requires a mass movement, self-defense, noninstitutional tactics, and total commitment. Individuals acting independently are powerless to bring about or resist change in confrontations with such potent and vigorous evil forces. An *omnipresent* devil is everywhere, involved in all that is evil, and thus requires constant vigilance and confrontation. And a *foreign* devil is unlike us in all matters of importance: anti-American, anti-Christian, anti-God, anti-free enterprise, antifamily, anti-freedom.

The notion of an omnipotent, omnipresent, foreign devil creates identification among movement members through antithesis by contrasting them with forces totally alien and without redeeming social value. For example, the "Manifesto for New York Radical Feminists" identified men as the devil:

> As radical feminists we recognize that we are engaged in a power struggle with men, and that the agent for our oppression is man insofar as he identifies with and carries out the supremacy privileges of the male role. For while we realize that the liberation of women will ultimately mean the liberation of men from their destructive role as oppressor, we have no illusion that men will welcome this liberation without a struggle.[46]

For the Radical Feminists, the world had two forces, men and women, in the struggle for liberation. Men were single, omnipotent, omnipresent, and foreign to everything that was feminine.

Identifying Conspiracies

Some social movements may perceive two or more of their devils to be plotting—conspiring—in secret to do something evil, sinister, or unlawful against them. The conspiracy is a kind of super devil because it combines evil forces into a single cause. For example, H. Rapp Brown and other black leaders of the 1960s condemned a white, genocidal conspiracy. Christian, evangelical groups in the 1990s spoke of the efforts of a secular humanist conspiracy to destroy the Christian foundations of the United States laid so carefully by the Founding Fathers. And militias warn of a conspiracy led by big government and big corporations to deprive Americans of their basic liberties set forth in the Constitution.

Whether a conspiracy is real or imagined, the rhetorical process is the same. A person or group notices a problem that is threatening and frightening, selects an enemy (men, government, internationalists, the Catholic Church, socialists) for attributing guilt, identifies the enemy and its action as secretive, draws links between the selected enemy and the problem, and makes the charge public. It is clearly *us* against *them*. The difference between a "real conspiracy" and "paranoia" is that the first provides audiences with a convincing argument, and the second does not.

Conspiracy can be powerful rhetoric for social movements because it appeals to Americans who have always been fearful of "foreign" plots to undermine our God-given, Constitutional rights and way of life. Our own government is somehow a foreign evil that cannot be trusted.[47] A letter from Patricia Ireland, President of the National Organization for Women, during the George Bush administration in the early 1990s lays out the conspiracy determined to end legal abortion in the United States:

> Just as surely as millions of women were denied the right to safe, legal abortion before *Roe v. Wade*, the antiabortion fanatics—aided and abetted by George Bush and his politicized Supreme Court—are today again denying that fundamental right to literally hundreds of thousands of women across this nation. Even though the Court claims that *Roe* still guarantees women their right to abortion.
>
> Ever since *Roe* was decided in 1973, right-wing extremists have vowed to overturn it. And from Ronald Reagan to George Bush, the antiabortion movement has controlled the political agenda. They also swore to prevent women from choosing abortion. And, unless we act now, they are likely to succeed beyond their wildest dreams.[48]

The conspiracy appeal is captivating rhetoric for some because it resembles a melodrama with an intriguing plot, a struggle between heroes and villains, good clashing with evil, and an unknown outcome that is precarious at best. It is an effective polarizing argument. On the one hand is a demonic, dangerous, and brutal plot by those with evil intentions, and on the other hand is a moral, fearless, and undeterable crusade by heroes with noble goals. Conspiracy argument is discussed at length in chapter 13.

Persuaders employ a variety of verbal and nonverbal tactics to polarize social movements from their oppositions—their devils. We will focus briefly on three: obscenity, ridicule, and vilification.

Obscenity

Obscenity is not a rhetorical staple of many social movements, but this is one of its strengths for protestors who choose to use it. Dan Rothwell claims that:

> The principle effect of verbal obscenity is polarization, which emanates from the social disapproval of this type of language. . . . The results of this polarization are sometimes profound and diverse. Few people are capable of remaining apathetic to the use of verbal obscenity by anyone, much less agitators. Consequently, the agitator wins at least a superficial, if not a consequential victory by forcing the majority into separate and opposing camps preparing for battle. . . . It is important that the agitator know his [her] allies and his [her] foes.[49]

Agitators of the 1960s and 1970s employed obscenity to set themselves apart from institutions, those over thirty years of age, and even those within the movement seen as too moderate or close to institutions and authority figures.

In most instances, institutions and countermovements cannot use similar or different obscenity in response to movement rhetoric because such words and gestures would separate them from their supporters and violate the customs, norms, and values they are attempting to sustain. Peter Farb maintains that the common denominator of all slang, whether obscenity, adolescent speech, or the jive talk of musicians, "is that it tests who belongs to the group and who is an intruder."[50] If this is so, then obscenity accomplishes what Lanigan calls "isolational polarization." This phenomenon, he writes, "is best viewed from two perspectives: (1) the isolation of the in-group versus the isolation of the out-group; and (2) the isolation of an elite leadership within the in-group by virtue of the external conflict existent between the in-group and the out-group."[51] For instance, when more radical, militant groups within the black rights, anti–Vietnam, and counterculture movements introduced the f-word into public discourse in the 1960s, they isolated themselves not only from institutions but from less militant elements within the movements themselves. Black Panthers, yippies, and the Weathermen saw themselves as elites within their respective movements.

Chapter 8 addresses at length how agitators employ obscenity to serve a variety of persuasive functions for social movements, the limits of obscenity as a rhetorical strategy, and the potential negative results of using obscenity.

Ridicule

Movement persuaders heap abuse upon their devils through ridicule, negative associations, and metaphors that may dehumanize them into pigs, rats, vermin, parasites, vultures, scum, and feces. Thus, ridicule is an effective means of polarizing the social movement and its opposition. For example, the Society for Cutting Up Men (SCUM) Manifesto identified the male as the polar opposite of the female. Unlike the female, the male is:

> a biological accident: the Y (male) gene is an incomplete X (female) gene, that is, has an incomplete set of chromosomes. In other words, the male is an incomplete female, a walking abortion, aborted at the gene state. . . . Being an incomplete female, the male spends his life attempting to complete himself, to become female. He attempts to do this by constantly seeking out, fraternizing with and trying to live through and fuse with the female, and claiming as his own all female characteristics.[52]

In short, ridicule can depict an ideal devil for the movement or countermovement to confront, for it is the epitome of evil that creates a need for urgent action and long-term commitment to the cause. The nature and persuasive functions of ridicule are discussed at length in chapter 8.

Vilification

Virtually all social movements attempt to polarize struggles through vilification or name-calling. Marsha Vanderford claims that vilification "formulates a specific adversarial force" by providing a "clear target for movement action." Vilification casts this target "in an exclusively negative light," "attributes diabolical motives to foes," and "magnifies the opponent's powers."[53]

Particularly intense rhetoric is directed at persons for whom the movement is fighting and who remain on the sidelines in the struggle. Bowers, Ochs, and Jensen write "those who sympathize with the activists but do not act with them are worse than useless. Action is the criterion for membership in an agitating group. Inactive members are counted as siding with the establishment."[54] A union song popular in the coalfields of the 1930s illustrates both the pressure to join the cause and the invective heaped on those who would not:

> Come all of you good workers, news to you I'll tell
> Of how the good old union has come in here to dwell.
> *Refrain* (repeated four times) Which Side are you on?
> They say in Harlan County, there are no neutrals there.
> You'll either be a union man, or a thug for J. H. Blair.
> *Refrain* (repeated four times) Which side are you on?
> Oh, workers, can you stand it? Oh, tell me how you can.
> Will you be a lousy scab, or will you be a man?[55]

Many contemporary movements have used similar epithets to stigmatize those who would not join the cause that was fighting for them. The black rights movement used Uncle Tom and handkerchief head for "Negroes" who had sold out to the white establishment; they were "oreos," black on the outside and white on the inside. Native-American activists called "Indians" Uncle Tomahawk and "apples," red on the outside and white on the inside. Similarly, Chicanos label institutional sympathizers Tio Tacos (Uncle Tacos) and Asian Americans have their "bananas."[56] While the SCUM Manifesto ridiculed men and dismissed them as irrelevant, it attacked other women as the real enemy:

> The conflict, therefore, is not between females and males, but between SCUM—dominant, secure, self-confident, nasty, violent, selfish, independent, proud, thrill-seeking, free-wheeling arrogant females, who . . . are ready to wheel on to something far beyond what it has been and nice, passive, accepting, "cultivated," polite, dignified, subdued, dependent, scared, mindless, insecure, approval-seeking Daddy's Girls, who can't cope with the unknown, who want to continue to wallow in the sewer that is at least familiar, who want to hang back with the apes, who feel secure only with big daddy standing by.[57]

In his analysis of radical feminist manifestos such as that of SCUM, Kimber Pearce concludes that "facing discordance in the movement similar to that which male authors of manifestoes experienced in the New Left, radical feminist writers could agree on the source of women's oppression in society [man], but not on which form were most damaging, and how feminists [opposed to other women] ought to respond with action to bring about a revolution."[58]

"If you are not with us, you are against us" is an underlying premise of social movement persuasion. As the song goes, "There are no neutrals there." Lanigan call this "confrontational polarization," the attempt by the "in-group to force uncommitted persons to choose within the polarity" through internal and external confrontations.[59]

Conclusions

This chapter has focused on how social movements strive to accomplish the apparently paradoxical but essential ends of creating "we and they" and "us" relationships simultaneously. In doing so, it pursued the question at the heart of the interpretive or social systems perspective: "Which *individuals*, conceiving themselves to be what *people* in what *environment*, use what *relational patterns* and what adaptive *strategies* with what *evolutionary* results?"

According to Kenneth Burke and other rhetorical theorists, language is the human vehicle for producing action and change by inducing cooperation in beings who are inherently separate. Division seems ever present, particularly when social movements arise to challenge traditions, institutions, beliefs, attitudes, and values. Burke claims that to persuade we must create a feeling of usness or weness, a feeling of being consubstantially or substantially the same as others. This identification comes about by talking the other person's language through "speech, gesture, tonality, order, image, attitude, idea."

Social movements employ a wide variety of identification strategies to transform "you and I" into "us." Some are as simple as establishing common ground by emphasizing similar backgrounds, memberships, social status, and work or using the implied we, plural pronouns, to create a feeling of togetherness rather than separateness. Others include creating groups, group actions, physical appearance and dress, choice of language, adaptation of content, appealing to common beliefs, attitudes, and values, creating visual symbols, and associating with famous people. All of these are efforts to lead members and sympathizers to identify with one another, the movement, and the cause.

But as Burke and others note, to identify as a people with a cause and as members of specific organizations within larger social movements also produces division. To identify with one is to separate from another. Thus, movements polarize society into a "we and they" relationship with those truly committed and active in the cause on one side and all others, including those for whom the movement is struggling but who refuse to join the cause, on the other. In a strange way, a rhetoric of polarization is meant to unite through division because human beings often unite over nothing else but a common enemy.

Social movements inevitably seek scapegoats upon whom they can cast all manner of failure, immorality, evil motives, and brutal actions. The scapegoats or devils of movements may be as vague as "they" (the opposite of the implied we), the rich, men, humanists, and globalists. On occasion movements name names. But regardless of the vagueness or specificity of these devils, they tend to qualify under Hoffer's criteria: one, omnipotent, omnipresent, foreign. Some movements see super devils in the form of organized and secret plots—conspiracies—to do evil or harm. Common rhetorical tactics designed to distance the devil from the movement are obscenity, ridicule, and vilification.

Thus, the seemingly paradoxical ends of creating "we and they" and "us" relationships simultaneously are essential in social movement struggles to unite and divide to further a cause. The two fundamental strategies are identification and polarization. Each enables individual true believers to see themselves as a people acting in a hostile environment with clearly identifiable relational patterns in a moral struggle for evolutionary change.

Endnotes

[1] Robert S. Cathcart, "Movements: Confrontation as Rhetorical Form," *Southern Speech Communication Journal* 43 (Spring 1978): 242.

[2] Cathcart, 246; Carol J. Jablonski, "Promoting Radical Change in the Roman Catholic Church: Rhetorical Requirements, Problems, and Strategies of the American Bishops," *Central States Speech Journal* 31 (Winter 1980): 289; R. R. McGuire, "Speech Acts, Communicative Competence and the Paradox of Authority," *Philosophy and Rhetoric* 10 (Winter 1977): 31 and 33.

[3] Rachel Holloway, *In the Matter of Robert J. Oppenheimer* (Westport, CT: Praeger, 1993): 31.

[4] Jacqueline Bacon, "Taking Liberty, Taking Literacy: Signifying in the Rhetoric of African-American Abolitionists," *Southern Communication Journal* 64 (Summer 1999): 271–287.

[5] Robert S. Cathcart, "New Approaches to the Study of Movements: Defining Movements Rhetorically," *Western Speech* 36 (Spring 1972): 86.

[6] Kenneth Burke, "Dramatism," *Communication Concepts and Perspectives*, Lee Thayer, ed. (Washington, DC: Spartan Books, 1967): 332.

[7] Kenneth Burke, *Permanence and Change* (New York: Bobbs-Merrill, 1965): xvii.

[8] Burke, *Permanence and Change*, xxxiii.

[9] Kenneth Burke, *A Rhetoric of Motives* (Berkeley: University of California Press): 21–45.

[10] Lawrence W. Rosenfield, "Set Theory: Key to Understanding Kenneth Burke's Use of the Term 'Identification'," *Western Speech* 33 (Summer 1969): 176.

[11] Burke, *A Rhetoric of Motives*, 55.

[12] Burke, *A Rhetoric of Motives*, 46.

[13] Burke, *A Rhetoric of Motives*, 20.

[14] Gregory Stephens, "Frederick Douglass' Multiracial Abolitionism: 'Antagonistic Cooperation' and 'Redeemable Ideals' in the July 5 Speech," *Communication Studies* 48 (Fall 1997): 175–194.

[15] Kenneth Burke, *A Grammar of Motives and A Rhetoric of Motives* (New York: 1952): 545.

16 Burke, *A Rhetoric of Motives*, 22.

17 Burke, *A Rhetoric of Motives*, 25.

18 Joseph R. Gusfield, *Protest, Reform, and Revolt: A Reader in Social Movements* (New York: John Wiley & Sons, 1970): 366.

19 www.resist.com, 26 January 2000.

20 Allan Carlson, "Twenty-Five Years Into the Culture of Death," *Vital Speeches of the Day*, 15 March 1998, 347–348.

21 Lafayette, Indiana *Journal and Courier*, 22 February 2000, C3.

22 "Hunger Strike Continues," *The Purdue Exponent*, 3 April 2000, 1.

23 *The Purdue Exponent*, 14 February 2000, 1.

24 Dorothy Mansfield, "A Blessitt Event: Reverend Arthur Blessitt Invites Youth to Tune In, Turn On, Drop Out," *Southern Speech Communication Journal 37* (Winter 1971): 165.

25 For speeches and excellent analysis, see "Stokely Carmichael: Two Speeches on Black Power," Wayne Brockriede and Robert Scott, *The Rhetoric of Black Power* (New York: Harper and Row, 1969): 84–131.

26 Frederick Douglass, "An Ex-Slave Discusses Slavery, July 4, 1852," *A Treasury of the World's Great Speeches*, Houston Peterson, ed. (New York: Simon and Schuster, 1965): 481.

27 From a video recording.

28 Richard J. Jensen and John C. Hammerback, "'Your Tools Are Really the People': The Rhetoric of Robert Parris Moses," *Communication Monographs* 65 (June 1998): 126–140.

29 Bert Klandermans, "The Social Construction of Protest and Multiorganizational Fields," *Frontiers in Social Movement Theory*, Aldon D. Morris and Carol McClurg Mueller, eds. (New Haven, CT: Yale University Press, 1992): 93.

30 March 12, 1963, from a tape recording.

31 September 14, 1985, from a video recording.

32 Hubert Humphrey, "Address at the NAACP Convention, July 6, 1966," Scott and Brockriede, 66.

33 Burke, *A Rhetoric of Motives*, 45.

34 Andrew A. King and Floyd Douglas Anderson, "Nixon, Agnew, and the 'Silent Majority': A Case Study in the Rhetoric of Polarization," *Western Speech* 35 (Fall 1971): 244.

35 Richard L. Lanigan, "Urban Crisis: Polarization and Communication," *Central States Speech Journal* 21 (Summer 1970): 108.

36 King and Anderson, 244.

37 John W. Bowers, Donovan J. Ochs, and Richard J. Jensen, *The Rhetoric of Agitation and Control* (Prospect Heights, IL: Waveland Press, 1993): 34–35.

38 Lanigan, 112.

39 Klandermans, 90.

40 Kenneth Burke, *The Philosophy of Literary Form* (Baton Rouge: Louisiana State University Press, 1941): 193.

41 Kenneth Burke, *The Philosophy of Literary Form* (Berkeley, CA: University of California Press, 1973): 39–40.

42 Kenneth Burke, *The Grammar of Motives* (Berkeley, CA: University of California Press, 1969): 407.

43 September 14, 1985, from a video recording.

44 Richard D. Raum and James S. Measell, "Wallace and His Ways: A Study of the Rhetorical Genre of Polarization," *Central States Speech Journal* 25 (Spring 1974): 32.

45 Eric Hoffer, *The True Believer* (New York: Mentor, 1951): 87.

46 Judith Hole and Ellen Levine, *Rebirth of Feminism* (New York: Quadrangle Books, 1971): 442.

47 Gary Wills, *A Necessary Evil: A History of American Distrust of Government* (New York: Simon & Schuster, 1999): 15–22.

48 Letter from Patricia Ireland (Washington, D.C.: National Organization for Women, 1992): n.pag.

49 J. Dan Rothwell, "Verbal Obscenity: Time for Second Thoughts," *Western Speech* 35 (Fall 1971): 240–241.

[50] Peter Farb, *Word Play: What Happens When People Talk* (New York: Bantam Books, 1975): 86.

[51] Lanigan, 108.

[52] Robin Morgan, ed. *Sisterhood Is Powerful* (New York: Random House, 1970): 514.

[53] Marsha L. Vanderford, "Vilification and Social Movements: A Case Study of Pro-Life and Pro-Choice Rhetoric," *Quarterly Journal of Speech* 75 (May 1989): 166–167.

[54] Bowers, Ochs, and Jensen, 36.

[55] Wanda Wilson Whitman, Ed. *Songs That Changed the World* (New York: Crown Publishers, 1969): 68–69.

[56] Bowers, Ochs, and Jensen, 36.

[57] Morgan, 516.

[58] Kimber Charles Pearce, "The Radical Feminist Manifesto as Generic Appropriation: Gender, Genre, and the Second Wave Resistance," *Southern Communication Journal* 64 (Summer 1999): 313.

[59] Lanigan, 111.

SLOGANS, OBSCENITY, AND RIDICULE IN SOCIAL MOVEMENTS

Symbols and symbolic acts provide shared meanings, perceptions, and security within social movements and social movement organizations. Verbal symbols or language, according to Richard Weaver, constitute a "Social and cultural creation functioning somehow within the psychic constitution of those who use it. . . . The question of stability in language cannot be considered apart from the psychic stability of the culture group."[1] The uses and styles of verbal symbols may signal conformity or rebellion in society. Although subtle in some cases and overt in others, symbols and symbolic acts create, sustain, and define role behavior and, as we discussed in chapter 7, may enhance identification or create division through polarization.

Every desire and emotion is a valid reason to initiate symbolic exchange. Emotional responses may be bad reasons for acting, but they are valid when grounded in one's reality. "The real art," Wayne Booth asserts, "lies always in the proper weighing—and what is proper is a matter finally of shared norms, discovered and applied in the experience of individuals whose very individuality is forged from other selves." "Every protest implies an affirmative ground for protest; every affirmation implies many negations."[2] Thus, emotional expressions through words and actions may contribute to social movement cohesiveness or division by affecting relational patterns.

Social Symbols

The intended and perceived meanings of social symbols—words, gestures, acts, signs, and signals—may be difficult to grasp and their impact or stimulation may differ among individuals, groups, and organizations. Hugh Duncan emphasizes "it is the ambiguity of symbols which makes them so useful in human society. Ambiguity is a kind of bridge that allows us to run back and forth from one kind of meaning to another until we take firm resolve to cross the bridge into new and fixed meanings."[3] The meaning of the V sign with two fingers has ranged from victory during World War II to peace during the Vietnam War. The clenched fist symbol meant power, independence, pride, and self-determination to members of the black power movement in the civil rights struggle, and these meanings were similar and different to its meanings when movements worldwide co-opted it in their struggles. News reports have shown women, students, Native Americans, anti–Vietnam protestors, and senior citizens in the United States as well as their counterparts in Japan, Africa, Italy, France, and Ireland exhibiting the clenched fist symbol. From "new and fixed meanings," we think, we feel, and ultimately we act.

Robert Brooks demonstrated the phenomenon of symbolic bridge crossing in his investigation of how three groups (black college students, white college students, and white police officers) interpreted the meaning of the phrase "black power."[4] He discovered three dominant dimensions. The first was aggression. Whites perceived aggression, violence, confrontation, and racial domination inherent in the concept of black power. The second was goals. Blacks associated various political goals such as equal rights and equal opportunity with the phrase. The third dimension was mystique. Blacks endowed black power with nonmaterial attributes such as self-identity, pride, and awareness. Words such as black power and its accompanying clenched fist serve as symbolic justifications for feelings and actions and provide a bridge or link to social action. Duncan concludes, "Symbols, then, create and sustain beliefs in ways of acting because they function as names which signify proper, dubious, or improper ways of expressing relationships."[5]

Because significant symbols often have standard meanings within groups and organizations, they serve both expressive and persuasive functions. Harold Laswell recognizes that influencing collective attitudes is possible by the manipulation of significant symbols such as slogans.[6] He believes that a verbal symbol might evoke a desired reaction or organize collective attitudes of "a people" toward a symbol. Murray Edelman writes "to the political scientist patterning or consistency in the contexts in which specific groups of individuals use symbols is crucial, for only through such patterning do common political meanings and claims arise."[7] Thus, symbols such as "Red power!" the gray panther logo, American flag, burning cross, clenched fist, beards and long hair, turtle costumes, red roses, and swastika evoke specific responses, and these symbols provide us with an index of group beliefs, attitudes, values, and conceptual rationales for claims.

A truism among social movement theorists and practitioners is that the *agent who controls language controls the world*. The language of symbols and symbolic acts that sanctifies actions and feelings, crosses the bridge into new and fixed meanings, sustains beliefs, and signifies proper, dubious, and improper means of expression is selected, reinforced, and maintained by social institutions such as schools, churches, courts, and legislative chambers. J. Vernon Jensen writes about how the British, including those who were sympathetic and antagonistic to the colonists, used the family metaphor when referring to and attempting to control colonists on the eve of the American Revolution. Members of Parliament called colonists "offspring," "children," and "sons" of the "mother country," and "homeland." They urged colonists to return to the "breast" or "bosom" of their mother, and chastised them as "recalcitrant children" for their "misconduct," "waywardness," and "mischief."[8] Philip Wander reveals how the pro-slavery movement in the South used the image of the "savage child" to argue that freeing adult slaves was dangerous both to society (to turn inferior, uneducated, and uncivilized savages loose in the states) and to the slaves themselves (to turn *children* loose who could not fend for themselves in any way without white, adult supervision and discipline).[9]

All social movements struggle to free themselves from symbols and symbolic acts (from movie portrayals of Native Americans as bloodthirsty savages to the tomahawk chop at baseball games) that degrade and consign them to lower rungs in the hierarchy—to gain control of their worlds. When protestors insist on being called blacks or African Americans instead of Negroes or niggers, Native Americans instead of Indians or redskins, black men instead of boys, and women instead of girls, they are demanding far more than political correctness. They are seeking equality, dignity, legitimacy, and the right to name themselves rather than live under names or labels attached to them by slave owners, European colonists, and a male-dominated society. When black nationalists such as Malcolm X substituted colony for ghetto, they communicated the notion of exploitation associated with colonialism and changed black Americans from a national minority to an international majority.[10] The gay rights movement of the 1990s struggled to replace sexual *preference* with sexual *orientation*, special rights with civil rights, and agenda with goals. Each of these changes altered how individual Native Americans, African Americans, gays, and lesbians perceived themselves to be what people. As Will Perkins, founder of an antigay rights organization in Colorado, declares, "Language doesn't shape the campaign—it is the campaign."[11]

Social movements also attempt to label events to cast them in a light to engage supporters—that is, to control or to alter perceptions of reality or the environment. For instance, when addressing a largely black audience at the Cobo Auditorium in Detroit in 1966, the young leader of SNCC, Stokely Carmichael, admonished listeners about what to call the violence that had taken place in several cities: "And don't you ever apologize for any black person who throws a Molotov cocktail. Don't you ever apologize. And don't you ever call those things riots, because they are rebellions! That's what they are."[12] Characterizing events as "insurrec-tions" and "rebellions," rather than random violence and looting by out-of-control citizens, transforms them into uprisings of exploited vic-tims who have grown sick and tired of their exploitation. Kurt Ritter reveals the genius of the colonists, particularly Samuel Adams, in labeling a minor riot by a handful of rowdies in Boston in 1770 as the "Boston Massacre." This label conjured up visions of a "horrid massacre" of many victims, soon to be martyrs for the cause of liberty, whose "innocent blood" cried "to God from the streets of Boston."[13] The contemporary animal rights movement refers to trapped and ranched animals as "mar-tyred victims" of "torture," of the "slaughter of the innocent" subjected to "sadistic" and "barbaric methods of capture and killing."[14] It calls mem-bers of the National Rifle Association who hunt with electronic devices and dogs "thrill-seeking killers."[15] James Andrews addresses the essen-tial roles of symbols in the persuasive efforts of social movements to alter perceptions, prescribe courses of action, and mobilize followers.

> The exciting, and frustrating, characteristic of a social movement is that it moves and what makes it move, in large measure, is the way language is manipulated to control or interpret events. In this sense, rhetoric makes moving possible—moving in all directions, pushing, shoving, lurching forward and falling backward as the movement encounters its environment. Growing out of the environment, intrud-ing into the environment, reacting to the environment, and becoming a part of the environment, the social movement is simultaneously a rhetorical response and a rhetorical stimulus.[16]

The remainder of this chapter focuses on three symbolic strategies common in social movements: slogans, obscenity, and ridicule. Protestors use these strategies to gain control of the symbols that define their world, who they are, relationships, dreams, demands, and actions.

Slogans

George Shankel defines a slogan as "some pointed term, phrase, or expression, fittingly worded, which suggests action, loyalty, or which causes people to decide upon and to fight for the realization of some prin-ciple or decisive issue."[17] Protestors have for centuries chanted, shouted, and sung slogans; printed them in leaflets, pamphlets, and social move-ment newsletters and newspapers; worn them on buttons, tee shirts, jack-ets, and the seats of their pants; and have written, painted, or pasted them on billboards, posters, banners, automobile bumpers, buses, subways, sidewalks, walls, and the Internet.

Slogans are so pervasive in today's society that it is easy to underesti-mate their persuasive power. They have grown in significance because of television, the Internet, and the advertising industry, which have made a science of sloganeering. Advertisers discovered long ago that it is easier to link product attributes to existing beliefs, ideas, goals, and desires of the consumer rather than try to change them. To say that a cookie tastes "homemade" does not tell us if the cookie is good or bad, hard or soft, but simply evokes fond memories of Mother's baking. An accompanying picture of "mother" taking appetizing cookies from an oven crystallizes the point implied in the slogan. The few words of a slogan may communicate a key idea or theme one wants to associate with an issue, group, product, or event.

Characteristics and Types

Slogans have a number of attributes that enhance their persuasive potential for social movements. They are unique and readily identifiable with a specific social movement or social movement organization. They are easy to say and to remember. Slogans are often fun because they contain active verbs and adjectives, are witty, and rhyme. Slogans are designed to be repeated or chanted. They release pent-up emotions and frustrations and act as a verbal surrogate for physical aggression. Finally, slogans may create a "blindering" effect by preventing audiences from considering alternative ways of thinking, feeling, and/or acting.[18] They tend to be definitive statements of the social movement's truths and rely on audience dispositions to achieve expected responses. By recognizing the symbols to which audiences have become conditioned to respond, social movement persuaders formulate slogans that have profound, persuasive, organizing effects.

Social movements use three types of slogans. *Spontaneous slogans* are original, impromptu creations of individual protestors improvised during demonstrations or gatherings. They are often short, rhythmical chants such as "Shut it down" (counterculture movement), "Freedom, freedom, freedom" (civil rights movement), "ROTC has to go" (antiwar movement), "Fur Is Dead" (animal rights), and "Support Human Rights" (Worker Rights Consortium). Other spontaneous slogans are longer and more issue oriented, such as "Housewives are unpaid slaves" (women's liberation movement) and "We have our Bible, we don't need your dirty books" (censorship movement).

Sanctioned slogans are official slogans of social movement organizations and are often placed on movement-produced materials. Examples are the civil rights slogan "Freedom Now" seen prominently in the giant Washington rally that featured King's "I Have a Dream" speech, pro-life's "Give to the unborn their first civil right—Life," "Never to laugh or love," and "We are Protestants, protesting abortion." Sanctioned slogans often appear on mastheads of publications. For instance, the masthead of *The Call*, published by the Marxist-Leninist October League, contains the slogan "People of the world unite to defeat imperialism;" and the Native-American newspaper *Wassaji* uses the slogan "Let my people know."

Advertising slogans are found most often on buttons, bumper stickers, and tee shirts. They tend to be short statements that emphasize a single demand or keep the social movement visible. Issue examples are "Recall Ralph Nader" (radical right groups) and "Solar employs, nuclear destroys" (antinuclear power movement). Organizational examples are "Gray Panthers" (gray power movement) and "The Wobblies are coming" (labor movement), and "Students Against Sweatshops" (worker rights). Whether spontaneous, sanctioned, or advertising, slogans perform a variety of persuasive functions for social movements.

Transforming Perceptions of Reality

Although the brevity of slogans limits their use in transforming perceptions of reality, some encapsulate an intolerable situation in a few striking, memorable words. They tend to address the here and now rather than the past or future, as illustrated in these examples:

"No playing today, kids—smog by General Motors" (environmental movement)

"You can't hug your children with nuclear arms" (antinuclear movement)

"Abortion: the American holocaust" (pro-life movement)

"War is not healthy for children and other living things" (antiwar)

"Thanksgiving Is Murder on Turkeys" (animal rights)

"Sweatshops Exist" (worker rights)

The Save the Whales slogan "Our looks can kill" attempts to make people aware that whales are slaughtered to make cosmetics. And the NORML (National Organization for Reform of Marijuana Laws) slogan "This little plant can turn your life upside down" warns audiences that violation of unfair marijuana laws might cost them their money and their freedom. In a mass demonstration in Columbia, South Carolina on Martin Luther King's birthday, January 17, 2000, an estimated 46,000 people protested the flying of the Confederate battle flag over the state capitol, many carrying signs reading "Your Heritage Is My Slavery."[19]

Protestors, particularly those in the pro-life, environmental, animal rights, and farm worker movements, include graphic pictures with slogans to enhance persuasiveness. For instance, the environmental movement's slogan "Ecology is for the birds" is accompanied by a picture of an oil-soaked duck. Pro-life slogans on bumper stickers and posters such as "Never to Laugh or Love" and "I Want to Live" portray a baby with a tear running down its cheek. "She's a Child Not a 'Choice'" is superimposed over the reddish picture of an embryo. Pro-life marchers in Washington, D.C., marked the twenty-seventh anniversary of *Roe v. Wade* by carrying placards with the slogan "Face It Abortion Kills!" surrounding the face of a young child.[20] The animal rights slogan "Did Your Food Have a Face" is on stickers portraying three baby chickens or a bloodied head of a slaughtered calf. A picture of a starving child in filthy surroundings accompanies the United Farm Worker slogan "Every grape you buy keeps this child hungry."

Some slogans attempt to redefine reality. The pro-life movement uses the slogan "Fetus is Latin for child." The movement against nuclear weapons claims "Peace is more than the absence of war." Women's liberation claims "Porn is violence disguised." And animal rights supporters display stickers and posters with the slogan "Pigs Are Friends Not Food."

An occasional slogan attempts to create negative expectancies in the minds of audiences by visualizing what will happen if change is initiated or stifled. The antinuclear weapons movement warns that "Nuclear war is nuclear suicide"; antinuclear power warns parents "In case of nuclear accident kiss your children goodbye"; and the environmental movement pleads "Save our grandchildren now, not when it's too late." Some movements play chronological ping-pong with adversaries. For example, pro-life warns that "Abortion today justifies euthanasia tomorrow," while pro-choice asks "Do you want to return to the butchery of back-alley abortion?" Antinuclear power groups advise "Better active today than radioactive tomorrow," while pro-nuclear power warns "No nukes, no heat, no lights."

Altering Self-Perceptions of Protestors

A surprisingly small number of slogans address self-perceptions. Movements struggling for dignity and equality such as gay rights, the elderly, Native Americans, and women are most likely to use slogans to enhance self-perceptions. The most common appeal is to self-worth, proclaiming I am somebody, I am important, or I should be in a position of power. Typical are these slogans:

Women are not chicks. (women's liberation)

Discover America with real Americans. (Native-American movement)

God loves Gays. (gay rights)

Seniors count too. (Gray Panthers)

Less direct but clever attempts to enhance self-concept are the women's liberation slogan "Trust in God, She will provide" and the gay rights slogan "I am your worst fear, I am your best fantasy."

Other slogans appeal to feelings of power and strength, such as the Gray Panther slogan "Panthers on the prowl." The simple but powerful slogan "Black power" generated a host of imitations: Brown power, Red power, White power, Gray power, Woman power, Senior power, Poor power, Gay power, and All power to the people. They enhance self-perceptions by expressing the social movement's ability and will to act. A women's liberation slogan declares "The hand that rocks the cradle should rock the boat;" a Hispanic slogan states "We are not a minority;" and a NORML slogan proclaims "You can change the world."

Some slogans appeal overtly to pride in self and the social movement and allow protestors to declare what people they are: "Say it loud, I'm black and I'm proud," "I am an Indian and I am pretty damn proud of it," and "I am lesbian and I am beautiful." Slogans that persuade self as well as others are important for social movements fighting for those who have been subservient for decades or centuries.

Some slogans challenge the self-esteem of members and nonmembers. For example, animal rights slogans attempt to show that wearing fur degrades its wearer and should lower self-esteem. The slogan "FUR shame" accompanied with the picture of a woman wearing a fur coat and a bag over her head appeared on a billboard in Times Square during the massive celebration on New Year's eve 1999–2000.[21] PETA's Web site entitled "meatstinks" contains the slogan "Hag in the Bag" with a drawing of the top of a fur coat with a paper bag where a woman's head would be. A large question mark adorns the sack. A KKK slogan and poster contains the slogan "Don't Be Half a Man, Join the Klan."

Legitimizing the Social Movement

Legitimizing the social movement is of critical importance to the success of protest efforts, so it is not surprising that movements engaged in frequent conflicts with institutions and countermovements use slogans to identify their devils, attack institutions, and challenge the legitimacy of institutional leaders as moral advocates. Anti–Vietnam War protestors chanted, "Hey, hey, LBJ, how many kids have you killed today?" Gay rights advocates used the slogans "Anita Bryant sucks oranges" and "Anita Bryant—Empress of the bigots" to attack the former actress and spokesperson for the Florida citrus industry who led a countermovement against gay rights in Florida. The United Farm Workers used the slogan "Boycott Campbell's cream of exploitation soup."

The majority of slogans that identify and attack devils identify nebulous, unnamed evil forces or things such as men, communism, the rich, and capitalists. Typical slogans are "Don't trust anyone over 30" (counterculture), "Bless those who declare war, they're usually too old to fight" (antiwar), and "Pill-em or kill-em groups make $'s from abortion" (pro-life). The unnamed devil allows the social movement to use the same slogan for years and in a variety of protest situations. The disappearance of a specific devil such as President Johnson, a college president, or the CEO of a corporation does not outdate the slogan; after all, the movement is opposing an institution over time, not merely a specific leader in the short-term.

Nearly all social movements employ slogans as signs of defiance that embolden members and sympathizers and threaten institutional legitimacy. Slogans are fun and relatively safe ways to agitate and threaten the powers that be. Protestors shout threatening slogans such as "Tell him what to do with the broom" (women's liberation), "Hell no, we won't go" (anti–Vietnam War), and "We will remember in November" (women's liberation). Some social movements go beyond defiance and mild threats with slogans such as "Kill the pigs" (counterculture), "Shut it down" (radical left), and "Buy more guns" (black rights).

Prescribing Courses of Action

Prescribing courses of action—usually demands and solutions—is the most common function of social movement slogans particularly among contemporary movements such as antinuclear power, black rights, and pro-choice. The brief slogan is an ideal means of calling attention to the key ideographs of movements such as equality, happiness, free speech, freedom, justice, rights, and peace.[22] Nearly all slogans that address demands and solutions are what Bowers, Ochs, and Jensen refer to as imperative statements: commands, edicts, or fiats.[23]

Some slogans are quite specific. For example, a radical right slogan demanded "Freedom for Rudolf Hess" (former German Nazi leader); an antiapartheid slogan urges institutions to "Ban the Krugerrand" (a South African gold piece); and a Native-American slogan demanded that authorities "Free the Wounded Knee 300."

One of the most important persuasive functions of slogans is the simplification of complex issues, problems, solutions, and relationships. Slogans bifurcate choices into "America—love it or leave it" (pro–Vietnam War), "America—Change It or Lose It" (anti–Vietnam War), "Make love not war" (anti–Vietnam War), and "Abortion kills babies—choose life" (pro-life). Other slogans propose simple solutions without recognizing the complicated steps involved or the difficulties of implementation: "No more nukes" (antinuclear power), "Dump Israel" (American Nazi party), "Humanize America" (radical left), "Go vegetarian" (animal rights).

While presenting demands, slogans often reveal the growing impatience and frustration of movement members and leaders. In John Wilson's words, protestors have grown "tired of being sick and tired."[24] This feeling is apparent in slogans such as "Freedom Now!" (civil rights), "Enough! Out Now" (anti–Vietnam War), "End the arms race now" (antinuclear weapons), "Equal rights now" (women's liberation), and "Stop All Abortion!" (pro-life).

Slogans espouse vague dreams, hopes, and visions. These include "Every child a wanted child, every mother a willing mother" (pro-choice), "For a bicentennial without colonies" (Native American), and "What if they gave a war and nobody came?" (antiwar).

Slogans, then, allow social movements to simplify and package their perceptions of the world that produce impressions of action, direction, analysis, and thoroughness. If, as Joseph Lelyveld claims, television has reduced the "attention span of the ordinary viewer" to "fractions of minutes" and "has made political communication a matter of fleeting impressions," then slogans are essential persuasive vehicles—sound bites—for social movements.[25]

While few slogans address *who* should bring about change, some champion the organization that is crusading for change or resistance to change, such as: "Gray Panthers: age and youth in action," "Young Americans for Freedom" (title and goal), and "The KKK likes Cubans, if they are in Cuba." Others name social movement leaders: "Viva Chavez" (United Farm Workers), "Free Huey" (black rights), and "We stand with Fr. Dan Berrigan" (anti–Vietnam War).

An important persuasive function of slogans is their potential for creating a strong personal identification with and commitment to a cause, particularly when protestors wear the slogans on buttons and tee shirts, place them on automobile bumpers, or carry them on placards. Examples include:

> I am an American Nazi (radical right)
>
> I am a secret member of the John Birch Society (radical right)
>
> Nurses for Life (pro-life)
>
> I Am the Face of Pro Choice America (pro-choice)
>
> Panthers on the Prowl (Gray Panthers)

These slogans provide both an opportunity for self-expression of beliefs and membership and a means of exhibiting commitment to a variety of audiences. Many movement sympathizers are reluctant to let others know of their feelings or support, and a simple button or bumper sticker may take them to a new level of commitment.

Mobilizing for Action

Since many slogans are created during enthusiastic mobilization periods, they often call upon members and sympathizers to take some sort of action. Slogans urge the faithful to repent, fight, picket, support, wake up, vote, help, or "do it." Some Klan rallies featured the slogan "Black Power Never!" and a recording played on jukeboxes in the South urged listeners to wear their "Never" buttons. Other slogans urge specific actions such as "Boycott Chiquita bananas" (United Farm Workers), "Sign up here to keep Taiwan free" (radical right), and "Occupy Seabrook" (antinuclear power). Some are designed to activate self and others through a bit of shaming: "Stand Up and Be Counted" (labor), "Be counted this time, march to end the war" (anti–Vietnam War).

A small number of slogans, such as the Native-American slogan "All for one, and one for all," appeal explicitly for unity. While few slogans call upon audiences to join specific social movement organizations, they do urge action on behalf of a cause or campaign. One radical right slogan proclaims, "I think it's time for us to stand up and be counted." A radical left slogan challenges audiences, "Dare to struggle, dare to win."

Unlike protest songs and other largely in-group persuasive efforts, slogans are often aimed implicitly or explicitly at nonmembers whose support is essential for social movement success. When the United Farm Workers demonstrate in front of supermarkets or liquor stores, for example, they carry signs and chant slogans such as "Don't buy Red Coach Iceberg lettuce," "Help the grape workers win their strike," and "Don't swallow Gallo's wine." These appeals are primarily to the public, retail customers, and the media. The same is true when Save the Whales protestors use the slogan "Wake up! to the alarming facts" and when environmental activists urge people to "Breathe deeply, then revolt." When prochoice unveiled its new slogan "Who Decides?" with a partial face of the Statue of Liberty in mailings to members and sympathizers, the National Abortion Rights Action League explained its importance this way:

> The logo you see below has been appearing all across America. *It's a logo that is critically important to you and millions of others who care about preserving every woman's right to make her own, personal decision about choosing abortion.* The logo symbolizes an effort of historic dimensions—the mobilization of literally millions of Americans in defense of Roe v. Wade, the 1973 Supreme Court decision that first recognized this right.[26]

The majority of slogans apply direct or indirect pressure on other social movements, institutions, or institutional agents. Nearly every demand is phrased as an imperative statement and shouted or displayed at rallies attended by hundreds or thousands of protestors in and around state legislatures, capitols, corporations, churches, courthouses, colleges, stores, beauty pageants, logging operations, abortion clinics, and nuclear power plants. Slogans such as "Ratify ERA now" (women's liberation), "No bus for us" (radical right), "Convert Rocky Flats" (antinuclear power), and "Hey [President] Beering!! It's time to join the Worker Rights Consortium" (sweatshop protest at Purdue University) pressure opposition. The same is true for expressions of power such as "Gray power," "White power," and "We are everywhere" (gay rights).

Social movement slogans act as social symbols and symbolic justifications to create impressions, alter perceptions of reality, transform perceptions of self, challenge the legitimacy of institutions and other movements, prescribe courses of action, and mobilize believers and sympathizers. The ambiguity of slogans and attending acts and images enables them to serve as symbolic bridges from one meaning to another.

Ambiguity allows individuals and groups to interpret slogans according to their own perceptions and needs. Slogans simplify complex problems, solutions, relationships, and situations while demanding instant corrective actions. Many slogans readily identify specific social movements and social movement organizations.

Obscenity

The act of swearing has always been a part of human social interaction. Sigmund Freud suggests that "the first human being who hurled a curse instead of a weapon against his adversary was the founder of civilization."[27] Obscenity is a form of swearing that makes use of indecent words or phrases and symbolic acts. It plays many roles within the realm of politics. Political scientist Harold Laswell refers to the use of obscenity as "the process by which the irrational bases of society are brought out into the open."[28] As Wendell Phillips, an antislavery agitator before the Civil War, observed:

> The scholar may sit in his [her] study and take care that his [her] language is not exaggerated, but the rude mass of men [women] is not to be caught by balanced periods—they are caught by men [women] whose words are half battles. From Luther down, the charge against every reformer has been that his [her] language is too rough. Be it so. Rough instruments are used for rough work.[29]

Obscenity is indeed a rough instrument because it is the ultimate form of symbolic conflict.

Obscenity may be verbal, nonverbal, or a combination of both, and usually appears as adjectives that constitute indecent words, phrases, and actions. It is a potentially powerful tool for social protestors. "Dissent," argue Ray Fabrizio, Edith Karas, and Ruth Menmuir, "has its own rhetoric, one that can be studied in its full range of tones—resentful or resigned, angry or agonized, irate or ironic, furious or downright funny."[30] Ashley Montagu observes that "swearing constitutes a species of human behavior so little understood, even by its most devoted practitioners, that an examination of its meaning and significance is long overdue."[31]

Rhetorical Characteristics of Obscenity

Verbal and nonverbal obscenity became a public issue during the protests of the 1960s and 1970s. Protestors against the war in Vietnam and U.S. culture used obscenities to express their rage, frustrations, and perceptions. They argued that obscene rhetoric was appropriate for describing and attacking an obscene society that was engaged in obscene actions. Early protestors of the civil rights and antiwar movements utilized traditional language strategies and forms of prose, but when these failed to change established policies and practices, they turned to less traditional methods, including obscenity. Denied the instruments of power and access to the mass media, protestors created a new language of protest to attract attention and publicity.

Saul Alinsky observes that "The passions of mankind have boiled over into all areas of political life, including its vocabulary."[32] Haig Bosmajian writes that "The dissenter wants to be heard, to be listened to, and if shouting obscenities is the only way he [she] can get people to listen to him [her], so be it."[33] A student who took part in the 1967 march on the Pentagon and the 1968 demonstrations at Columbia University commented, "I and the others had reached the point where we could no longer tolerate being disregarded. I and the others had to own our lives."[34] An obscene word, phrase, or gesture can provide a summation of the group situation that lends emotion to the group's political and social interests and reifies and magnifies issues at hand. The use of obscenity, then, reflects a political reality of frustration with and separateness from institutions and an environment protestors can no longer tolerate.

No symbol is intrinsically or literally *dirty*. Obscenity, like beauty, is in the eye and mind of the beholder. Words become dirty or taboo because of social conventions, not logical bases of argument. Specific words, phrases, and gestures may be viewed as more or less obscene over time. The contextual elements of who and where are vital to the use of obscenity. For instance, sex, position, age, and status influence our perceptions of taboo symbols. Obscenities by women, children, teenagers, and high-status individuals are more shocking than when used by middle-aged men or dockworkers. Police officers have reacted most angrily to obscenities by young protestors, particularly females. Murray Edelman argues "the politically relevant setting is not merely physical but also social in character" and "is fundamental to symbol formation."[35] The outrageousness of obscenity, particularly when used in public or sacred places (churches, libraries, courtrooms, classrooms) and by young people, women, and professionals jolts people into awareness that a significant number of people are disaffected enough with society to violate its fundamental rules of conduct and its value system.

Obscenity is metaphorical because it implies meanings and disengages the word from the thing signified. Verbal obscenity implies a link between a person, group, or object to some religious, sexual, or excretory reality. For instance, calling someone a "son of a bitch" implies more than birth heritage because it attacks an individual by linking the person to a socially negative construct. The strength of obscenity, then, lies in the linking or comparative process. Michael Hazen observes:

> By making comparisons with those things which are at the heart of a culture's values, a verbal obscenity draws on the strength and vitalness of a society. The values that are being drawn on are those which are important to society. Sex, body functions, and religion are at the

heart of how we perceive ourselves and our relationship to the world. Thus, the verbal obscenity, as a metaphor, draws its strength from the culture's definition of what is proper in several inherent realms of human values.[36]

Verbal and nonverbal obscenities violate societal norms and expectations. And the more obscene the word or gesture, the greater the violations and the potential impact upon an audience. Within the realm of social protest, obscenity is emotional and intense because it expresses inner feelings and reflects the extent of a persuader's pessimism, futility, and anger. Obscenities may serve a variety of persuasive functions for social movements.

Transforming Perceptions of Reality

During the Vietnam War, antiwar protestors used obscenity to alter the way Americans viewed the military conflict and society. Jerry Rubin, a founder of the Yippies, argued that a new language of protest was critical because institutions controlled the old language and thus perceptions of the war and its opposition:

> When they control the words, they control everything, and they got the words controlled. They got "war" meaning "peace;" they got "fuck" being a "bad word;" they got "napalm" being a good word— they got decency that to me is indecent. The whole thing is like backwards, and we gotta turn it around.[37]

To turn it around, Theodore Windt writes, antiwar protestors resorted to verbal obscenities and public sexual acts to communicate their belief that "while sex is natural and creative" and exhibits love, "war is unnatural and destructive" and exhibits hatred.[38] Jerry Farber wrote a popular and highly controversial essay entitled "The Student as Nigger" to influence the way readers viewed the U.S. educational system, particularly universities. He wrote "In California state colleges the faculties are screwed regularly and vigorously by the Governor and the Legislature." For students "There is a kind of castration that goes on in schools."[39] Protestors used all of these obscenity-laden arguments to convince audiences that reality was the exact opposite of that which institutions portrayed and espoused.

Altering Self-Perceptions of Protestors

Protestors may attempt to enhance self-concept and self-esteem by employing obscenities to discredit and humiliate the opposition. Richard Gregg writes that "By painting the enemy in dark hued imagery of vice, corruption, evil, and weakness, one may more easily convince himself [herself] of his [her] own superior virtue and thereby gain a symbolic victory of ego-enhancement."[40] When members of the labor movement sang the song entitled "You Low Life Son of a Bitch," they were undoubtedly "establishing, defining, and affirming" their selfhood by "engaging in a rhetorical act" against employers and industrialists. The sexual mocking of authority figures may relieve the protestor of personal feelings of inadequacy and reduce authority figures below the protestor's own perceived social worth. Each obscenity gives the user the power to mock and challenge the most powerful of foes in relative safety. Rarely is the boss, president, draft board, or institutional agent, aside from police officers, present to answer the charges hurled.

Obscenity may also demonstrate the user's "sexual, social, and political liberation" from a repressive, "parental establishment."[41] Steven Spender writes that obscenity "is based on speaking the unspeakable. It is a style of protest, the basic protest being against censorship: not just official censorship which inhibits you from saying anything you like to anyone anytime."[42] For instance, radical gay rights groups such as Act-Up and Queer Nation appear half-naked and exhibit erotic lovemaking during demonstrations and marches. Such obscenity demonstrates social and political independence, exhibits freedom over one's mouth and body, and is a tactic institutions cannot co-opt. It enables protestors to reject old and create new relational patterns in what they perceive to be an obscene environment.

Legitimizing the Social Movement

Persuaders use obscenity to challenge the legitimacy of institutions. A first step may be to distinguish the social movement from its opposition and to goad the opposition into a delegitimizing and ultimately self-destructive action. Agitators employ obscenity in a variety of ways to establish distinctions between movements and institutions.

Social movement persuaders heap obscenities upon their perceived devils to discredit and humiliate them. Students at Kent State University called National Guard members "fascist bastards;" students at Jackson State College called police "motherfuckers."[43] Eldridge Cleaver, a leader of the Black Panthers, exclaimed in a speech on the UCLA campus that his hatred and hostility was for a "fucked up system, that has fucked up our lives, and fucked up the world we live in, that we have to deal with for ourselves and for posterity."[44] Such obscenities are not purposeless, gutter profanities. They enable social movements to define and stereotype the opposition as vile, hypocritical, impotent, and stupid—literally as obscene. They exhibit a profound contempt for and revolt from established institutions, norms, and values that are responsible for an obscene situation.

Social movements attempt to goad institutions into exhibiting their true natures for all to see. Scott and Smith write that the confronter communicates to opponents, "We know you for what you are. And you know that we know."[45] And "the confronter who prompts violence in the language or behavior of another has found his collaborator. 'Show us how ugly you really are,' he [she] says, and the enemy with dogs and cattle prods, or police billies and mace, complies. Protestors in Chicago during the 1968 Democratic National Convention bombarded the police with nonstop verbal and nonverbal obscenities. These continual taunts eventually resulted in what *The Walker Report to the National Commission on the Causes and Prevention of Violence* called "unrestrained and indiscriminate police violence," a "police riot." Police gassed, clubbed, kicked, and used motorcycles to run over innocent onlookers, pedestrians, residents, delegates to the Democratic Convention, photographers, and reporters as well as the protestors who provoked the hatred. The police officers resorted to the ugly rhetoric of the demonstrators by charging into crowds with cries of "Let's get these fucking bastards" and "Get out of the park you motherfuckers."[46] The demonstrators in Chicago had indeed found their collaborators. Members of the establishment discredited and humiliated themselves because they lost control, an unforgivable sin for institutions and their agents.

Expressing Contempt

Social movements that employ verbal and nonverbal obscenities consciously divorce themselves from societies they believe have no values or norms worth redeeming. They may have no solutions or courses of action to prescribe, so obscenity is a means of putting down the system and escaping the responsibility of finding a replacement. Protestors after the 1968 Democratic Convention carried signs reading "Bullshit!"—no demands or solutions, merely a condemnation of everything.[47] Before the convention, Abbie Hoffman advocated "revolution for the hell of it," and remarked:

> They know something's up, something's going on down there, something's happening, some change coming on in this country . . . . We won't tell 'em what it is. What do you want to tell them for? Don't tell 'em shit. Never . . . . That's the problem you have when you focus in on an issue, when you make a demand. They can deal with a demand. We put a finger up their ass and tell them, 'I ain't telling you what I want,' then they got a problem.[48]

H. Rapp Brown, who succeeded Stokely Carmichael as leader of SNCC, outlined a somewhat different strategy for confusing enemies of black power: "If white folks say gray suits are fashionable, you go buy a pink one. If they say america [sic] is great, you say america [sic] ain't shit. Chairman Mao says, 'Whatever the enemy supports, we oppose. Whatever the enemy opposes, we support.'"[49]

Obscenity-laden strategies preclude meaningful courses of action or dialogue with institutions, but they do express an extreme contempt for society's standards and a burning desire for revolutionary change. "Civility," Dan Rothwell observes, "is an instrument of the status quo; verbal obscenity is a symbol of rebellion against the power structure. Agitators seek profound change, and profanity offers a profound change from the accepted style of dissent."[50] But is change possible with a total absence of dialogue?

Resorting to Diatribe

When orthodox means of persuasion fail to gain attention, social movements may resort to what Windt calls the "diatribe." Diatribe is an abusive and bitter moral drama played out theatrically with the intention of assaulting sensibilities, turning thought upside-down, turning social mores inside-out, and committing in language the same barbarisms or obscenities protestors condemn in the social environment.[51] Obscene words and actions may gain attention and support, and perhaps bring about dialogue, when more temperate words and actions fail.

Obscenity is a way to gain and control media attention. Jerry Rubin explained efforts to manipulate the mass media. "We're living TV commercials for the revolution," he wrote. "We're walking picket signs. Every response to longhairs creates a moral crisis for the straights. We force adults to bring all their repressions to the surface, to expose their raw feelings."[52] Rubin, Abbie Hoffman, and other agitators of the 1960s and 1970s learned quickly that obscenity not only attracted media attention but gave protestors a degree of control. Radio, television, and the press could not broadcast or print obscenities or pictures of obscene acts, but all three could report the sights and sounds of violent police reactions to obscenities. Speaking in Lincoln Park in Chicago during the Democratic convention, Abbie Hoffman instructed demonstrators on media control and coverage:

> If you don't want it on TV, write the word "Fuck" on your head, see, and that won't get on TV, right? But that's where the theater is at, it's TV. I mean our thing's for TV. We don't want to get on Meet the Press. What's that shit? We want Ed Sullivan, Johnny Carson Show, we want the shit where the people are lookin' at it and diggin' it. . . . The media distorts. But it always works to our advantage.[53]

Ugly, obscene, and sometimes violent confrontations and media exposure may have an important byproduct. They make moderate social movement elements and critics within the system more respectable. Windt writes that, "Just as Stokely Carmichael legitimized the moderate, nonviolent posture of Martin Luther King, Jr., so too, the violent acts of the Weatherpeople and the absurd acts of the Yippies contributed to acceptance of traditional criticism of the war and enhanced the ethos of those critics who held positions of power."[54] Thus, institutions may open dialogues with moderate movement elements because of fear or as efforts to counteract radical elements.

Obscenities may enhance the credibility of movement leaders among members and sympathizers because they have the nerve to shout what others only feel. For instance, Rothwell notes "the Black Panthers' obscene vilification of police apparently expresses the private feelings of many black Americans. Although they may not approve of the Panther terminology, they may admire those who have the courage and audacity to insult policemen."[55]

Obscenity may contribute to social movement cohesiveness. Humans have a basic need to identify with others in similar circumstances, and obscenity can create a sense of interpersonal identification and establish relational patterns among protestors and potential sympathizers and legitimizers. Alinsky explains why he uses the obscene:

> Every now and then I have been accused of being crude and vulgar because I have used analogies of sex or the toilet. I do not do this because I want to shock, particularly, but because there are certain experiences common to all, and sex and toilet are two of them. Furthermore, everyone is interested in those two—which can't be said of every common experience.[56]

Group chanting of obscenities makes everyone equal, involves everyone in the protest, and both shares and reduces the risk involved.

Obscenity allows movement members to release pent-up hostility and fear. Psychologist Chaytor Mason asserts that obscenity serves as a safety valve that helps society function without excessive frustration.[57] Verbal aggression is often a surrogate for physical aggression and, consequently, may have a therapeutic value for society by sparing it from bloodshed. Verbal aggression permits protestors to challenge society verbally to expand the boundaries of expression.

Adverse Effects of Obscenity on Social Protest

While obscenity may be an effective means of performing persuasive functions for some social movements, it may have serious adverse effects. First, although obscenity may capture the attention of the public and the media, it may draw attention to itself and away from the social movement's demands. The issue becomes not *what* is being said but *how* it is being said and by whom. David Dellinger, the defender of the Chicago Seven on trial following the 1968 Democratic National Convention, warned the movement:

> We become intoxicated by the slogan "By any means necessary," and forget the interrelationship of means and ends. Like the hot-rod who was caught in traffic and bottomed out racing across a field, we rush into shortcuts that take us for an exciting ride but don't get us where we want to go. The movement falls into its own brand of tokenism, preferring the showy symbolism of insulting a "pig" or trashing a window to the reality of winning over the people to resist the authority of the state and the corporation.[58]

Saul Alinsky berates those who forget the cause, the end for which the social movement is fighting: "These rules make the difference between being a realistic radical and being a rhetorical one who uses the tired old words and slogans . . . and has so stereotyped himself [herself] that others react by saying, 'Oh, he's [she's] one of those,' and then promptly turn off."[59]

Second, attention gained through obscenity tends to be short-lived. As Windt writes, "Once attention has been gained and criticism voiced, the diatribe diminishes in usefulness. People demand serious remedies, seriously treated. Moral dramaturgy must give way to conventional rhetorical forms."[60] When the shock of seeing and hearing obscenities wears off, there is nothing left. The Yippie movement is an excellent illustration of this hollowness. Many recall their vulgar and weird language, actions, and dress but little or nothing of what they stood for, demanded, or attained.

Third, since obscenity is the most extreme form of verbal aggression, the social movement cannot become more radical without resorting to actual violence. People soon grow tired of the same old words. As Alinsky warns, "A tactic that drags on too long becomes a drag."[61]

Fourth, the social unacceptablity of verbal and nonverbal obscenity relegates its use to minorities in both society and social movements. "Most people castigate those who dare to speak obscenities in the public forum," Rothwell writes, "despite the fact that a substantial portion of the 'Silent Majority' seems to have little aversion to private cursing."[62] The repugnance for the public use of profanity denies to social movements the support of important legitimizers outside of and moderates within movements. Neither group can condone or be associated with elements that resort to obscenity. Tom Hayden chastised his fellow SDS (Students for a Democratic Society) members, "There's no reason to continue to verbally put down white liberals for only contributing money or legal defense and going no further. There's no reason to verbally antagonize anyone unnecessarily—that is a form of pseudo politics, a substitute for action."[63] Verbal obscenity tends to become both contagious and noxious to growing numbers of people as protest escalates in intensity and time.

Fifth, obscenity may produce violent reactions that members do not anticipate. Shortly after noon on May 4, 1970, a group of approximately fifty protestors approached a line of Ohio National Guardsmen on the Kent State University campus. The protestors were shouting obscenities, and a photograph clearly shows several students making obscene gestures. The Guard moved forward to dispel the students from the Commons; confrontations occurred; and at 12:25 the Guardsmen lowered their rifles and fired into the crowd. Seconds later four students lay dead and nine were wounded.[64] Some of the victims were hundreds of yards away from the confrontation and were either watching the activities or going to class. On May 14, 1970, a group of between seventy-five and two hundred students at Jackson State College in Mississippi confronted state and local police after two days of throwing rocks and bottles and yelling obscenities. Shortly before midnight police fired into a crowd and into nearby dormitory windows. Two students were killed and twelve were wounded.[65] During the five days of the Democratic National Convention, 192 police officers and approximately 1,000 demonstrators and non-demonstrators were treated for injuries; 668 people were arrested.[66]

And sixth, many social movements do not find obscenity an accept-able means of protest. Their beliefs, attitudes, and values prevent them from delving into the obscene, and their publics would withdraw support if the movements did so. Contemporary movements such as animal rights, pro-life, pro-choice, environment, the far right, and the militias are striving for respectability and acceptability. They want to show they are more civilized and moral than the actions and elements they oppose. Obscenity would destroy these efforts.

Whether the advantages of capturing attention, distinguishing friends from enemies, enhancing self-image, and liberating the social movement from a repressive establishment outweigh the disadvan-tages—and for how long—depends upon the particular movement or movement element, the environment in which it operates, and the evolu-tionary results it hopes to achieve.

Ridicule

Alinsky claims "ridicule is man's [woman's] most potent weapon" because "it is almost impossible to counterattack ridicule. Also it infuriates the opposition, who then react to your advantage."[67] Ron Roberts and Rob-ert Moss write that ridicule is a form of humor usually employed by social movements and countermovements "to demean the status of another indi-vidual or group." They claim "Ridicule has been used with some success in keeping people 'in their place'."[68] What, then, is this potent rhetorical tool?

Dictionaries tell us that to ridicule is to make a person, group, place, thing, action, or idea an object of laughter and even of scorn.[69] Ridicule generally follows a process similar to the following: to ridicule is to mock or make fun of; to make fun of is to exaggerate every real or alleged fault or weakness; to exaggerate every fault and weakness is to distort, deform, and uglify; to distort is to make someone or something appear absurd, laughable, or outrageous; and to make outrageous is to dehumanize. It is obvious from this process that ridicule is a persuasive strategy and, as Alinsky noted, a potent weapon for social agitators who desire change or the stifling of change.

Ridicule attacks the basic worth and credibility of persons and ideas and thus endangers any assigned or claimed legitimacy. A target of verbal assaults, even those laced with obscenity and invective, can take some com-fort in the notion that the attack signals importance or a threat. There can be little comfort in being the object of laughter—of ridicule—because few peo-ple take seriously persons, acts, or groups that appear laughable or absurd.

Levels of Ridicule

Social movements and countermovements employ ridicule in speeches, essays, songs, poetry, slogans, and cartoons. Ridicule can make fun of a person, group, place, thing, action, or idea for being (1) inconsistent, (2) illogical, (3) inept, (4) silly, (5) monstrous, and (6) inhuman.

Cartoonists are particularly adept at portraying *inconsistencies and self-contradictions* in institutional or movement beliefs, claims, and actions. For instance, a cartoon during the antiapartheid movement of the 1980s depicted a South African police officer beating a black citizen while the South African Prime Minister lectures, "How many times do I have to tell you? We won't talk to any black leader who doesn't renounce violence."[70] A cartoon in 1999 following the violent protests during the World Trade Organization's meeting in Seattle depicted a sign-carrier protesting world trade. It labeled the ink on his sign made in India, wooden shaft made in Nova Scotia, hat made in Bangladesh, earring made in Singapore, marijuana cigarette made in Colombia, necklace made in the Philippines, jacket made in Malaysia, watch made in Japan, slacks made in Indonesia, and shoes made in China.[71] Numerous cartoons have noted contradictions between pro-life's beliefs and the murder of physicians in Florida, New York, and elsewhere. One portrays a man holding a Bible in one hand and a gun in the other near a clinic; the caption reads "The right-to-lifers have spoken."[72] A second depicts the words "RESPECT LIFE" written with bullet holes on a blood-stained wall and an outstretched hand in a pool of blood near a stethoscope.[73] And a third, in two parts, contains a top portion showing the trail of a sperm with the caption "Life Begins at Conception . . . " and the bottom portion portraying a pro-choice physician lying in a trail of blood with the caption ". . . And Ends at Assassination."[74] Ridicule at this level attacks beliefs, claims, and actions directly and persons or groups indirectly. The assault is more ideological than personal but reveals glaring inconsistencies and self-contradictions that challenge a movement's or institution's trustworthiness by mocking or making fun of its alleged sincerity, honesty, and fairness— important credibility traits in American society.

At the second level of ridicule, persuaders get more personal while mocking a group's ideas, actions, and statements as *illogical, irrational, or unreasonable*. An anti–Vietnam War poster and bumper sticker reads, "Join the army; travel to exotic, distant lands; meet exciting, unusual people and kill them."[75] A Native-American cartoon printed at Thanksgiving portrays a colonist walking away from three Indian braves, one of whom is saying, "They've shot twenty-nine of our braves, polluted all the rivers, killed most of the game, and raped the chief's sister. Now he wants us to drop over next Thursday for turkey dinner will all the fixin's."[76] And a cartoon that ridicules the far right's agenda shows a large mushroom-shaped cloud in the background as an angry figure shaking a fist while holding his Bible in the other hand shouts, "Blast! I suppose this pre-empts our giant antiabortion, support James Watt, and put prayer back in the schools, book burning rally tomorrow!"[77] These exaggerated irrationalities of the Army, colonists, and far-right members attack their competence by ridiculing their powers of reasoning, judgment, and fairness.

Not all ridicule is aimed at the opposition. Persuaders may taunt their own supporters and sympathizers. At a "Free Huey" rally (demanding the release of Huey Newton, a leader of the Black Panther party), Bobby Seale provoked his audience to cheers rather than jeers:

> For over four hundred years, he taught you white nationalism, and you lapped it up. You taught it to your children. You had your children thinking that everything black was bad. Black cows don't give good milk. Black hens don't lay eggs. Black for funerals, white for weddings. That's white nationalism. Santy Claus, a white honky who slides down a black chimney and comes out white.[78]

Malcolm X employed this tactic frequently in speeches to predominantly black audiences. In "The Ballot or the Bullet" speech in Detroit, he addressed the need for black capitalism and the foolishness of many black would-be entrepreneurs:

> You can't open up a black store in a white community. The white man won't even patronize you. He's not wrong. He's got sense enough to watch out for himself. It's you who don't have sense enough to look out for yourself. The white man is too intelligent to let someone else come and gain control of the economy of his community. But you will let anybody come in and control the economy of your community, control the housing, control the education, control the jobs, control the businesses under the pretext you want to integrate. No, you're out of your mind.[79]

The intent of such assaults on audience abilities to reason and make good judgments is not to demean but to activate, to alter audiences' perceptions of reality, and to shake them into doing something about it. It is the proverbial wake-up call. Rebecca Leonard writes that "black liberation" agitators of the 1960s "actually insulted their audiences in an apparent attempt to motivate them to act in defiance of the agitator's insult."[80]

At the third level of ridicule, persuaders get increasingly personal as they make fun of the opposition as *inept, stupid, or senseless*. One Native-American cartoon depicts Columbus landing in the New World being met by a male and a female native; the male comments to the female, "That's a laugh . . . This guy thinks we're Indians."[81] Cartoonists and others portrayed militia movement members during the 1990s as stupid and paranoid. One cartoon depicts a tiny militia member hiding behind his bed with gun in hand. His wife yells from the bathroom, "Who left the toilet seat up?" and her husband replies "The government."[82] A Friend of Animals advertisement in magazines shows pictures of a lynx, fox, and raccoon wearing female wigs; the caption reads, "YOU LOOK JUST AS STUPID WEARING THEIRS."[83] Anti–civil rights recordings played on jukeboxes in the South during the 1960s are clones of the old Amos and

Andy radio show. The recordings play on a whole repertoire of black stereotypical features: lazy, ignorant, stupid, cowardly, drunken, and corrupt. White supremacist Web sites on the Internet contain cartoons that depict African Americans, Hispanics, Jews, and "wiggers" (white American "race traitors" who support equal rights) as stupid, inept, and immoral.[84] This level of ridicule brings into question a wide range of credibility traits: intelligent, knowledgeable, mentally alert, honest, rational, dynamic, and industrious. Charges of ineptness and stupidity not only demean the opposition, but imply obvious superiority of the attacker.

The fourth level of ridicule attacks the opposition as *silly, trivial, or comical*. A cartoon during the student protests in England portrays a placard-carrying group of students marching down a street while a well dressed, older couple looks on. The caption has the woman saying to her husband, "I don't think it's anything intellectual, dear—they're from the university."[85] Anti-United Nations cartoons have shown members blowing Halloween whistles, wearing buckets and lampshades on their heads, and having a water faucet coming out of an ear. Arlo Guthrie wrote and performed one of the most famous songs of the 1960s student and antiwar movements following his arrest in New England while he was a vacationing college student. His rambling "Alice's Restaurant Massacre" that runs more than twenty minutes portrays the police chief, police officers, a blind judge, military recruiters, and psychiatrists as silly, outrageous, and ridiculous. This level of ridicule attacks persons and their actions more than ideas and claims and depicts oppositions as unworthy of serious consideration because they are so trivial and comical. Institutional and uninstitutional collectives must sustain perceptions that they are forces to contend with, otherwise they will be neither feared nor respected, only ignored. And to be ignored is to cease being an agent of change or resistance.

The fifth level of ridicule attacks the opposition as *monstrous, bizarre, and grotesque*. Opponents are not silly buffoons but ugly monsters. An anticapitalist cartoon depicts an incredibly gross and bloated male in a suit saying, "Starvation's God's way of punishing those who have little or no faith in capitalism."[86] An anti–pro-life cartoon portrays two ugly, "dirty old men" carrying protest signs reading "Outlaw Abortion" and "Keep Em Barefoot and Pregnant."[87] In the late 1990s when the Reverend Jerry Falwell attacked the Teletubby Tinky Winky as gay and Southern Baptists called upon a boycott of all Disney attractions because Disney provided benefits for gay employees, cartoonists depicted them as monstrous and bizarre. One cartoon portrayed an angry, grotesque Southern Baptist holding a Bible and yelling at the Seven Dwarves, "Sodomites!"[88] The anti–Vietnam War song "Masters of War," sung by Bob Dylan, attacks those who build the big guns, best planes, and bombs to destroy and kill while hiding in their mansions as "the young people's blood flows out of their bodies and is buried in the mud."[89] This level of ridicule shows oppositions not merely as inconsistent, illogical, inept, or silly but as vicious, evil human monsters who will do anything to fulfill their desires and beliefs. They are not merely incompetent but dangerous to humanity, particularly because they are industrious and vigorous in their efforts to exploit and harm others under their control.

The sixth level of ridicule attacks oppositions as *inhuman and brutish.* Movements portray their targeted enemies or devils as animals, insects, and diseases. For example, males are "chauvinist pigs" and "rats" (women's liberation); liquor dealers are "rummies" (temperance movement); American Nazis are "cancers" (anti–hate group movement); black males are "bucks." One cartoon depicts the American Nazi Party as helmeted, hideous varmints emerging from under a rock, while the White Aryan Resistance Web site includes cartoons depicting Jews as hideous, poisonous spiders with the Star of David replacing the hour glass of the Black Widow.[90] This level of ridicule dehumanizes the opposition by portraying it as animalistic or an inanimate object. The enemy is the epitome of evil without the abilities to reason, know, make judgments, or act fairly and sympathetically.

The Functions of Ridicule

The six levels of ridicule support Richard Gregg's claim that "the primary appeal of the rhetoric of protest is to the protestors themselves, who feel the need for psychological refurbishing and affirmation."[91] An implied comparison is present in all instances of ridicule. If the opposition is irrational, the movement is rational; if the opposition is stupid, the movement is intelligent; and if the opposition is monstrous, the movement is natural and attractive. Gregg writes that "Throughout all these interactions a person constructs an order; he weighs, evaluates, and orients toward goals so that a symbolic hierarchy is established in which he locates himself."[92]

The more the villain is demeaned and reduced from an intelligent, rational force to an irrational, monstrous animal or thing, the more the movement member is transported up the social hierarchy, and the greater is one's self-concept. Indeed, depicting the opposition as inhuman places it below the scale of a social and symbolic hierarchy. Denise Bostdorff identifies several figures of speech that make the cartoon an effective rhetorical agent in enhancing selfhood. For example, metaphor identifies the cartoon villain as a threat when seen as a spider, snake, or vermin-infested rat. Irony connects the villain with cultural icons such as the flag, Bible, schools, and churches.[93] But the power of ridicule lies not merely in reducing the worth of the opposition but in the act itself. Gregg claims that "The rhetoric of attack becomes . . . a rhetoric of ego-building, and the very act of assuming such a rhetorical stance becomes self-persuasive and confirmatory."[94]

The act of ridicule gives persuaders feelings of power, control over their environment and lives, and superiority. As a persuasive strategy often tied to music, drawings, or photographs and to phrasing that give it a mean-spiritedness on many occasions, ridicule is both a common ground and a confrontational strategy.

Ridicule is an important weapon in the struggle over legitimacy. It challenges the five powers of legitimacy by characterizing adversaries "as ungenuine and malevolent advocates." Marsha Vanderford writes that "Rather than differentiating opponents as good people with a difference of opinion, vilification [such as ridicule and name-calling] delegitimizes them through characterizations of intentions, actions, purposes, and identities."[95] How can an institution or social movement claim the *power to reward* those who conform to norms and values and to punish those who do not when it appears to violate the very norms and values it claims to espouse? Is it not guilty of hypocrisy and sanctimoniousness? How can an institution or social movement claim the *power of control* over information and persuasion when it appears to be self-contradictory, illogical, and stupid in its actions and rhetoric? How can an institution or social movement maintain the *power of identification* with sacred symbols, codes, and myths when it is identified with what is trivial, grotesque, and brutish? Are they the successors of a society's founding fathers, prophets, and high priests, or its demons? How can an institution or social movement sustain or attain the *power of terministic control* when depictions of its rhetoric and actions are the opposite of respected behavior such as order, nonviolence, reason, restraint, sensitivity, and justice? How can an institution or social movement claim the *power of moral suasion* when it appears to be irrational, monstrous, and inhuman, the very epitome of immorality and evil?

Conclusions

The symbols and symbolic acts unique to slogans, obscenity, and ridicule enable participants in social movements and social movement organizations to share meanings, perceptions, and security. They are substitutes for and challenges to the language symbols and symbolic acts that institutions select, reinforce, maintain, and impose. Protestors are aware that the agent who controls language controls the world.

Social movements and countermovements employ a variety of language strategies such as slogans, obscenity, and ridicule to create impressions, alter perceptions of reality and self, attain legitimacy, elicit emotional responses, make demands, attain and sustain commitments to causes, and pressure oppositions. The ambiguity of words, phrases, caricatures, symbols, and symbolic acts allow them to serve as verbal bridges from one meaning to another and allow individuals and groups to interpret them according to their own perceptions. They simplify complex problems, solutions, situations, and peoples while demanding instant corrective actions. And they help to determine the legitimacy granted to and stripped from institutions and social movements. In short, selecting and adapting symbols and symbolic acts enable individuals to perceive themselves to be a particular people, establish meaningful relationships, gain a degree of control in a hostile environment, and envision the evolutionary results for which they are striving.

Selecting and performing symbolic acts are not without perils for social movements, however. Such powerful language strategies as slogans, obscenity, and ridicule unite and divide, placate and antagonize, attract and repulse, impress and trivialize. Protestors must adapt strategies carefully to the fundamental nature of their movements, environments, relationships, and evolutionary stages. Perhaps it is fitting to close a chapter dealing with slogans, obscenity, and ridicule by altering the old adage about swords to read "the agent that lives by the symbol may die by the symbol."

Endnotes

1   Richard Weaver, *Language as Sermonic* (Baton Rouge: Louisiana State University Press, 1970): 120–121.

2   Wayne Booth, *Modern Dogma and the Rhetoric of Assent* (Chicago: University of Chicago Press, 1974): 164 and 193.

3   Hugh Duncan, *Symbols in Society* (New York: Oxford University Press, 1968): 8.

4   Robert D. Brooks, "Black Power: The Dimensions of a Slogan," *Western Speech* 34 (Spring 1970):108–114.

5   Duncan, 22.

6   Harold D. Laswell, "The Theory of Propaganda," *American Political Science Review* 21 (1927): 627.

7   Murray Edelman, *The Symbolic Uses of Politics* (Urbana: University of Illinois Press, 1967): 115.

8   J. Vernon Jensen, "British Voices on the Eve of the American Revolution: Trapped by the Family Metaphor," *Quarterly Journal of Speech* 63 (February 1977): 43–50.

9   Philip C. Wander, "The Savage Child: The Image of the Negro in the Pro-Slavery Movement," *Southern Speech Communication Journal* 37 (Summer 1972): 335–360.

10 Karlyn Kohrs Campbell, "The Rhetoric of Radical Black Nationalism: A Case Study in Self-Conscious Criticism." *Central States Speech Journal* 22 (Fall 1971): 151–160; Robert L. Scott, "Justifying Violence—The Rhetoric of Black Power," *Central States Speech Journal* 19 (Summer 1968): 96–104.

11 Lawrence Ingrassia, "Fighting Words," *The Wall Street Journal*, 3 May 1993, Al.

12 Stokely Carmichael, "Black Power," speech delivered in Detroit, 30 July 1966, from a tape recording.

13 Kurt W. Ritter, "Confrontation as Moral Drama: The Boston Massacre in Rhetorical Perspective," *Southern Speech Communication Journal* 42 (Winter 1977): 114–136.

14 *Say No to Torture* (Washington, DC: Animal Welfare Institute, n.d.); Vivisection . . . (New York: CIVIS, n.d.); *A Time to Choose* (Neptune, NJ: Friends of Animals, n.d.).

15 Letter from Cleveland Amory, Fund for Animals, February 1995, n.pag.

16 James R. Andrews, "History and Theory in the Study of the Rhetoric of Social Movements," *Central States Speech Journal* 31 (Winter 1980): 274.

17 George E. Shankel, *American Mottoes and Slogans* (New York: Wilson, 1941): 7.

[18] Ashley Montagu, *The Anatomy of Swearing* (New York: Macmillan, 1967): 2.

[19] "46,000 decry Confederate flag," Lafayette, Indiana *Journal and Courier*, 18 January 2000, A1.

[20] "Activists mark 27th anniversary of 'Roe vs. Wade,'" Lafayette, Indiana *Journal and Courier*, 23 January 2000, A3.

[21] Reported in PETA's Web site meatstinks.com.

[22] Michael C. McGee, "The 'Ideograph': A Link between Rhetoric and Ideology," *Quarterly Journal of Speech* 66 (February 1980): 7.

[23] John W. Bowers, Donovan Ochs, and Richard J. Jensen, *The Rhetoric of Agitation and Control* (Prospect Heights, IL: Waveland Press, 1993): 28.

[24] John Wilson, *Introduction to Social Movements* (New York: Basic Books, 1973): 89–90.

[25] Joseph Lelyveld, "The Selling of a Candidate," *New York Times Magazine*, 18 March 1976, 16.

[26] Letter from Kate Michelman, Executive Director of NARAL, n.d.

[27] As reported in "A Good Word for Bad Words," *Time*, 14 December 1981, 77.

[28] Harold Lasswell, *Psychology and Politics* (Englewood Cliffs, NJ: Prentice-Hall, 1960): 184.

[29] As reported in Mary G. McEdwards, "Agitative Rhetoric: Its Nature and Effects," *Western Speech* 32 (Winter 1968): 38.

[30] Ray Fabrizio, Edith Karas, and Ruth Menmuir, *The Rhetoric of No* (New York: Holt, Rinehart and Winston, 1970): vi.

[31] Montagu, 5.

[32] Saul Alinsky, *Rules for Radicals: A Practical Primer for Realistic Radicals* (New York: Vintage, 1971): 48.

[33] Haig A. Bosmajian, "Obscenity and Protest," *Dissent: Symbolic Behavior and Rhetorical Strategies* (Boston: Allyn and Bacon, 1972): 299.

[34] As reported in Bosmajian, 299.

[35] Edelman, 103.

[36] Michael Hazen, "The Rhetorical Functions of Verbal Obscenity in Social Protest: The Limits of Cultural Values," unpublished paper presented at the annual convention of the National Communication Association, San Antonio, Texas, November 1979.

[37] As reported in Theodore Windt, Jr., "The Diatribe: Last Resort for Protest," *Quarterly Journal of Speech* 58 (February 1972): 10.

[38] Windt, 11–12.

[39] Jerry Farber, "The Student as Nigger," in Fabrizio, Karas, and Menmuir, 414, 416, 417.

[40] Richard B. Gregg, "The Ego-Function of the Rhetoric of Protest," *Philosophy and Rhetoric* 4 (Spring 1971): 82.

[41] Bosmajian, 298.

[42] Stephen Spender, *The Year of the Young Rebels* (New York: Random House, 1969): 7–8

[43] *The Report of the President's Commission on Campus Unrest* (Washington, DC: U.S. Government Printing Office, 1970): 266 and 439; Daniel Walker, *Rights in Conflict: The Violent Confrontation of Demonstrators and Police in the Streets of Chicago During the Week of the Democratic National Convention* (New York: Bantam Books, 1968): 135, 146, 154.

[44] Eldridge Cleaver, Speech at UCLA, 4 October 1968, from a tape recording.

[45] Robert L. Scott and Donald K. Smith, "The Rhetoric of Confrontation," *Quarterly Journal of Speech* 55 (February 1969): 7 and 8.

[46] See for example, Walker, 1, 5, 8, 139, 154, 158, and 181.

[47] Mitchell Goodman, *The Movement Toward a New America: The Beginnings of a Long Revolution* (Philadelphia: Pilgrim Press, 1970): 95; Walker, 41, 43.

[48] Walker, 46.

[49] J. Dan Rothwell, "Verbal Obscenity: Time for Second Thoughts," *Western Speech* 35 (Fall 1971): 234

[50] Rothwell, "Verbal Obscenity," 234.

[51] Windt, 7–8.

[52] As reported in Windt, 13.

[53] Goodman, 361–362.

[54] Windt, 14.

[55] Rothwell, "Verbal Obscenity," 236.

[56] Alinsky, 83–84.

[57] Rothwell, *Telling It Like It Isn't*, 106.

[58] As reported in Bosmajian, 296.

[59] Alinsky, xviii.

[60] Windt, 8–9.

[61] Alinsky, 128.

[62] Rothwell, "Verbal Obscenity," 232–233.

[63] As reported in Bosmajian, 296.

[64] *Report of the President's Commission*, 265–410.

[65] *Report of the President's Commission*, 421–444.

[66] Walker, 351–358.

[67] Alinsky, 128.

[68] Ron E. Roberts and Robert Marsh Kloss, *Social Movements: Between the Balcony and the Barricade* (St. Louis: C.V. Mosby, 1974): 154.

[69] *Webster's New Collegiate Dictionary* (Springfield, MA: G. & C. Merriam, 1977): 996; *The Oxford Universal Dictionary on Historical Principles* (Oxford: Clarendon Press, 1955), 1736; *Roget's International Thesaurus* (New York: Thomas V. Crowell, 1958), 584–585, 632, and 636–637.

[70] Cartoon from *Newsday*, Los Angeles Times Syndicate.

[71] A Darcey cartoon from the *Plain Dealer* reprinted in *Newsweek*, 13 December 1999, 27.

[72] Cartoon by Olpihant, *The Denver Post*, Los Angeles Times Syndicate.

[73] Cartoon by SAOC, *Star Tribune*.

[74] Newsweek, 28 December 1998/4 January 1999, 104.

[75] Poster by Rosner.

[76] Cartoon from *Playboy*, 1969.

[77] Cartoon by Oliphant.

[78] Bobby Seale speech from a tape recording of the rally.

[79] Malcolm X speech from a tape recording.

[80] Rebecca Leonard, "The Rhetoric of Agitation in the Abolition and Black Liberation Movements," unpublished master's thesis, Purdue University, 1970, 93.

[81] Cartoon by Werk.

[82] Cartoon by Smith, *Las Vegas Sun*, 1995.

[83] Friends of Animals (Darien, CT: n.d.).

[84] See Internet addresses such as *http://www.aryan* resistance.com.

[85] Cartoon from *Punch*, London.

[86] Cartoon from *Sawyer Press*.

[87] Cartoon by Bill Mauldin, *Chicago Sun Times*.

[88] *Newsweek*, 29 December 1997/January 1998, 124.

[89] From a tape recording.

[90] Cartoons by Oliphant and from White Aryan Resistance Web site.

[91] Gregg, 75–76.

[92] Gregg, 75–76.

[93] Denise M. Bostdorff, "Making Light of James Watt: A Burkean Approach to the Form and Attitude of Political Cartoons," *Quarterly Journal of Speech* 73 (February 1987): 48.

[94] Gregg, 82

[95] Marsha L. Vanderford, "Vilification and Social Movements: A Case Study of Pro-Life and Pro-Choice Rhetoric," *Quarterly Journal of Speech* 75 (May 1989): 166.

MUSIC IN SOCIAL MOVEMENTS

The persuasive potential of music has attracted attention for centuries, particularly when social agitators have composed, performed, or sung protest songs. Plato warned in *The Republic*, written in the fourth century B.C., that "any musical innovation is full of danger to the whole state, and ought to be prohibited."[1] Jeremy Collier, famous for his controversial pamphlets and moral essays that demanded social reforms in seventeenth-century England, remarked that music is "as dangerous as gunpowder."[2] In the early 1900s, the militant Industrial Workers of the World (known as the Wobblies) sang songs "on the picket lines, in jail, at trials and defense meetings, at free speech demonstrations, at the Patterson Pageant, at membership rallies, and in the union halls."[3]

Slaves on southern plantations before the Civil War used songs disguised as religious hymns ("Steal Away," "Run to Jesus," "Follow the Drinking Gourd," and "Many Thousand Gone") to urge slaves to run away from plantations, tell them when to escape, explain how to locate the underground railroad through the northern states to Canada, and celebrate the arrival of those who had traveled safely to freedom. More than a century later, "We Shall Overcome" and "We Shall Not Be Moved" helped thousands of Americans confront institutional violence and hatred while carrying the civil rights struggle forward during the 1950s and 1960s.

Although reformers and agitators have used music for centuries to aid their efforts to bring about or to resist change, researchers did not begin to study the persuasive nature and effects of protest music until the 1960s and 1970s. Songs of this period demanded civil rights for African Americans, criticized U.S. society, condemned the war in Vietnam, and raised the consciousness of women. For the first time in American history, protest music became popular and commercially lucrative. Records by the Kingston Trio; the Chad Mitchell Trio; Peter, Paul, and Mary; Simon and Garfunkel; and Bob Dylan sold in the millions. Establishment elements became frightened when leftist singers of the 1930s such as Pete Seeger, Woody Guthrie, and The Weavers (blacklisted during the Senator Joseph McCarthy era as communists) were "rediscovered" and "whitewashed" into union or labor singers so they could became popular folk singers. College and high school students loved folk music. David Noebel of the Christian Crusade warned in his book, *The Marxist Minstrels: A Handbook on Communist Subversion of Music*, that "The communist infiltration into the subversion of American music has been nothing short of phenomenal and in some areas, e.g., folk music, their control is fast approaching the saturation point under the able leadership of Pete Seeger."[4]

Near panic set in when "The Eve of Destruction," sung by Barry McGuire, reached the number-one position on popular music charts in 1965 and remained there for weeks. The lyrics, voice, and instrumentation painted in dark-hued colors a world filled with hatred, prejudice, destruction, and hopelessness—and institutions that were incapable of reform. Resistance to this song began immediately. Established groups feared that millions of young people would drop out of schools and society; they reasoned that if young people bought the record, they bought the message. The future of the United States was at stake. Decca Records countered with "The Dawn of Correction" and "Better Days Are Yet to Come," sung by the Spokesmen. These songs portrayed the good in society and how things could get better if we all believed in the system and tried to create a better world. Atomic bombs, for instance, assured the peace and would not destroy the world because no one was crazy enough to use them and the Peace Corps was helping to make the world a better place. The American Broadcasting Company warned affiliates they might lose affiliation if they insisted on playing music that was dangerous to society. The Federal Communication Commission reminded radio and television stations of their responsibility and accountability to the public, a veiled threat to revoke or not renew broadcasting licenses if stations played the wrong kind of music. David Noebel declared that "The Eve of Destruction" was "obviously aimed at instilling fear in our teenagers as well as a sense of hopelessness. Thermonuclear holocaust, the button, the end of the world, and similar expressions are constantly being used to induce the American public to surrender to atheistic, international communism."[5] The impact and danger of popular protest songs were greatly exaggerated, however. Sociologist R. Serge Denisoff discovered in a study of the "The Eve of Destruction" that only 36 percent of young listeners interpreted the song in the composer's terms, while 23 percent totally misconstrued the lyrics. Of the 73 percent that assimilated all or part of the message, only 44 percent approved of the message; 39 percent disapproved.[6]

While protest music may not produce the cataclysmic results institutions and the public often fear, music does have a number of advantages over speeches, leaflets, editorials, and essays. For example, "Songs are created and designed for repetition, and they are often sung (perhaps with the addition of timely lyrics) throughout the life cycles of social movements."[7] They have powerful nonverbal (voice, instruments, rhythm) as well as verbal (words, lyrics, repetition) components. Songs give persuaders a poetic license to challenge, exaggerate, and pretend in ways that audiences would find unacceptable, unbelievable, or ridiculous if spoken or written in prose.[8] Since protestors often sing songs *together* or *along with* a leader, they become active participants in the persuasive process rather than passive listeners to speeches or readers of printed or electronic materials. Active participation may aid self-persuasion. Stephen Kosokoff and Carl Carmichael discovered that a combination of song and speech was more persuasive than either medium by itself, and they found "significant attitude change as a result of the speech-song combination condition. "In every case there was significant attitude change after exposure to the combined media, even when the song or the speech alone did not produce such change."[9]

This chapter focuses on how the verbal and nonverbal elements of protest music perform critical persuasive functions throughout the life cycle of social movements. These functions include transforming perceptions of reality, altering self-perceptions, legitimizing movements, prescribing courses of action, mobilizing for action, and sustaining the movement. What follows reveals which functions dominate protest music, how they are performed, the ways they vary from stage to stage of long-lived social movements, and how they differ between moderate and radical elements of movements.

Presenting Past, Present, and Future in Song

Protest songs rarely deal solely with the past. An exception is a ballad of the black rights movement entitled "Gray Goose" that deals metaphorically with the plight and invincibility of the black man. Most historical references are brief portions of songs and portray the past as a time of misery, suffering, privation, anguish, and despair. For instance, the civil rights song "Freedom Is A Constant Struggle" exclaims that "we've struggled so long," "cried so long," "sorrowed so long," and "died so long." The socialist song "The Long-Haired Kings" describes the brutal life under the "warrior kings of old" who "polished off the natives."

Even songs of social movements that present the past as preferable to the present do not dwell on history. For example, only occasionally does a labor song look to the pre-industrial era prior to "wage slavery," or an antiwar song refer to times of peace and tranquillity, or a counterculture song relate how the United States was pristine before its corruption. There are a few exceptions. For instance, the anti–civil rights song "Johnny Reb" tells of Johnny's heroic exploits against Union soldiers in the Civil War. "We're Not for Integration" declares that "Our southland got along just fine until those integrators came down here stirring up the mess with outside agitators." Another anti–civil rights song asks, incongruously, "when we whites gonna have our day" in spite of more than two centuries of subjugating African Americans with slave and Jim Crow laws, customs, and violence. The following verses of the woman's rights song "Don't I Wish I Was a Single Girl Again" contrast an innocent past with the brutal present of the late nineteenth century:

> When I was single, I went dress'd fine,
> Now I am married, go ragged all the time.
> Lord, don't I wish I was a single girl again.
> When I was single, my shoes they did screak,
> Now I am married, my shoes they do leak.
> Lord, don't I wish I was a single girl again.

There are no apparent differences in references to the past between songs of moderate and radical elements or songs popular during different stages in the life cycle of movements. Twentieth-century songs are a bit more concerned with the past than nineteenth-century songs, perhaps because more history is available for reference and expectations remain unfulfilled. In general, protest songs tend not to look back at either a glorious or a miserable past.

The majority of protest songs focus on the present; most of them communicate suffering and misery. Titles reflect this bleak state: "Hard Is the Fortune of All Woman Kind" (women's rights), "Cotton Farmer Blues" (farm), "Cold Iron Shackles" (black rights), "Father's a Drunkard, and Mother Is Dead" (temperance), and "Only a Pawn in Their Game" (counterculture). The antislavery song "Sometimes I Feel Like a Motherless Child" describes the psychological plight of the slave:

> Sometimes I feel like a motherless child (repeated three times)
> A long ways from home, a long ways from home.
> Sometimes I feel like I'm almost gone (repeated three times)
> A long ways from home, a long ways from home.
> Sometimes I feel like a feather in the air (repeated three times)
> A long ways from home, a long ways from home.

The anti–civil rights song entitled "The Great Society" describes the terrible state of the country in the sixties. The satirical anti–Vietnam War song "Kill for Peace" exclaims that when Americans do not like the way people walk, talk, or threaten their status, they "kill, kill, kill, burn, burn, burn." The counterculture song "Pollution" describes life in the crowded, dangerous, polluted city:

> Just go out for a breath of air,
> And you'll be ready for Medicare.
> The city streets are really quite a thrill,
> If the hood don't get you, monoxide will.
> Pollution, pollution,

Wear a gas mask and a veil,
Then you can breathe long as you don't inhale.

Notice the "sense of immediacy" created in each of these songs. There is an urgent problem that needs addressing *now*.

The life cycle of social movements determines the emphasis on the present. For instance, most songs of movements such as the black rights and farm movements that have rarely gone beyond the stage of social unrest focus on the present compared to songs of the civil rights and populist movements that have had lengthy periods of enthusiastic mobilization. Social movements devote more attention to transforming perceptions of reality when they are attempting to create awareness of an urgent problem in the environment and less attention to such perceptions once they become dynamic forces clashing with institutions.

Protest songs do change over time. In a comparative study of labor songs of the 1930s and 1940s and counterculture songs of the 1960s, Ralph Knupp discovered "Labor portrays itself as unjustly excluded from its share of the pie of economic and social advantage" while "protest songs of the 1960s call into question the validity of the entire pie."[10] An aura of hope in labor songs ("There is power in a union") is replaced with despair in counterculture songs (we're "on the eve of destruction").

While more songs address the future than the past, the numbers are far smaller than ones focusing on the present. Unlike treatments of either the past or the present that tend to be dreary, most portrayals of the future are positive. For example, the eight-hour movement song "Divide the Day" envisions a day when there will be work for all, plenty of food, and joy in the homes of the workers. In "When the Revolution Comes," socialists sing of a future when robbers, editors, policemen, landlords, and capitalists will no longer frighten workers and will have to "live by honest labor!" And "Dawn of Correction" counters the "Eve of Destruction" with a future full of peace, inventions, medical breakthroughs, and a better life for all.

Not all portrayals of the future are positive, however. Anti–civil rights and counterculture movements portray gloomy visions of the future in songs such as "Darling I'm Growing Old," "Black Power Never!," "Trouble Comin' Everyday," and "Child of Our Times." The antinuclear power movement alludes often to the future because, except for a few nuclear power plant accidents, it has only the future to warn about. "No Seabrook Over Me" is sung to the tune of the civil rights song "Oh, Freedom" and contains such verses as:

No radiation getting' me . . .
No fail-safe systems failin' me . . .
No human errors wastin' me . . .
No radioactive garbage dumped on me . . .
No thermal pollution cookin' me . . .

The majority of both negative and positive portrayals of the future are brief. For example, the antislavery song "My Father, How Long" alludes to a time when "The Lord will call us home . . . where pleasure never dies" and "We'll walk the golden streets of the New Jerusalem." Research has not located any song that is devoted solely or predominantly to transforming perceptions of the future.

If, as Elizabeth Kizer theorizes, "Protest lyrics and their music line have a synergistic effect" by complementing "each other to produce a sum greater than their parts," then verbal and nonverbal elements of protest music can be effective combinations to help social movements transform perceptions of reality.[11] Instruments such as drums, trumpets, guitars, and harmonicas can create a somber, forbidding, haunting, and even apocalyptic mood. Rhythm may reduce inhibitions and defense mechanizations and make audiences more susceptible to rhetorical elements that portray an intolerable situation that warrants urgent attention and action. Cheryl Thomas argues rhythm can have a subliminal effect to push the message more strongly." [12] Repetition, claimed by some to be the heart of persuasion, is a traditional characteristic of music that allows the persuader to reinforce again and again the miserable plight of the slave, laborer, woman, student, white citizen, or gay person. James Irvine and Walter Kirkpatrick discovered that "repeated patterns in the melodic structure tend to produce an almost instant light hypnosis" and, "when combined with the physiological responses," may "create a situation in which the listener [singer] has almost no control over the potential persuasion inherent in the lyrical structure of the musical message."[13]

Song and Self-Image

The majority of protest songs emanate from self-directed social movements striving for personal freedom, equality, justice, and a fair share of the American dream. In these songs, members identify themselves— workers, African Americans, Hispanic Americans, whites, women, wives, gays, farmers, senior citizens—as innocent victims of circumstances and forces beyond their control.[14] The guilty forces range from humans (white folks, husbands, bosses, preachers, landlords, rumsellers, and bankers) to things (idol gold, rum, and mushroom clouds), to an all encompassing they. Songs identify the innocent victims for whom the movement is struggling as slaves, wage slaves, factory slaves, white slaves (prostitutes), and slaves of the slaves (women). Some songs try to enhance self-perceptions by claiming the protestors were duped, deceived, lied to, embezzled, or framed. For every innocent victim, there is an evil and overpowering victimizer taking advantage of naïveté, trust, powerlessness, or ignorance.

Social movements that feel a critical need to establish or to defend self-identity or self-worth delve into the self through music. Songs dealing with self-perception cry out: we are somebody; we are important; we make contributions. The "Farmer Is the Man" contains the following verses:

> Oh the farmer is the man who feeds them all.
> If you'll only look and see, I think you will agree
> That the farmer is the man who feeds them all.

Some songs describe the achievements or contributions of the social movement's primary audience. For example, the socialist "Hymn of the Proletariat" asks:

> Who hammers brass and stone?
> Who raiseth from the mine?
> Who weaveth cloth and silk?
> Who tilleth wheat and vine?
> Who worketh for the rich to feed,
> Yet lives himself in sorest need?
> It is the men who toil, the Proletariat.

Many protest songs declare singers and audiences are strong and powerful. These declarations dominate many songs such as "I Am Woman," with the following verses:

> I am strong, I am invincible.
> If I have to, I can do anything.
> I am woman, hear me roar in numbers too big to ignore.

Similar songs are "Don't Put Her Down," and "The Liberated Woman's Husband's Talking Blues" of the women's liberation movement; "A Hayseed Like Me," and "The Hand that Holds the Bread" of the populist movement; and "Okie from Muskogee," "Segregation Wagon," and "Nigger Hatin' Me" of the anti–civil rights movement.

Protest songs attempt to counteract commonly held negative stereotypes about groups such as African Americans, gays, women, and elderly Americans. The Gray Panther song "Over 65" paints a picture of senior citizens quite different from the public stereotype. Here are sample verses:

> Over sixty-five and I'm not only alive,
> I'm up and at it,
> Where some have had it.
> Not only out and doing,
> Indeed the blood's renewing.
> There's no glimmer of a rocker,
> Next week I'm starting soccer.
> And the fastest Knickerbocker beware!
> Though I'm retired,
> I'm more inspired and more admired than ever before.
> I've taken up Karate, So I'll take on anybody, foul or fair!

The majority of protest songs that treat self-concept overtly attempt to activate audiences rather than to enhance feelings of self-identity or self-worth. The primary focus is on relational patterns. One tactic is to challenge singers and listeners to "show the world you're a man" (anti–civil rights); "Be brave, be human, not a slave" (socialist); "Come forth and prove your manliness . . . come forth, ye women, be true mothers" (labor 1865–1900); and "Dare to be a union man: Dare to stand alone" (labor 1865–1900).

A second tactic is to pose challenging rhetorical questions. The labor song of the 1930s and 1940s entitled "Which Side Are You On?" asks, "Will you be a lousy scab, Or will you be a man?" The civil rights version of this labor song asks, "Will you be an Uncle Tom, Or will you be a man?" A labor song popular from 1865 to 1900 asks, "Shall we yield our manhood, and to oppression bow?" The song "Freedom," sung by the eight-hour workday movement, asks, "Has nature's thrift given thee naught but honey's gift? See! the drones are on the wing, have you lost your will to sting?"

A third tactic is to relate personal conversion experiences. The populist song "A Hayseed Like Me" begins the first verse with "I was once a tool of oppression" and the last verse with "But now I've roused up a little." The gay liberation song "Second Chance" contains the following verse:

> You know once I was something like you,
> I was scared to try anything new.
> Well then love it conquered,
> Let's see what it can do for you.

The 1930s labor song "Boom Went the Boom" tells how "I thought the boss was my best friend" but "I wish I had been wise, next time I'll organize."

A fourth tactic is to arouse guilt feelings. For example, the anti–Vietnam War song "Better Days" admits "I remember I was smiling as they sent you off—to where? I don't remember." The civil rights song "The Ballad of Bill Moore" relates the bravery of an assassinated civil rights protestor and notes, "he dared to walk there [Alabama] by himself, none of us here were walking with him." "Radiation Blues," an antinuclear power song, has a child of the future asking:

> Tell me Papa why you didn't say no,
> To Nuclear power years ago.
> Tell me Papa why you didn't say no,
> You let it slip away.

Labor movement songs of the nineteenth century allude to the bravery of the American revolutionaries and the cowardliness of their children. For example, "The Working Men" song declares, "To break, we should be ashamed, the bond our fathers framed." And the song "Swell Our Ranks" laments:

> Oh, ye old and peerless heroes!
> Who did battle for us all,
> In the days of freedom's life-throes,

> Look not earthward on our fall!
> Look not on your servile offspring,
> Who to brothers bend the knee,
> Afraid to utter thoughts within them,
> Or do battle with the free.

A fifth tactic is to portray the terrible status of the oppressed. "Woman Is Nigger of the World" relates how society forces women to behave, dress, look, and think while turning them into "the slave of the slaves." The black rights song "Ain't It Hard to Be a Nigger" describes how blacks are treated in society and at work. One verse reads:

> Nigger and white man,
> Playin' seven-up;
> Nigger win de money,
> Skeered to pick it up.

The importance for social movements to polarize society by creating we-they distinctions is undisputed. However, social movement music seems to be more effective in creating and attacking devils than in enhancing the virtuous selves. A study of the ego function of protest songs notes that the often repeated image of an innocent, duped victim, while satisfactory for the early consciousness-raising stages of a movement, must be replaced with an image of bravery, power, unity, importance, and virtue as the movement progresses to later stages of the life cycle. "A rhetoric that emphasizes these points is essential for locating protestors positively in the social hierarchy, for extricating them from symbolically defensive positions in a hostile environment, and for achieving a new unity, identity, and condition."[15]

Music may enable victims to enhance self-perceptions because of its unique characteristics. For example, Ralph Knupp writes that "Protest songs provide a forum in which a movement can talk about itself at its best and its opponents at their worst, without accountability to provide reasons."[16] Irvine and Kirkpatrick note that "A steady line in the progression of chords induces in the listener a sense of confidence and/or well-being."[17]

Achieving Legitimacy through Song

As noted in chapter 3, social movements must employ co-active persuasive strategies to demonstrate that they deserve legitimacy by worth and right. While most protest songs do not appeal directly for outside support and legitimacy, many are modeled after or sung to the tune of traditional religious hymns such as "The Old Rugged Cross." R. Serge Denisoff writes that this practice enables the social movement to establish important links to institutions:

> The use of religious music adds an appeal to tradition which social
> movements generally require. Movements, by their very nature, of
> advocating social change, are generally not tied to tradition. Hymns,
> in part, appear to tie the movement to a national heritage, regardless
> of the programs they advocate.[18]

On the other hand, Denisoff notes, some movements such as radical labor
and leftists have "alienated the very people" they "desired to mobilize"
by producing and singing parodies of religious hymns.

Other protest songs use the patterns or melody of well known, popular, and perhaps patriotic songs to identify with tradition and societal values. These include "Casey Jones," "Battle Hymn of the Republic,"
"Marching Through Georgia," "America," "Dixie," and "Swanee." The
civil rights movement had its version of "Yankee Doodle:"

> Freedom Riders came to town
> Riding on the Trailway,
> Mississippi locked them up
> Said you can't even use Trailways.
> Mississippi, you are wrong,
> You've gone against the nation
> We'll keep coming big and strong
> And we'll end segregation.

Thomas, Irvine, and Kirkpatrick claim that use of such songs, or varia-
tions of them, can transfer legitimacy to the social movement from religious, social, and political institutions.[19] Counter or resistance
movements maintain close identification with institutions by singing
institutional songs. For instance, Roman Catholic protestors have
marched to pro-life Operation Rescue sites singing "Ave Maria," one of
the best known and loved of Catholic hymns. Others sing the "National
Anthem" and "America."

Some social movements attempt to attain legitimacy within and
beyond the social movement by employing altered versions of songs used
by successful social movements. "We Shall Overcome," for instance,
began as "We Will Overcome," a southern labor song in the 1920s and
1930s. It was revised slightly for the civil rights movement, became an
important song for black nationalist movements in Africa, and was eventually the anthem for the Catholic rights movement in Northern Ireland.
Black slaves wrote "Oh Freedom" prior to the Civil War, and black regi-
ments marched to it during the Civil War. In the 1960s, SNCC resurrected
"Oh Freedom" with revised verses that substituted segregation, shooting,
burning churches, and Jim Crow for earlier yearnings. In the 1970s and
1980s, as noted previously, the antinuclear power movement produced its
version of this song entitled "No Seabrook Over Me."

During the 1960s and 1970s, several social movements gained legitimacy, particularly among audiences under thirty, by producing or revis-

ing popular songs that earned high ratings and substantial revenues. These included "Eve of Destruction," "If I Had a Hammer," "Sounds of Silence," and "Where Have All of the Flowers Gone." Denisoff warns that "what is popular cannot at the same time be deviant or in opposition to the *status quo*, since popularity is the *status quo*."[20]

Denisoff raises an important question for contemporary social movements: can a social movement become too similar to or identified with what is popular or institutional? As the gulf between the mainstream popular culture and the counterculture widened during the late 1960s, some radio broadcasters recognized a shrewd business opportunity. FM radio stations had languished for years, used mostly for "wallpaper music" and nonprofit classical music. Many thought of FM as the radio without commercials. Nationwide Communications saw the wisdom in programming their radio stations for the counterculture audience. These stations abandoned the stylized disc jockey act, the three-minute length restriction on songs, the Top 40 play list, and rigid formats. Instead, they played album cuts by unknowns such as the Grateful Dead, Jefferson Airplane, and Country Joe and the Fish. Suddenly, these FM stations had listeners; listeners meant advertisers, and advertisers meant profits. Ironically, establishment corporations such as Nationwide owned many of these counterculture stations. Before long FM stereo took over the broadcasting of music and left AM radio with news, sports, and talk shows. Thus, institutional interest in profit motivated them to provide wider circulation for the counterculture's music and views. But at what price does a movement such as counterculture obtain this exposure? What happens to its messages and noninstitutional status?

The majority of protest songs identify the social movement's devil, its major antagonist. Not surprisingly, movements engaged in frequent conflicts with institutions and other social movements and generally regarded as radical and revolutionary contain the most devil appeals, while songs of moderate, less confrontative social movements contain the fewest devil appeals. Most devils are nebulous, unnamed evil forces, groups, or things. Examples include capitalists, men, bankers, bosses, landlords, integrators, masters of war, war machines, generals, nuclear power plants, and demon rum.

Lack of specificity in identifying devils in songs is not surprising. First, few protest songs, unlike speeches or editorials, are created for specific situations or events. Songs are sung in a variety of situations over a period of years or decades and do not become dated when an antagonist dies or resigns or an event fades from memory. Indeed many songs are passed from one social movement to another. Second, the citation of specific devils (persons or groups) can be dangerous for members of social movements such as antislavery and labor who are susceptible to legal, social, and economic retaliation. Third, social movements tend to be more concerned with large problems such as suffrage, civil rights, animal rights, gay rights, and working conditions than with individuals or specific organizations.

When a social movement or social movement organization is in direct conflict with a specific person or group, songs may identify this devil. Songs name Henry Ford (labor movement of the 1920s and 1930s); President Lyndon Johnson (anti–Vietnam War movement); Martin Luther King, Jr. (anti–civil rights movement); the Pullman Palace Car Company and its owner (labor movement of the 1890s); the Nuclear Regulatory Commission (antinuclear power movement); and Governor George Wallace of Alabama, Governor Ross Barnet of Mississippi, and Police Chief "Bull" Connor of Birmingham (civil rights movement). Some songs are devoted entirely to devils. For example, antinuclear power groups sang "The Meldrim Thompson Song" (Governor of New Hampshire) and "The Lemon Tree" (attacking the Public Service Company) during their efforts to stop construction of the nuclear power plant at Seabrook, New Hampshire.

Few songs contain conspiracy appeals—claims that two or more groups are making secret and concerted efforts (literally conspiring) to harm the movement. The populist movement and the 1900–1940 period of the labor movement use conspiracy appeals most frequently. Populists sing about "the cursed snare—the Money Ring," spying and plotting by landlords, banks, and merchants, and the banding together of monopolies. Labor songs refer to members being "framed up by the law," mine owners "framing men to jail," and "The bosses' justice" ordering "cops and thugs to give them lead." Even social movements such as the I.W.W. (Industrial Workers of the World), socialists, women's rights, and civil rights that clash frequently with a variety of institutions and resistance movements, encounter organized opposition, and have a paranoid flavor in their persuasive efforts, do not sing of conspiracies. Conspiracy appeals may be too complex for brief songs; it is simpler to list a devil or two.

Songs employ surprisingly mild language toward the opposition. About one in four songs contains invective, and this is almost always aimed at the social movement's devils who are tyrants, usurpers, thugs, agitators, oppressors, masters, and lords. Some songs are more original and identify "race hate fascists," "ghouls of gain," "mule-hearted screwers," "fornicating preachers," and "mean . . . wicked . . . heartless . . . cruel deceivers." Only a few approach the level of verbal venom exhibited in the labor movement's "You Low Life Son of a Bitch" with its profanity and references to the boss as thief, snitch, skunk, pimp, swine, snake, cheat, and "baby-starving . . . organizer of death." Protestors who perceive themselves locked in a no-holds-barred mortal conflict with vicious institutions or other social movements resort to invective far more often than reform-oriented movements noted for moderate persuasive tactics.

Although many practitioners and students of social protest agree with Saul Alinsky's claim that ridicule is the most potent weapon (see chapter 8), few songs employ ridicule. As we might expect, radical-revolutionary movements and organizations use ridicule most often, and moderate reform movements that try to minimize confrontations use no ridicule, including black rights, civil rights, farm, temperance, and antinuclear power movements. When ridicule occurs in social movement music, it tends to be heavy-handed degradation in an effort to strip the opposition of its legitimacy. Thus, civil rights advocates are niggers, apes, and jigaboos; police are pigs; factory owners are cowardly fobs; and workers and blacks who do not join or support the movement are scabs, Uncle Toms, stools, cruel knaves, or slackers. Anti–civil rights songs such as "Banjo Lip," "Who Likes a Nigger," and "That's the Way a Nigger Goes" contain vicious caricatures of black Americans. Labor songs such as "The Scabs Crawl In," "Casey Jones the Union Scab," and "Scissor Bill" ridicule nonunion workers, especially ones who helped owners break strikes.

Some songs employ satire or parody, and most of these appear in two twentieth-century movements: anti–Vietnam War and moderate counterculture. Antiwar protestors, for instance, sing "The Draft Dodger Rag," "With God on Our Side," "Feel Like I'm Fixin' to Die Rag," and "Kill for Peace." Counterculture protestors sing "The Merry Minuet," "Mine Eyes Have Seen the Horror of the Coming of the Reds," and "Hex on Sex." "The Lament of a Minor Dean," sung to the tune of "Oh What a Beautiful Mornin'," pokes fun at institutional rules and claims that all protestors are part of the communist movement:

> There are five million Reds in the plaza.
> The mike is so loud, and it's drawing a crowd,
> And I'm sure that our rules say it's just not allowed.
> It's open revolt on campus.
> We're crawling with Reds 'neath our desks and our beds,
> And I wish that the Chancellor would call out the Feds.

Interestingly, most music of these two movements, unlike social movement music of earlier periods, is composed and sung by professional commercial artists. Abolitionists had a special version of "My Country" that condemned slavery in verses such as:

> My country 'tis for thee,
> Dark land of slavery,
> For thee I weep;
> Land where the slave has sighed,
> And where he toiled and died,
> To serve a tyrant's pride,
> For thee I weep.

Labor movement members of the 1865–1900 period sang a similar parody called "America":

> Our country, 'tis for thee,
> Sweet land of knavery,
> Of thee we sing!

Sweet land of Jobs and Rings,
And various crooked things —
Our social system brings,
Full many a sting.

The majority of social movement songs, however, are either devoid of humor or employ a meat cleaver approach to ridicule that appeals to the guttural instincts of movement members rather than a scalpel approach of satire and parody that would appeal to a variety of audiences and, perhaps, gain a larger degree of legitimacy.

What, Who, and How in Song

The majority of social movement songs contain demands, but most are ambiguous references to Michael McGee's "ideographs" (discussed in chapter 3), freedom, liberty, justice, equality, reform, fair share, human rights, and dignity. Many demands are vague allusions to ending the war, gaining civil rights, killing Jim Crow (southern segregation laws), achieving integration, attaining fair compensation (rewards for toil, higher wages, just pay), working shorter hours, obtaining leisure time, and having peaceful homes with quiet firesides. Thomas writes that "The ambiguity of the lyrics serves the song well by leaving it open to various individual and personal interpretations."[21]

A few songs contain specific demands such as equal pay for equal work, a limit to the workday (ranging from four to twelve hours), the right to vote, collective bargaining, greenbacks and bonds, and an end to nuclear tests and nuclear power plants. Highly specific demands appear in songs from single-issue social movements (an eight-hour workday from the eight-hour movement and universal suffrage from the suffrage phase of the women's rights movement) and in songs written for specific social movement campaigns ("No Seabrook" in the antinuclear power effort to end construction of the Seabrook power plant and "60 Cents a Ton" during a coal miner's strike in the 1900–1940 period of the labor movement).

Few songs include solutions, and solutions addressed are simple and nondetailed.[34] For example, the I.W.W. proposes "One Grand Union"; an anti–Vietnam War song proposes to "Stop the War, right now"; an antinuclear power song recommends that the United States "look toward the sun and the wind" for power; socialists propose a "worker's commonwealth"; and two versions of the same song ("Talking Union" and "Talking Lesbian") urge listeners and singers to "build you a union." An occasional song provides some detail. For instance, "Arise Ye Garvey Nation," a song popular during Marcus Garvey's back to Africa movement of the 1920s, mentions getting ships and materials strong enough to withstand the storms of the seven seas, training Black Cross nurses, and creating a motor corps to "take up the wounded dead" from future battlefields. Songs tend to be activity oriented rather than reflective of demands, needs, and solutions.

Knupp argues that solutions are few because "Problems are more rhetorically fruitful for movements than solutions."[22] Others suggest, however, that detailed demands and solutions are few because they are inappropriate and almost impossible for brief, poetic songs. As Gerald Mohrmann and Eugene Scott write, "A song is, after all, a song, and it is an unsuitable medium for complex persuasive appeals."[23]

Some protest songs mention the movement, organization, leader, or elite (true believers) who must bring about or stifle change. Most refer to unnamed organizations or movements, but a few name specifics such as the Knights of Labor, the I.W.W., and the Weathermen. Highly organized social movements and ones espousing organization as a means to an end refer to organization most often. For example, the song "Knights of Labor" touts the achievements of their Order:

> I'll sing of an order that lately has done
> Some wonderful things in our land;
> Together they pull and great battles have been won
> A popular hard working band.
> Their numbers are legion, great strength they possess,
> They strike good and strong for their rights;
> From the North to the South, from the East to the West
> God speed each assembly of Knights.

Very few songs mention specific leaders, but some name Martin Luther King, Jr., Marcus Garvey, and James Sylvis (founder of the National Labor Union in the 1860s). A few name leader-heroes such as Coxey and his army of unemployed workers, Eugene V. Debs and the Pullman Strike, and Joe Hill and his miners. The typical protest song contains no references to leaders, perhaps because songs are timeless and not anchored to the here-and-now like speeches, newspapers, pamphlets, and leaflets.

Heroic elites of true believers who are carrying out the social movement's cause appear in some songs. For example, civil rights songs mention freedom riders and freedom fighters; radical counterculture songs praise the Weathermen; and the I.W.W. lauds the Wobblies, as they called fellow I.W.W. members. Few songs praise the elite more profusely than the "Noble Knights of Labor" in the post-Civil War labor movement. One verse reads:

> Oh, the great Knights, the noble Knights of Labor,
> The true Knights, the honest Knights of Labor,
> Like the good old Knights of old, they cannot be bought or sold,
> The great Knights, the noble Knights of Labor.

Highly organized movements and ones confronting established institutions refer to elites most frequently, and they do so during the enthusiastic mobilization stage.

Protest songs prescribe strategies, tactics, and communication channels movements should employ to accomplish their ends. Recommenda-
tions include picket lines, marches, demonstrations, strikes, boycotts,
votes, sit-ins, stand-ins, agitation, singing, nonviolent protest, disruptions, freedom rides, talk, thoughts, organization, and running away.
Some suggestions are original. The song "Over 65" by the gray power
movement explains, "And when a nose needs tweaking, I'm right at it
and critiquing everywhere." The anti–civil rights song "Black Power
Never!" urges audiences to "wear your never buttons, and wave your
rebel flags." The labor song "Stick 'Em Up" recommends placement of
black and red stickerettes "on every slave-pen in the land, on every fence
and tree" so "No matter where you look you'll see a little red stickerette."

Contrary to social movement stereotypes, few songs advocate violence. One anti–civil rights song recommends running civil rights leaders
out of town on a rail, and another proposes shipping "twenty million jigaboos" back to Africa on leaking boats so they will drown on the way.
One women's liberation song, "Don't Say Sister (Until You Mean It),"
urges violence in self-defense: "When they stab you in the back, Give me
a knife and watch me use it." Only one movement, radical counterculture,
advocates violence over persuasion. For example, this movement advocates assassination in "Stop Your Imperialist Plunder," gasoline bombs in
"We Are the Trashmen," armed struggle and riots in "White Riot," and
attacks on police in "Fa La La La La."

The most frequently recommended strategy in songs is the ballot box.
Even socialists who advocated revolutionary change and the I.W.W. with
its radical image propose the ballot as the primary means of bringing
about change. All phases of the labor movement advocate change through
peaceful, constitutional means. A Knights of Labor song entitled "The
Grand Labor Cause" declares that "the ballot's our only salvation."
Another song declares, "Not by cannon nor by saber . . . , Thought is stronger far than weapons." Although society often perceives social movements as collectives of bomb-throwing, gun-toting radicals, most social
movement songs advocate moderate and legitimate means of change.

Highly organized social movements in the stage of enthusiastic mobilization and preoccupied with means refer most frequently to strategies, tactics, and channels. For example, civil rights songs cite strategies and tactics
more often than do black rights songs of the earlier period of black protest.
Denisoff claims that as social movements have become less ideological during this century, their songs have grown less ideological.[24] If what, who,
and how are the primary elements of ideology, twentieth-century protest
songs are neither more nor less ideological than their nineteenth-century
counterparts. Songs do present highly simplified versions of movement ideology, and they appear not to have changed much since the nineteenth century. Degree of organization, movement life cycle, and cause appear to be
more influential in whether or not ideology is present than historical period.

Requesting Action through Song

The majority of protest songs call upon audiences to act in some way: sing, march, demonstrate, picket, vote, organize, strike, talk, disrupt, agitate, and run away. A few challenge listeners to "stand up and be counted," "go tell it on the mountain," "give your hands to the struggle," or "dump the bosses off your back." Actions are often dangerous because of possible institutional reactions and sometimes embarrassing for conservative groups that have always had a reverence for the law and avoided calling attention to themselves in public. The antislavery song "Follow the Drinking Gourd" was written so that slave owners would think the singing slaves were speaking of dying, going to heaven, and meeting God. The message for slaves was very different.

> Follow the drinking gourd! [the big dipper]
> For the old man is a-waitin' to carry you to freedom. [underground railroad]
> The riverbank will make a very good road, [Ohio River and others]
> The dead trees show you the way. [instructions for escaping North]

"Steal Away" contained very important but disguised instructions for when to escape—during a storm when few people were out and tracks could not be seen or followed:

> My Lord—calls me.
> He calls me by thunder,
> The trumpet sounds within my soul,
> I ain't got long to stay here.
> My Lord calls me,
> He calls me by the lightening.

Rhythm of music may "reduce the inhibitions and defense mechanisms" of singers and listeners and make them more willing to lie down in front of an abortion clinic, sit-in a dean's office, be dragged to a police van, or face the taunting jeers and threats of those unsympathetic with animal rights or gay rights.[25] Singing can also give protestors the courage to demonstrate and continue the fight in the face of violence or arrest. A Georgia NAACP organizer comments "the people were cold with fear until music [broke] the ice."[26] Martin Luther King, Jr. commented in a television interview that "The [civil rights] movement has also been carried on by these songs because they have a tendency to give courage and vigor to carry on."[27] Most movements have songs that create this courage and vigor in the face of resistance. Civil rights has "We Shall Overcome" and "We Shall Not Be Moved"; the abolition movement has "Many Thousand Gone" and "I'm on My Way"; and women's liberation has "I Am Woman" and "I've Got a Fury."

Protest songs are also an important means of unifying a social movement and instilling a determination to keep the struggle going—critical goals during the enthusiastic mobilization and maintenance stages. Concerning music during the civil rights movement, Martin Luther King commented that "These freedom songs serve to give unity to a movement, and there have been those moments when disunity could have occurred if it had not been for the unifying force of freedom songs."[28] The most common pleas are to join and unite in the struggle against evil. "The Liberty Tree" of the American Revolution proclaims, "Let the far and the near, All unite with a cheer, In defense of our Liberty Tree." The civil rights song "Keep Your Eyes on the Prize" exclaims, "The only chain that a man can stand, Is that chain of hand in hand."

A number of theorists have pointed to the unifying factor of music that comes from singing as a group rather than as individuals. Thomas writes that the sing along nature of social movement music creates and reinforces feelings of unity, togetherness, and camaraderie—meaningful relational patterns.[29] Kizer notes that protest music reinforces and promotes "a sense of community among followers."[30] Knupp states "The promotion of group unity through rhetoric is the enduring contribution of protest music in social movements."[31] And Bloodworth claims that music is effective in uniting a group behind a certain cause.[32] Singing allows the individual to become an active part of the whole—a people—that is the social movement.

Because songs are usually sung either by highly credible sources or by audiences themselves, they present excellent opportunities for self-persuasion through statements of personal intent. As Irvine and Kirkpatrick write, The "new amplificative meaning generated includes identification and commitment from the auditor. The new meaning is personalized and, therefore, self-persuasive."[33] Songs enhance first person commitment. For example, a black rights song declares, "Well now I shall not be moved." The song was changed to "We Shall Not Be Moved" during the civil rights movement, perhaps an effort to stress the need for collective action and unity rather than individual initiatives. Some songs include personal pledges or intentions to remain committed to the cause. A women's rights song pledges not to be silenced: "No, I will speak my mind if I die for it"; a civil rights song exclaims, "I gotta fight for my freedom"; a labor song proclaims, "I'm too old to be a scab"; an antinuclear power song declares, "I'm gonna stand here and protest"; a gray power song warns, "so I'll take on anybody, foul or fair"; and a migrant worker's song intones, "The picket sign, the picket sign, I carry it all day long."

Songs may unite movement members and maintain commitment by polarizing (1) the movement and institutions and (2) those striving for the movement and those failing to do their part or actively working against the movement. One of the most famous is Pete Seeger's "Which Side Are You on Boys?" written for the labor movement of the 1930s.

> My daddy was a miner
> And I'm a miner's son,

And I'll stick with the union
'Til every battle's won.
Chorus: Which side are you on?
Which side are you on?
Don't scab for the bosses,
Don't listen to their lies.
Us poor folks haven't got a chance
Unless we organize.

Almost thirty years later, James Farmer of CORE (Congress On Racial Equality) rewrote this labor song for the civil rights movement. "Which Side Are You On?" contains such verses as:

Come on You freedom lovers and listen
While I tell of how the freedom riders came to Jackson to dwell, oh,
Chorus: Which side are you on, boys,
Which side are you on?
My daddy was a freedom fighter and I'm a freedom son
I'll stick right with the struggle until the battle's won.
Chorus: Don't Tom for Uncle Charlie, don't listen to his lies
'Cause black folks haven't got a chance until they organize.
Chorus: They say in Hinds County, no neutrals have they met
You're either for the freedom ride or you 'tom' for Ross Barnett.

Notice how each version of this song polarizes the movement and its devils and distinguishes true believers from those unwilling to join or persevere until the battle is won.

Twentieth-century songs contain personal intents more frequently than do nineteenth-century songs, perhaps because social movements of this century have faced less brutal repression and have moved into later stages of their life cycles. In fact, many of them are essentially continuations of social movements started last century, particularly black rights, women's rights, labor, and animal rights-welfare.

Appeals beyond the Movement

Denisoff argues, however, that songs designed to promote cohesion within the membership of a movement "may have little effect on nonmembers and in some circumstances may negatively affect nonparticipants."[34] Following a comparison of samples of labor songs with anti–Vietnam War songs, Knupp concludes "The rhetorical patterns in protest songs suggest that they are largely in-group activities."[35] Other studies support this conclusion because only a handful of songs appeal overtly to outsiders or to potential legitimizers for sympathy or assistance.

Occasionally a song appeals to the feelings or consciences of outsiders. For example, the labor song "Thirty Cents a Day" tells of a young maiden dying from long hours, brutal work, and starvation. The last verse begins, "Too late, Christian ladies! You cannot save her now; She breathes out her life, See the death damp on her brow." The antislavery song "A Pilgrim of God" describes the condition of slaves and their pleas for help. It ends:

> But while your kindest sympathies
> To foreign lands do roam,
> I would ask you to remember
> Your own oppressed at home.

"Links on a Chain" by Phil Ochs appeals to labor unions to help blacks in their struggle for equal rights and jobs.

Few songs make overt threats to established institutions or their agents. The antislavery song "Nat Turner," written shortly after Nat Turner's bloody slave uprising, warns slave owners:

> You might be as rich as cream,
> And ride you a coach and four-horse team;
> But you can't keep the world from moving around,
> And Nat Turner from gaining ground.

The I.W.W. tune "Harvest War Song" warns, "We are coming home, John Farmer, We are coming home to stay." The civil rights song "Oh Wallace" warns the Alabama governor: "Oh Wallace, you never can jail us all, Oh Wallace, segregation's bound to fail." And the gay rights song "Leaping" contains these verses:

> Here come the lesbians,
> Here come the leaping lesbians.
> We're going to please you, tease you,
> Hypnotize you, try to squeeze you.
> We're going to get you if we can,
> Here come the lesbians.
> You can't escape, you're in our hands,
> Here come the lesbians.

Although threats appear in some songs, social movement music talks a great deal more about the opposition than to the opposition. Most songs are for in-house consumption.

Victory Is Near

Some songs assure singers and listeners that victory is at hand for the social movement. For instance, the black rights song "One Day Old and No Damn Good" portrays a hard present and then reassures, "This nightmare, babe, can't last the night; We'll end it soon, both black and white." Other songs proclaim that "Freedom's comin' and it won't be long"; "Oppression's expiring, and soon will be past"; "The joyful hour is coming, 'tis the dawn before the day"; and "It's coming fast—our turn, at last—the social revolution."

The majority of social movement songs tend to be dreary and pessimistic, particularly twentieth-century songs. All songs with the fewest references to immediate victory are in the twentieth century, perhaps because many struggles have gone on too long to believe success is imminent.

Commitment to the Movement

Although protest songs do not attempt to address setbacks and delays (too complex a topic for songs), they do aid in sustaining social movements. Protest songs, attempt to reinforce commitment for the long haul. As years turn into decades for many movements, songs assure listeners that "perseverance conquers all," that "the union makes us strong," and that "our hearts and hands in union strong, not fear or threats can swerve." Other songs urge listeners to remain committed to the cause, to "stick together," to "hang in there a little bit longer," to "hold the fort," to "fight on undaunted," and to "be firm and valiant-hearted." And still other songs involve audiences in singing pledges of commitment. A Revolutionary War-era song proclaims, "We are the troop that will never stoop to wretched slavery." A Ku Klux Klan song promises, "we always can be counted on, when there's a job to do." A civil rights song pledges, "We're gonna keep on fighting for freedom, in the end we will be free."

Social movement songs tend to urge people to remain committed or to include collective pledges rather than resort to potentially persuasive personal pledges. These preferences may reduce opportunities for the influence of highly credible sources or self-persuasion, but they emphasize collective action and commitment as essential for bringing about significant change. It is also safer to take a group rather than a personal pledge in the face of potential retaliatory actions and violence from resistance movements and institutional agents and agencies.

Ultimate Victory

Some protest songs assure movement supporters that victory will come if they sustain their efforts. When victory will come is left ambiguous. For example, perhaps the most famous of all social movement songs, "We Shall Overcome," proclaims "We shall overcome someday" and "we'll walk hand in hand someday." The temperance song "Victory" predicts that "In the sweet by and by, we'll conquer the demon of rum." The song "Better Days Are Yet to Come" (the counter to "Eve of Destruction") pleads "Listen to me everyone, better days are yet to come." The Knights of Labor song "The Good Time Coming" begins with this verse:

> There's a good time coming, boys,
> A good time coming;

> We may not live to see the day,
> But earth shall glisten in the nay,
> Of the good time coming.

Optimism is higher in nineteenth-century songs than in twentieth-century songs and more frequent in songs of highly organized and less confrontational movements. The overall level of optimism, however, is lower than one would expect of protest songs, perhaps because many struggles have faced too many setbacks and gone on too long for expressions of optimism. Women's rights, animal welfare, labor, and African American rights have their roots in the early decades of the nineteenth century and, while they have achieved many important changes, no end is in sight as they move into the twenty-first century.

The Movement's Heritage

A number of writers have claimed that social movement songs rely heavily upon references to past heroes, martyrs, victories, and tragedies to sustain commitment of supporters and the movement's forward progress. However, less than 15 percent of songs mention heroes or martyrs. The majority of these songs refer to one of three groups (1) assassinated leaders or followers such as Medgar Evers, Bill Moore, Malcolm X, and Martin Luther King, Jr. of the civil rights movement; (2) persons unfairly arrested and convicted or executed such as Joe Hill, Sacco and Vanzetti of the labor movement, and the Scottsboro boys and Ferguson brothers of the black rights movement; and (3) victims such as peasants in Vietnam, coal miners, "labor's sons and daughters," child factory workers, and mythical workers such as John Henry.

A small number of protest songs do refer to heroes such as the Founding Fathers, Abraham Lincoln, Mother Jones (an early labor leader), Momma Rosa Parks (see chapter 6) James Meredith (the first black student at the University of Mississippi), and Harriet Tubman (a black antislavery leader).

Very few songs refer to tragedies or victories. For instance, some labor songs relate the details of disasters such as "The Ludlow Massacre," "1913 Massacre at Calumet, Michigan," "The Marion, North Carolina, Massacre," and "The Ballad of the Chicago-Memorial Day Massacre of 1937." Each was precipitated by thugs hired by owners and industrialists or by agents of institutions such as police and the National Guard. A few songs recall victories such as successful strikes, passage of important legislation such as an eight-hour law in Illinois, or the bringing down of Chicago during the 1968 Democratic National Convention.

Most songs are composed during the social unrest and enthusiastic mobilization stages before most tragedies and victories take place and before most heroes and martyrs are enshrined. When movements sing during the maintenance stage, they apparently select from among the movement's traditional songs such as "We Shall Overcome," "Solidarity Forever," and "We Shall Not Be Moved" rather than compose new ones. Often these are performed by noted performers or choirs at national conventions, anniversaries such as the birth of Martin Luther King, Jr., and memorial services for former leaders or the movement's martyrs.

Conclusions

Protest songs enable social movements to perform a variety of essential persuasive functions throughout their life cycles. Most songs perform all major persuasive functions of social movements rather than a single function. Thus, although songs are simplistic, brief, and poetic in nature, they are more complex persuasive channels than theorists suggest.[36]

Most song lyrics describe the present, identify devils, list demands and solutions, and urge movement members to act and remain committed to the cause. They tend to be negative rather than positive, pessimistic rather than optimistic, general rather than specific, and mild rather than abrasive in language. Most songs address the in-group rather than potential legitimizers or the opposition. Songs attempt to enhance self-concept (identity or self-worth) and praise the movement and its leaders. Songs contain few threats and prescribe few violent actions. Rather, they plead for fair treatment and urge followers to use lawful means, primarily the ballot box, to bring about or resist change.

The persuasive content of songs varies considerably from song to song within the same movement, between movements, and over time. Although many differences are not explainable, there are some apparent patterns. For instance, twentieth-century songs refer to the past and to movement heritage more often than do nineteenth-century songs, perhaps because there is more of each to talk about. Twentieth-century songs include tasteful satire more often (perhaps because of involvement of commercial composers in the 1960s and 1970s), more statements of personal intent, and a greater degree of pessimism. The songs of highly organized social movements exude more optimism and are more movement centered. Songs of single-issue movements or composed during social movement campaigns are more specific, especially when identifying devils and treating demands and solutions. Songs of radical social movements and ones in desperate struggles with institutions deal more with the opposition and employ more ridicule and invective. Attempts to transform perceptions of reality appear more often in songs composed during the social unrest stage of social movements. The purposes of songs such as "We Shall Overcome" are different when sung during the enthusiastic mobilization and maintenance stages.

The nonverbal elements of music complement the verbal. For example, instruments help to create the somber, forbidding, and haunting views of reality presented in lyrics. Rhythm may reduce inhibitions and defense mechanisms to aid movement members in viewing reality and social relationships in prescribed ways and make them willing to act in spite of dangers, social pressures, and social inhibitions. Repetition drums the movement's versions of reality, the evil of devils, the plight of victims, movement demands, and the necessity of unity into the consciousness of members. The steady line in the progression of chords may induce a sense of confidence and well-being. Since singing is often a group activity, it promotes feelings of togetherness—relationships—and enhances self-persuasion more than other channels such as speeches, leaflets, and newsletters.

Endnotes

[1] Plato, *The Republic*, Book IV, B. Jowett, trans. (New York: Modem Library, n.d.): 424, 135.

[2] R. Serge Denisoff, *Sing a Song of Social Significance* (Bowling Green, OH: Bowling Green University Popular Press, 1972): 19.

[3] David A. Carter, "The Industrial Workers of the World and the Rhetoric of Song," *Quarterly Journal of Speech* 66 (December 1980): 371.

[4] David Noebel, *The Marxist Minstrels: A Handbook on Communist Subversion of Music* (Tulsa: American Christian College Press, 1974): 1.

[5] Denisoff (1972), 137.

[6] Denisoff (1972), 137–145.

[7] Charles J. Stewart, "The Ego Function of Protest Songs: An Application of Gregg's Theory of Protest Rhetoric," *Communication Studies* 42 (Fall 1991): 241. See also David M. Rosen, *Protest Songs in America* (West Lake Village, CA: Aware Press, 1972): 21–23; R. Serge Denisoff, *Great Day Coming: Folk Music and the American Left* (Urbana: University of Illinois Press, 1971): 18–39; and Stephen Kosokoff and Carl W. Carmichael, "The Rhetoric of Protest: Song, Speech, and Attitude Change," *Southern Speech Communication Journal* 35 (Summer 1970): 295–302.

[8] John David Bloodworth, "Communication in the Youth Counter Culture: Music as Expression," *Central States Speech Journal* 26 (Winter 1975): 304–309.

[9] Kosokoff and Carmichael, 301.

[10] Ralph R. Knupp, "A Time for Every Purpose Under Heaven: Rhetorical Dimensions of Protest Music," *Southern Speech Communication Journal* 46 (Summer 1981): 383–384.

[11] Elizabeth J. Kizer, "Protest Song Lyrics as Rhetoric," *Popular Music & Society* 9 (1983): 6.

[12] Cheryl Irwin Thomas, "'Look What They've Done to My Song, Ma': The Persuasiveness of Song," *Southern Speech Communication Journal* 39 (Spring 1974): 261.

[13] James R. Irvine and Walter G. Kirkpatrick, "The Musical Form in Rhetorical Exchange: Theoretical Considerations," *Quarterly Journal of Speech* 58 (October 1971): 275–276.

[14] Stewart, 242–243.

[15] Stewart, 251.

[16] Knupp, 377–389.

[17] Irvine and Kirkpatrick, 276.

[18] Denisoff (1972), 57.

[19] Thomas, 263; Irvine and Kirkpatrick, 279.

[20] Denisoff (1972), 39.

[21] Thomas, 267.

[22] Knupp, 383.

[23] Gerald P. Mohrmann and F. Eugene Scott, "Popular Music and World War II: The Rhetoric of Continuation," *Quarterly Journal of Speech* 62 (April 1976): 145–156.

[24] Denisoff (1972), 78–79.
[25] Irvine and Kirkpatrick, 277.
[26] Denisoff (1972), 57.
[27] Denisoff (1972), 76.
[28] Denisoff (1972), 75.
[29] Thomas, 262–263, 265.
[30] Kizer, 7.
[31] Knupp, 389.
[32] Bloodworth, 309.
[33] Irvine and Kirkpatrick, 278, 274.
[34] Denisoff (1972), 61.
[35] Knupp, 388.
[36] Mohrmann and Scott, 156.

POLITICAL ARGUMENT IN SOCIAL MOVEMENTS

With this chapter, our discussion of social movement persuasion turns in a new direction. Since defining social movements and describing the systems perspective in the first two chapters, we have focused on the communication processes that characterize the growth and decline of individual movements. Remember the part of the definition presented in chapter 1 that stated a movement "promotes or opposes change in societal norms or values" and encounters "opposition in a moral struggle." We will now analyze conflicts as arguments between opposing points of view. This chapter will explain the concept of "argument" as it is used in rhetorical studies in general and then present a typology of arguments—a set of recognizable "moves" that recur in social movement persuasion—so that we can better understand the various ways that movements propose and oppose change.

The Nature of Argument

"Argue" is a familiar verb. Your parents argue. You had an argument with the person you are dating. The news is full of arguments among politicians. As used in general conversation, "arguing" is hostile, destructive, and unreasonable. Consequently, we tend to avoid it whenever possible. But communication theories, such as the interpretive systems model presented in chapter 2, remind us that humans reason and that two individual humans cannot reason identically all the time. When two (or more) parties reason differently about a subject that concerns them both, the result is a conflict in reasoning—an argument. Viewed from this perspective, arguments can be hostile or friendly, destructive or constructive,

225

unreasonable or reasonable. Those of us who study and teach about human communication in democratic societies cling to the belief that even serious differences in reasoning can often (although not always) be friendly, constructive and reasonable. Even when one of the parties, frustrated by unsatisfying discussions and debates, feels it necessary to go beyond the normal means of discussion to demonstrate, threaten, or revolt it seems wise to explore the underlying conflict in reasoning that caused the uproar.

Like most writers on the subject, we will use the term "argument" in two ways, both of which may be a bit different from your understanding. First, an argument is a linking of ideas in support of identifiable proposition.[1] Second, arguments involve a clash in reasoning between parties. In his essay, "Where Is Argument?," Wayne Brockriede observed "Human activity does not usefully constitute an argument until some person perceives what is happening as an argument." [2] Two people may disagree but not perceive themselves to be arguing, or they can be in basic agreement but perceive themselves as arguing (perhaps because they dislike one another or because each wants to assert dominance over the other).

The connection between these two uses of the term argument becomes clearer when we consider British social psychologist Michael Billig's idea that human thought is an internal argument:

> All too often, psychologists have ignored the essentially rhetorical and argumentative dimensions of thinking. Human thinking is not merely a matter of processing information or following cognitive rules. Thinking is to be observed in action in discussions, in the rhetorical cut-and-thrust of argumentation. To deliberate upon an issue is to argue with oneself, even to persuade oneself. It is no linguistic accident that to propose a reasoned justification is rightly called "offering an argument." [3]

Sometimes we make part of that internal conversation public by stating an argument—casting it out as bait on the waters of human interaction to see if we get a bite. Chaim Perelman directs our attention to the way this bait attracts "adherents."[4] If they swallow the argument and make it their own, then the two arguers are joined by the argument that they then take forth in search of new adherents.

We mull over all relevant thoughts and values in an internal conversation, anticipate differences between our reasoning and the reasoning of those likely to hear us and then make a statement that links ideas to support our position and/or to oppose their position. Either through agreement or disagreement we position ourselves relative to the proposed/opposed change.

Because social movements, by definition, propose or oppose changes, we will present a typology of arguments related to the kinds of changes sought by the arguers. A typology of political argument based on the theme of change enables us to study the types of argument that recur in various movements and in ordinary systemic political rhetoric. Much as the chemist looks for the combination of known elements, the rhetorical analyst can study the ways different social movements use and combine basic kinds of argument.

Traditional analysts have relied on the writings of Aristotle and his successors to describe recurrent rhetorical techniques. But, as Herbert Simons suggested many years ago, social movements and the people who carry their arguments can rarely afford to use the logic of polite discussion or university seminars.[5] If we want to taste the distinctive flavor of a social movement's persuasion, we need to approach it on its own terms by studying how the flavor derives from the unique blend of the arguments available to it. A typology of political arguments can help us understand the kinds of ingredients from which the movement's persuasion is blended.

Rossiter's Political Spectrum

Clinton Rossiter created a typology of seven political philosophies based on orientation toward change to discuss *Conservatism in America*.[6] The first, *Revolutionary Radicalism*, sees societal institutions as "diseased and oppressive, traditional values dissembling and dishonest; and it therefore proposes to supplant them with an infinitely more benign way of life." *Radicalism* is "dissatisfied with the existing order, committed to a blueprint for thoroughgoing change, and thus willing to initiate reform, but its patience and peacefulness set it off sharply from the revolutionary brand." *Liberalism* is generally satisfied with the existing order and believes that the status quo can be improved "substantially without betraying its ideals or wrecking its institutions." *Conservatism*, like liberalism, is satisfied with the existing order but is suspicious of change "The Conservative," says Rossiter, "knows that change is the rule of life ... but insists that it be sure-footed and respectful of the past.... [The Conservative's] natural preferences are for stability over change, continuity over experiment, the past over the future." *Standpattism* prefers today over either past or future; it opposes any change, no matter how respectful of the past. "Despite all evidence to the contrary," "society can be made static." *Reaction* "sighs for the past and feels that a retreat back into it, piecemeal or large scale, is worth trying." Reaction is unlike Standpattism in two ways: it is unwilling to accept the present, and it is amenable to changing the present state of society. Reaction, like radicalism, limits the means it will employ to effect that change. But *Revolutionary Reaction* is willing and anxious to use subversion and violence to overthrow established values and institutions and to restore the era it views as the "Golden Age."

Rossiter's typology has several important rhetorical implications. First, it reveals that "revolutionaries" have much in common, whether they seek a New Age or a return to a Golden Age. They are willing to subvert and to kill, and they disdain discussion and compromise.

A second rhetorical implication is that philosophies adjacent to one another share enough fundamental assumptions that their disagreements can be argued in roughly compatible worldviews. The believers in adjacent philosophies appear reasonable to one another in that each regards the other as a potential, if misguided, ally. They concur enough to converse but differ enough to argue.

The third rhetorical implication is that philosophies opposite one another share no common assumptions. Believers in opposite philosophies make little sense to one another. These partisans have great difficulty persuading one another because their fundamental differences preclude compromise and constrain their ability to adjust to the other's assumptions. Indeed, they are more likely to talk about one another than with one another.

The fourth rhetorical implication of Rossiter's spectrum is consistent with the social judgment approach to attitude change: we distort our comparative judgments when we are ego-involved.[7] This is particularly important to the study of social movements where we are likely to find an abundance of ego-involved persons. When we are ego-involved in a topic, we distance ourselves from all those with whom we disagree and lump them into one perceptual category, even if they disagree with one another. We presume that they must agree with one another if they disagree with us. People also exaggerate their agreement with people whose positions are close to their own.

But despite its usefulness, Rossiter's spectrum has several shortcomings. His categories are too narrow to capture most political arguments. Moreover, he ignores apathy, ambivalence, and indecision in political theory and argument, thus omitting from his model the intensity and fervor that are so important to social movement rhetoric. Finally, Rossiter overlooked the fact that each of the philosophies he described was an argument with some other philosophy. This is so because, as Billig writes, the process of thinking is itself argumentative.[8]

Thus do people create, rediscover, and rehearse arguments in anticipation of a chance to voice them. Every argument faces in some direction and implies disagreement with at least one other position. This is not to say that all arguments are well chosen or supported; indeed, they may not even be voiced. But the set of arguments heard from a social movement provides evidence of their individual and collective thinking.

The Types of Political Argument

We can retain the advantages of Rossiter's spectrum while overcoming its disadvantages by (a) bending his spectrum of philosophies into a circle so that revolutionary radicalism and revolutionary reaction are adjacent to one another (see Figure 10.1), (b) considering the area of the circle as well as its perimeter, and (c) regarding the center of the circle as apathy, ambivalence, and/or indecision and the perimeter as intense or vehement argument. The alterations allow us to conceive of Rossiter's seven philosophical types as spokes on a wheel rather than points on a circle, with the pure philosophical stances located on the rim and apathy at the hub. We can imagine various arguments (a) located along some spoke and (b) facing some other philosophical position. The arguments of radical speeches and pamphlets would cluster toward the rim, while dispassionate academic discussions of social injustice might cluster toward the center.

Arguments along the seven spokes—Revolutionary Radical, Radical, Liberal, Conservative, Standpat, Reaction, and Revolutionary Reaction—attempt to reinforce, sustain, intensify, or energize that philosophical stance. It is through this "in-group" argument that, for example, radicals decide just how radical they wish to be. The arguers agree about the nature of change, but disagree about the intensity of their beliefs or about the need for action.

Figure 10.1   Rossiter's Political Spectrum

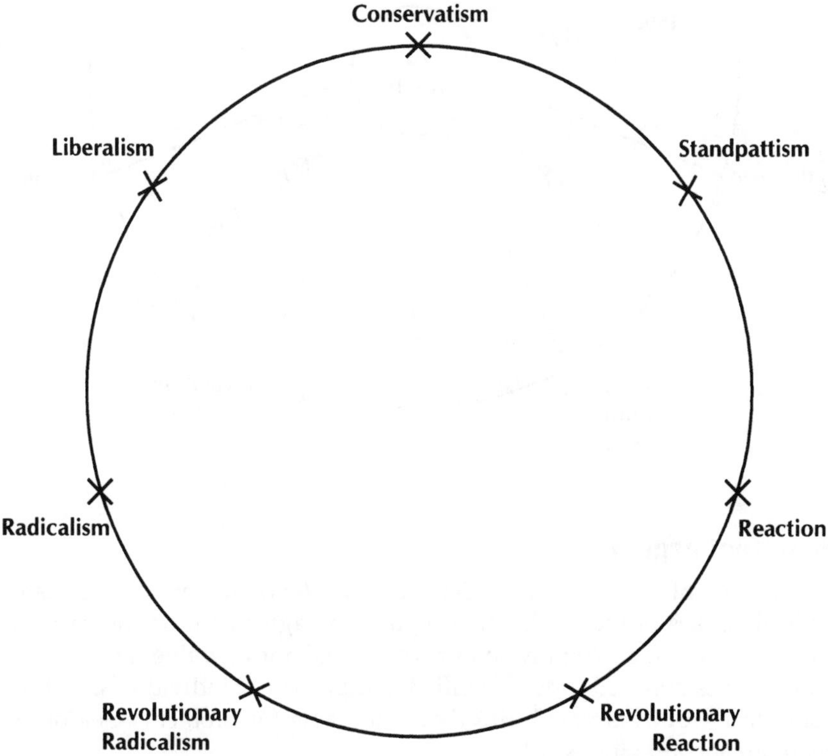

But the spokes of the Rossiter-based wheel delineate seven additional types of political argument. An argument found between the spokes— between Radical and Liberal positions, for example, or between the Revolutionary Radical and Revolutionary Reaction positions—is an argument that reflects the arguer's anticipated differences with the audience's philosophical assumptions. These seven types of argument delineated by Rossiter's philosophical stances are Insurgent, Innovative, Progressive, Retentive, Reversive, Restorative, and Revolutionary See Figure 10.2. Let us examine each in turn.

Figure 10.2   Typology of Political Argument

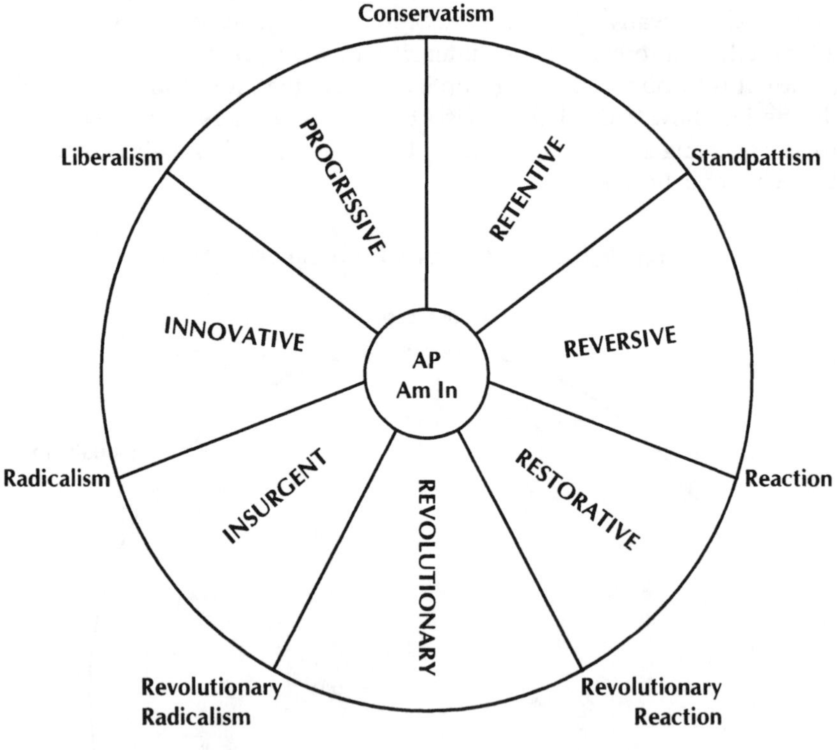

Insurgent Argument

Insurgent argument falls between the Revolutionary Radical and Radical spokes of the model. It is typified by agreement on the corrupt, mendacious, and exploitative nature of societal norms, values and institutions. The established order is vilified and particular individuals, institutions, and groups are held directly accountable for problems. Seldom is heard an encouraging word.

The Industrial Workers of the World (I.W.W.) blamed employers, as a group, for social conditions in the United States. The preamble to their Constitution of 1908 declared that:

> The working class and the employing class have nothing in common. There can be no peace so long as hunger and want are found among the millions of working people and the few, who make up the employing class, have all the good things in life. Between these two classes a struggle must go on until the workers of the world organize as a class, take possession of the earth and the machinery of production, and abolish the wage system.[9]

The I.W.W.'s position that "there can be no peace" anticipates the call for patience or hope for incremental improvement in circumstances. Labor leader John Swinton was more specific in his denunciation of President Grover Cleveland for breaking the Pullman Strike of 1894:

> [President Cleveland] has this year stood out as a servile, mercenary and pusillanimous politician, the ally of money against manhood, fully ready to exercise his power, real and assumed, for the enslavement of the laborious masses who elected him to office.[10]

Roughly fifty years later, Black Muslim leader Malcolm X blamed the American government in its totality for the condition of Black America. In "The Ballot or the Bullet" he argued that:

> You and I in America are faced not with a segregationist conspiracy, we're faced with a government conspiracy. Everyone who's filibustering is a senator—that's the government. Everyone who's finagling in Washington, D.C. is a congressman—that's the government. You don't have anyone putting blocks in your path but people who are part of the government. The same government that you go abroad to fight and die for is the government that is in a conspiracy to deprive you of your voting rights, deprive you of your economic opportunities, deprive you of decent education.[11]

The I.W.W., John Swinton, and Malcolm X all attributed blame for undesirable social conditions to a group or class of people, an important individual, or institution. Insurgent arguments imply that destroying the perpetrator can cure social ills, and they warn audiences to beware of outsiders who council cooperation, moderation, or patience.

Because radicalism is one boundary of the insurgent category, insurgent arguments rarely call explicitly for violent change. Indeed, most insurgent argument is antiviolent. These advocates are not willing to let the new order evolve slowly and naturally, but neither are they prepared to shed blood. Abolitionist William Lloyd Garrison in 1844 exhorted his followers:

> Up, then, with the banner of revolution! Not to shed blood, not to injure the person or estate of an oppressor, not by force of arms to

resist any law, not to countenance a servile insurrection, not to wield
any carnal weapons! No, ours must be a bloodless strife, . . . to overcome evil with good. . . . Secede, then, from the government. Submit
to its exactions, but pay it no allegiance, and give it no voluntary aid.[12]

In his 1934 proletariat play, "Waiting for Lefty," Clifford Odets has a disillusioned wife tell her cabdriver husband how to fight the "bosses:"

JOE: One man can't . . .

EDNA: I don't say one man! I say a hundred, a thousand, a whole
million, I say. But start in your own union. Get those hack boys
together! Sweep out those racketeers like a pile of dirt! Stand up like
men and fight for the crying kids and wives . . . . Get brass toes on
your shoes and know where to kick![13]

Insurgent argument need not be as violent as kicking. For example, People For the Ethical Treatment of Animals (PETA) announced a campaign
for the summer of 2000 to discourage children from fishing, a position
that challenges the traditional image of Grampa spending quality time
with the kids, teaching them about wholesome fun:

In a campaign aimed at getting kids to leave rods and reels behind as
they leave for summer vacation, "Gill the Fish" —PETA's six-foot-tall
"Save Our Schools" mascot—will distribute "Look Don't Hook" toy
binoculars to students after school . . . Why the flap over fishing? Fish
feel pain—they have neurochemical systems like humans and sensitive nerve endings in their lips and mouths. They begin to die slowly
of suffocation the moment they are pulled out of the water. And fishing hurts other animals, too, like birds and otters who swallow hooks
and plastic bait or get tangled in lost fishing line. PETA is urging kids
to give fish a break and, instead, learn about turtles, birds, and other
wildlife by viewing them in nature[14]

Mild as the message may be, the PETA campaign is a direct assault on some
of the widely shared values and activities that shape summer vacations.

Insurgent argument may challenge recollections of what was or
images of what could be. For example, many African Americans recall the
effects of segregation at the hands of white officials, employers, and
unions. But the United Autoworkers Union's Web site tells of the Union's
history, including their shared struggle for fairness:

The UAW approached unionism as a big part of a larger struggle for
equity and justice in society: Worker rights and civil rights were two
sides of the same coin. After all, unequal treatment for any group
undermines the standards of equality unionism rests on. As early as
1946, UAW President [Walter] Reuther set up labor's first civil
rights department—then called the UAW Fair Employment Practices and AntiDiscrimination Department, and he named himself a
co-chair of it.[15]

Rather than looking to their past, the United Farm Workers Union points out that Union representatives in California's strawberry fields could enforce pesticide laws better than can the government:

> Strawberry workers in a union could act as marshals overseeing the use of pesticides more effectively than stretched and absent government agencies. They could do the same for issues of health, safety, child labor and wages. Moreover, union strawberry workers would work to take responsibility for their own condition, seeking better wages and benefits that would ripple through their communities. Union strawberry workers would bring sanity to the field hiring system. Willingness to provide sexual favors or not question conditions would no longer be a criteria [sic] for hiring. In addition to providing strawberry workers with the ability to speak up for themselves, their legitimate concern about their companies' success could bear fruit for the industry.[16]

Insurgent argument, then, is confrontational. It focuses upon one or more social ills and blames them on persons, institutions, or values that are integral parts of the established order. Strategically, insurgent argument calls for strong action.

Innovative Argument

Innovative argument falls between the Radical and Liberal spokes of the Rossiter model. It is characterized by a nagging dissatisfaction with the existing order and a preference for experimental change. There is an almost equal aversion to violence and the status quo. Fundamental questions include: Is the political system part of the problem or part of the solution? Can normal channels produce sufficient change? Can actual practice be made to conform to traditional values?

Ralph Smith and Russell Windes suggest that it is advisable for social movement persuaders to identify discrepancies between traditional values and current practice and to argue that their innovation is, in fact, more traditional than the status quo.[17] This is a recurrent feature of innovative arguments. American Federation of Labor founder Samuel Gompers tied the goals and tactics of his movement to "Americanism." In a 1908 article, he explained that:

> We American trade unionists want to work out our problems in the spirit of true Americanism—a spirit that embodies our broadest and highest ideals. If we do not succeed, it will be due to no fault of ours. We have been building the A. F. of L. in conformity with what we believe to be the original intent and purpose of America.[18]

Similarly, Martin Luther King's "I Have a Dream" speech grounded his call for integration in both Americanism and Christianity:

> I still have a dream. It is a dream deeply rooted in the American dream. It is a dream that one day this nation will rise up and live out

the true meaning of its creed: "We hold these truths to be self-evident; that all men are created equal." I have a dream that one day every valley shall be exalted, every hill and mountain shall be made low, the rough places will be made plane and crooked places will be made straight, and the glory of the Lord shall be revealed, and all flesh shall see it together.[19]

A 1993 mailing from the Native American Rights Fund (NARF) begins with an observation by Twila Martin-Kekanhbah, former Chairperson of the Turtle Mountain Band of Chippewa, that voices America's professed values: "Every Chippewa is taught from birth that these seven basic qualities must guide us as individuals and tribal members: honesty, respect, generosity, kindness, fairness, sharing and spirituality. Only by keeping this path can we meet our responsibilities to ourselves and to one another."[20] The letter from NARF's Executive Director, John Echowak, proceeds quickly to argue that his people often stand alone with these values: "Because my people are abused by a system of government that is not honest with us, is not respectful of our culture or our fundamental rights; a government that continues to degrade and abuse the land on which we all depend."[21] The problem is that the practices of institutions are unfaithful to the fundamental values that are being upheld by the social movement. "I ask you," writes Echowak, "can America continue to stand proud as a nation revered for its freedoms when its government allows religious freedom—the first freedom enunciated in the First Amendment—to be just a hollow promise to the *first* Americans?"[22]

Of course, innovative arguments are frequently met by the response that their innovation is unwise or impractical. Many innovative arguments anticipate this response by differentiating the situation in question from similar situations in the past. In a familiar but often misquoted passage, industrialist Henry Ford dismissed history as a standard by which to assess proposed innovation:

> What do we care what they did 500 or 1000 years ago? It means nothing to me. History is more or less bunk. It's tradition. We don't want tradition. We want to live in the present and the only history that is worth a tinker's damn is the history we make today.[23]

Yet sometimes "the history we make today" is an innovation based upon the past.

Social movements frequently seek to have the larger society commemorate their historic moments and personages. The Martin Luther King, Jr. and Labor Day holidays are two familiar examples. In California the United Farm Workers Union is leading efforts to have a holiday honoring their founder, Cesar Chavez. Their call for support argues for adherence to the proposal based upon shared respect for Chavez:

> Time and again, Cesar Chavez sacrificed for farm workers and all Americans. Today, men and women of good will can help insure that

California makes the United Farm Workers founder the first Mexican
American and labor leader to be honored with a paid state holiday.[24]

Stephen Browne has studied how Crispus Attucks, one of the casualties
of the Boston Massacre, became memorialized in Boston through a determined campaign to transform him from "a figure virtually without identity into a major symbol of African-American resistance." He relates that
"By 1860 Crispus Attucks had not only been retrieved from the oblivion
of the Boston Massacre Orations; he had been inspirited and transformed
into a living icon of a 'new' history, the telling of which had become the
business of annual commemorations." [25]

Innovative argument, then, seeks substantial changes in the norms,
values, or institutions of society without violent action. It grounds its proposals in the society's dominant creeds or values and rejects as irrelevant
the suggestion that the innovation cannot or will not work. It is easy to
see that innovative argument is safer than insurgent argument. Innovators embrace rather than scorn the principles upon which the society is
founded, and they claim a moral advantage over both their insurgent and
institutional adversaries. This enables innovators to confront the immediate but transient manifestations of the social order such as a corrupt official, a discriminatory law, or an unfair labor practice without confronting
the social order itself.

The danger of innovative argument is that the more moderate elements of society often mistake innovative argument for insurgency
because it seeks major change, sometimes through the use of "unpleasant" tactics. Just as King's dream contrasts with Malcolm X's indictment;
so any innovative argument should be advanced as a reasonable alternative to insurgency. It argues that major changes are necessary for the
established order to fulfill its own destiny. But when innovative arguments fail to present such a clear contrast, they are vulnerable to charac-
terization as "subversive" or "revolutionary."

Progressive Argument

Progressive argument is a clearly "systemic" approach to political
argument. By this we mean that unlike insurgent arguments that seek to
replace the established means for reconciling differences or innovative
arguments that believe in the underlying values but object to the ways
that society acts on those values, progressive argument takes established
procedures as givens.

The philosophies of liberalism and conservatism agree that change of
some sort is inevitable and that the established system for resolving disagreements should be used. Neither liberalism nor conservatism pursues
change through "extra-systemic" or proscribed means such as subversion,
violence, or illegal strikes. Progressive argument is therefore conducted
within the "rules of the game." Robert Cathcart has described this as "man-

agerial" rather than "confrontational" rhetoric.[26] The United Farm Workers Union has often been confrontational, but in 1998 they used California's ballot initiative provision to work toward a new way to protect their jobs by protecting farmland from saltwater. Their Web site's discussion of the measure would do credit to any Washington public relations firm:

> Measure K, a United Farm Workers-sponsored initiative on the Nov. 3, 1998 ballot, was approved by voters in the Pajaro Valley Water Management Agency. It requires greater emphasis on conservation in solving serious salt-water intrusion in the coastal basin around Watsonville. More importantly, Measure K gives farm workers and other rural residents a greater voice in water use and acquisition.[27]

The ability to use progressive argument effectively is important when the social movement seeks to institutionalize the concessions won from the system.

Lyndon Johnson's answer to critics who charged that "The System" was responsible for poverty, discrimination, and other social ills was a "War on Poverty." In his first State of the Union address, Johnson told Congress and the nation that:

> We have in 1964 a unique opportunity and obligation—to prove the success of our system; to disprove those cynics at home and abroad who question our purpose and our competence. If we fail, if we fritter and fumble away our opportunity in needless, senseless quarrels between Democrats and Republicans, or between the House and the Senate, or between the South and North, or between the Congress and the administration, then history will rightfully judge us harshly.[28]

Johnson offered his audience an implicit choice: keep pride in your established system by making serious efforts to change socioeconomic conditions, or keep socioeconomic conditions as they are at the expense of proving the insurgents and innovators correct.

Progressive argument often attempts to stress the feasibility of patience and compromise with "The System." President Lyndon Johnson did this in his 1968 State of the Union address:

> A moment ago I spoke of despair and frustrated hopes in the cities where the fires of disorder burned last summer. We can—and in time we will—change that despair into confidence, and change those frustrations into achievements. But violence will never bring progress.[29]

In her stirring keynote address to the 1976 Democratic National Convention, African-American Congresswoman Barbara Jordan made it clear that she believed in the political system and the Democratic Party. She also distanced herself from the insurgent argument of Malcolm X and, more subtly, from the innovative argument of Martin Luther King: "We cannot improve on the system of government handed down to us by the founders of the Republic, there is no way to improve upon that. But what we can do is to find new ways to implement that system and realize our destiny." [30] But the rules of the game Johnson and Jordan supported were not static: the system Jordan praised in 1976 was not identical to the one faced by Dr. King in 1963 nor by Malcolm X in 1965.

Labor unions today are usually able to resolve grievances through collective bargaining—the system for which they struggled prior to the New Deal. Detroit was an important center of labor union activity throughout the twentieth century and, consistent with that culture, the faculty of Wayne State University in Detroit unionized as members of the American Association of University Professors and the American Federation of Teachers (AAUP-AFT). The following excerpt from the Union Local President's letter to the University President announced their intent to strike in terms far different from the labor tensions of the 1930s:

> Our fair-share proposal . . . will add newly hired faculty and academic staff to the union for a short time, giving us a fair opportunity to recruit them as long-term members. Perhaps more significantly, it will give an unmistakable signal to the administration, faculty, and staff of this university that the antiunion days are over . . . . All members of our bargaining unit want a fair compensation package. The offer your administration has put on the table does not meet that simple test. Our union recognizes that the university has many unmet needs. For over a decade, the leadership of our union has called for greater investment in technology and has warned of the university's dangerously heavy dependence on state appropriations for revenue. So we are not naïve about the economics of the university, and we did not go into negotiations asking your administration to match the raises that faculties at some other state universities are receiving.[31]

The letter is interesting because it clearly positions the union and its members as insiders: they recognize that the University has unmet needs, and they imply that they share a commitment to the same code of fairness. Thus, yesterday's insurgency and innovation can become today's progressivism.

The established order often refuses to listen to the arguments of insurgent and revolutionary persuaders. Because progressive argument follows established procedures, it more easily gains an audience. Progressive argument often refers to the threat of insurgency in order to press for moderate change.

Retentive Argument

Retentive argument revolves around conservative and standpat efforts to preserve important elements of the status quo. It bridges the distance between the standpatter who wants to maintain the status quo and the conservative who may be suspicious of change but recognizes its inevitability. The conservative prefers the present to the proposed future and attempts to insure that only necessary and practical changes are instituted. Retentive argument concerns cautious, minimal change, and it will therefore often seem trivial to radicals and reactionaries, both of whom want substantial changes.

Since retentive argument seeks to retain important procedures or qualities that are under attack, it often exhibits an ominous tone. In his memoirs, Senator Barry Goldwater reveals his hope that, "If what I have to say strikes a response in the hearts and minds of other Americans, perhaps they will enlist in the cause to keep our country strong and to restrain those who seek to diminish the importance and significance of the individual." [32] Segregationists argued for retention of the old ways by wearing buttons that said simply, "NEVER!" and (as we will see in chapter 11) the New Right Movement coalesced around arguments to retain control over the Panama Canal.

Retentive argument is heard in presidential campaigns when we are warned about opponents. Gary Allen, who frequently wrote for the John Birch Society, warned in 1976 that:

> If even half of the Carter program is adopted, the average worker in America will face crippling new taxes, horrendous new regulations, and a spiraling rate of inflation that could wipe out any savings he hopes to have. It is a program for Big Government and "efficient Socialism." It is enough to make any sensible person wring his hands in horror.[33]

Jimmy Carter Democrats in 1980 and Walter Mondale Democrats in 1984 said comparable things about the anticipated effects of the Reagan programs on the poor, the elderly, and delicate foreign relations, and many Bush supporters in 1992 echoed Allen's critique of Carter. All three campaigns lost, a sign that threatening apocalyptic visions often reflect more fear than they generate.

Not all retentive argument is threatening. While Governor of California, Ronald Reagan ridiculed criticism of socioeconomic conditions in America by dwarfing social ills with material accomplishments:

> I think if you put your minds to it you could match the Soviet Union's achievements. You would only have to cut all the paychecks 75 percent, send 69 million people back to the farm, tear down almost three-fourths of the houses in America, destroy 69 percent of the steel-making capacity, rip up fourteen of every fifteen miles of road, two-thirds of the railroad track, junk 85 percent of the autos, and tear out nine out of ten telephones.[34]

The politically conservative Reagan, in this passage, focused on retaining good things about American life. But we should not assume that only conservatives try to conserve.

Anarchists recently used retentive argument in relation to control of the Internet and biotechnology. "What people value most about the Internet," says the Black Ribbon Campaign comes from its anarchistic character: the free exchange of information and ideas among people around the world, without the intervention of a governing body. Capitalists and other authoritarians would like to end this: they want nothing more than to attempt to carve up the Internet into an array of corporate/government fiefdoms, to make it just another commodity.[35]

The anarchists are similarly concerned that biotechnology companies seeking to alter the world's food production techniques are getting out of control:

What right do these companies have to tinker with the DNA of these life forms for private gain, when the changes they make can (and do) have unforeseen consequences and will continue in perpetuity? Can the scientists-for-hire who do the gene tinkering for these firms see into the future and definitively say that no threat exists from biotechnologically-mutated life forms? They can't, of course, and they don't, if they wish to remain employed by the firm! You have the foundations for very poor decision making all there, a recipe for disaster.[36]

In short, retentive argument seeks to save or to preserve as much of the present as possible. It may range from Allen's alarm to Reagan's ridicule. In either case, retentive argument usually presents an unattractive picture of its adversaries, impugns their motives, and reduces progressive, innovative, and insurgent argument into one pattern that it characterizes as ill-conceived, evil, and/or dangerous.

Reversive Argument

Reversive argument concerns efforts to return to a previous societal or political condition. Rather than urge retention of "today," it uses the proposed "tomorrow" to argue that society has gone too far and that the tide must be reversed. In reversive argument, standpatters struggle against the reactionary's call for reversive change just as they struggle against the conservative's call for careful, respectful change.

One Right to Life pamphlet urges its audience to reverse the *Roe v. Wade* decision's legalization of abortion because of the precedent it set:

The U.S. Supreme Court has excluded an entire group of humans from legal personhood and with it their right to life. . . . How long will it be before other groups of humans will be defined out of legal existence when it has been decided that they too have become socially burdensome? Senior citizens beware! Minority races beware! Crippled children beware! It did happen once before in this century you know. Remember Germany? Are you going to stand for this?[37]

William Rusher, publisher of the conservative *National Review*, painted a bleak picture of America's future in 1975:

If we succeed, we will have accomplished a mighty thing. We will have reversed . . . the whole downward-spiraling tide of the 20th century. There is no reason why this country's great experiment with freedom must end in failure. It was men and women who created the opportunity, and they who have botched it; and they can rescue it, even now, if they only will.[38]

In a similar vein, Senator Jesse Helms lamented that:

For forty years an unending barrage of "deals" . . . have regimented our people and our economy and federalized almost every human enterprise. This onslaught has installed a gigantic scheme for redistributing the wealth that rewards the indolent and penalizes the hard-working.[39]

But, said Helms, this onslaught can be reversed: "I believe we can halt the long decline. There is nothing inevitable about it. There is a way back." [40]

Let us not presume from these examples that reversive arguments are heard only on the American Right. Several powerful pieces of reversive argument attack the Right itself. Liberal Republican Nelson Rockefeller, a defeated candidate for his party's presidential nomination, addressed the 1964 Republican Convention to propose that the platform condemn extremism:

There is no place in the Republican Party for such hawkers of hate, such purveyors of prejudice, such fabricators of fear, whether Communist, Ku Klux Klan, or Bircher. . . . These people have nothing in common with Republicanism. These people have nothing in common with Americanism. The Republican Party must repudiate these people.[41]

Rockefeller's call to reverse the trend toward extremism of all sorts was drowned out by the booing of an audience unworried by what it regarded as the right kind of extremism. The next evening the audience cheered as conservative presidential nominee Barry Goldwater exclaimed, "Extremism in defense of liberty is no vice!" Contemporary anarchists object to the CIA's creation of a Web page for children. Their language positions it as a "last straw" signaling that the CIA and its supporters have gone over the brink:

Isn't it pretty sick and twisted that the CIA has a Web page for kids? As if this murderous, secretive organization was some cuddly lil' agency you'd be happy to let near your kids? Sheesh. Basically, the page attempts to sanitize (and propagandize) the CIA, to get kids used to its existence and accepting of its mission—after all, they're the next generation of taxpayers![42]

Reversive argument may be near the middle of the typology, but it is hardly moderate in tone. Indeed, it is frequently quite vehement as befits its function of reversing societal direction. It is not unlike shifting into reverse at 65 mph. Reversive argument must direct its audience to (1) see the current direction of society as dangerous, (2) see an alternative direction as desirable, and (3) provide some vehicle for facilitating the necessary change in direction. It cannot rely upon foot dragging, stubbornness, or apathy. Instead, the willingness of the people simply to "go along" with trends is part of the problem. Reversive argument seeks action, and it can fail either because it sounds too "radical" to standpatters and conservatives, or because it is insufficiently inspiring to accomplish its three objectives.

Restorative Argument

Restorative argument urges a full-scale return to a previous state of affairs. The relative merits of that Golden Age are no longer debated: it is clearly preferable to the existing order. Restorative argument centers upon questions of when and why society went astray and how restoration can be accomplished. Reactionaries typically propose legislative or electoral solutions, a change in funding or enforcement of existing means, or a reconstitution of values to conform more closely to an earlier ideology. Revolutionary reactionaries urge more abrupt tactics for the overthrow of the existing order and restoration of the Ancient Regime.

Believing that our national problems stemmed from the intrusion of the federal government into unnecessary ventures, a campaign was advanced during the 1960s on behalf of "The Liberty Amendment" to the U.S. Constitution which would have prohibited government engagement in "any business, professional, commercial, financial, or industrial enterprise except as specified in the Constitution."[43] All such enterprises would be sold to private entrepreneurs, and the federal government's right to tax would be repealed. Supporters of the Amendment argued that:

> We can renew the effectiveness of our Constitution. . . . We can restore the efficiency of our capitalist economy. The Liberty Amendment will accomplish both these purposes, by reducing the functions and powers of the Federal Government, and by restoring the abilities of people to take care of themselves, . . . and by curtailing destructive intervention in our free enterprise economy.[44]

No fan of taxes himself, Senator Jesse Helms argued that the critical turning point in our demise was the ban on prayer in public schools. He explains that:

> It is hardly coincidence that the banishment of the Lord from the public schools has resulted in their being taken over by a totally secularist philosophy. Christianity has been driven out. In its place has been enshrined a permissiveness in which the drug culture has flourished, as have pornography, crime, and fornication . . . . I think there is no more pressing duty facing the Congress than to restore the true spirit of the First Amendment.[45]

And Robert Welch of the John Birch Society encouraged his followers to work toward restoration of the nature of America in the latter half of the twentieth century. He prescribed that America:

> Push the Communists back, get out of the bed of a Europe that is
> dying with the cancer of collectivism, and breathe our own healthy
> air of opportunity, enterprise, and freedom . . . . And despite the bad
> scars and the loss of some muscles, this young, strong, great new
> nation, restored to vigor, courage, ambition, and self-confidence, can
> still go ahead to fulfill its great destiny, and to become an even more
> glorious example for all the earth than it ever was before.[46]

All three of these authors feel strongly the need to restore an earlier and
better day, but there is some disagreement as to whether to get there by
cutting taxes, restoring prayer to the schools, or emphasizing individualism and laissez-faire capitalism.

Restorative argument, in short, alludes to an era or condition that was
preferable to the present in one or more respects. Like reversive argument, it is characteristically immoderate; unlike reversive argument, it
often presents a goal to be pursued.

Revolutionary Argument

Revolutionary argument urges total overthrow of the existing order
but disagrees as to the form and/or nature of the new regime. While revolutionary radical and revolutionary reactionary groups frequently ter-
rorize one another, they agree that the existing order is intolerable,
corrupt, and burdensome. They also agree that its despicable nature justifies violent overthrow. Thus, some reactionaries migrate from radical to
reactionary variants of revolutionary argument, and back again. It is possible to become a revolutionary radical from either direction: a frustrated
radical or a disenchanted revolutionary reactionary. Revolutionary argument is clearly the most confrontational form of political argument; it
relies heavily on brute force to destroy the persons and established institutions that it holds responsible for the problems of society.

For revolution to be considered, the prevailing regime must be seen
as beyond redemption. A master of this was nineteenth century anarchist
Pierre Proudhon. In the following passage, Proudhon allows government
no redeeming value:

> To be governed is to be watched, inspected, spied upon, directed,
> law-driven, numbered, regulated, enrolled, indoctrinated, preached
> at, controlled, checked, estimated, valued, censured, commanded, by
> creatures who have neither the right nor the wisdom nor the virtue to
> do so. To be governed is to be at every operation, at every transaction,
> noted, registered, counted, taxed, stamped, measured, numbered,
> assessed, licensed, authorized, admonished, prevented, forbidden,
> reformed, corrected, punished. It is, under pretext of public utility,
> and in the name of the general interest, to be placed under contribu-
> tion, drilled, fleeced, exploited, monopolized, extorted from,
> squeezed, hoaxed, robbed; then, at the slightest resistance, the first

> word of complaint, to be repressed, fined, vilified, harassed, hunted down, abused, clubbed, disarmed, sacrificed, sold, betrayed, and, to crown all, mocked, ridiculed, derided, outraged, dishonored. That is government; that is its justice; that is its morality.[47]

Nevertheless, revolutionary argument depends upon dramatic rhetorical depictions of its violent acts for its effect. This is why several terrorist groups (often rivals) may claim responsibility for the same bombing—the destruction of property is generally less important than the symbolic mileage gained from it.

Socialist Eugene V. Debs, who ran five times for President of the United States, proclaimed that, "The working class must get rid of the whole brood of masters and exploiters, and put themselves in possession and control of the means of production. . . . It is therefore a question not of reform, the mask of fraud, but of revolution."[48] Clifford Odets concluded "Waiting for Lefty" with this speech by a tough insurgent cab driver:

> AGATE: Christ, we're dyin' by inches! For what? For the debutantes to have their comin' out parties at the Ritz! . . . It's slow death or fight. It's war! . . . Hello America! We're stormbirds of the working class. Workers of the world . . . our bones and our blood! And when we die they'll know what we did to make a new world![49]

Perhaps the most prominent advocate of revolutionary argument was the anarchist Johann Most. While others simply blew buildings to pieces, Most savored violent acts through language. In a pamphlet on dynamite, he wrote:

> Dynamite! Of all the good stuff, that is the stuff! . . . Place this in the immediate vicinity of a lot of rich loafers who live by the sweat of other people's brows, and light the fuse. A most cheerful and gratifying result will follow. In giving dynamite to the downtrodden millions . . . science has done its best work. . . . A pound of this stuff beats a bushel of ballots all hollow—and don't you forget it.[50]

On another occasion, Most proclaimed in his famous speech, "The Beast of Property," that, "If the people do not crush them, they will crush the people, drown the revolution in the blood of the best, and rivet the chains of slavery more firmly than ever. Kill or be killed is the alternative. Therefore massacres of the people's enemies must be instituted"[51]

Dennis Kearney, a California labor leader during the 1870s, sought to rid California of Orientals who constituted a source of cheap labor. But his violence was directed not only at the Orientals, but also at his own union:

> The first time you find a man in the ranks who is not true to the core take him by the nape of the neck and chuck him into the street and then take the bloody shrimps by the throat and tell them you will put big stones around their necks and throw them in the bay.[52]

Of course, exhorting people to violence entails risks to both the speaker and the audience. Anarchist Albert Parsons, a master of revolutionary argument, exhorted his audience:

> If we would achieve our liberation from economic bondage and acquire our natural right to life and liberty, every man must lay by a part of his wages, buy a Colt's navy revolver, a Winchester rifle, and learn how to make and use dynamite. Then raise the flag of rebellion, the scarlet banner of liberty, fraternity, equality and strike down to the earth every tyrant that lives upon this globe.[53]

Lest his audience hesitate, Parsons reminded hearers that, "Until this is done you will continue to be robbed, to be plundered, to be at the mercy of the privileged few." Parsons was hanged in connection with the 1886 Haymarket Square bombing in Chicago. As Carl Smith, professor of American studies points out:

> It [the latter half of the nineteenth century] was a time of terrible cultural tension and anxiety, in which an appalling miscarriage of justice took place. . . . At the trial, the defense argued that although the defendants preached dynamite, there was no evidence to link them to this bomb. The trial was a travesty because the anarchists were convicted for their words, not their deeds.[54]

Revolutionary argument also offers praise to others for their violence. In May of 2000, a Pittsburgh lawyer went on a shooting rampage, killing and injuring a number of people. The Web site of the white supremacist Posse Comitatus organization said:

> Another White Male, Richard Scott Baumhammers, that couldn't take the darkening of Amerika takes ACTION in Pittsburg [sic], Pennsylvania! Kills 5 non-Whites including one jewess bastard! Ah, what's up Scott . . . couldn't find a queer? You ask, "what's wrong? "What's WRONG is that the jew bastards are destroying our once Great White Christian Republic and replacing it with a multicultural cesspool! Each of us must ask what we ARE contributing to STOP this rising MUD FLOOD? What are we doing to let the rest of our brethren know the plight of our RACE & NATION?[55]

Revolutionary argument recommends violent actions against the established order. It is possible for such terrorist rhetoric to be largely devoid of social or political ideology; such is the case today with the Irish Republican Army, the skinheads and the neo-Nazis. While the threat of violence may pave the way for less extreme advocates, actual violence more often polarizes negotiations and renders reasoned, moderate argument exceedingly difficult. Of course, this is rarely important to the revolutionary, who sees moderation as part of the problem.

Conclusions

Seven types of argument—insurgent, innovative, progressive, retentive, reversive, restorative, and revolutionary—are found throughout political controversies. Many social movements have engaged in revolutionary, insurgent, and progressive arguments, while others have sought to preserve the status quo, reverse trends, or restore various Golden Ages. Each type of argument serves a different purpose, and each is a response to a changing social relationships and rhetorical situations.

Insurgent argument addresses the corrupt, mendacious, and exploitative nature of societal norms, values, and institutions. It vilifies institutions, groups, and individuals accountable for problems. *Innovative argument* reveals dissatisfaction with the existing order and preference for experimental change. There is an aversion to both violence and the status quo. *Progressive argument* takes established procedures and values as givens but recognizes that change is inevitable through proper channels and means. *Retentive argument* addresses the importance of preserving significant elements of the status quo. Cautious, minimal change may be accepted grudgingly. *Reversive argument* proposes a return to a previous societal or political state. Society has gone too far and must reverse dangerous trends. *Restorative argument* urges a full-scale return to a previous, ideal state of existence. *Revolutionary argument* demands the complete overthrow of the existing order, by violent means if necessary. The preference is for either a glorious past or a glorious future totally different from the present.

Our illustrative examples show that each of the seven types of argument can be found in the discourse of almost any social movement. But when a social movement or a social movement organization relies disproportionately on one type of argument, we can detect rhetorical patterns that differentiate it from other movements or movement organizations.

Endnotes

1   Roderick P. Hart, *Modern Rhetorical Criticism* (Glenview, IL: Scott Foresman, 1990): 117.

2   Wayne Brockriede, "Where Is Argument?," in Robert Trapp and Janice Schuetz, eds., *Perspectives on Argumentation: Essays in Honor of Wayne Brockriede* (Prospect Heights, IL: Waveland Press, 1990): 4.

3   Michael Billig, *Ideology and Opinions: Studies in Rhetorical Psychology* (Newbury Park, CA: Sage Publications, 1991): 17.

4   See Chaim Perelman and L. Olbrechts-Tyteca, *The New Rhetoric: A Treatise on Argumentation*, trans. by John Wilkinson and Purcell Weaver (Notre Dame, IN: University of Notre Dame Press, 1969).

5   Herbert W. Simons, "Persuasion in Social Conflicts: A Critique of Prevailing Conceptions and a Framework for Future Research," *Speech Monographs* 39 (November 1972): 227, 247.

6   Unless otherwise noted, all references to Rossiter's typology refer to Clinton Rossiter, *Conservatism in America* (New York: Vintage Books, 1962): 11 and 14.

7   See Stephen W. Littlejohn, ed. *Theories of Human Communication* 6/E (Belmont, CA: Wadsworth Publishing, 1992): 148–150, for a helpful summary of social judgment theory; or Muzafer Sherif and Carl Hovland, *Social Judgment: Assimilation and Contrast Effects in Communication and Attitude Change* (New Haven: Yale University Press, 1961).

8   Billig, 17.

9   "Preamble of the I.W.W. Constitution as amended in 1908," *The American Labor Movement*, Leon Litwack, ed. (Englewood Cliffs, NJ: Prentice-Hall, 1962): 42.

10 John Swinton, *Striking for Life: Labor's Side of the Question* (Westport, CT: Greenwood Press, 1970): 104 and 110.

11 Malcolm X, "The Ballot or the Bullet?" *Malcolm X Speaks*, George Breitman, ed. (New York: Ballantine Books, 1965): 31.

12 William Lloyd Garrison, "No Union with Slaveholders," *William Lloyd Garrison*, George M. Frederickson ed. (Englewood Cliffs, NJ: Prentice-Hall, 1968): 54.

13 Clifford Odets, "Waiting for Lefty," *Modern American Plays*, Frederick Cassidy, ed. (Freeport, NY: Books for Libraries Press, 1949): 195.

14 "'Gill the Fish' Urges Kids to Boycott Fishing," 10 May 2000 *(http://www.peta-online.org/news/500/500gillbill.html)*.

15 United Autoworkers Union, "1960's: The UAW Marches Side By Side With Martin Luther King, Jr.," *(http://www.uaw.org/History/civil2.html)*.

16 The Strawberry Workers Campaign, "Five Cents for Fairness: The Case for Change in the Strawberry Fields," United Farm Workers Union White Paper, November 1996 (http://www.ufw.org/paper1.htm/Barons at war with the workers).

17 Ralph Smith and Russell Windes, "The Innovational Movement: A Rhetorical Theory," *Quarterly Journal of Speech* 61 (April 1975): 143. Although we disagree with their conception of innovational movement, we find their characteristics of such movements useful for understanding innovational argument.

18 Samuel Gompers, *Seventy Years of Life and Labor*, quoted in *Samuel Gompers Credo* (New York: American Federation of Labor Samuel Gompers Centennial Committee, 1950): 37.

19 Martin Luther King, Jr. "I Have a Dream," *Contemporary American Public Discourse*, 3/E, Halford R. Ryan, ed. (Prospect Heights, IL: Waveland Press, Inc., 1992): 214–217.

20 Quoted in John C. Echowak, letter (Boulder, CO: Native American Rights Fund, n.d. 119931).

21 Echowak, 1.

22 Echowak, 3.

23 Henry Ford, "History Is More or Less Bunk," *Henry Ford*, John B. Rae, ed. (Englewood Cliffs, NJ: Prentice-Hall, 1969): 53.

24 "Call for Action on SB 984," *(http://www.ufw.org/galloact.htm)*.

25 Stephen H. Browne, "Remembering Crispus Attucks: Race, Rhetoric, and the Politics of Commemoration," *Quarterly Journal of Speech* 85 (May 1999): 171 and 175.

26 Robert S. Cathcart, "Movements: Confrontation as Rhetorical Form," *Southern Speech Communication Journal* 43 (Spring 1978): 237 and 238.

27 Research Office of the United Farm Workers, AFL-CIO, "Stop the Salt, Save Our Jobs." White Paper, September 1999 *(http://www.ufw.org/waterwp.htm)*.

28 Lyndon B. Johnson, "Annual Message to the Congress on the State of the Union," *Public Papers of the Presidents of the United States: Lyndon B. Johnson*, 1963, 1964, Book I (Washington, DC: U.S. Government Printing Office, 1965): 113.

29 Lyndon B. Johnson, "Annual Message to the Congress on the State of the Union," *Public Papers of the Presidents of the United States, Lyndon B. Johnson* Book I (Washington, DC: U.S. Government Printing Office, 1970): 31.

30 Barbara C. Jordan, "Democratic Convention Keynote Address," reprinted in Ryan, 230 and 231.

31 Letter from AAUP-AFT President M. Marlyne Kilbey to WSU President Irvin D. Reid, September 3, 1999 *(http://home.msen.com/~mikemci/aaup/notice_letter.htm.)*.

32 Barry M. Goldwater, *With No Apologies* (New York: William Morrow, 1979): 14.

[33] Gary Allen, *Jimmy Carter, Jimmy Carter* (Seal Beach, CA: 76 Press, 1976): 68.

[34] Ronald Reagan, "Free Enterprise," in Ryan, 273.

[35] The Anarchist Black Ribbon Campaign, "Join the Anarchist Black Ribbon Campaign," May 12, 2000 *(http://www.radio4all.org/anarchy/black.html)*.

[36] "Beware Biotechnology!" May 10, 2000 *(http://www.radio4all.org/anarchy/biotech.html)*.

[37] Dr. and Mrs. J. C. Wilke, "The U.S. Supreme Court Has Ruled It's Legal to Kill a Baby . . ." (Cincinnati: Hayes Publishing, n.d.), 4.

[38] William A. Rusher, *The Making of the New Majority Party* (Ottawa, IL: Green Hill, 1975): 161 and 162.

[39] Jesse Helms, *When Free Men Stand Tall* (Grand Rapids, MI: Zondervan, 1976): 11.

[40] Helms, 12.

[41] Nelson A. Rockefeller, "Address to the Third Session of the 1964 Republican National Convention in Moving Adoption of the Amendment to the Report of the Committee on Resolutions on the Subject of Extremism," Cow Palace, San Francisco, California, July 14. 1964. *Public Papers of Governor Nelson A. Rockefeller, 1964*, 1330.

[42] Anarchy for Anybody, "Random Hostile Thoughts," May 12, 2000 *(http://www.radio4all.org/anarchy/black.html)*.

[43] Lloyd G. Herbstreith and Gordan van B. King, *Action for Americans: The Liberty Amendment* (Los Angeles: Operation America, 1963): inside cover.

[44] Herbstreith and King, 105.

[45] Helms, 108.

[46] Robert H. W. Welch, *The Blue Book of the John Birch Society* (Boston: Western Islands, 1961): 39.

[47] Pierre Joseph Proudhon, "General Idea of the Revolution in the Nineteenth Century," quoted on Geocities' "Anarchist Sampler" page *(http://www.geocities.com/CapitolHill/5065/state.html)*.

[48] Eugene V. Debs, "Outlook for Socialism in the United States," Debs, Ronald Radosh, ed. (Englewood Cliffs, NJ: Prentice-Hall, 1971): 21.

[49] Odets, 192.

[50] Quoted in Louis Adamic, *Dynamite: The Story of Class Violence in America* (New York: Chelsea House, 1958): 47.

[51] Johann Most, "The Beast of Property," reprinted in Charles W. Lomas, *The Agitator in American History* (Englewood Cliffs, NJ: Prentice-Hall, 1968): 39.

[52] Dennis Kearney, "The Chinese Must Go!" reprinted in Lomas, 29.

[53] Albert Parsons, "The Board of Trade: Legalized Theft," reprinted in Lomas, 44.

[54] Quoted in Robert Freed, "Making History," *Northwestern* (fall 2000): 40.

[55] "Newsflash," May 12, 2000 (http://posse-comitatus.org).

ARGUMENT FROM NARRATIVE VISION IN SOCIAL MOVEMENTS

This chapter examines how people use stories or narratives as frameworks for interpreting reality. It will consider how some people construct stories to help other people see the world "properly." Two case studies demonstrate how a social movement can challenge an institution's narrative, how the interpretive frameworks and events are interdependent, and how a rhetorical form can become a political resource.

Narrative and Rhetorical Vision

David Carr writes, "Human existence and action . . . consist not in overcoming time, not in escaping it or arresting its flow, but in shaping and forming it.[1] He maintains that each person lives in a remembered past and acts in expectation of a future that is a projection of past and present. We cast ourselves in an unfolding story and act it out, and because we choose the story and our role in it, we can switch stories at any time.

Howard Kamler explains that stories help us to "know" and to protect what we "know" from counterargument. Stories structure our lives by contextualizing otherwise ambiguous episodes, and they allow us to believe what we need to believe by defining what constitutes relevant evidence. Kamler also writes that we communicate by making our private stories public and public stories (such as myths) our own.[2] Moreover, storytelling invites audiences to agree for the sake of the story, unlike arguments that invite debate. Thus, individuals search for self-understanding by imposing narrative structure on their lives.

Earlier chapters discussed the importance of perceived environments and the need for social movements to transform perceptions. These functions are normally accomplished through narratives. Each narrative structures the past, projects a future, and prescribes a preferred course of conduct from a particular vantage point. Each narrative has an author, a narrator, a protagonist, and an audience; but it is the narrator's vantage point in time, intellect, wisdom, values, and character that positions the story for the audience. The reader-narrator identification is central. Readers who identify with the narrator step into the story, enact it, and retain the experience. Stories that facilitate these processes, in turn, foster identification. Readers can ignore an ill-defined or unconvincing narrator, and an audience repelled by the narrator may use the narrative to construct an opposing vision. The narrator's image and audience appeal are so important to the narrative that personal identification overpowers logical rigor.[3]

Carr theorizes that we organize our social relationships and communities through the telling and retelling of stories. Stories or myths link us to our contemporaries and to our predecessors and successors.[4] Storytelling engages people in a communicative relationship defined by the narrator-audience relationship. The narrator and listener create a "we" through their identification; "my story" becomes "our story" through co-creation. Interpretive communities coalesce around stories as each "we" acquires its own folklore and narrators. Narrators embellish the story by emphasizing different characters, motives, events, chronology, and plot lines. Carr distinguishes between stories that endure ("retentions") and those that can be remembered if necessary ("recollections").[5] Differences develop when one person's retention is another's mere recollection. Social movements often weave a variety of recollections into a new story to raise them to the level of retention.

If history is the creation of explanatory stories, and if communities form around their stories, then some of these narrative groups must inevitably conflict. Consider the historic conflicts among Christian denominations, all based upon their varying interpretations of the story of Jesus of Nazareth. Likewise, most U.S. social movements offer conflicting narratives of the "meaning of America" and the essence of "the American Dream."

Fisher suggests that each narrative enacts a set of values and that these enacted values govern the narrative's audience appeal. Each narrative is judged by its narrative coherence (does the story work?) and by its narrative fidelity (does the story use the audience's beliefs and values?). He says that audiences look for good reasons, which they regard as stories that are consistent with what they know and value, appropriate to the pending decision, promising in effects for themselves, and consistent with what they regard as an ideal basis for conduct.[6] This view of persuasion hinges less on changing beliefs, attitudes, or values than on integrating beliefs and behaviors into a story regarded by the audience as coherent, relevant, compatible, promising, and proper.

The narrative position is largely compatible with the popular rhetorical perspective of symbolic convergence, sometimes known as "fantasy theme analysis." Ernest Bormann built upon Robert F. Bales's observation that individuals working together frequently dramatize or act out a "fantasy" (a recollection or an estimation of the future).[7] The verbalizing, expressing, or dramatizing of a fantasy orients listeners to the present by drawing upon their pasts and futures. Some fantasies fall flat, but when listeners recognize a fantasy as one of their own, they respond emotionally as well as cognitively. They hitchhike on the original comment and extend the fantasy by polishing the image, adding examples, and extending it. Then a third person recognizes and joins the shared fantasy. Soon the individuals are drawing on their separate pasts and futures to create a shared present. Thus, they develop a common orientation to the present that binds them to one another by the shared vision and by the process of creating it. This process is called "chaining" (as in "they created an elaborate fantasy chain" or "the fantasy chained out to the entire group").

Bormann's primary contribution is his suggestion that fantasy-chaining transcends the small-group experience. If small groups create shared identities through group fantasizing, he reasons, so might large groups such as audiences, organizations, social movements, and societies. Bormann identifies rhetorical visions as "the composite dramas which catch up large groups of people in a symbolic reality."[8] They arise through communication and provide the themes, heroes, villains, values, and motivations that are invoked in later communication. Rhetorical visions are particularly pertinent where clear explanations are elusive. Bormann observes that:

> When the authentic record of events is clear and widely understood, the competing visions must take it into account . . . [But] Whenever occasions are so chaotic and indiscriminate that the community has no clear observational impression of the facts, people are given free rein to fantasize within the assumptions of their rhetorical vision.[9]

Narrative and rhetorical vision are not identical frameworks. The narrative model is more perceptually grounded, more cognitive, and offers more analytical guidance. Fantasy theme analysis draws more heavily upon imaginings than recollections, although most would agree that our fantasies and imaginings grow out of our experiences. But the connection between narrative and rhetorical vision should be evident. Fantasies and rhetorical visions are narrative in form. Some fantasies stimulate recognition and empathy, thereby enhancing audience-narrator identification, inviting the audience to join in the creative process by participating in the story itself, fostering identification with like-minded auditors, and motivating listeners to remember the story. We shall coin the term "narrative vision" to encompass both Carr's sense of configured time and Bormann's collective imagining with respect to two social movement episodes.

We will first examine the story told by the contemporary militia or patriot movement to see how a social movement situates itself, characterizes its legitimacy, and transforms the prevailing perceptions of reality. We will then explore the New Right's use of the Panama Canal controversy of the 1970s to mobilize a movement, gain control of the Republican Party, and to shape U.S. foreign policy in the 1980s.

Patriot Movement or Domestic Terrorism?

Ruby Ridge, Waco, and Oklahoma City quickly became defining episodes in the stories of the militia or patriot movement. This section considers three elements of the militia narrative—claim to historic legitimacy, the sanctity of weapons, and characterizations of the 1995 Oklahoma City bombing—to understand better the interpretive stance of this contemporary social movement.

The Militia Movement as Historically Legitimate

The militia or patriot movement anchors itself in the U.S. Constitution, and the clash between the militias and the United States government results from their divergent interpretations of this foundational document. There is little disagreement that colonists such as George Washington, John Adams, Benjamin Franklin, and Thomas Jefferson led a revolutionary movement to overthrow British rule and then established the United States of America to replace it. The disagreement is that today's government sees itself as the living extension of Washington, Jefferson, and the Constitution, and they see the militia not as patriots but as misguided terrorists who put the Constitution at risk. But the militia story portrays today's federal government as an occupying force comparable to the British, with the militia themselves being heirs to the tradition of Washington and Jefferson. Their conflicting understandings of "true Americanism" frame strikingly divergent narratives of today's "problem" and "solution".

One voice of the movement, the "Belligerent Claimant" Web site, states "We have been living in occupied enemy territory for a very long time."[10] Dave Delany of Dave Delany's Freedom House also develops the historic roots of the militia, writing "The militia is a 'grass roots' tool of the people, designed to check the abuse of its own internal government, *and* to defend against the incursions of a foreign enemy . . . We are now at odds with our history."[11]

Delany quotes Founders John Hancock, Josiah Quincy, Joseph Warren, and Benjamin Rush on the dangers of having a professional military that follows orders. Their ideal, he says, was a citizen militia committed to defending their own rights and property. "When the force directed against you is the army of the federal government or one of its fingers," he warns "you can hardly call upon the hand of the federal government to protect you! Do you somehow think that the commander in chief is immune from the abuse of power?" In his view the growth of a professional military is not a source of protection but a threat to all Americans: "Rather than replacing the local militia, the growth of the federal army requires the increase in the strength of the local militia. The local militia is the only defense against the tyranny of a standing army."[12] Thus, True Americans must be ever vigilant. Delany closes by quoting Benjamin Rush from 1787:

> "The American war is over, but this is far from being the case with the American revolution. On the contrary, nothing but the first act of the drama is closed." He was speaking then of the weakness of our nation. I am writing now of the weakness of our nation also. "Hear her proclaiming, in sighs and groans, in her governments, in her finances, in her trade, in her manufactures, in her morals and in her manners," (do you hear them?) "'The Revolution is not over.'" If we are to remain free, it never will be. God bless the militia.[13]

Although Delany's position is grounded in the writings and addresses of the Founders, other militia voices have used the patriotic uprising story to develop historical lessons from scratch.

The Turner Diaries is a novel about a 1991–93 American revolution by "The Organization" against the Zionist Occupied Government (ZOG). It is fiction presented as the diary of one Earl Turner. Because it is fiction, the author has a free hand with the narrative. Because it looks like a diary, it invites a suspension of disbelief. Because it is the reminiscence of a "freedom fighter," it invites us to transfer the author's insights to our contemporary lives. The narrative persona of Earl Turner was created by Andrew Macdonald, the pen name of physicist William Pierce. Priscilla Meddaugh has pointed out that Pierce frequently identifies himself as "Dr. William Pierce" without explaining the relevance of his academic credentials in physics to his white supremacist argument.[14] Pierce used the Macdonald/Turner persona for a particular kind of discourse. "Dr. Pierce" is his voice for making the white supremacist case in logical, nonfictional terms while "Macdonald/Turner" is his voice for telling a story of revolution that invites identification and eschews logical argument.

Whereas Delany views the present from the perspective of the Founders, the voice of Macdonald/Turner looks at the United States from the post-revolutionary vantage point:

> All in all, it has been depressingly easy for the System to deceive and manipulate the American people—whether the relatively new "conservatives" or the spoiled and pseudo-sophisticated "liberals." Even the libertarians, inherently hostile to all government, will be intimidated into going along.[15]

From his perspective in the fictional future, Turner can say that Americans deserved to lose their freedom because they failed to act when there was still time.

> Americans have lost their right to be free. Slavery is the just and
> proper state for a people who have grown as soft, self-indulgent, care-
> less, credulous, and befuddled as we have. . . . Indeed, we are already
> slaves. We have allowed a diabolically clever, alien minority to put
> chains on our souls and our minds. These spiritual chains are a truer
> mark of slavery than the iron chains which are yet to come.[16]

Thus, Pierce recommends a course of action to his readers by moving
them into a fictional future and then providing a flashback.

The Belligerent Claimant Web site extends that critique. In their view,
the problem is not so much a matter of national weakness as an enemy
occupation of America:

> The entirety of this Web site is to prove that we are AT WAR with the
> very government who calls us their chattel, and have been that way for
> over a century. Call it the United Nations, the United States, The New
> World Order, the Masons, the Jews, the Illuminatti [sic], the CFR
> [Council on Foreign Relations], the Trilateral Commission, or that furry
> thing from Star Wars . . . . We are at war with an Occupied Enemy.[17]

Who, then, is this occupying enemy?

> [They] have called themselves Yankees more often than not. If you
> believe in a strong and oppressive government, then you are a Yankee.
> If you believe in Life, Liberty and the pursuit of your own Happiness,
> then you are an American at heart. This is not about the Mason-Dixon
> Line or where you were born. It has nothing to do with the northern
> or southern, eastern or western States, except that they are all under a
> government's control who could care less about the American people
> and our rights. Now is the time to Call to Arms! We have waited far
> too long to act upon their aggression, AMERICA IS AT WAR![18]

The voices of the contemporary militia movement therefore conceive
of themselves as direct descendants of the citizen militias that overthrew
the power of the Crown in the eighteenth century. They identify with
George Washington less as a general and a president than as the land-
owner and slave owner who risked everything to stand up to the oppressive power of the State. Theirs is a libertarian worldview in which
legitimacy comes not from the legal authority of executives, legislatures,
police, and judges but from the inalienable rights each person possesses
and loans—temporarily and grudgingly—to the government. Beyond the
political beliefs expressed, note the language used. The tone of the language is blunt, aggressive, and uncompromising. It seems unlikely to
appeal to happy people or to those who dislike confrontation. Thus, it
invites identification with some people and alienates others.

The Inalienable Right to Bear Arms

As heirs to the citizen militias of the 1700s, today's activists believe,
perhaps first and foremost, in the role of private gun ownership as the

guarantor of freedom. They claim that the freedom fighters who wrote the Constitution did not write the Second Amendment to protect target shooters and deer hunters but to insure that an armed citizen militia could protect the security of their newly won independence and government. The institutional position is that circumstances have changed in 200 hundred years, and the armed forces and the police now perform the function originally assigned to the militia. Militia voices perceive any form of gun control as the Government's effort to take away the most revered individual right.[19]

A statement posted on the Web captures the grandeur and the totality of the militia movement's causal link between gun ownership and freedom:

> The Soviet Union established gun control in 1929. From 1929 to 1953, 20 million political dissidents, unable to defend themselves, were rounded up and exterminated. Turkey established gun control in 1911. From 1915 to 1917, 1.5 million Armenians, unable to defend themselves, were rounded up and exterminated. Germany established gun control in 1938. From 1939 to 1945, 13 million Jews, Gypsies, homosexuals, mentally ill people, and other "mongrelized peoples," unable to defend themselves, were rounded up and exterminated. China established gun control in 1935. From 1948 to 1952, 20 million political dissidents, unable to defend themselves, were rounded up and exterminated. Guatemala established gun control in 1964. From 1964 to 1981, 100,000 Mayan Indians, unable to defend themselves, were rounded up and exterminated. Uganda established gun control in 1970. From 1971 to 1979, 300,000 Christians, unable to defend themselves, were rounded up and exterminated. Cambodia established gun control in 1956. From 1975 to 1977, 1 million "educated people," unable to defend themselves, were rounded up and exterminated.[20]

In short, seven countries instituted gun control in this century and almost immediately rounded up and slaughtered 55 million innocent people. The posting dares the reader to call this a coincidence. The implied relationship is clearly causal: 55 million people would have lived if they had kept their guns.

The horror of gun control is prominent in the fictional *Turner Diaries*. Turner wonders:

> Why didn't we rebel 35 years ago, when they took our schools away from us and began converting them into racially mixed jungles? Why didn't we throw them all out of the country 50 years ago, instead of letting them use us as cannon fodder in their war to subjugate Europe? More to the point, why didn't we rise up three years ago when they started taking our guns away? Why didn't we rise up in righteous fury and drag these arrogant aliens into the streets and cut their throats then? Why didn't we roast them over bonfires at every street corner in America? Why didn't we make a final end to this obnoxious and eternally pushy clan, this pestilence from the sewers of the East, instead of meekly allowing ourselves to be disarmed?[21]

Clearly, Turner's narrative attributes political legitimacy to individual citizens who are entitled to violate a gun control law. Far more importantly, his story invites readers to conclude that they are entitled to kill brutally those who support and enforce such laws.

The dominant militia theme is that citizens need to be able to use weapons to protect themselves. When the enemy has the upper hand, some militia voices urge premeditated or pre-emptive illegal acts. The Belligerent Claimant Web site, for example, offers tips to its readers:

> *TIP #1:* Visit your local auto dealership as a shopper and learn where they store the keys at night for the trucks on the lot. Do some research to locate any other important 'bounty' required for self-defense when the time comes.
>
> *TIP #2:* Research weaponry if you have no knowledge of the current firearms and ammunitions, etc. . . . If you do not have a modern gun, keep in mind that captured weapons and guns from dead enemies (& compatriots) work fine too.[22]

In short, the militia voices regard guns and other weapons as essential to protect basic rights, and they express no qualms about the means used to acquire those weapons.

Although militia groups cherish their Constitutional rights to bear arms and to form a militia, the National Rifle Association has been careful to separate its own defense of gun ownership from the need for a militia. One militia member downloaded and shared with his colleagues the NRA's position on militias and guns:

> the individual right to own firearms is guaranteed by the Constitution, but the right to own firearms is not at all dependent upon the militia clause. The militia clause of the Second Amendment merely adds to the reason for the right, which is a common law right rooted in the right of protection of self, family and community. The Second Amendment guarantees an individual's right to arms; participation in a citizen militia organization does not make that right more valid nor any stronger.[23]

Of course, guns are most useful when the gun wielder has a clear view of the target. One might reasonably infer, then, that the importance of bearing arms is linked clearly to a well-defined Other that threatens rights and property. Indeed, Richard Hofstadter's landmark essay on "The Paranoid Style in American Politics" posited an enemy that was, "clearly delineated: he is a perfect model of malice, a kind of amoral superman: sinister, ubiquitous, powerful, cruel, sensual, luxury-loving."[24] But a clearly delineated image of such an Evil Other did not emerge from Priscilla Meddaugh's study of the "Other" in hate group Web sites.[25] Indeed, the Evil Others discussed so far in this essay have included the United Nations, the United States, the New World Order, the Masons, Jews, the Illuminati, the Council on Foreign Relations, the Trilateral Commission and the governments of the Soviet Union, Turkey, China, Nazi Germany, Guatemala, Uganda, and Cambodia. Against which of those enemies are private guns thought to be useful?

As a story of villainy, the militia sites give us not vivid evidence of some Freddie Krueger or Chucky slashing victims—those are the kinds of individual villains against which hand to hand use of personal guns might prove useful. Instead, the militia stories provide us with tales of the Blair Witch and signs of evil in the woods. Their villain is a generalized evil that manifests itself in a variety of forms. It is precisely such fears of invisible targets that often lead frustrated armed people to shoot blindly into the night. Whatever they hit becomes, after the fact, the target. Sometimes, such random violence is rationalized. *The Turner Diaries* tells of the militia's arrest near a university campus of a "white girl, about 19, a bit flabby but still pretty. . . . Informed that she was about to pay the price for defiling her race by living with a Black lover . . . wailed, 'But why me?'"

> The answer is simply that her name happened to be on our list and Helen's didn't [although Helen, too, had "defiled her race"]. There's nothing fair about that—or unfair either. The girl who was hanged deserved what she got. Helen probably deserved the same fate—and she is undoubtedly suffering the torments of the damned now, in fear that she will be found out and forced to pay the price her friend did.[26]

That price was to be a violent death at the hands of self-appointed executioners whenever her name became the random target hit by the violent act.

This execution taught the fictional Turner a lesson in the value of arbitrary political terror. Pierce tells the reader through Turner, "Its very arbitrariness and unpredictability are important aspects of its effectiveness. There are a great many people in Helen's situation, whose fear that lightning may strike them at any moment will keep them walking on eggs."[27] Yet Pierce and Turner fail to notice that there is little one can do to escape lightning or random violence. Indeed, it is precisely when arms are used to commit violent acts that kill and injure innocent people that the militia narrative fragments.

Militia Accounts of Violence: The Oklahoma City Bombing

We have seen that many militia voices characterize themselves as heirs to the libertarian tradition of individual sovereignty and that they perceive the Second Amendment's arms and militia protections as the only way to protect and/or recover individual rights. This creates a rhetoric of virtual violence, as in *The Turner Diaries*. But what does their rhetoric say about *actual* violence and destruction, as in the 1995 bombing of the federal building in Oklahoma City?

Militia voices told four different stories to explain the 1995 bombing of the Federal Building in Oklahoma City. The "Revolution: Ammo for Freedom Fighters" Web site integrated the bombing into the violent narrative exemplified by *The Turner Diaries*. A reporter interviewed Ross Hullett, identified as the "commander of the Oklahoma brigade" who said:

> there are 20 militia members underground for every one in the open. . . . There are four or five different groups in the shadows around here and we're talking about dangerous people. I mean savage, vicious people. I am one of them. . . . Our government has been lying to us for too long, and Waco was the last damned straw," said the Texan, a veteran of US Special Forces. "Now we're telling them that they'd better straighten out this government and they had better straighten out Waco because, if they don't, it is going to get ugly. . . . You think you've seen terror? You haven't seen shit yet."[28]

This militia spokesman's account characterized the Oklahoma City bombing as a microcosm of the type and magnitude of terrorism that the militias will produce. It is reminiscent of colonial propagandists such as Sam Adams who did their best to maximize the movement's resources and resolve. This can help mobilization and confrontation, but it also invites institutional retaliation by admitting/claiming participation in a revolutionary act.

Other militia voices put a second, very different spin on the Oklahoma City bombing. Pierce's radio commentary turned the tables on government officials:

> I listened to the expressions of pious outrage by Bill Clinton and Janet Reno and the other government gangsters on television that evening, and I thought, "You hypocrites! What do you expect? You are the real terrorists. When a government engages in terrorism against its own citizens, it should not be surprised when some of those citizens strike back and engage in terrorism against the government. You are the ones responsible for this bombing, for the deaths of these children."[29]

Unlike the first example, Pierce's account distanced his followers from the bombing. He understands and justifies the hatred of government that could lead people to commit such acts, but he denounces the bombing and attributes ultimate blame for it to the President and the Attorney General. There is no claim of militia strength or of any interest in flexing muscle through bombings.

The third view decried the bombings and focused on the "government and media campaign" to discredit the militias. One Internet posting stated "I am incapable of saying anything which would adequately express 1/100th of the disgust I feel for anyone who would do such a thing, or the sorrow I feel for the victims. However, the government, with massive help from the media, will use this opportunity to attack and murder more citizens and further restrict our rights—all in the name of 'security'—all under the cloak of emotional hysteria."[30]

A fourth militia response to the bombing charged that the federal government itself destroyed the building. A *Stormfront* article by Eustace Mullins pulls no punches:

J'Accuse! This is the title of the French Novelist Emile Zola's trenchant work of the nineteenth century, which accused the Government of France of brazen corruption. Today, in the United States, I accuse the federal government of planning and perpetrating the most horrible crimes, a series which culminated in the April 19, 1995 bombing of the federal building in Oklahoma City. This was a deliberate conspiracy by corrupt and treasonous elements in the federal agencies in Washington as part of a plan to provoke martial law, confiscate legal guns from American citizens, and to wipe out the citizens militia of the several states.[31]

A group called The Prophecy Club advertises a video called *Cover-up in Oklahoma*, billed as "a highly acclaimed video tape which is singularly effective at exposing the massive government/media cover-up of the Murrah Building bombing."[32]

Cover-up in Oklahoma convincingly demonstrates that the Murrah Building was destroyed from within by demolition charges placed on the critical support columns by people with free access to that building. But most shocking to many viewers is this video's revelation that the huge 30' wide X 8' deep bomb crater alleged by government and media is a hoax.[33]

All four militia versions of the Oklahoma City bombing underscore mistrust of government and encourage support for the militia itself. As Duncan put it:

In the aftermath of the bombing, it's important to examine our reasoning processes and emotions very carefully. We must remain vigilant of overzealous politicians, regulators, and federal agents. We must not be blinded by fear. A strong, nationwide emotional reaction is exactly what the Administration (and its puppet-masters in the UN) need to grab what's left of our Rights. The media will play their part because sensationalism always jacks up the ad rates. In both cases, it's all about money and control.[34]

Thus, the militia, like movement voices across the political spectrum, responded to the Oklahoma City bombing with four different stories: (1) the bombing shows that militia forces are stronger than previously thought and prepared to act, (2) the bombing was a regrettable but understandable reaction to government terrorism at Waco, (3) the bombing is regrettable but will be used by the government and the corporate media to attack the militia and (4) the bombing was conducted by the government to warrant suppression of the militia.

Weaving the Story

How have the militia voices used language to tell their story? How has their story arrested the flow of time and shaped circumstances to reflect militia reality? And, finally, how has their story protected members of the militia movement from counterargument and attack?

The militia story connects members to the Founders of the United States. Because the story still regards the nation as an enemy-occupied territory, it suggests almost immediate derailment with the government betraying the ideals of the Founders. Their story is comparable to George Orwell's *Animal Farm* in which the revolutionary pigs become a totalitarian order more vile than the order they had overthrown. The occupying force—be it the British, the New World Order, the United Nations or ZOG—intrudes upon the individual sovereignty that, they say, was at the heart of the Founders' revolution.

In this never-ending struggle over individual rights, the militia's central commitment is to the sanctity of weapons. They talk frequently of stockpiling guns and other weaponry to defend or to take back their rights and property from the occupying force, and they advertise training manuals so that they can be well prepared to use arms when the time comes. But their aggressive and uncompromising narrative splinters in the face of real violence when their varied accounts fail to live up to the bravado of their call to arms.

Every social movement is large in scope, and it is the variety of stories and people who believe them that gives each movement its character. Most of these stories are shared by word of mouth, and the chaining-out process creates links among believers. This seems especially likely when the story is one of ideals betrayed, of heroism and martyrdom, and of "real truths" that corrupt institutions keep from us. Although such stories may not appeal to a large number of listeners, they do invite very intense feelings among those devoted to the cause who then propel and sustain a movement.

The centrality of weapons to the militia movement has important theoretical implications. The militia movement faces a strategic trilemma. Their first problem is that their divergent accounts of Oklahoma City undermined the credibility of their extreme rhetoric, while the pictures of bloodied children did little to win mainstream popularity. The second problem is that a full rhetorical retreat from Oklahoma City for public relations purposes invites several questions: If not Oklahoma City, then what sort of militia warfare would they support? After all, if the federal government has not infringed upon their rights, then who has? And, therefore, if violence against the federal government is not in order, then against whom do they plan to use their arms? And if they do not plan to use their arms to protect and to reclaim their rights, then (a) how are they like the Founders, and (b) why are they acquiring their weapons and training? The third problem is that any attempts to resolve the first two problems with divergent accounts undermines the importance of narrative unity and discipline and thus undercuts the need for quasi-military operations from the outset.

This section has emphasized the Militia narrative; but it is not realistic to consider any narrative in isolation because there are always an infinite number of stories available to the public, especially with the advent of Internet sites and chat rooms. As Bormann would remind us, it is the convergence of people around narratives and the divergence among narratives that lead to the rise and fall of social movements and to a movement's ability to win its struggle. We turn, therefore, to the comparison of two narratives that engaged one another in a struggle for dominance in the late 1970s.

The Panama Canal Controversy

New Right organizer Richard Viguerie boasted in 1981 that "No political issue in the last 25 years so clearly divided the American establishment from the American people as the Panama Canal treaties." The proposed treaties were truly supported by the establishment: two Democratic and two Republican presidents, the Democratic leaders in both houses of Congress, the Joint Chiefs of Staff, "Big Labor, Big Business, Big Media, the big international banks, and just about every liberal political and cultural star you could name." Opposed to the treaties were "the American people—about 70 percent of them . . . probably 85 percent of registered Republicans" and a coterie of conservative spokespersons who would become known as the "New Right": Senators Paul Laxalt, Jake Garn, and Bill Scott, Congressmen Philip Crane, Larry McDonald, and Mickey Edwards, and organizers Paul Weyrich, Howard Phillips, William Rhatican, Terry Dolan, and Viguerie himself.[35] The treaties passed the Senate by a two-vote margin, a significant victory for President Carter. But many citizens remained deeply opposed to the treaties.[36]

The "New Right" movement used the proposed Panama Canal treaties to energize the conservative imagination. By advancing a narrative that made treaty ratification illogical, rather than arguing technicalities, the New Right engaged less active conservatives in group fantasizing.

To defeat the treaties and/or mobilize a new conservative majority, the New Right needed a rhetoric that would appeal to a variety of interpretive communities. Specifically, the New Right had four rhetorical tasks. First, they needed to incorporate the enduring symbols and beliefs of foreign policy conservatives, many of them Democrats, as the core of the antitreaty coalition. Second, they needed to enhance U.S. recollections of the Panama Canal. Third, they needed to dramatize latent fantasies about a perilous world to keep Americans from trusting other nations. Fourth, and most delicately, they had to separate the concept of "Republican Party" into two parts: linking the Ford-Kissinger-Rockefeller-Nixon wing with Carter and the Democrats while linking their own wing with treaty opposition, the New Right, and public opinion.

Ronald Reagan used the canal issue to with the 1976 North Carolina primary, and he continued to be a prominent antitreaty voice. Unconvinced by a private briefing from the negotiators, Reagan told the Young

Americans for Freedom that the treaties "would eliminate the rights of sovereignty we acquired in the original treaty. . . . Without these rights we must ask what is to prevent a Panamanian regime one day from simply nationalizing the canal and demanding our immediate withdrawal. . . . Secrecy, of course, is no longer the issue. Security is."[37] By using a narrative structure Reagan invited his young, unbriefed, conservative listeners to fantasize. Instead of telling them what he had learned from the negotiators, Reagan asked his audience to allay his fears.

An antitreaty letter in Reagan's name was sent out on Republican National Committee letterhead in late October. The letter advanced nine propositions:

1. In the process of giving up our Canal, Mr. Carter has also surrendered our rights to build a new one if needed.

2. There's no guarantee our Naval Fleet will have the right of priority passage in time of war.

3. The U.S. does not have the right to intervene to defend the Canal.

4. We must close down 10 of our military bases, Americans in the Zone will be under Panamanian rule, and we must pay [General Omar] Torrijos millions more each year for the Canal.

5. These treaties could cost Americans hundreds of millions . . . Plus we'll pay higher prices . . . [Torrijos] maintains close ties with Fidel Castro and the Soviet Union.

6. [Torrijos] seized power by gunpoint . . . [and] controls the press, he's outlawed all political parties but the Marxist party and he controls the military.

7. Once we pull out, what's to stop Torrijos or his successor from nationalizing the Canal and ordering us out at once?

8. Panama is one of the most unstable countries in Latin America.

9. From the beginning, Mr. Carter negotiated this treaty without consulting Congressional leaders.[38]

It is difficult to imagine the Republican National Committee sponsoring this mailing if President Ford had won the 1976 election, because five of the nine statements refer to Carter while none mention that Republican Presidents Ford and Nixon agreed with him. By so strongly opposing the treaties, the Republican National Committee significantly disadvantaged the future prospects of Republican treaty supporters such as Ford.

The Reagan letter was the New Right's first major victory in its efforts to lead mainstream Republican opposition to the Carter administration. The Republican leadership had significant political and organizational needs that provided incentives for them to oppose the treaties now advocated by the Democrats. Nevertheless, the Reagan letter was flawed because it was a propositional rather than a narrative argument. By detailing nine propositions, Reagan invited disagreement, which he received from many quarters because many Republican conservatives did not oppose the treaties.

The most trenchant response to Reagan came in a letter from actor John Wayne, an icon of patriotism and military heroism. Wayne's personal cover letter to "Ronnie" expressed his regrets: "If you had given time and thought on this issue, your attitude would have gained you the image of leadership that I wished for you, rather than, in the long run, a realization by the public that you are merely making statements for political expediency." He told Reagan "I'll show you point by God damn point in the Treaty where you are misinforming people." Wayne then gave an important warning: "If you continue these erroneous remarks, someone will publicize your letter to prove that you are not as thorough in your reviewing of the Treaty as you say or are damned obtuse when it comes to reading the English language." Attached to the cover letter was a four-page cut-and-paste summary of Reagan's nine points under the title "SCARE LETTER FROM THE HONORABLE RONALD REAGAN" along with Wayne's quite specific and technical responses. His responses were replete with phrases such as "the truth is," "completely misleading," "complete untruth," and "How dare you continue to make these statements." Wayne's conclusion spoke directly to Reagan's use of the Canal as a vehicle for fund raising. "Quite obviously," said Wayne, "you are using . . . [the Panama Canal Treaty] as a teaser to attract contributions to our party. I know of our party's need for money; but if your attitude in order to get it is as untruthful and misleading as your letter, we haven't a chance."[39] (The tone of Wayne's letter may seem surprising in the post-Reagan era. But it must be read in the context of 1977 when the treaties had been supported by Nixon, Ford, and the Joint Chiefs of Staff, and Senator Barry Goldwater was moving toward support.)

Wayne's letter highlights the rhetorical dilemmas facing the New Right in late 1977. Reagan was their best prospect for winning the presidency in 1980 and the Panama issue was their best chance for mobilizing support. But Reagan's arguments against the treaties could destroy his credibility. The rhetorical leadership of the antitreaty forces passed from Reagan to Illinois Congressman Phillip Crane, a historian by profession, in January 1978.

President Carter avoided a televised Canal speech in 1977 even though speechwriter James Fallows feared that this would leave "all the public argumentation to the other side . . . and by letting their crazy charges go unanswered for the moment we suggest that we don't have any answers."[40] Fallows agreed with advisor Harlan Strauss that the basic problem was "the McGuffey Reader Complex":

> Since early this century . . . the myth that the Panama Canal and its surrounding territory was ours "in perpetuity" was taught as a truism in the classroom and in the grammar school textbooks. [The Pres-

ident must re-educate] the over 50, the grade school only, and
Republican [audiences about manifest destiny, the Monroe Doctrine,
and the "in perpetuity" clause].[41]

Herein lay Carter's rhetorical predicament. The New Right was constructing a coherent antitreaty narrative out of the retentions that older,
conservative, Republican citizens had acquired early in life. Even if that
narrative were as erroneous as claimed by Strauss and Wayne, it was nevertheless consistent with everything they had learned about the canal,
and a narrative's persuasiveness hinges largely on its fidelity to its audience's experiences. On the other hand, the President was being urged to
tell this audience that the facts they had learned in grade school were
wrong—facts that were being used and reinforced almost daily by the
antitreaty advocates. Although Fallows agreed with Strauss's analysis, he
recognized the predicament and its risks.[42]

On January 25, 1978, Fallows outlined a Fireside Chat. It was to be a
short (10 to 15 minute) address, "confident, positive, and forward looking" as well as "simple (7th grade this time)." But his outline suggested 28
points and sub-points distributed over four sections.[43] Their discussions
led to 13 additional points, leaving Fallows with an average of fifteen to
twenty seconds per point—not counting the introduction and conclusion.

By contrasting pro- and antitreaty narratives from 1974–1978, we can
see how the New Right movement used the canal issue to weave diverse
public recollections and fantasies into a narrative vision that aroused and
united conservatives and, ultimately, reoriented U.S. foreign policy. We
will pay particular attention to the narratives of Crane (the movement's
primary spokesman and legitimizer) and President Jimmy Carter (who
spoke for the foreign policy establishment, the leadership of both parties,
the diplomatic corps, the State Department, the CIA, and the Pentagon).[44]
Carter and Crane advanced comparable narratives. Each recounted our
past, depicted our present situation, envisioned desirable and undesirable futures, dramatized and reconciled significant U.S. values and symbols, and espoused a preferred course of action consistent with the
narrative and its values.

The Past: America's Claim to the Canal

President Carter's narrative found the original 1903 Hay-Bunau-
Varilla Treaty to be out of step with a sense of fairness and morality.
Whereas "No person from Panama ever saw that treaty before it was
signed" or "was involved in the signing of that treaty"[45] the new treaties
would reaffirm U.S. fairness because ratification "is what is right for us
and what is fair to others."[46] Further, Carter argued that even the unfair
treaty failed to grant the United States sovereignty over the canal; if Panama retained sovereignty even under an unfair treaty, we should affirm
that fact with a fair treaty.

Crane agreed that the original treaty was unfair, saying that it was advantageous to the United States and disadvantageous to Panama because it was a clever and legal treaty granting the United States sovereignty over the Canal Zone. Our claim epitomized shrewdness and opportunism, because "When any nation goes to the bargaining table it does so with the determination to act in its own best interests and to derive as many benefits as possible."[47]

Crane further maintained that the original treaty ceded all sovereignty over the Canal Zone to the United States. But the thrust of Carter's argument was that the treaty provided for Panamanian sovereignty and U.S. jurisdiction *as if* we had sovereignty. Crane cited several examples of acts usually associated with sovereignty, and he inferred that "the very yielding to Panama of certain small pieces of control proves that the United States has full control—de facto sovereignty—in the first place."[48] Carter's concern was the discrepancy between our *de facto* sovereignty and Panama's *de jure* sovereignty. His best handling of this issue came three months before Crane's book and four months before the Fireside Chat. Carter explained to a Denver audience:

> We have never owned the Panama Canal Zone. We've never had title to it. We've never had sovereignty over it . . . the Supreme Court has confirmed since then that this is Panamanian territory. People born in the Panama Canal Zone are not American citizens. We've always paid them an annual fee, since the first year of the Panama Canal Treaty that presently exists, for the use of their property. . . . People say we bought it; it's ours; we ought not to give it away. We've never bought it. It's not been ours. We are not giving it away.[49]

These points Crane never directly engaged.

Crane and Carter argued their positions differently. Crane's account sidestepped the treaty's grant of control *as if* the United States held sovereignty despite reprinting the text of Article III of the 1903 treaty in his book. It states that, "The Republic of Panama grants to the United States all the rights, power and authority within the zone . . . which the United States would possess and exercise *if* it were the sovereign of the territory within which said lands and waters are located" [emphasis added].[50] He focused instead on signs of sovereignty and exploited the fact that few knew that the original treaty preserved Panamanian sovereignty in principle. For his part, Carter too often summarized and asserted while Crane used detailed extrinsic support such as testimony and court decisions. Carter's claim that "the Supreme Court has confirmed since then that this is Panamanian territory," for example, seems to be refuted with Crane's specific references to *Wilson v. Shaw* (1907), *The United States v. Husband* (1972), and a "veteran American diplomat and international law authority."[51]

Carter and Crane presented strikingly divergent histories that forced their audiences to choose. If the United States held sovereign control over the Canal Zone, then any sharing of that power would be surrender, retreat, or a giveaway; but if Panama held sovereignty, there was nothing for the United States to surrender. Fisher's first test for good reasons is the degree to which the narrative is "true to and consistent with what we think we know and what we value."[52] Crane's history met the first narrative test better than did Carter's—even though it misused its own evidence—because it fit neatly with the McGuffey Reader Complex and dramatized U.S. cleverness and power.

The Present: The Western Hemisphere Today

President Carter characterized Panama as one of our "historic allies and friends" headed by a "stable government which has encouraged the development of free enterprise" and would hold democratic elections.[53] But Crane described a "banana republic" dominated by "forty influential families" where "poverty is abysmal" and in which General Omar Torrijos runs a "corrupt, vicious police state . . . built with the help of his Marxist allies" and kept from bankruptcy only by "the New York banking community."[54] Carter described legitimate disaffection in the hemisphere and depicted the canal as "the last vestige of alleged American colonialism."[55] He eagerly anticipated this "new partnership" and spoke of defending the canal with Panamanian forces "joined with us as brothers."[56] In the Carter vision, the United States was a powerful, fair, generous neighbor ready and willing to demonstrate those admirable traits by sharing the canal with the Panamanians.

But Crane painted a future based upon the proper places of property and generosity. Crane bluntly differentiated his world from Carter's: "The world is not a Sunday school classroom in Plains, Georgia. It is a violent, conflict-ridden place where peace and freedom only survive when they are protected. . . . Peace comes only to the prepared and security only to the strong."[57] Generosity among friends is noble; generosity in a jungle is foolish and cowardly.

The Carter and Crane narratives dramatized divergent values. Carter told of a friendly, honest, rational, democratic, capitalist nation worthy of being our military and economic partner. Crane described a hostile, corrupt, childish, socialist nation unworthy of partnership with the United States. Accuracy aside, Crane's story built upon his audience's belief in U.S. superiority and generosity but asked them to be suspicious and protective in this particular case. Carter's account played on his audience's perceptions of our traditions of fairness and military strength and asked his audience to demonstrate its trusting and generous nature in this particular case.

The Future: The Kind of Power We Wish to Be

Carter and Crane agreed that the canal decision would demonstrate "the kind of great power we wish to be."[58] Carter claimed that Theodore

Roosevelt "would join us in our pride for being a great and generous people, with the national strength and wisdom to do what is right for us and what is fair to others."[59] He said that ratification would be "a show of strength . . . national will . . . fairness and . . . confidence in ourselves." He explained that we need not "run over a little country. It's much better for us to show our strength and our ability by not being a bully and by saying to Panama, let's work in harmony."[60] Carter said that ratification would demonstrate that "we are able to deal fairly and honorably with a proud but smaller sovereign nation . . . [because] we believe in good will and fairness, as well as strength." He spoke of the "new partnership" as a "source of national pride and self-respect."[61]

But Crane saw ratification as "one more crucial American step in a descent into ignominy—to the end of America's credibility as a world power and a deterrent to aggression."[62] Crane's future envisioned neither friendship nor generosity but a reputation for cowardice and weakness. A "surrender in Panama would appear as not a noble act of magnanimity, but as the cowardly retreat of a tired, toothless paper tiger."[63]

The futures Carter and Crane envisioned diverged. Crane saw danger, Carter security. Crane wanted superiority, Carter partnership. Crane implied force and punishment, Carter generosity and kindness. Crane found the United States weak, Carter thought us strong. Crane saw shame in "surrender," Carter in continued imperialism. Each believed that the other side in the controversy indirectly helped U.S. enemies.

Outgrowth of the Narrative

In the end, the treaties were ratified. But the New Right aroused public sentiment and developed a massive public relations machine, defined its identity, created a list of villains, and transformed treaty ratification into a rhetorical success. As Viguerie explained:

> Our campaign to save the Canal gained conservative converts around the country, added more than 400,000 new names to our lists, encouraged many of the movement's leading figures . . . to run for public office, and produced significant liberal defeats. The New Right came out of the Panama Canal fight with no casualties, not even a scar. Because of Panama we are better organized. We developed a great deal of confidence in ourselves, and our opponents became weaker. That November [1978] the New Right really came of age.[64]

In short, the New Right campaign accomplished four of the five functions of social movement persuasion despite losing the treaty vote. It enabled them to transform perceptions of reality, transform perceptions of society, prescribe courses of action, and mobilize for action.

The Panama Canal controversy shows how a social movement can critique a bipartisan consensus and mobilize supporters by dramatizing their fears. The New Right's narrative enabled them to take over the rhetorical agenda of a Republican National Committee that hungered for a set of arguments with which to mobilize voters against Carter and the Democrats.

New Right organizers used the canal issue as a symbolic vehicle for energizing their movement. Because the debate was between narrative visions, defenders of the institutional narrative risked losing their entire policy framework. The New Right undermined public confidence in the assumptions underlying U.S. foreign policy and provided an alternative narrative framework through which subsequent events in Iran, Afghanistan, Nicaragua, Grenada, El Salvador, and the Persian Gulf would be interpreted.

Dramatic rhetorical narratives that excite the imagination are more persuasive than those that are more technical in nature. Both Crane and Carter claimed to have "the facts," and both established their authority and expertise. But Crane was better able than Carter to involve his audience in the process of collective fantasizing because his narrative provided themes that his audience interpreted as "good reasons."

Let us appraise the narratives with respect to Fisher's four criteria of narrative rationality. First, Crane's narrative dramatized U.S. heroism, strength, generosity, legality, and cleverness while Carter's narrative required us to revise our sense of history and national character to admit that Teddy Roosevelt was a bully who tricked our neighbors. Crane's narrative was more consistent with what we "knew," "believed," and "valued" than Carter's. Ironically and importantly, the social movement built on existing perceptions of history, while the institutional version sought to change them.

Second, both narratives were appropriate to the ratification decision because they framed the issues and compelled a conclusion. But Crane's account was self-supporting. His conflict with the defense establishment clouded the decision and made caution seem more prudent than trust. Carter, like Ford, tried to respond with administrative rhetoric, but this required him to allay the fears aroused by the movement. This left citizens with two questions: "After fourteen years of negotiating, what's the hurry?" and "If you are right, Mr. President, why is this convincing congressman so worried?"

Third, Crane's narrative was the more promising in its effects for his audience. It promised that the path of alleged cowardice and weakness would lead to friendship without respect, while resolve would lead to both power and respect. Carter's narrative promised that the choice of generosity and honor would lead to friendship, respect, and security while intransigence would lead to greater antagonism and vulnerability. Crane's account invites audience fantasizing because its stakes were so dramatic.

And fourth, Crane's narrative was the more internally consistent because of its simplicity. Carter's narrative presented several apparent inconsistencies. Why should we grant anything to people who are increasingly resentful? How are these resentful people developing this new sense of mutual purpose and trust with the United States? If Panama is friendly and stable, why need we worry about defending the canal? If we need to worry about defending the canal, why voluntarily relinquish any of our claim to it? Carter answered these questions reasonably well, but his answers were complex and strung-out over several months. Crane's narrative provided few apparent inconsistencies. He did commit a critical logical error by arguing that the presence of all the signs of U.S. sovereignty over the canal proved sovereignty. But this inconsistency was buried deep in his argument, and it was obscured by his references to memoranda and court decisions on related points.

In short, President Carter advanced a technically sound argument for treaty ratification that did not meet the tests of good narrative. Crane's arguments against ratification, flawed as they were, met the narrative tests and involved audience members in the social movement. The treaty was ratified on administrative and technical grounds, but the social movement established its narrative framework as a viable alternative and used it a year later to frame events in Iran and Afghanistan and to over-throw the Ford-Carter-Kissinger "friendly giant" narrative.

Conclusions

A choice between narrative frameworks ultimately boils down to the question of believability, and believability hinges on the individual's personal inventory of words, meanings, experiences, associations, social influences, values, needs, and sense of causation. People believe what they need to believe to keep themselves afloat in the world. A narrative that embodies and dramatizes experiences and fantasies "makes sense" because it has coherence and fidelity. It excites us, and we wonder why no one noticed it before. We share it excitedly with our associates and create through the act of collective fantasizing a sense of community that is embodied in the shared vision.

The militia movement adopted the story of the American Revolution and recast it with their members as the patriots and the federal government as the occupying force. Like the Founders, contemporary militia talk about the need to resist gun control and stockpile arms so that they can resist the encroachment of the Yankees, ZOG, the United Nations, and the government of the United States. But the cohesive narrative fragmented with the Oklahoma City bombing; there was no consistent story to tell. They did it, or they didn't do it but they understood why it was done, or it was a despicable act exploited by the government, or it was a horrific act of an unprincipled federal government. Without a consistent account of such a high profile incident, the movement will be hard pressed to sustain itself.

The New Right transformed the controversy over the Panama Canal into a social movement vs. establishment conflict. Crane's office legitimized his advocacy, and his reliance upon old memoranda, court cases, testimony, and reprinted treaties created what Barnet Baskerville once called "the illusion of proof."[65] When Crane's narrative accounted for subsequent developments in Iran and Nicaragua, moderate Republicans such as Richard Nixon and Gerald Ford were perceptually exiled to the Carter position.

In a debate between narratives, the struggle over images, heroes, villains, values, and motives is central. These symbolic struggles determine how Americans, whether policymakers or ordinary citizens, will order the world around them and how they will perceive their policy alternatives. Narrative visions are the frameworks within which specific people, motives, and incidents are interpreted. As people recognize, share, and apply their vision, they recruit members and consolidate them into a working group.

This analysis of the Militia and New Right movement narratives illustrates six important points about social movements and argument from narrative vision. First, activists coalesce around a narrative framework for interpreting political realities. Second, movements often ground their narratives in mainstream history. Third, an emerging social movement with a clear and convincing narrative can credibly challenge even a logical institutional narrative advanced by the president. Fourth, a narrative's unity or fragmentation can impact the movement's development. Fifth, the movement's narrative transcends its particular subject, and short-term losses can become long-term wins. Finally, because narratives help us to interpret events, and because events help us to validate our choice of narrative, political history is a series of struggles for narrative dominance.

Endnotes

[1] David Carr, *Time, Narrative, and History* (Bloomington: Indiana University Press, 1986): 89.

[2] Howard Kamler, *Communication: Sharing Our Stories of Experience* (Seattle: Psychological Press, 1983): 27–58.

[3] Walter R. Fisher, *Human Communication as Narration: Toward a Philosophy of Reason, Value and Action* (Columbia, SC: University of South Carolina Press, 1987): 66–67.

[4] Carr, 1–113.

[5] Carr, 23.

[6] Fisher, 194.

[7] Ernest G. Bormann, "Fantasy and Rhetorical Vision: The Rhetorical Criticism of Social Reality," *Quarterly Journal of Speech* 58 (December 1972): 396–407; and "Fantasy and Rhetorical Vision: Ten Years Later," *Quarterly Journal of Speech* 68 (August 1982): 288–305. See also Dan Nimmo and James E. Combs, *Mediated Political Realities* (New York: Longman, 1983); and Murray Edelman, *Constructing the Political Spectacle* (Chicago: University of Chicago Press, 1988).

[8] Bormann (1971), 398.

[9] Bormann (1972), 405.

[10] "Belligerent 'Claimant' Page: A Call to Arms," (http://www.geocities.com/Yosemite/Gorge/8270/).

[11] Dave Delany, Dave Delany's Freedom House. (http://www.constitution.org/piml/piml.htm).

[12] Delany.

[13] Delany.

[14] Priscilla Marie Meddaugh. *The Other in Cyberspace Discourse on White Supremacy.* Unpublished doctoral dissertation. Detroit: Wayne State University, 1999,132.

[15] [William L. Pierce] Andrew Macdonald, *The Turner Diaries,* 2nd ed. (New York: Barricade Books, 1978).

[16] Macdonald, 33.

[17] Belligerent 'Claimant' Page. (http://www.geocities.com/Yosemite/Gorge/8270/).

[18] Belligerent 'Claimant' Page. (http://www.geocities.com/Yosemite/Gorge/8270/).

[19] Kenneth S. Stern, *A Force Upon the Plain* (Norman: University of Oklahoma, 1997): 108–118.

[20] Jim Cook, MIT Center for Space Research, Cambridge, MA: n.d.

[21] Macdonald, 33–34.

[22] Belligerent 'Claimant' Page. (http://www.geocities.com/Yosemite/Gorge/8270/).

[23] Downloaded from GUN-TALK [703-934-2121] a service of the National Rifle Association Institute for Legislative Action Fairfax, VA 22030.

[24] Richard Hofstadter, "The Paranoid Style in American Politics," in *The Paranoid Style in American Politics and Other Essays* (New York: Alfred A. Knopf, 1965): 31–32.

[25] Meddaugh.

[26] Macdonald, 167.

[27] Macdonald, 167.

[28] "Revolution: Ammo for Freedom Fighters," (http://www.douzzer.ai.mit.edu:8080/revolution/multi/terrorism/okc/militia.html).

[29] William L. Pierce, "Radio Commentary," (April 29, 1995) from (http//:www.stormfront.org).

[30] Ric Duncan. #0 @176:200/36 via 176:400/0 PRNet.

[31] Eustace Mullins, "J'Accuse!," (http://www.stormfront.org).

[32] "The Prophecy Club," (http://www.prophecyclub.com/video/coverup.html).

[33] "The Prophecy Club," (http://www.prophecyclub.com/video/coverup.html).

[34] Ric Duncan #0 @176:200/36 via 176:400/0 PRNet.

[35] Richard A. Viguerie, *The New Right: We're Ready to Lead* (Falls Church, VA: The Viguerie Company, 1981): 65–67.

[36] Although both Carter and Crane refer to 70-80% public opposition to the treaties, an August, 1977 Gallup Poll reports only 47% opposition. See American Institute of Public Opinion, *The Gallup Poll: Public Opinion, 1972-1977,* Vol. 2 (Wilmington, DE: Scholarly Resources, 1978): 1181–1183. In his memoirs, *Keeping the Faith* (New York: Bantam Books, 1982), Carter calls his efforts to win support for the Canal treaties his most difficult political battle (184).

[37] E. Pace, "Reagan Declares Canal Treaties Should Be Rejected by the Senate," *New York Times,* 26 August 1977, 1.

[38] John Wayne, "Scare Letter from the Honorable Ronald Reagan," November 11, 1977. Fireside Chat, 2-1-78, Box 17, Staff Office Files, Speechwriters' Chronological, Jimmy Carter Library.

[39] Wayne, letter.

[40] James Fallows, Memo to Hamilton Jordan, September 4, 1977. Fireside Chat, 2-1-78, Box 17, Staff Office Files, Speechwriters' Chronological, Jimmy Carter Library.

[41] Harlan J. Strauss, Letter to Jim Fallows, September 6, 1977. Staff Office Files, Speechwriters, James Fallows Files, Jimmy Carter Library.

[42] James Fallows, Letter to Harlan Strauss, September 19, 1977. Staff Office Files, Speech Writers, James Fallows Files, Jimmy Carter Library.

[43] James Fallows, Memorandum to Zbigniew Brzezinski, January 27, 1978 and Suggested Outline: Panama Canal Speech, 1-25-78. Fireside Chat, 2-1-78, Box 17, Staff Office Files, Speechwriters' Chronological, Jimmy Carter Library.

[44] Phillip M. Crane, *Surrender in Panama: The Case Against the Treaty* (New York: Dale Books, 1978): 1–2; and Jimmy Carter, "Panama Canal Treaties," *Public Papers of the President of the United States: Jimmy Carter, 1978* (Washington, DC: United States Government Printing Office, 1979): 259. About 100,000 copies of Crane's book were distributed in January, 1978 by Richard Viguerie's associates.

[45] Jimmy Carter, "Radio-Television News Directors Association," *Public Papers of the Presidents: Jimmy Carter, 1977* (Washington, DC: United States Government Printing Office, 1978): 1597 (referred to hereafter as 9-15-77).

[46] Carter, "Panama Canal Treaties," 262, 263.

[47] Crane, 41.

[48] Crane, 37.

[49] Jimmy Carter, "Denver, Colorado," *Public Papers of the Presidents: Jimmy Carter, 1977* (Washington, DC: United States Government Printing Office, 1978): 1886 (referred to hereafter as 10-22-77).

[50] Quoted by Crane, 136.

[51] Crane, 36–37.

[52] Fisher, 194.

[53] Carter, "Panama Canal Treaties," 262.

[54] Crane, 56–57, 71, and 66.

[55] Carter, "Panama Canal Treaties," 258, 261.

[56] Carter, "Panama Canal Treaties," 260, 262.

[57] Crane, 113–114.

[58] Carter, "Panama Canal Treaties," 262.

[59] Carter, "Panama Canal Treaties," 263, emphasis added.

[60] Carter, 10-22-77, 1890.

[61] Carter, "Panama Canal Treaties," 259 and 262.

[62] Crane, 113.

[63] Crane, 1.

[64] Viguerie, 70–71.

[65] Barnet Baskerville, "The Illusion of Proof," *Western Journal of Communication* 25 (Fall 1961): 236–242.

ARGUMENT FROM TRANSCENDENCE
IN SOCIAL MOVEMENTS

As a social movement challenges established norms, values, hierarchical relationships, and symbols; adapts rhetorical strategies; and proceeds from the genesis and social unrest stages to the enthusiastic mobilization stage, it "creates doubts about the legitimacy and morality of the establishment."[1] Established institutions cannot ignore this threat. They confront the social movement, often in conjunction with resistance or countermovements, by challenging its fragile claim of legitimacy, means and ends, norms and values, and credibility.

Many theorists claim that confrontation is essential for the rise of a social movement. Robert Cathcart, for instance, argues that confrontation is "the necessary ingredient" for a social movement to come into being and to proceed with its cause (see also chapter 1). Kenneth Burke notes "drama requires a conflict."[2] Building on Burke's writings, Leland Griffin claims "The development of a countermovement is vital: for it 'is the bad side that produces the movement which makes history, by providing a struggle.'"[3]

As necessary as confrontation may be for social movements, however, its results are often a mixture of blessings and curses. On the one hand, confrontations with institutional forces and countermovements serve three essential functions. They establish the social movement as a serious threat; they contrast the two collectives; and they reveal the ugly side of institutions and their collaborators. On the other hand, the resistance rhetoric of institutions and countermovements threatens the social movement's existence by attacking its foundations, ideology, methods, ends, structure, and legitimacy. Unless the social movement is able to develop an effective rebuttal strategy, it may be pushed back to an earlier stage, stall, or perish. If for every persuasive action there is a reaction, it is always possible that the reaction may overwhelm the social movement's action.

Argument from Transcendence

Social movements rely heavily upon a *rhetoric of transcendence* to challenge institutions and to counter the persuasive efforts of institutions to meet threats to norms, values, and hierarchical relationships. In a rhetoric of transcendence, persuaders argue that a person, group, goal, thing, right, action, or proposal *surpasses*, is *superior* to, or was *prior* to its opposite. Karl Wallace notes, for example, that in considering relative merits "the point is, what is good and what is evil, and of good what is greater, and of evil what is the less."[4]

When operating at the *highest level* of transcendence, persuaders claim that a goal, group, or right, for instance, is superior to or greater than *all* other options. The goal, group, or right has attained (through development, achievement, statute, discovery, or dogma) the *ultimate* state of perfection. When operating at the *lowest level* of transcendence, persuaders argue that a goal, group, or right is superior to or greater than *one* or *some* of its kind.[5] Aristotle wrote centuries ago that "The acquisition of a greater in place of a lesser good, or of a lesser in place of a greater evil, is also good, for in proportion as the greater exceeds the lesser there is acquisition of good or removal of evil."[6] Thus, the goal, group, or right has not reached an ultimate state of perfection but is *more perfect* or *more preferable* than its competitors.

Burke describes transcendence as the building of a language "bridge whereby one realm is *transcended* by being viewed *in terms* of a realm 'beyond it'."[7] Theorists from Cicero in ancient Rome to the twentieth century have identified four common points of comparison in establishing transcendence, quantity (more–less, large–small), quality (good–bad, excellent–poor), value (important–unimportant, desirable–undesirable), and hierarchy (high–low, above–below).[8]

Argument from Quantity

Persuaders base arguments on *quantity*, writes Burke, when contending that one group is larger than a competing group or that one organization is more inclusive than one or more organizations with which it is identified.[9] For instance, PETA (People for the Ethical Treatment of Animals) and the International Fund for the welfare of animals claim to be the largest and fastest growing organizations within the animal rights movement.[10] A person advocating censorship may claim a right to speak for the *American people* that transcends political parties, special interest groups, or liberals. Leaders of an industrial union that is open to all workers may claim that their organization transcends a *trade union* that represents only one trade such as carpenters, plumbers, or control tower operators. For example, Terence Powderly compared the Knights of Labor to the steam locomotive of the day and the trade union with the "stage coach of half a century ago." Workers of "different trades and callings," he claimed, "have had their eyes opened "to the fact that the organization composed of but one trade or calling does not meet their wants, and must give way for a grander, mightier association, which recognizes the right of every honest man to come within its protecting folds."[11] Thus, many protest groups struggle to become (or claim to be) the largest or most inclusive of all grassroots, people's, workers', professional, reform, or political organizations.

Argument from Quality

Persuaders use the comparative point of *quality* when arguing that one goal, proposal, or strategy, for instance, is good while a competing goal, proposal, or strategy is bad or evil. Truth is contrasted with falsehood, justice with injustice, freedom with slavery, equality with inequality, nonviolence with violence, rationality with irrationality, reason with emotion, prejudice with tolerance or respect, moral development with moral underdevelopment. Aristotle noted that when "people agree that two things are both useful but do not agree about which is the more so, the next step will be to treat of relative goodness and relative utility."[12] Thus, a persuader may contend that one proposal promises a *greater good* than a competing proposal or that one strategy is *less evil* than another strategy. Debaters, litigants, and legislators often argue about "comparative advantages" or "comparative disadvantages" of proposals and actions. Persons warning of the potential catastrophic results of acid rain may recognize that solutions will cause economic hardships for some companies and workers; persons advocating censorship of textbooks or gun control measures may admit that their proposals will place some limits on constitutional rights; and persons arguing against using animals for medical research may admit that some research might be more difficult to perform without animals. But in each case, persuaders argue that the potential benefits outweigh the potential harms. For instance, animal rights advocates warn that demeaning animals demeans humans and that "this crime against nature and humanity" adversely affects "human health, world hunger, natural resources, and the environment."[13]

Argument from Value

Persuaders use the point of *value* when arguing that a group's ends are so important that any means (vilification, dishonesty, obscenity, espionage, disruptions, violence, terrorism) are justified or that the need to meet a crisis takes precedence over factional differences. For example, government agencies use "national security" to justify spying on U.S. citizens and the issuance of "disinformation." Political parties justify mudslinging and dirty campaign tricks by arguing it is for "the good of the people." Militant elements of social movements may use justice, freedom, equality, and independence to rationalize bombings, assassinations, and terrorism. Roxanne Dunbar, a staff member of the Southern Female Rights Union, said the group seriously considered assassinating a man to make their *presence* known. Becoming known became a more important value than a human life. They dropped the idea not because of the nature of the act but because the male victim would become important because their group had selected him.[14] His potential fame and martyrdom would transcend the recognition the Union might achieve. Attaining a goal or preventing a change, persuaders argue, is more important—is of greater value—than the means used, resulting factional differences, ideological disputes, or which movement leader or organization takes the lead or gets the credit. Barry Brummett notes "one may *avoid* guilt by engaging in *transcendence*. This avoidance of guilt puts the sin into a perspective which redefines it as 'not a sin,' as a virtue or as the requirement of some higher or nobler hierarchy."[15] All kinds of questionable actions are executed by institutions and social movements "in the name of God."

Argument from Hierarchy

Persuaders use the point of *hierarchy* when attempting to establish that one person, group, thing, act, right, or ideal exceeds another because it is of a higher order along a gradation or continuum: one human race or ethnic group above another race or group, human above animal, animal life over comfort or style, spiritual over temporal, supernatural over natural, universal over the individual or local, ethical over utilitarian.[16] White supremacist groups see white European descendants as superior to those of African, Asian, Native-American, Middle Eastern, or Hispanic descendants. Medical scientists argue that it is ethical to experiment on animals because experiments eventually help save the lives of humans, a higher order of life. Animal rights activists, on the other hand, argue that the suffering and mutilation of animals is evil for what it does to living, feeling beings superior to inanimate objects and plants. Persons of some religious organizations refuse to recite the Pledge of Allegiance or go to war for their country because these human, political acts violate religious principles that are of a higher order. The notion of *hierarchy* is a versatile argumentative tactic for collectives such as social movements. For instance, if a member or leader does something to discredit the movement, a persuader might argue that the "power of truth" for which the movement is fighting "transcends the limitations of the personal agent who propounds it."[17] To counteract feelings of guilt or accusations of blame for the consequences of a movement's actions, a persuader might argue that the act was not an "inferior kind of crime" (breaking and entering, trespassing, petty theft, vandalism, killing in a drunken brawl) but a "transcendent kind of crime" actually "required by traditional values" or to further a just cause.[18] Most movements claim they are *grassroots efforts*, stating or implying that grassroots collectives are more American, high-minded, and democratic than others—institutional or uninstitutional.[19]

The strategy of transcendence provides social movements with a variety of lines of argument for defending organizations, enhancing positions, countering other movements, and avoiding the necessity of denying the undeniable. Argument from transcendence strengthens a movement's support among "the people" and important legitimizers because it refutes the opposition by identifying the movement symbolically (including its ideology, prescribed course of action, mobilization efforts, and claims to legitimacy) with what is large, good, important, and of the highest order. It identifies the opposition with what is small, evil, unimportant, and of a lower order. Burke writes:

> Hence, to some degree, solution of conflict must always be done purely in the symbolic realm (by "transcendence") if it is to be done at all. Persons of moral and imaginative depth require great enterprise and resourcefulness in such purely "symbolic" solutions of conflict (by the formation of appropriate "attitudes").[20]

The Abortion Conflict as a Case Study

The conflict over abortion is centuries old, but the current conflict in the United States began with the forming of pro-choice and right-to-life organizations during the late 1960s to enhance and to resist increasing efforts to liberalize state laws governing abortion.[21] On 22 January 1973, the United States Supreme Court dealt the fledgling pro-life resistance movement an "unqualified legal defeat."[22] In *Roe v. Wade*, the Supreme Court decided (1) that a woman's constitutional right of privacy precludes a state from prohibiting her from obtaining an abortion on demand during the first trimester of pregnancy, (2) that a state could regulate abortions during the second trimester only for the purpose of protecting the woman's life, and (3) that a state could regulate abortions during the third trimester to preserve the life of the child.[23] Thus, the Supreme Court viewed fetal life as a viable human only after the first six months of pregnancy. The pro-choice movement had apparently won the war over abortion.

Right-to-life forces recovered quickly from the shock of the Supreme Court defeat and began to create a powerful revivalistic social movement to make abortion unlawful under all circumstances and to reaffirm society's respect for all human life. Their primary solution proposed during the early decades was a constitutional amendment defining human life as beginning at the moment of conception and prohibiting the termination of a "child's" life except in situations in which the "mother's" life is in grave danger. This amendment would overturn the Supreme Court decision and preclude further court and legislative actions (state and national) to liberalize abortion.

When the likelihood of a constitutional amendment passing both houses of congress and being ratified by a sufficient number of states dwindled, the National Right to Life Committee, its affiliates in all fifty states, Baptists for Life, the American Life League, Women Exploited By Abortion, American Life Lobby, Americans Against Abortion, Catholic and evangelical churches, the Moral Majority, and allied groups mobilized massive political pressure from the grassroots level. Their goals were to support the passage of restrictive federal and state laws and to deny federal and state financial aid for abortions. They became involved in political campaigns at all levels to elect candidates (including Presidents Reagan and George Bush, Sr.) who would support their positions through legislation, Executive Orders, and appointment of antiabortion justices to the Supreme Court to overturn *Roe v. Wade*.

More militant tactics became common in the mid–1980s, particularly Operation Rescue's efforts to blockade abortion clinics, to discourage pregnant women from obtaining abortions through "sidewalk counseling," to pressure hospitals and physicians into refusing to perform abortions, and to clog the jails by prompting police officers into massive arrests. Violence such as bombings, arson, vandalism, and shooting into clinics became commonplace. In 1994, a number of clinics received powder-laced letters alleging that the recipients had just been exposed to anthrax. The ultimate violence first occurred on March 10, 1993 when Dr. David Gunn was murdered by a pro-life militant in Pensacola, Florida.[24] Other assassinations of physicians and clinic workers followed in both the United States and Canada.[25] Wanted posters featuring the faces of physicians who performed abortions and Web sites modeled after the Nuremberg Files at the end of World War II have informed antiabortion forces of the names, addresses, and phone numbers of "abortionists." When Dr. Barnett Slepian was gunned down in his kitchen by a sniper in 1998, his name was crossed off a national Web site list.[26]

The pro-choice movement transformed itself literally overnight in the mid-1970s into a resistance movement to counter the efforts of pro-life groups. Before *Roe v. Wade*, NARAL was the acronym for National Association for Repeal of Abortion Laws. After *Roe v. Wade*, it changed its name to the National Abortion Rights Action League and worked closely with the Religious Coalition for Abortion Rights (RCAR), Planned Parenthood, the National Organization for Women (NOW), and allied organizations to protect the woman's right to choose. For several years these groups presented their cases primarily through leaflets, mailings, and advertisements in magazines and newspapers. Pro-choice became increasingly active as the pro-life movement pressured physicians and hospitals into refusing to perform abortions, achieved many legislative successes, and seemed near victory with conservative, pro-life appointments to the Supreme Court. The movement held mass rallies in Washington, D.C. and other cities, campaigned actively for pro-choice candidates, brought pressure on state legislatures and Congress, presented court cases, protected abortion clinics, and formed escorts for women trying to enter clinics surrounded by pro-life activists.

The election of President Clinton in 1992 and the possibility of appointment of pro-choice justices to the Supreme Court tilted the conflict once more toward the pro-choice countermovement, spurring the pro-life movement into greater efforts to end legalized abortion. Rather than the struggle lessening, it entered a new and more militant phase.

The raging conflict over legalized abortion in the United States provides an excellent case study of how movements and countermovements use argument from transcendence. Although the conflict has been increasingly punctuated with violence, disruptions, coercive tactics, terrorism, and murder, both movement and countermovement have relied primarily on symbols and symbolic actions to attain and maintain public support and to win victories in living rooms, voting booths, courtrooms, legislative chambers, and executive offices.[27] An analysis of dozens of leaflets, pamphlets, mailings, books, newspaper essays, and advertisements reveals that, for nearly forty years, the pro-life and pro-choice movements have relied heavily on arguments from transcendence.[28] These movements use the four points of comparison to define fundamental issues, present and defend cases, resolve dilemmas, enhance their credibility, attack one another, and refute charges made against their ideologies, tactics, organizations, and memberships. The remainder of this chapter focuses on how the pro-choice and pro-life movements have used arguments from transcendence in their clashes over personhood, rights, reality, and respective movements.

The Clash over Personhood

The key premise on which all pro-life and pro-choice arguments from transcendence rest is the debate about exactly when a *life* or a *person* comes into existence. Both social movements expend a great deal of rhetorical energy trying to establish the moment of *personhood* and to discount the other's claims. If a person exists at the moment of conception, abortion is murder. If a person does not exist until the moment of birth or viability, abortion is not murder but a medical procedure to terminate an unwanted pregnancy.

Pro-Choice

Pro-choice advocates pose several arguments to support their stand on personhood. First, they argue that the fetus has never been recognized legally, constitutionally, or historically as a *full-fledged person* but only as a *potential human being*.[29] Choice persuaders contend that even the Bible declines to identify the fetus as a person. For instance, Exodus 21:22–23 regards the fetus not as a person but as belonging to the father; the killing of a woman but not of the fetus would warrant avenging. The New Testament does not address the issue.[30] Second, the pro-choice movement claims that no one really knows when personhood begins. Persuaders assert that "medical, legal, and religious experts cannot, and will never, agree!"[31] The belief that personhood begins at conception, they contend, has been "disputed by theologians for centuries": even the Roman Catholic Church did not espouse this belief until the mid-nineteenth century.[32] Third, pro-choice advocates point out that the lack of agreement "means determining when life begins—which no one knows—must ultimately rest on man-made definitions more arbitrary, philosophical and religious than scientific."[33] Contrary opinions are *theological* or *religious* beliefs held by the Roman Catholic Church and a few other denominations, not *biological* or *absolute facts* as pro-life proponents assert.[34]

These three claims place the opposition's belief of personhood at the moment of conception at the bottom of a hierarchy of beliefs: below scientific or biological facts, legal or constitutional statutes and decisions, biblical teachings, and prevailing theological beliefs. It is reduced in *importance* and in a *hierarchy* of beliefs to *merely* an arbitrary, man-made, religious issue among *religious denominations*.[35] Thus, pro-choice persuaders conclude that antiabortion advocates give "a fertilized egg or a fetus legal standing equal to that of a pregnant woman" whose personhood is undisputed.[36] They argue that "a qualitative distinction must be made between its [the fetus] claims and the rights of a responsible person made in God's image who is living relationships with God and other human beings." To do otherwise would be "to dehumanize the woman, to consider her a mere 'thing' through which the fetus is passing."[37] The woman (a recognized person) is clearly superior to (transcends) the fetus (recognized arbitrarily as a person only by a few religious denominations) she is carrying and thus deserves higher legal and constitutional standing and concern.

Pro-Life

Pro-life advocates argue that life begins at the moment of conception, that "Human life is a continuous developmental process that begins at conception and ceases at death."[38] In support of this claim, pro-life persuaders offer detailed chronologies (often with photographs) of development from conception, through three weeks when the heart starts beating, to the moment of birth.[39] They counter that, contrary to pro-choice claims and the Supreme Court decision that declared the unborn to be "not persons at all," scientists, medical authorities, every Protestant theologian since Calvin, the Catholic church, most Protestant denominations, and the Bible agree that life begins at conception, the moment the sperm and egg meet.[40] Thus, the pro-life position is not merely *church* dogma or a *religious* issue but is a *scientific fact*, a basic human issue.[41]

If human life exists from the moment of conception, persuaders conclude, the fetus is a person, one of us, and not a "poorly functioning adult" but a "splendidly functioning baby."[42] The act of abortion, then, is not removing, as pro-choice claims, "a mass or blob of tissue," a "POC—product of conception," or a "clump of cells" but the destruction, killing, murdering of "an innocent human life," "pre-born children," and the "defenseless little child living in the mother's womb."[43] In the hierarchy of living beings, the fetus or baby is equal to its mother and higher than, transcends, all nonpersons. Because the fetus is both innocent and defenseless, it deserves special protection against its mother's (an equal but not superior) desire to kill it.

The Clash over Rights

The establishment of the personhood and hierarchical status of the woman or the fetus allows each movement to develop a case for which rights are most important and which are being violated or are in danger of being violated. Persuaders use the comparative points of value and hierarchy in their clashes over rights.

Pro-Choice

Pro-choice defenders argue that "every woman in a free society" has the fundamental, constitutional right guaranteed by the Supreme Court to a safe, legal abortion because it is crucial to her health and well-being.[44] "The welfare of the mother," a universally recognized person, "must always be our primary concern," pro-choice advocates argue, and freedom of choice (reproductive freedom) is fundamental.[45] This choice, free from unwarranted governmental intrusion into our private lives, is the "most precious of individual rights."[46]

Persuaders claim that the right to privacy, upon which the Supreme Court based its decision in *Roe v. Wade* in 1973, is guaranteed by the 1st, 9th, and 14th amendments to the Constitution. Any effort by religious groups to limit this choice is a direct threat to religious liberty and the constitutional provision of separation of church and state. The pro-choice slogan, "Not the church, not the state, women must decide their fate," sums up the movement's fundamental beliefs in freedom and privacy.[47] Pro-choice advocates contend, then, that the value of the woman's health and well-being exceeds (transcends) that of a nonperson, and the rights of privacy and freedom of choice are the most important of all human rights. These rights are essential to our religious liberty and reproductive freedom. All other rights are lower in the hierarchy and of less importance.

Pro-Life

Pro-life advocates argue that the fetus is a living human being and must be guaranteed the right to life—the "most basic value of our society," the "most fundamental right," the "paramount right," "the most basic human right bestowed on us by God."[48] This premise allows pro-life supporters to argue from the highest level of transcendence and to claim that "If all of our rights are to be protected, we must defend this first and most basic right—the right to life."[49]

Pro-life champions do not argue against women's rights, the freedom of choice, or religious liberty, but they place those values lower on the rights hierarchy and dependent upon the right to life. A leaflet entitled *The Abortion Connection* exclaims that in contrast to the right to life, "There is NO 'constitutional' right to abortion. There is only a Supreme Court-created right from a split decision in *Roe v. Wade* on January 22, 1973."[50] In a leaflet bearing a picture of an unborn but fully developed fetus, the author asks, "does her [the woman's] rights include dealing out a death sentence to another human being who is completely defenseless?"[51] The point appears to be a reverse value argument: the end (preserving a woman's right of privacy or choice) does not justify the means (depriving the fetus of the right to life).

Pro-life persuaders use a combination value and hierarchy argument when they point to state and federal laws designed to protect the defenseless. For example, one writer notes that state laws guarantee "the right of inheritance, to damages received while yet unborn, to get a blood transfusion over the mother's objection, to have a guardian appointed, and other rights of citizenship" but not the "most basic right of all—the right to life."[52] Newspaper advertisements entitled "Eagles, Beagles, Babies and 'There Oughta Be a Law'" contain large pictures of a bald eagle, two beagle puppies, and a fetus. A caption reads: "Ours is a peculiar society. We have laws protecting wildlife and dogs, but not defenseless human beings."[53] The advertisements report that stealing one eagle egg may result in a $5,000 fine, one year in jail, or both and that both houses of Congress overwhelmingly approved a federal law prohibiting the use of dogs in tests of chemical, biological, and radioactive warfare materials. While these laws protect the life and rights of eagles and beagles, the advertisements note, "Last year . . . more than 1,000,000 unborn babies were 'terminated' through 'abortion on demand.' Terminated means killed. Killed without penalty. Unless someone got a parking ticket in front of an abortion mill." The lines of argument are clear. Although states and the federal government have laws to protect the rights of privacy and choice for the mother and the lives and well-being of animals, no laws guarantee the unborn child the human right to life—the right at the pinnacle of the human rights hierarchy that transcends all other rights.

The Clash over Realities

The pro-choice and pro-life movements offer very different views of reality. Essentially the first portrays the present as the best of times and the second portrays the present as the worst of times, but each also takes a look backward and a look forward in presenting their cases for resisting or bringing about change. Arguments tend to be from quality and value.

Pro-Choice

Pro-choice defenders trace abortion practices back to ancient Egypt and conclude that there have always been and always will be abortions.[54] The only issue, persuaders argue, is whether abortions will be legal and safe or illegal and brutal. Early pro-choice leaflets contain police photographs of mutilated, dead women on bathroom floors from self-induced and "back-alley" abortions and abused or murdered unwanted babies, including the body of a deformed baby that had been thrown into a furnace.[55] Later leaflets and mailings write of the "horror," "slaughter," and "butchery" of past abortions in which women had used knitting needles, coat hangers, Lysol, and soap suds to induce abortions, often in filthy conditions.[56]

In a letter to pro-choice sympathizers, actress Joanne Woodward writes of a haunting part she played in which a woman faced the evils of a back-alley abortion.[57] Kate Michelman (Executive Director of NARAL) relates her personal story about receiving an abortion. First, she was treated in the most demeaning fashion by medical and legal officials; second, she had to be declared an unfit mother even though she had three small children and; third, she had to receive her husband's permission even though he had abandoned the family and refused to pay child support.[58] In the past, persuaders claim, the wealthy could get hospital abortions because they could afford to travel long distances and pay large sums of money. The poor, on the other hand, had to turn to the butchery of the back alley even when they were the "innocent victims of rage and violence" such as child abuse, rape, and incest.[59]

The pro-choice movement contrasts the horrors of the past with safe, legal abortions since 1973. All women, including the poor, now receive "safe and skilled treatment in hospitals and clinics," children are wanted and eagerly awaited, maternal and infant health has improved markedly, and countless women have been saved from injury and death.[60] Advocates claim that death from legal abortion is rare, that the abortion procedure is actually safer than childbirth, and that there has been no detectable increase in mental illness or psychological stress resulting from abortions.[61] Clearly the *quality* of life for women and infants since *Roe v. Wade* transcends the past to which the pro-life movement would have all Americans return. Pro-choice persuaders have increasingly warned audiences that the previous administrations, Congress, and state governments, in support of the pro-life cause, have placed unwarranted and evil restrictions on the woman's right to choose. They cite gag rules on counselors, parental and spouse consent laws, class discrimination against the poor who cannot get federal funds for abortions, and denial of abortions to institutionalized women, military wives and women, Peace Corps workers, and even children pregnant from incest.[62] They warn against slipping slowly back to the butchery of the past.

The pro-choice movement increasingly peers into the future and describes the horrors that will take place if its resistance efforts fail. Since laws and constitutional amendments will not eliminate abortions, persuaders claim, women will be "dragged back" to the untold suffering—the nightmare—of illegal abortions. Women would have to choose between compulsory pregnancy or death at the hands of quack abortionists.[63] Extending the opposition's argument about protecting the rights of the fetus legally, persuaders describe the chaotic impact such laws might have on our "entire system of civil and criminal laws." The woman would have to register her fetus with a "fetus-protection agency," and if the fetus were to die from disease, be miscarried, or be killed in an auto or sporting accident, the woman could be charged with premeditated murder and be jailed for life or executed. Physicians could be convicted of homicide for performing an abortion and suffer the same fate.[64]

Pro-choice advocates warn that in addition to the horrors of criminalizing abortion, infant and maternal mortality would increase, intolerable governmental intrusion into the private lives of pregnant women would be legal, and religious liberty would diminish because "one particular theology would become civil law."[65] The rhetoric of the pro-choice movement attempts to do what a resistance movement must do—convince audiences that the present must be preserved at all cost because it is *far better* than, transcends, the past or the future the opposition desires.

Pro-Life

Pro-life rhetoric dwells little on the past and never claims there were few or no abortions prior to *Roe v. Wade* in 1973. A publication by Americans Against Abortion does argue that 84 to 87 percent of so-called back-alley abortions of the past "were not done in back alleys at all" but by "reputable physicians" in medical facilities.[66] Pro-life persuaders dwell mostly on what has happened in the past when humans were labeled as nonpersons. They offer Nazi Germany and the extermination of six million Jews as indisputable evidence of what happens when some humans are judged to be inferior.[67] A number of sources refer to the treatment of Native Americans as savages and of African Americans who, as nonpersons, could be bought, sold, or killed, particularly after the Dred Scott decision of 1857.[68] Thus, pro-life advocates imply that the instances of abortion prior to 1973 were inconsequential and use historical accounts of Native Americans, slavery, and Nazi Germany as lead-ins to lengthy accounts of the horrors of the present. The past was obviously better than the present, at least for the unborn.

Pro-life rhetoric abounds with accounts and pictures of the cruel, bar-barous slaughter and even cannibalism of the unborn, what is called the "hidden holocaust." This evil is perpetrated for insignificant or unimpor-tant reasons. Persuaders claim that 98 percent of abortions are for social and professional reasons, literally killing unborn humans "on a whim."[69] Millions die every year merely because pregnancy is inconvenient or the mother wants to get rid of an annoying problem. Nurses and physicians tell stories about when they had to starve, smother, or bash in the head of an aborted fetus when it refused to die, and these stories are often accom-panied by gory, full-color pictures of tiny bodies torn apart by a variety of abortion methods and dumped in buckets and trash cans.[70] The most spectacular and controversial effort to show life and death in the womb is a video entitled "The Silent Scream" that purports to show the struggle for life of a fetus being "murdered" by a vacuum aspirator. Joseph Scheidler, founder and director of the Pro-Life Action League, narrates this struggle: "She retreats frantically from the device. But it pulls her legs off. Then it disembowels her. She struggles violently with her arms. Her head falls back; her mouth opens in anguish."[71]

The battleground of the late 1990s became centered on late-term abor-tions, those in the third trimester of pregnancy. Pro-life champions have termed these procedures "partial-birth" abortions or "partial-birth infanti-cide" and described them in horrific detail.[72] They offer clinical descrip-tions and firsthand testimony of nurses and physicians that portray the "heinous" or "gruesome" procedures performed on near-term fetuses who are often alive at the time of their "murder."[73] After citing a step-by-step late-term abortion described in the *New York Times Magazine*, Tom Bethell, the Washington correspondent for *The American Spectator* exclaimed: "Mur-der, is what it was. The infant was within a few inches of drawing its first breath. Instead, it was stabbed in the back of the head by the attending 'doc-tor'."[74] These doctors, he noted, "are the American successors to Mengele, who performed experiments in Nazi Germany." Bethell astutely noted that this procedure shifted the focus of the abortion debate from "'a woman's right to choose' to what is being chosen: infanticide."[75] The shift was from a right high on the good scale (free choice) to an act high on the evil scale (murder and infanticide). The pro-life movement's campaign against late-term abortions has attracted many supporters and met with considerable success. Some twenty-eight states had outlawed such procedures or stopped them temporarily by mid-1998. Congress passed legislation in the same year to ban all late-term abortions, but President Clinton vetoed it. The House of Representatives voted 296 to 132 to override the veto, and the Senate came within three votes of doing the same.[76] Pro-life has found a battle in the abortion war that resonates well with a sizable majority, some estimates are 80 percent, including many nominal pro-choice supporters.

Pro-life advocates claim that all acts of abortion, not just partial-birth, are so heinous that pro-abortion forces have created euphemisms to mask reality. These include "terminating a pregnancy," "post-conceptual planning," "menstrual extraction," and "exercising a woman's right to choose." And they claim that the tragedies of the present, largely unreported and covered up, go beyond the unborn. Women who have been "exploited by abortion" suffer life-threatening complications and even death, serious mental and psychological problems, and increases in sterility, miscarriages, tubal pregnancies, and premature babies. Persuaders argue that abortion-on-demand has caused child abuse to increase by 500 percent.[77] The conclusion is obvious: this is the worst of times. The past may have been imperfect, but it was better than the present with its hidden tragedies for both the unborn and the mothers that destroy them.

What about the future? Pro-life persuaders predict a chain reaction because, "Once we permit killing of the unborn child, there will be no stopping."[78] The list of nonpersons may grow to include anyone considered to be a burden because if the state can legalize murder of some, it can do so for the many. One leaflet warns:

> How long will it be before other groups of humans will be defined
> out of legal existence when it has been decided that they too have
> become socially burdensome?
> SENIOR CITIZENS BEWARE
> MINORITY RACES BEWARE
> CRIPPLED CHILDREN BEWARE
> Once the decision has been made that all human life is no longer
> an unalienable right, but that some can be killed because they are a
> social burden, then the senile, the weak, the physically and mentally
> inadequate and perhaps someday even the politically troublesome
> are in danger.
> It did happen once before in this century you know. Remember
> Germany?[79]

The message is clear. The United States must return to a better past to stop the evils of the present and to avoid even greater evils of the future.

The Clash over Competing Social Movements

The pro-life and pro-choice movements use a variety of arguments from transcendence to establish their size and stature and to justify their motives and methods while shrinking the opposition and painting it as evil. The transcendent points of quantity, quality, and hierarchy are common in these competing rhetorical efforts.

Pro-Choice

Pro-choice advocates describe their movement as a "massive state-by-state grassroots campaign" and mobilization that has the "overwhelming support" of the "vast majority" of Americans. They claim that polls continually show that four out of five Americans, including the majority of Roman Catholics and almost all Protestant and Jewish groups, support the pro-choice position that "there are situations in which abortion may be a moral alternative."[80] They talk about the size of NARAL's membership, the hundreds of thousands who have marched for pro-choice in Washington, D.C., the 38 religious organizations that belong to the Religious Coalition for Reproductive Freedom (originally the Religious Coalition for Abortion Rights), and the 8,000 members of Clergy for Choice "representing over 25 mainstream denominations." In contrast, they claim the pro-life movement is an "anti-choice minority," a "tiny, fanatical minority," a "vocal, powerful minority."[81] Compared to the pro-choice movement that represents most Americans and mainline religious groups, pro-life consists of a small group of religious zealots, a few small Protestant denominations, Orthodox Jews, and the Roman Catholic hierarchy allied with the political right-wing and anti-women's rights organizations.[82] Thus, they argue, pro-choice is superior in both size (quantity) and stature (hierarchy).

Advocates claim the pro-choice community is being heard and heeded in elections throughout the country because its motives, goals, and methods are virtuous (quality) and desirable (value). The pro-choice movement disputes opposition claims that the movement advocates abortion. In fact, some sources claim, we "don't know anyone" connected with the movement "who is 'pro-abortion.'"[83] Instead, the movement is pro-family, for reproductive freedom, for peace among nations, and an advocate of help for the poor, a sound educational system, and a clean environment while struggling against racism, classism, and sexism. Its methods are limited to electing pro-choice candidates and preserving abortion rights through the courts. As a result, the pro-choice position has received the endorsement of such highly credible groups as the American Medical Association, the American Bar Association, hundreds of doctors of obstetrics and gynecology, the President's Commission on Population Growth and the American Future, the National Conference of Commissioners on Uniform State Laws, the U.S. Commission on Civil Rights, and the National Academy of Scientists Institute on Medicine.[84]

Pro-choice champions contrast their membership with that of the pro-life movement, which consists of religious sects, church-supported lobbying groups, the hierarchy of the Roman Catholic Church (not Catholics themselves), the ultra right, spineless and pandering politicians, and arch conservatives such as Senators Jesse Helms of North Carolina and Orin Hatch of Utah and the reverends Jerry Falwell and Jimmy Swaggart. The cover of one leaflet is the picture of weeping, pro-life advocate Reverend Jimmy Swaggart on television admitting to having consorted with prostitutes.[85] Pro-life advocates are identified as dangerous extremists, ruthless fanatics, mobs, terrorists, and irrational, moral zealots who will stop at nothing until they achieve their evil, self-serving goals: return women to a position of subservience, force their religious dogma on the American people, foster class discrimination, end sex education in the schools, and outlaw all forms of birth control.[86] A letter from the Religious Coalition for Reproductive Choice charges that "In their violence toward women and their doctors, they are terrorists cut from the same cloth as KKK night riders who used terror to stop African-American citizens from exercising their right to vote."[87]

Pro-choice literature chronicles the ruthless guerrilla and terrorist tactics of so-called right-to-life groups who "have an iron disregard for life" and are often in "a frenzy amounting to hysteria."[88] These acts include death threats, claims of spreading deadly anthrax germs in clinics, threats to kidnap children, arson, bombings, shootings into clinics while patients and staff are inside, acid sprayed into clinics, hate campaigns, obscenity shouting, blockades of clinics, stalking of physicians and physicians' families, and threats to hospitals where abortions might take place. After Dr. David Gunn was murdered by a pro-life advocate outside a clinic in Pensacola, Florida in March 1993, pro-choice supporters said they had been expecting this to happen as terrorist tactics had escalated:

> Anyone who wants to check the fertile soil in which fanaticism grows has only to listen to the leaders' responses to the assassination of the 47-year-old doctor and father of two: "While Gunn's death is unfortunate," said Don Treshman of "Rescue America", "it's also true that quite a number of babies' lives will be saved." While it is wrong to kill, said Randall Terry [leader of Operation Rescue], "we have to recognize that this doctor was a mass murderer." "Praise God," said a protestor at a clinic in Melbourne, Florida, "one of the (baby) killers is dead!"[89]

Following the murder of Dr. Barnett Slepian in 1998, the media quoted Reverend Donald Spitz, founder of Pro-Life Virginia, who called Slepian's killer a "hero" because "We as Christians have a responsibility to protect the innocent from being murdered. Whoever shot the shot protected the children." Spitz claimed the killers of physicians were "being forced into it" because the government had limited other means of protest.[90] An editor of *The Progressive* concluded, "Religious fundamentalism is morphing into religious vigilantism before our very eyes."[91]

Thus, the rhetoric of the pro-choice movement claims that it transcends the pro-life movement that destroys life in the name of protecting life. The pro-life movement is smaller (quantity), consists of and is supported by evil persons and groups (quality), and employs evil means to achieve evil and self-centered goals (quality).

Pro-Life

Pro-life champions claim their movement is not a narrow, conservative, religious and political movement but a "great people's movement," "the largest grassroots; citizens movement in recent history," a "majority movement" that transcends all religions and political parties. One source claims "Millions have joined the National Right to Life Committee and many more millions will join when they realize how big the problem is."[92] Persuaders argue that polls cited in pro-choice literature are highly misleading and present their own interpretations of results: 65 percent of Americans believe abortion is morally wrong, 52-55 percent approve of abortion only for hard cases, 77 percent of Americans oppose abortion for social, nonmedical reasons, and most Americans approve of only 2 percent of abortions performed today. One writer notes that if the following question were asked, results would favor the pro-life position: "Should an innocent human being be killed for the crime of another?"[93] Recent sources note that "Perhaps 75 to 80 percent of the people nationwide oppose partial-birth abortions."[94]

Pro-life defenders contend their movement is not a small political/ religious coalition, but a massive movement that represents the true beliefs of the United States. This "majority movement," advocates claim, is supported by "some of the finest minds in the country"; "people from all across the country and in every walk of life"; "moms, dads, business people, retired people and children"; nurses, physicians, lawyers, courts, state and federal legislators of both parties, and presidents Reagan and Bush.[95]

Pro-life persuaders portray the pro-choice movement as "abortionists," "social engineering advocacy groups," tiny minorities, and the "abortion industry." One leaflet argues that, since it is possible for eleven people in the National Council of Churches to convey an "official stand" for thirty-three denominations with forty-two million members, the "religious" support for the pro-choice stance should be discounted.[96] The late-term abortion conflict has enabled pro-life persuaders to attach the "extremism" label to pro-choice adherents. One writer claims only "zealots" oppose the banning of "partial-birth abortions," and that opposing argument "comes from National Abortion Rights Action League fanatics who fear that any slippage in the defense of an already extremist position is likely to lead to more slippage."[97] Thus, persuaders argue, pro-life exceeds pro-choice in both quantity and quality.

The pro-life movement also argues that it is superior to the pro-choice movement in motives for acting. In a "VERY URGENT" action-gram to committee members in 1987, president Dr. John Willke declared that the NRLC's sole purpose was to stop the wholesale slaughter of unborn babies in their mother's wombs, while "Planned Parenthood, NARAL and the National Organization for Women exist to make sure that unborn babies don't live. That's a very sorry reason."[98] Defenders contrast their unselfish crusade to save unborn lives with the abortionists' motive to maintain the abortion-on-demand industry for financial profit, alleging that pro-choice is only interested in the $700 million a year they get from killing babies and selling these bodies for soap and cosmetics.[99] Joseph Sobran of the American Life League claims the hidden agenda of the pro-choice movement is to subvert Christian morality in the United States. Proof, he claims, lies in the partial-birth conflict:

> Now, in the current debate over "partial-birth abortions," the advocates of legal abortion have shown themselves willing to defend the most hideous abortions of all, in which nobody can doubt that a child is being killed and, moreover, dying in agony. They express moral indignation not against the "abortion providers" who perform such atrocities, but only against those who insist on describing these abortions in accurate detail.[100]

David Mall, in his book entitled *In Good Conscience: Abortion and Moral Necessity*, reviews the moral development principles and theories of philosopher Jean Piaget and psychologist Lawrence Kohlberg and asserts that pro-life advocates have reached a high level of moral development in which they struggle for the rights and welfare of others while pro-choice advocates never advance beyond an immature, self-centered stage of moral development and are willing to kill their unborn to achieve social and professional benefits. Mall writes:

> There appear to be two contrary psychological forces at work in the abortion debate: one pulls toward genuine moral growth and development and the other toward moral decay and dissolution. The struggle is really between a moralizing process that is authentic and one that is not. Moralizing that favors abortion is really an anti-development. A parallel is to be found in the relationship between the symbolic and the diabolic, a relationship with deep religious significance. . . . One leads to life and the other leads to death.[101]

Perhaps the greatest rhetorical dilemma facing the pro-life movement is the growing militancy that has resulted in the killing of several physicians who had performed abortions in the United States and Canada. Since the 1970s, there have been seven murders, sixteen attempted murders, more than 200 bombings and arsons, 750 death and bomb threats, and hundreds of acts of vandalism, stalking, and burglary.[102] It is risky, however, for *pro-life* movement members and leaders to condemn violence unconditionally. They risk fragmenting the movement.[103] Some pro-life groups take the risk for moral and practical reasons. A *Newsweek* poll following the murder of Dr. Slepian revealed that 86 percent of Americans believed such killings hurt the pro-life movement.[104] For example, a consortium of pro-life groups in New York offered a $5,000 reward for information leading to those responsible for bombing an abortion clinic, and the Reverend Jerry Falwell (founder and leader of the Moral Majority) called violent elements "common criminals" and warned that violence does "great damage to the antiabortion cause."[105] Helen Alvare, director of planning and information for the U.S. Bishop's Secretariat for Pro-Life Activities, declared in a statement following the murder of Dr. Gunn, "As we abhor the violence of abortion, we abhor violence as a dangerous and deplorable means to stop abortion. In the name and in the true spirit of pro-life, we call on all in the pro-life movement to condemn such violence in no uncertain terms."[106] Bob Behn, who regularly held pro-life prayer vigils outside Slepian's clinic, said the killing was a loss not a victory for the movement. He said he and Slepian "were just getting a dialogue going" on the abortion issue when he was murdered.[107]

Some leaders of pro-life organizations deny that their members have committed violent acts and urge followers to refrain from violence. Willke of the NRLC issued this appeal to members: "Let us witness peacefully in work, in picketing, by sit-ins, in letters, by prayers, and at the ballot box. It is they who live by violence and the modern sword, the suction curette. Violence is not our way."[108] Some pro-life leaders in statements following the death of Gunn blamed the pro-choice movement for having created the violent climate through abortion. John Burt, regional director of Rescue America, remarked: "I think all life is sacred, and Dr. Gunn and Michael Griffin [Gunn's confessed killer] are both victims of abortion."[109]

Although many moderate movement leaders and followers condemn militancy, some use arguments from transcendence to justify militancy for the cause of life. First, they vindicate militant pro-lifers because militants defend *higher principles* and do not act through self-interest. A writer in the *National Right to Life News* claims "the appeal of the pro-life movement is to those principles of justice and nondiscrimination which transcend self-seeking."[110]

Second, pro-life apologists argue that violence for *noble purposes* transcends violence for ignoble purposes and, thus, is acceptable. Cal Thomas of the Moral Majority compares pro-life violence with the civil rights riots of the 1960s and concludes that both were "equally wrong, but served a higher and nobler purpose in that they moved lethargic government leaders to action."[111]

Third, pro-life argues that militancy is justified in defense of a *higher law*. For example, Monsignor Thomas C. Corrigan defended the "Cleveland Eleven" who were arrested for disrupting an abortion clinic by contending that when "the laws of God (which say that abortion is wrong) are in opposition to the laws of man (which say abortion is legal), people are justified in siding with the Gospels and challenging man-made laws."[112]

Fourth, persuaders claim that the *end justifies or transcends the means used*. During his trial for trespassing in an abortion clinic sit-in, Dabien Avila of Fort Wayne, Indiana, declared that "when life or property is in danger . . . a person does have a right to go in. He has a right to attempt in a reasonable manner to stop the destruction of life or property."[113] The Cleveland Eleven concluded, "It's a small price to pay in view of the millions of lives annually being snuffed out."[114]

Fifth, advocates argue that *lesser violence* is justified if it stops a *greater violence*. Jan Carroll of the National Right to Life Committee refuses to apologize for violence because "violence that goes on inside the clinic is much more damaging to the moral fiber of the nation."[115] This is how some pro-life leaders reacted to the death of Dr. Gunn; it was the lesser of two evils. Others seemed to argue this way with reluctance. John Burt said, "We don't condone this, but we have to remember that Dr. Gunn has killed thousands and thousands of babies."[116]

Sixth, some advocates contend that *extraordinary circumstances* justify violent means that are ordinarily considered unacceptable in society. Elsie Lewis, active in the American Life League, explains that:

> For the most part, where there is an unjust law, you obey it, and you try to change it. But when they are killing two million babies a year— it is so heinous an injustice. While working to change the law, many lives are being lost. Since 1973 a holocaust has been going on . . . If you believe that an abortuary is murdering thousands of babies and thirty are scheduled for tomorrow, how can you condemn someone for destroying it?[117]

Thus, pro-life persuaders defend militant tactics ranging from trespassing to murder by using six lines of argument that develop three of the four points of comparison that establish transcendence: hierarchy (higher principles, higher law), quality (noble purposes, lesser crime or evil), and value (end over means, extraordinary circumstances, life over a building). These points allow persuaders both to condemn and to praise militant actions and thereby to answer challenges from pro-choice and avoid factionalizing the movement over tactics. Violence, like war, is generally to be condemned, they argue, but there are circumstances when violence is the lesser of two evils and the only viable course of action.

Conclusions

Social movements argue from transcendence when they claim that an organization, group, goal, thing, right, act, or proposal surpasses, is superior to, or is prior to that of the opposition. It is a comparative argument based on quantity (more–less), quality (good–bad), value (important–unimportant), and hierarchy (high–low).

The pro-choice and pro-life movements rely heavily upon argument from transcendence to establish their positions on fundamental issues, to attack one another, and to defend themselves. They employ the comparative points of value and hierarchy when establishing their positions on personhood (the issue upon which all subsequent arguments rest) and to attack opposition claims regarding personhood of the fetus or woman. They employ hierarchy and value points when arguing which rights are most basic (at the top of the rights hierarchy) and which are most important. They employ the points of value and quality when presenting their versions of reality: the past, present, and future. Pro-choice, as a resistance social movement, claims that the present is the best of times while both the past and future have been or might be full of horrors. Pro-life, as a revivalistic social movement, implies that the past was the best of times while the present is full of horrors and the future is likely to be worse. They employ the points of quantity, quality, and hierarchy when establishing themselves (including size, motives, morals, and methods) as the superior movement in the abortion conflict.

Each movement's argument from transcendence is a fragile interdependent network of premises based on a single major premise: either the woman is a full-fledged person while the fetus is a potential person or the fetus is a person from the moment of conception and deserves special protection because of its innocence and vulnerability. Neither movement rests comfortably on the moral high ground to which it has laid claim. True believers of each movement are extremists in the sense that they accept no compromises or exceptions to life or choice. Each fears that acceptance of some abortions (due to incest or rape, for instance) or some restrictions (late-term abortions, for instance) will lead to a plunge down a slippery slope on which they will lose their struggle for life or choice. The majority of Americans, including many of each movement's sympathizers, has reservations about and supports exceptions to or qualifications of these premises. If the recipient of a pro-choice or pro-life message seriously questions or denies the central premise, the network of transcendent arguments crumbles. Thus, neither the woman nor the fetus has the inalienable rights claimed. The past, present, and future was not, is not, and will not be as bright or dark as portrayed.

Social movements suffer from limited resources and often find it difficult to prove that an institution, competing movement, norm, or value is utterly without value. Transcendence allows a movement to address *degrees* of size, importance, goodness, or risk. For instance, a social movement need not establish that it, its cause, or its methods are without flaw but only that it is larger than an institution or opposing movement claims, that it is more honorable than established institutions or countermovements, that its plan is safer than current or proposed policies, or that its tactics are less evil than ones employed by institutions or countermovements. Social movements must also strive to maintain unity among supporters of the cause and attract support from the public, legitimizers, and established institutions.

Argument from transcendence allows a social movement, or a faction of a movement, to stress its superiority, explain its ideology, and justify its tactics without having to destroy other factions or antagonize institutions that might be potential allies. A social movement does not have to deny competing rights but only to claim that such rights are less important or lower on a hierarchy of rights. Thus, a movement may reduce the risk of fracturing the movement by antagonizing varying elements within or scaring away potential supporters.

This chapter has illustrated how the pro-choice and pro-life movements have employed argument from transcendence in their continual conflict over legalized abortion. The four points of comparison—quality, quantity, value, and hierarchy—have enabled both movements to establish, attack, and defend positions on personhood, competing rights, visions of reality, and organization (including membership, motives, and tactics). It is difficult to imagine how social movements could carry forward their struggles and meet oppositions without relying upon this essential language bridge.

Endnotes

[1] Robert S. Cathcart, "Defining Social Movements by Their Rhetorical Form," *Central States Speech Journal* 31 (Winter 1980): 271.

[2] Robert S. Cathcart, "New Approaches to the Study of Social Movements," *Western Journal of Speech Communication* 36 (Spring 1972): 88; Kenneth Burke, "Catharsis—Second View," *Centennial Review* 5 (1961): 130; Leland M. Griffin, "A Dramatistic Theory of the Rhetoric of Movements," *Critical Responses to Kenneth Burke*, William Rueckert, ed. (Minneapolis: University of Minnesota Press, 1969): 456.

[3] Griffin, 464.

[4] Karl R. Wallace, *Francis Bacon on Communication and Rhetoric* (Chapel Hill: University of North Carolina Press, 1943): 65.

[5] *Readers Digest Oxford Complete Word Finder* (New York: Oxford University Press, 1996): 1623.

[6] Aristotle, *The Rhetoric*, W. Rhys Roberts, trans. (New York: Modern Library, 1954): Book 1, 1362a37–1362b2.

[7] Kenneth Burke, *Language as Symbolic Action* (Berkeley: University of California Press, 1966): 187.

[8] Marcus Tullius Cicero, Topics, H. M. Hubbell, trans. (Cambridge: Harvard University Press, 1959): 433; *Aristotle, Book I*, 1363b5–13; Kenneth Burke, *A Rhetoric of Motives* (Berkeley: University of California Press, 1969): 231–279.

[9] Burke, *Rhetoric of Motives*, 11–12; Kenneth Burke, *Dramatism and Development* (Barre, MA: Clark University Press, 1972): 23–24.

[10] *Join Us and Make A Difference* (Washington, DC: PETA, n.d.; Brian Davies, letter for the International Fund for Animals, October 1987.

[11] Terence Powderly, "Address of the Grand Master Workman," Proceedings of the General Assembly of the Knights of Labor, 7 September 1880, 176.

[12] *Aristotle, Book I*, 1362a37–b2 and 1363b5–13; Wallace, 60–65.

[13] Charles J. Stewart, "Championing the Rights of Others and Challenging Evil: The Ego Function in the Rhetoric of Other-Directed Social Movements," *Southern Communication Journal* 53 (Winter 1999): 101.

[14] Roxanne Dunbar, "Women's Liberation: Where the Movement Is Today and Where It's Going," reprinted in *On Speech Communication*, Charles J. Stewart, ed. (New York: Holt, Rinehart and Winston, 1972): 312.

[15] Barry Brummett, "Burkeian Scapegoating, Mortification, and Transcendence in Presidential Campaign Rhetoric," *Central States Speech Journal* 32 (Winter 1981): 256.

[16] Kenneth Burke, *A Grammar of Motives* (Berkeley: University of California Press, 1969): 424, 425, and 428; Burke, *Rhetoric of Motives*, 14, 16, 76, and 138; Kenneth Burke, *The Rhetoric of Religion* (Berkeley: University of California Press, 1970): 58, 83, and 156.

[17] Burke, *Rhetoric of Motives*, 76.

[18] Burke, *Rhetoric of Religion*, 230; Brummett, 256 and 259.

[19] Stewart, 98.

20 Kenneth Burke, *The Philosophy of Literary Form* (Berkeley: University of California Press, 1973): 312.

21 See for example, Frederick S. Jaffe, Barbara L. Lindheim, and Philip R. Lee, *Abortion Politics: Private Morality and Public Policy* (New York: McGraw-Hill, 1981); Marilyn Falik, *Ideology and Abortion Party Politics* (New York: Praeger, 1983); "America's Abortion Dilemma," *Newsweek*, 14 January 1985, 20–29; "The Future of Abortion," *Newsweek*, 17 July 1989, 14–20; "Abortion Angst," *Newsweek*, 13 July 1992; 16–20.

22 Richard D. Orlaski, "Abortion: Legal Questions and Legislative Alternative's," *America*, 10 August 1974, 50.

23 *United States Supreme Court Reports*, vol. 35 (Rochester, NY: Lawyers Co-Operative Publishing Company, 1974): 147–149.

24 "The Death of Doctor Gunn," *Newsweek*, 22 March 1993, 34–35.

25 "The Abortion Wars Come Home," *Newsweek*, 9 November 1998, 34–35.

26 "The Abortion Wars Come Home," 34.

27 Randall A. Lake, "Order and Disorder in Anti-Abortion Rhetoric: A Logological View," *Quarterly Journal of Speech* 70 (November 1984): 425–443; Celeste Condit Railsback, "The Contemporary American Abortion Controversy: Stages in the Argument," *Quarterly Journal of Speech* 70 (November 1984): 410–424; Marsha L. Vanderford, "Vilification and Social Movements: A Case Study of Pro-Life and Pro-Choice Rhetoric," *Quarterly Journal of Speech* 75 (May 1989): 166–182; Celeste M. Condit, *Decoding Abortion Rhetoric: Communication Social Change* (Urbana: University of Illinois Press, 1990); Faye D. Ginsburg, *Contested Lives: The Abortion Debate in an American Community* (Berkeley: University of California Press, 1989).

28 Fifty leaflets, pamphlets, mailings, and newspaper advertisements produced by each movement from 1970–1999 were the primary sources for this study. Additional materials included thirty issues of *The Communicator*, the Indiana Right to Life newspaper, thirty issues of the *Tippecanoe County Right to Life* newsletter, and magazine articles dealing with the abortion issue.

29 *Saving Abortion* (New York: Association for the Study of Abortion, n.d.): 2; *Legal Abortion: Arguments Pro & Con* (New York: Westchester Coalition for Legal Abortion, 1978): n.pag.; *Sponsors & Members* (Washington, DC: Religious Coalition for Abortion Rights, 1978): n.pag.

30 *The Abortion Dilemma* (Washington, DC: Religious Coalition for Abortion Rights, n.d.): n.pag.

31 Mailing from the Religious Coalition for Abortion Rights, n.d., n.pag.

32 *Abortion: Why Religious Organizations in the United States Want to Keep It Legal* (Washington, DC: Religious Coalition for Abortion Rights, 1979): n.pag.

33 *Saving Abortion*, 2–3; mailing from the Religious Coalition for Abortion Rights, n.d., n.pag.

34 *What Is the RCAR* (Washington, DC: Religious Coalition for Abortion Rights, 1979): n.pag.; *The Abortion Dilemma*, n.pag.; *Sponsors & Members*, n.p.; *Legal Abortion*, n. pag.

35 *Abortion: Why Religious Organizations in the United States Want to Keep It Legal*, n.pag.; mailing from Fredrica F. Hodges, Executive Director of the Religious Coalition for Abortion Rights, n.d., n.pag.; *Wouldn't a Law Prohibiting Abortion Violate Religious Liberty?* (Washington: DC: Religious Coalition for Abortion Rights, n.d.): n.pag.

36 *Sponsors & Members*, n.pag.; *What Is the RCAR?*, n.pag.

37 *We Affirm: Excerpts from Statements about Abortion Rights as Expressed by National Religious Organizations* (Washington, DC: Religious Coalition for Abortion Rights, 1978): n.pag.; *Abortion: Why Religious Organizations in the United States Want to Keep It Legal*, n.pag.

38 *Abortion: Questions and Answers* (Washington, DC: Committee for Pro-Life Activities, 1983): n.pag.; *Abortion: Death Before Life* (Washington, DC: NRL Educational Trust Fund, 1985): n.pag.; *Some Surprising Facts . . . about Your Right to Life* (Washington, DC: National Right to Life Committee, n.d.): n.pag.

39 *We Care, We Love, We Are PRO-LIFE* (Conway, AR: Conway Mother & Unborn Baby Care, n.d.): n.pag.; *The U.S. Supreme Court Has Ruled It's Legal to Kill a Baby . . .* (Cincinnati:

Hayes Publishing Company, 1976): n.pag.; *Where Do You Stand?* (Cincinnati: Willke & Hiltz Publishing Company, n.d.): n.pag.

40 *Why People Vote Pro-Life* (Lafayette, IN: Tippecanoe County Right to Life, n.d.): n.pag.; *Aborted Baby Discarded in Hospital Bucket* (n.p., n.d.), n.pag.; Melody Green, *Children— Things We Throw Away* (Lindale, TX: Last Days Lifeline, 1979): n.pag.

41 *Abortion: Death Before Life*, n.pag.; *Abortion: A Catholic Issue* (Minneapolis: For LIFE, 1977): n.pag.

42 *Abortion: Questions and Answers*, n.pag.; *What Is the Key Question?* (Minneapolis: For LIFE. 1977): n.pag.; *The Facts of Death* (Glendale, CA: Committee of Ten Million, 1973): n.pag.

43 *The Hidden Holocaust* (Taylor, AZ: The Precious Feet People, n.d.): n.pag.; *Their Life Is in Your Hand* (Lafayette, IN: Tippecanoe County Right to Life, n.d.): n.pag.; mailing from Judie Brown, President, American Life Lobby, Stafford, VA, n.d., n.pag.

44 *Do You Want to Return to the Butchery of Back-Alley Abortion?* (New York: NARAL, n.d.): n.pag.; *A Mobilization Bulletin* (Washington: National Organization for Women, n.d.): 1; mailing from Patricia Ireland, President, National Organization for Women, n.d., 1–2.

45 Mailing from Kenneth Edelin, Planned Parenthood Federation of America, n.d., 1; We Affirm, n.pag.; mailing 4 from Faye Wattleton, President, Planned Parenthood Federation of America, n.d., 1.

46 "Special Advisory Memorandum" from Kate Michelman, Executive Director, NARAL, April 19, 1988, 1–4.

47 *Constitutional Aspects of the Right to Limit Childbearing* (Washington: NARAL, n.d.): n.pag.; mailing 1 from Molly Yard, President, National Organization for Women, n.d., 1–4; mailing from Sarah Weddington, RCAR, n.d., n.pag.

48 *We Care, We Love, We Are Pro-Life*, n.pag.; mailing from Judie Brown, 2–4; *Abortion: A Catholic Issue*, n.pag.

49 *Why Vote Pro-Life*, n.pag.; *Abortion: A Catholic Issue*, n.pag.

50 *The Abortion Connection*, n.p., n.d., n.pag.

51 *Is This Life Worth a Postage Stamp?* (n.p., n.d.): n. pag.

52 Ken Unger, *What You Don't Know Can Hurt You!* (Ashtabula, OH: Protestants Protesting Abortion (n.d.): n.pag.; *Children—Things We Throw Away?*, n.pag.; *The Facts of Death*, n.pag.

53 Lafayette, *Indiana Journal and Courier*, 22 January 1979, A-8; 22 January 1980, B-4; 11 May 1980, B–7.

54 Mailing 1 from Molly Yard, President, National Organization for Women, 1990, 1–2; mailing 2 from Molly Yard, President, National Organization for Women, 1991, 2–3; Mailing from Edelin, 2.

55 *Do You Want to Return to the Butchery of Back-Alley Abortion?*, n.pag.

56 Mailing from Edelin, 1; mailing 1 from Joanne Woodward, n.d., 1; Congressional Action in Violation of Reproductive Freedom: 1978 (Washington, DC: NARAL, 1978): 1.

57 Mailing 2 from Joanne Woodward, n.d., 1.

58 Mailing from Kate Michelman, Executive Director, NARAL, July 25, 1988, 1–2.

59 *What Is RCAR?*, n.pag.; *Abortion: Why Religious Organizations in the United States Want to Keep It Legal*, n.pag.; *Legal Abortion: Arguments Pro & Con*, n.pag.; *We Affirm*, n.pag.

60 *Abortion Q & A* (Washington, DC: NARAL, n.d.): n.pag.; *Abortion Fact Sheet* (New York: NARAL, n.d.): n. pag.; mailing from Edelin, 3–4.

61 *The Abortion Dilemma*, n.pag.; *Legal Abortion: Arguments Pro & Con*, n.pag.; *Abortion Q & A*, n. pag.

62 Mailing 2 from Faye Wattleton, President, Planned Parenthood Federation of America, n.d., 1–4; mailing 3 from Faye Wattleton, President, Planned Parenthood Federation of America, n.d., 1–3; mailing from Karen Mulbauser, Executive Director, NARAL, n.d., 2.

63 Mailing from Gloria Steinem, n.d., 1; mailing 2 from Molly Yard, 1–2; mailing 1 from Joanne Woodward, 1.

64 Mailing 3 from Molly Yard, President, National Organization for Women, n.d., 2–3; saving Abortion, 1–3; *Constitutional Aspects of the Right to Limit Childbearing*, n.pag.

[65] *Sponsors & Members*, n.pag.; *Abortion: Why Religious Organizations in the United States Want to Keep It Legal*, n.pag.

[66] *Americans Against Abortion*, Summer, 1986, 2.

[67] *Life or Death* (Cincinnati: Hayes Publishing, n.d.): n.pag.; *Children – Things We Throw Away?*, n. pag.; *The Hidden Holocaust*, p.pag.

[68] *What Is the Key Question?* (Minneapolis: For Life, 1977): n.pag.; *Heartbeat*, September/October 1991, 2–3; Paul Marx, *The Mercy Killers* (Palos Verdes Estates, CA: Right to Life, 1974): 1–11.

[69] *Abortion: Public Opinion* (Washington, DC: NRL Educational Trust Fund, 1985): n.pag.; *The Hidden Holocaust*, n.pag.; *Sex Discrimination Before Birth* (Jefferson City, MO: Easton Publishing, 1985): n.pag.

[70] See for example, *Aborted Baby Discarded in a Hospital Bucket*, n.p., 1973, n.pag.; *Children—Things We Throw Away?*, n.pag., Gary Bergel, *Abortion in America* (Washington, DC: National Right to Life, 1990): 11–5.

[71] *Newsweek*, 14 January 1985, 25.

[72] Allan Carlson, "Twenty-Five Years Into The Culture of Death," *Vital Speeches of the Day*, 15 March 1998, 345; Tom Bethell, "A Heinous Procedure," *The American Spectator*, April 1998, 20.

[73] Bethell, 20; Robert W. Lee, "The Partial Birth 'Choice': Pro-Aborts Are Pushing a Particularly Gruesome Form of Child Murder," *The New American*, 15 April, 1996, 4–8; "When Abortions Come Late in a Pregnancy," *U.S. News & World Report*, 19 January 1998, 31.

[74] Bethell, 20.

[75] Bethell, 21.

[76] "Back-Alley Antiabortion," *The Nation*, 16 November 1998, 5.

[77] *Before You Make the Decision* (Moreno Valley, CA: Women Exploited by Abortion, 1984): n.pag.; *Abortion: Death Before Life*, n.pag.; *Aborted Baby in a Hospital Bucket*, n.pag.; *Rape* (Jefferson City, MO: Easton Publishing, 1986): n.pag; *Incest* (Jefferson City, MO: Easton Publishing, 1987): n.pag.

[78] Marx, 16.

[79] *The U.S. Supreme Court Has Ruled It's Legal to Kill a Baby*, n. pag.

[80] *Religious Freedom and the Abortion Controversy* (Washington, DC: RCAR, 1978): n.pag.; mailing #3 from Kate Michelman, Executive Director, NARAL, n.d., 2; Woodward, mailing 2, 2; Yard mailing #2, 2–4; letter from the Religious Coalition for Reproductive Freedom, n.d., n.pag.

[81] *Abortion Q & A*, n.pag.; Weddington mailing, n.pag.; Wattleton mailing 4, 1–3.

[82] Wattleton mailing 1, 1-2; *What Is RCAR?*, n.pag., Ireland mailing, 1–4.

[83] *You Know Them as the Right to Life People. They Oppose Abortion. But Did You Know . . .* (Washington, DC: NARAL, n.d.): n. pag.; *The Abortion Dilemma*, n.pag.

[84] *How to Become a Pro-Choice Activist*, n.pag.; *Twelve Abortion Facts* (Washington, DC: NARAL, n.d.): n.pag.; *Saving Abortion*, 3.

[85] Yard, mailing 3, 1–4; *Legal Abortion: Arguments Pro & Con*, n.pag.; *Listen to the Anti-Choice Leaders. Then Help Us Stop Them Before It's Too Late* (New York: Planned Parenthood Federation of America, n.d.): n.pag.

[86] *You Know Them as the Right to Life People*, n.pag.; Steinem, 1; Edelin, 1–4.

[87] Letter from the Religious Coalition for Reproductive Freedom.

[88] Mulhauser, 1; Steinem, 1-4.

[89] Ellen Goodman, This Time, However, the Word 'Terrorism' Is Perhaps too Mild, Lafayette, Indiana *Journal and Courier*, 16 March 1993, A4.

[90] "Preachers of Hate," *The Progressive*, December 1998, 8; "The Abortion Wars Come Home," *Newsweek*, 9 November 1998, 34.

[91] "Preachers of Hate," 8.

[92] *The Communicator*, June 1978, 2; and May 1977, 2.

[93] *Abortion: Public Opinion*, n.pag.; Brown, 1–3; *Americans Against Abortion*, 3 & 16.

[94] Bethell, 20.

[95] *The Communicator*, September 1978, 2; November/December 1977, 2; October/November, 1980, 3.

[96] *Abortion: Public Opinion*, n.pag.; *Heartbeat*, 1–3; *Abortion: A ~~Catholic~~ Issue*, n.pag.

[97] Bethell, 20, 21.

[98] John Willke, President, National Right to Life Committee, "Action-Gram," 9 February 1987, n.pag.

[99] *Abortion: Death Before Life*, n.pag.; *The Hidden Holocaust*, n.pag.

[100] Joseph Sobran, "The Tactics of Subversion," *The New American* 15 April 1996, 15.

[101] David Mall, *In Good Conscience: Abortion and Moral Necessity* (Libertyville. IL: Kairos Books, 1982): 41.

[102] "Preachers of Hate," 8; "The Abortion Wars Come Home," 35.

[103] *New York Times*, 11 March 1993, 1310.

[104] "The Abortion Wars Come Home," 35.

[105] "More Ads, No More Bombs," *America*, 8 February 1986, 82; "Violence Against Abortion Clinics Escalates Despite the Opposition of Pro-life Leaders." *Christianity Today*, 1 February 1985, 45.

[106] *The Sunday Visitor*, 21 March 1993, 1 & 4; see also Bill Price, President, Texans United for Life, *New York Times*, 12 March 1993, A17.

[107] "The Abortion Wars Come Home," 35.

[108] John Willke, "Violence—The Answer?" *The Communicator*, May 1978, 2.

[109] *The Sunday Visitor*, 21 March 1993, 1; *Newsweek*, 22 March 1993, 34–35; *New York Times*, 11 March 1993, BIO.

[110] *Indiana Right to Life*, n.p., n.d., 3, reprinted from *National Right to Life News*, Feb. 1980, n.pag.

[111] *Violence Against Abortion Clinics*, 45–46.

[112] Cleveland, Ohio *Catholic Universe Bulletin*, 17 September 1976, 2, col. 4.

[113] *The Communicator*, January 1978, 3.

[114] *Catholic Universe Bulletin*, 17 September 1976, 2, col. 2.

[115] *Violence Against Abortion Clinics*, 46.

[116] *Newsweek*, 22 March 1993, 34–35.

[117] Judith Adler Hennessee, Inside a Right-to-Life Mind, *Mademoiselle*, April 1986, 261.

13

ARGUMENT FROM CONSPIRACY IN SOCIAL MOVEMENTS

Rhetorical theorists agree that conspiracy arguments become widely disseminated and accepted "when they explain an otherwise ambiguous evil" or "a pattern of anomalies."[1] A pattern or repetition of events intensifies the search for an explanation and increases the likelihood that people will begin to suspect a conspiracy is at work. Steven Goldzwig writes, for example, "The ideological explanation" of conspiracy argument "restructures an ambiguous, inexplicable situation by explaining it in a plausible, unifying, and coherent way to audiences."[2]

The past half-century has witnessed an abundance of ambiguous evils and anomalies, including wars, economic crises, declines in traditional social morals and values, assassinations, natural and technological disasters, terrorism, and massacres. The long-awaited and prayed-for demise of the worldwide communist threat to U.S. freedoms and existence in a nuclear age appeared to some to be succeeded immediately by a greater threat, a New World Order with evil roots traced to the Illuminati founded in 1776.[3] It is little wonder, then, that argument from conspiracy, in Kenneth Burke's words, has become "as natural as breathing."[4]

Humans have an insatiable need for order, reason, and "explanation of all human phenomena," so they have limited tolerance for explanations ranging from uncontrolled chaos and a world with no one in charge to coincidence, accident, mistake, bad luck, or stupidity.[5] Inevitably, some will argue that a conspiracy—a combination of two or more people plotting to do something illegal or to harm people in some way—is responsible for the phenomenon they find frightening, worrying, disconcerting, or confusing. Richard Hofstadter claims that persons who see conspiracies as explanations do not see events as "part of the stream of history" but as "the consequences of someone's will." With someone in charge, the world of conspiracy "is far

299

more coherent than the real world, since it leaves no room for mistakes, failures, or ambiguities."[6] Dan Nimmo and James Combs address what attracts many to conspiracy theories in an uncertain and often dangerous world. "To explain historical chaos as simply chaos does not appeal to dramatic sensibilities," they write. "History is much more understandable, interesting, and exciting if it is a grand romantic melodrama, full of adventure, mystery, peril and threat and wherein there is a moral to the story."[7]

A growing body of literature has focused on the argumentative structures or forms persuaders have employed to prove, for example, that a conspiracy was behind the Oklahoma City bombing, the *Challenger* disaster, the assassinations of John Kennedy and Martin Luther King, Jr., and the downing of Korean Airline Flight 007 by Russian fighter planes. This body of literature enables us to understand better how those who would have us believe that conspiracies are responsible for unexplained or poorly explained phenomena argue their cases. Persuaders develop arguments from cause-to-effect, narrative, hypothesis, generalization, sign, and syllogism.[8] Syllogisms with stated or implied premises (enthymemes) appear to be most prevalent after a conspiracy has been "proven" through evidence-driven, inductive, argumentative patterns and the conspiracy charges have been around for some time.

Rhetorical theorists typically, and often with good reason, dismiss conspiracy arguments as loaded with argumentative fallacies and masses of irrelevant detail designed to seduce paranoid, noncritical, and ignorant audiences. Marilyn Young, Michael Launer, and Curtis Austin claim, for instance, that conspiracy theorists build their arguments on hypothetical premises and hypothetical evidence.[9] It is easy to understand such criticism and skepticism if you read publications that claim, for example, that the Vatican plotted and carried out the assassination of Lincoln, U.S. Representatives Phil Gramm and Newt Gingrich created a contract to destroy America, and President Reagan and Pope John Paul II ("a couple of ANTICHRIST DEVILS") conspired to commit genocide.[10]

In spite of outrageous claims and preposterous "evidence" presented in many conspiracy arguments, do not forget that there are *real* conspiracies. The Soviet Union did conspire to take over eastern European countries; John Wilkes Booth and his comrades did conspire to assassinate President Lincoln, Vice President Andrew Johnson, and members of the cabinet; the CIA and other forces did conspire to depose Cuban leader Fidel Castro and bring down his communist government; police forces in the United States did conspire to destroy the Black Panther Party; and there was a Watergate conspiracy during the Nixon administration. Conspiracies to set prices among "competitors," to commit fraud, and to commit murder are prosecuted in the United States every year. The U.S. government has published a document to assist in prosecuting conspiracies. It sets forth the history of conspiracy, the essential elements of the crime, defenses, the process of prosecution, and the liability for substantive offences.[11] The authors believe that all of us should maintain a healthy skepticism toward conspiracy theories: examine the evidence, the assumptions, and the logical connections before deciding if they are true or the bogus creations of paranoid persuaders for paranoid audiences.

While understanding argumentative forms and fallacies is helpful in critiquing specific conspiracy arguments, a deeper understanding of argument from conspiracy is possible if it is studied as a *process* in *relation* to competing argument. David Zarefsky claims that conspiracy "argument responds to a situation by asserting that things are not really what they seem" and "transforms the situation into one presenting a clear-cut choice of alternatives."[12] Its persuasive function is to induce polarization. In most situations, then, conspiracy argument is developed after an official or institutional explanation of a phenomenon has been widely disseminated and generally accepted. Those dissatisfied with an official explanation, or lack of it, may proceed to develop a counter-rhetoric with conspiracy as its centerpiece and "focus on what is *secret* as a basis for inducing polarization."[13] Thomas Goodnight and John Poulakos observe "The struggle characteristically emerges between two parties: those who claim to be aware of a conspiracy . . . and those who argue these claims to be preposterous and malevolently inspired."[14]

A persuader intent on weaving an argument claiming that a conspiracy is the *cause* or the *best explanation* of an event or body of facts starts from a decidedly underdog position. "The initial odds of winning such a battle" are "stacked in favor of the challenged authority" who has a head start and both legitimacy and credibility that goes with institutional agents and their rhetoric.[15] Relatively few audiences are truly paranoid or totally ignorant of events or facts widely disseminated in the press, and most audiences trust official or institutional explanations until someone proves otherwise. Thus, those who would sell a conspiracy argument to the U.S. public must perform three essential persuasive functions. First, they must undermine trust in the institution's ability and willingness to locate and tell the *truth*. Second, they must challenge the believability of the official explanation or story. Third, they must offer a *more believable* explanation or story.

Sowing Distrust

The persuader who would replace an official explanation of an event with one centered on the actions of a conspiracy must arouse *serious doubt* in the minds of targeted audiences. How can we trust an explanation, the persuader asks, if we cannot trust the institutional storyteller?

Capitalizing on Distrust

On occasion, persuaders are able to capitalize on a sense of distrust and suspicion that permeates social interactions. For example, in the early

1950s, "distrust, suspicion, and panic permeated all social interactions, and few Americans ventured to openly question the premise of domestic Communist subversion."[16] Hans Toch writes:

> Into this predisposing situation emerged Senator Joseph McCarthy and his Communist Conspiracy. McCarthy's "stab in the back" formula dealt directly with the events of the previous half-decade, and provided an explanation for them which was not only *coherent* and *face-saving*, but also an obvious *depository of accumulated feelings.*[17]

This situation also enabled the John Birch Society, Billy James Hargis's Christian Crusade, and Carl McIntire's Twentieth Century Reformation Hour to flourish in the 1950s and 1960s as forces dedicated to exposing and confronting the communist conspiracy that had allegedly taken over much of U.S. society, including mainline churches, education, entertainment, and the military. In his studies of the "radical right," Dale Leathers noted that the dominant value of this rhetoric was "mistrust," and that its "startling contention" was that "all institutionalized voices in America are to be mistrusted."[18] All of these individuals and groups appealed to the centuries-old fear in the United States that the real threat to our republic and way of life would come from within.[19]

If there is not widespread distrust, there is nearly always distrust of specific institutional *agents* or *agencies*. Gary Wills, in his recent book entitled *A Necessary Evil: A History of American Distrust of Government*, cites Henry David Thoreau's famous statement, "That government is best which governs least." Wills writes that:

> We are pious toward our history in order to be cynical toward our government. We keep summoning the founders to testify against what they founded. Our very liberty depends so heavily on distrust of government that the government itself, we are constantly told, was constructed to instill that distrust . . . . Since human nature cannot be trusted, power must be so insecurely seated that even slight opposition to it can stymie it.[20]

Persuaders may call an explanation into question by *associating* the official version of an event or situation with distrusted, even hated, agencies such as the U.N., the Supreme Court, Congress, the CIA, FBI, ATF, or IRS. Young and Launer, for instance, theorize that "Association/disassociation is probably the most powerful tool of persuasiveness and the most basic human thought process."[21]

Distrust is also enhanced by associating institutional explanations with distrusted or hated *groups* such as liberals, humanists, internationalists, advocates of the New World Order, and communists. Bernard Duffy claims, for example, that the antihumanist rhetoric of the religious right attempts to make "the audience skeptical of all opposing claims, even those made by the most disinterested observers; they too may be humanists."[22] Bob Fletcher, a representative of the Montana Militia, exhibited such associative distrust at the 1995 Senate hearings on the militia movement called in response to the Oklahoma City bombing. He agreed with radical-right literature that claimed the FBI and IRS were headed by "lesbians, sex perverts, child molester advocates, Christian haters, and the most doctrinaire of communists."[23] George Lincoln Rockwell, founder of the American Nazi Party, told an audience at the University of Kansas how, as a Naval officer, he had become curious about Senator McCarthy and proceeded to read the complete transcripts of the Senate Hearings.[24] Instead of the "louse" he expected to find in Senator McCarthy, he discovered a "sissy," a "super, easygoing nice guy" who was confronting "arrogant, and obnoxious, and vicious" witnesses and the media. As he investigated further, he discovered that the "entire media of public information were lying," and that every group seemed to have those that were "pro-McCarthy" and those that were "con-McCarthy." Every group that is except one, "and that one group was fanatically, unanimously anti-McCarthy. And this group was the Jewish group" led by the violently anti-McCarthy American Jewish Committee. His research took him into the world of art where "A rose, is a rose, is a rose" was considered fine poetry and paintings by an ape in the Baltimore Zoo were called "beautiful" and "sensitive" by critics unaware of the painter's identity. Since the creators of such art were both Jewish, Rockwell proclaimed that "it will take a miracle for white, Western, Christian civilization to survive" the Jewish communist conspiracy.

Creating Distrust

Often persuaders must create distrust in institutional explanations of phenomena, and the key to undermining trust appears to be the claim that the institution is attempting "to thwart the search for the truth."[25] Institutions may inadvertently fuel this claim by classifying information too quickly as secret or top secret, by refusing to change secret classifications even after credible sources challenge the necessity or legality of the classifications, and by refusing to reveal some or part of the classified information that might verify the official explanation or undermine a growing conspiracy theory. On other occasions, institutions refuse to reveal sources or to explain how information was discovered that serves as the basis for the institution's case.

In the introduction to his book entitled *Others Unknown*, Timothy McVeigh's defense attorney, Stephen Jones, writes that "The real story" of the Oklahoma City bombing remains a mystery for "many reasons, but perhaps the most important has been the U.S. government. And in the end, the Oklahoma City bombing conspiracy may not be merely the crime itself but also the systematic, deliberate attempt of our federal government to prevent all of us from finding out what exactly happened on that terrible morning."[26] Jones relates that when he agreed to take over

McVeigh's defense, Susan Otto, one of the original defense attorneys, commented to him, "When you know everything I know, and you will soon enough, you will never think of the United States of America again in the same way."[27] The obvious message is that the institution is untrustworthy, if not downright evil, and is attempting to hide something from the American people. Why else would an institution refuse to reveal sources, share documents, provide information, and explain its investigative methods? Jones relates again and again how the *government*, rarely identified as the *prosecution*, tried to hide vital information it was required by law to share with the defense. He continually turned to the judge to force the "government" to cooperate. Even then the "government" tried to change testimony and discoveries to avoid its legal, ethical, and moral obligations. His claims of obstruction and repeated use of the word "government" played upon a growing mistrust of the institution in the United States and seemed to lend credence to his counterconspiracy theories that one of two social movements with foreign roots, or perhaps both, were the true perpetrators of the horrible bombing of the Murrah Federal Building in Oklahoma City.

Some persuaders cite historical examples of institutional deception to establish that U.S. institutions and agents are not always trustworthy. The *American Patriot Network's* Web site claims, for instance, that in the 1794 Jay Treaty, the United States agreed to pay 600,000 pounds sterling to King George even though the colonies had won the Revolutionary War.[28] According to the *American Patriot Network*, the Senate ratified the treaty in "secret session" and ordered that it "not be published." Americans learned about this outrageous, secret agreement only because Benjamin Franklin's grandson ignored the order and published it. The "exposure" from this publication "and resulting public uproar so angered Congress that it passed the Alien and Sedition Acts (1798) so federal judges could prosecute editors and publishers for reporting the truth about the government." The *American Patriot Network* also reports that the Library of Congress has 349,402 uncatalogued books and 13.9 million uncatalogued rare manuscripts, and notes ominously: "There may be secrets buried in that mass of documents even more astonishing than a missing Constitutional Amendment."

Other persuaders report the discovery of previously denied or unrevealed documents as evidence that the institution cannot be trusted to tell the whole truth about an event under scrutiny. Ralph de Toledano, in an article entitled "Was *Challenger* Sabotaged?" asked, "But are we being told everything that is so far known? I suggest that we are not." He then added, "This is not idle conjecture on my part but is based on information I have received from a source I consider reliable who has access to the intelligence community. And that information is very disturbing."[29]

Conspiracy theorists also create doubts in the minds of audiences by describing aspects of events, institutional actions (or lack of them), and explanations as mysterious, curious, strange, suspicious, weird, and unexplainable. In his effort to prove that the Soviets sabotaged the shuttle *Challenger*, Kirk Kidwell writes of a Delta rocket "mysteriously" experiencing a "shut down," the "mysterious disappearance" of a top Air Force expert on rocket self-destruct procedures, and the "absolute mystery" why Soviet spy ships steamed at "flank speed" away from Cape Canaveral the morning of the *Challenger* disaster.[30] The frequent repetition of such words as mysterious, suspicious, and strange is clearly designed to sow mistrust and suspicion.

Official silence and secrecy are offered as proof of cover up, deception, or manipulation of the truth. Zarefsky writes that Abraham Lincoln used sign reasoning to connect Stephen Douglas to the conspiracy to expand slavery into new states. Lincoln claimed that "Although Douglas promised to investigate the matter, he has made no report. Since he would stand to gain by clearing himself, his silence is a sign that he is implicated."[31] Secret meetings, often in secret locations, with outcomes and actions unknown except to *insiders* feeds the notion of a conspiracy and raises doubts about the truthfulness of official explanations. In his study of *The Wanderer's* (an ultraconservative Roman Catholic publication) theo-political conspiracy rhetoric, Goldzwig identifies both mystery and secrecy as key elements:

> By working through the various connections between liberal bishops, seemingly handpicked advisors, and other mysteriously nefarious events in the implied network of intrigue, *The Wanderer* is able to dramatically establish the conspiratorial tone of the discourse. The idea that things are being hatched in "some quarter" by these church bureaucrats gives audiences reason to believe in "actual conspiracies" also "documented" in *The Wanderer* rhetoric.[32]

The Principle of Reversal

The creation of mistrust enables persuaders to employ one of their most effective tactics when presenting and defending conspiracy arguments, the principle of reversal. "To trust appearances is *naïveté*," they claim, because "everything is the opposite of what it appears to be."[33] When "confronted with potentially dissonant information," the persuader merely applies the principle of reversal "to arrive at a conclusion different from that of" one who believes or espouses the institutional version of events. There is no need to refute or distort evidence to reach or maintain conspiracy claims.[34] Denial of a conspiracy confirms it "since what conspirators profess is not what they believe, and appearances are not real because appearances are deliberately manipulated by untrusted sources."[35] A John Birch Society leaflet employed the principle of reversal when attacking Senator William Fulbright's proposal for improving relations with the Soviet Union: "What Senator Fulbright calls myths are realities, and what he calls realities are myths. One of his realities is: 'The

Soviet Union, though still a formidable adversary, has ceased to be totally hostile to the West.'"

Mistrust enables the persuader to employ the principle of reversal to address all sorts of unpleasant questions. If proof of a conspiracy is elusive, that shows how powerful the conspiracy is. If investigators cannot locate conspirators, that proves they are everywhere. If accused conspirators do not appear to be evil or part of a damnable plot, that proves how clever they are. Like many interchangeable elements of conspiracy argument, advocates not only use the principle of reversal to verify a conspiracy but also to vilify the conspiracy by accusing it of using the principle they use.[36] A pamphlet entitled *A Cross Section of the Truth* accuses the communist conspiracy of using the principle of reversal for devious reasons. It is a "tactical thread which runs through all Communist strategy:"

> But the basic tactic has many parallel or affiliated forms: In the midst of stealing something, be the first to cry "stop thief" at somebody else; always accuse your enemies, first and loudly, of the very crimes you are yourself committing; knock a rival down by some foul and hidden blow, then jump on him as a weakling for having fallen . . . . Variations of this theme are countless and commonplace in the orchestration of the Conspiracy. And a great deal of the strategy which the *Insiders* have developed since 1800 can be more quickly understood if this principle of reversal is kept in mind.[37]

Mistrust allows the arguer to use the principle of reversal tactic as proof a conspiracy exists and as proof the conspiracy is diabolical. There is no acknowledgment of a possible argumentative inconsistency in the two-sided use of this principle.

Challenging Plausibility

Once trust in institutional sources and storytellers is questioned, it is an easy transition to challenge the plausibility or believability of the report or story.

Implausible Labels

Persuaders attempt to make words such as accident, mishap, coincidence, and circumstantial sound ridiculous or deceptive. For instance, Kidwell entitled his article on the *Challenger*, "What a Coincidence! The *Challenger* Fits a Pattern of 'Accidents.'" In the article he reported eight unexplained disasters involving American and French launch vehicles considered among the most reliable in the world. In order to substitute a Soviet conspiracy to sabotage the shuttle *Challenger* for the government's "accident" or "malfunction" argument, Kidwell claims that "Now, a number of experts, in and out of the government, are beginning to consider the possibility that the thread of sabotage is woven through all these disasters." He quotes one of his unnamed U.S. sources as stating that "Simple logic demands at least the possibility of foul play," and an unnamed French source as saying "It requires more faith to believe these disasters were all coincidence than it does to believe they were caused deliberately."[38]

Failure to Consider Alternative Explanations and Evidence

Those who see conspiracy at work express dismay that institutions have failed to consider obvious explanations. Kidwell, for example, notes that in spite of the numerous rocket failures around the world, "At present, no official government agency is even investigating the possibility of sabotage."[39] De Toledano claimed he was "not asserting that the *Challenger* was sabotaged—only that this possibility should be given serious consideration and not brushed aside as an Ian Fleming fantasy."[40] He noted that it took only one "deliberately careless person" to cause such a tragedy "and NASA does not seem to be inquiring."

Other persuaders charge institutions with ignoring important evidence. Bob Fletcher of the Montana Militia claimed at Senate hearings that militia sources had located the famous John Doe #2 in the Oklahoma City bombing and was aware of his name and location, but "for some reason the FBI is steering away from this gentleman."[41] Jones, Timothy McVeigh's defense attorney, repeatedly questions the lack of governmental interest in critical events, clues, or people related to the same bombing. For instance, there was evidence of a call that came to the Justice Department in Washington reporting the bombing thirty minutes before it happened, but the FBI had not pursued it. Some "believed the caller had been McVeigh," Jones writes, "I had my doubts. But whether it had or hadn't been Tim, the FBI's lack of interest was—again—surprising. But the FBI's lack of interest in a lot of things continued to be surprising."[42] Conspiracy authors Jonathan Vankin and John Whalen identify eighteen links between the CIA and the Reverend Jim Jones's Jonestown prior to the massacre of hundreds of men, women, and children—a great many by apparent suicide and others apparently shot. In spite of such information, they write, "The House Permanent Select Committee on Intelligence announced that there was 'No evidence' of CIA involvement at Jonestown."[43]

Simplicity of Explanations

Persuaders also attempt to show the extreme simplicity, and therefore unbelievability, of the official version of an event. Ironically, this is the same argument institutions use to debunk conspiracy arguments by social movements and skeptics. For instance, Jones questioned the plausibility that two untrained loners with limited knowledge of bomb-making and no network to assist them in planning, carrying out, and escaping from the bombing could have carried out the worst act of domestic terrorism in U.S. history. He identifies seven deadly terrorist acts against American troops and personnel around the world that always fit the same pattern and remained "unsolved and unprosecuted." "Given all this," he asks, "does it seem so far-fetched that what happened in Oklahoma City might not be as simple as the government said?"[44] No, he tells readers of his book, "The real story of the bombing, as the McVeigh defense pursued it, is complex, shadowy, and sinister. It stretches weblike, from America's heartland to the nation's capital, the Far East, Europe, and the Middle East, and much of it remains a mystery."

Bob Fletcher of the Montana Militia claimed to have a lengthy report from a former FBI agent that disputed the single fertilizer bomb in a rental truck theory for the Oklahoma City bombing. He stated that evidence showed there was more than one bomb inside the building, and the government's argument was "absolute baloney."[45] Norman Olson of the Michigan Militia suggested the possibility of a more complex conspiracy explanation to replace the government's simplistic single bomber theory: "It very well may be that there was a conspiracy at higher levels. People behind those people who we have been fed by the press to accept or believe that perhaps it was one angry individual."[46]

Selling the Conspiracy

If the conspiracy persuader can cause audiences to lose trust in institutional ability and willingness to be totally open and truthful and raise doubts about the believability of official explanations, audiences may be more willing to listen to a competing conspiracy argument. The persuader must create a competing argument that appears to be more plausible and to be based on data superior to that of the institutional explanation of a phenomenon.

A Coherent Pattern

The conspiracy argument typically ties together numerous bits of information or examples into a "coherent pattern" or "mosaic," usually resulting in argument from hypothesis, example, sign, or cause to effect.[47] Evidence and associations contained in conspiracy argument are often those readily available to institutions and the public but are selected and organized to support a different claim—a claim that a conspiracy rather than an accident, mechanical failure, human error, or coincidence best explains an event. Stephen Browne writes that the conspiracy narrative gives "the sense of being better able to account for the full sweep and complexity of events."[48] Similarly, Young, Launer, and Austin conclude that conspiracy argument "provides a worldview which is complete, capable of answering . . . all uncomfortable questions. Its apparent internal cohesiveness provides the narrative fidelity and probability which make it persuasive."[49] Thus, conspiracy argument is an argumentative exercise in connecting the dots to lead an audience to a reasonable explanation and, in doing so, to undermine the official explanation by offering a more plausible one. For example, in a follow-up article on the *Challenger* disaster entitled "The Question Persists: Was Shuttle Sabotaged?" Ralph de Toledano identified nine interconnected, serious effects of the tragedy, including destruction of 25 percent of shuttle capability, halt of military research and missions, and direct blow to President Reagan's antiballistic missile Strategic Defense Initiative program (dubbed Star Wars program by many). "Putting it all together," he concluded, "it 'amounts to valid reasons' for Soviet sabotage."[50]

Overwhelming Proof

Rhetorical theorists note that the conspiracy "charge is also virtually impossible to disprove," that "Oftentimes the mere accusation of conspiracy is enough to 'prove' it," and that once a conspiracy argument is underway it cannot "be easily dispelled."[51] This is a sort of rhetorical tar baby effect. Whoever or whatever touches a conspiracy gets stuck to it; the more one struggles to get free, the more one is associated with it. Recall the principle of reversal discussed earlier.

A basic principle of argumentation is known as the "burden of proof"—the notion that each of us has an obligation to prove what we claim. Normally, we reject the argument of a persuader who tries to shift his or her burden of proof to others by challenging them to disprove an unsupported claim. It is important to recognize that many, perhaps most, conspiracy advocates attempt to fulfill rather than to shift their burden of proof. Conspiracy arguers are noted for carefully accumulating and arranging large amounts of evidence, some say "overwhelming proof," to establish claims. After all, the persuader who would establish a conspiracy explanation must accept the burden of proof, a burden that requires not only proving one case but also *disproving* another—the competing official or institutional explanation widely disseminated by the mass media. The attempt may be to persuade by out-proving or overwhelming the opposition and winning over skeptical audiences.

For instance, Robert Welch began the John Birch Society with a two-day speech that detailed the communist conspiracy and the dangers of big government to his hand picked audience of eleven businessmen. His speech became the 165-page *Blue Book of the John Birch Society*. Stephen Jones devoted forty-seven pages of his book to establishing two meticulously traced counterconspiracy theories for the Oklahoma City bombing. The first traced Terry Nichols's (McVeigh's alleged co-conspirator) connections and numerous contacts with Islamic radicals in the Philippines and the Middle East. The second traced a conspiracy of white supremacists in Arkansas with connections in Europe.[52] A pamphlet entitled *Why Don't You Believe*

What We Tell You? contains thirty-seven pages of quotations from Jewish leaders and publications from 1883 to 1976 to prove that a Jewish/Zionist/ Communist conspiracy is attempting to create a new world order.[53]

Some theorists, such as Richard Hofstadter, attack conspiracy arguers for "obsessively" accumulating "evidence."[54] The suggestion is that much of this evidence may be bogus. The amassing of overwhelming "proof" may not be a characteristic of the "paranoid style" Hofstadter developed in the 1950s or of rhetorical crackpots, as others would suggest. In a study of evidence in paranoid (conspiracy) and non-paranoid discourse, Craig Smith discovered that

> Overall, the "paranoid" discourse contained significantly more references to general, specific, and documented others (extrinsic evidence) and significantly fewer non-attributed assertions (intrinsic evidence) than did "non-paranoid" discourse. . . ."
>
> The political "paranoid's" conspiratorial worldview should lead him to distrust his audience. The "paranoid" would therefore attempt to combat this perceived hostility with cold, hard facts—verifiable references to credible others.[55]

Critics of conspiracy argument should look more to how evidence is employed to support claims than the quantity and quality of evidence offered.

Overwhelming support and a coherent narrative or pattern are insufficient, however, to sell a conspiracy argument to replace an institutional explanation. The persuader must establish *motivation* and *evilness*.

Motivation

Zarefsky claims that "Like many other argument patterns, conspiracy charges depend upon an analysis of motives. The argument will not be persuasive unless the alleged conspirator is shown to have a motive for participating in the plot."[56] In other words, the persuader who weaves a conspiracy argument must be able to answer the "why" question: Why would the Soviet Union want to sabotage the shuttle *Challenger*? Why would white supremacists, or connections in the Philippine Islands, or (as some militia leaders claimed) the Japanese government want to blow up the federal building in Oklahoma City? Why would President Reagan and Pope John Paul II want to conspire to commit genocide? If there is no motive, there is no conspiracy, but the greater the motive the greater the believability of the conspiracy argument.

Kidwell claims a source reported to him "There exists a very strong presumption among defense, aerospace, and intelligence experts that the Soviets are attempting to scuttle the SDI [Reagan's antimissile Strategic Defense Initiative] through active measures."[57] The Soviet inability to counter SDI technologically, militarily, and economically provided sufficient motive for sabotaging the *Challenger* and numerous other U.S. and

European rockets. The net effect of these "mishaps," Kidwell concluded, was a great curtailment of SDI research and destruction of U.S. capability to launch crucial satellites to monitor Soviet troop movements and nuclear deployments. De Toledano claimed the "shuttle taxis" repeated successes had "driven Soviet scientists wild" and that "the USSR" was "driven by a desperate need to retard Mr. Reagan's Star Wars" [SDI program].[58] Thus, the Soviet Union had significant motivation to launch a conspiracy to destroy the *Challenger*.

When Iranian dissidents were attempting to overthrow the Shah in Iran, members of the Iranian Students Association in the United States were often arrested during demonstrations and protests. They saw conspiracies between the Shah and Savak (the Shah's secret police) and the U.S. government, police, and CIA. Pamphlets and fliers distributed on college campuses cited the motives for this unlikely conspiracy. They centered on *control* (the CIA had created Savak in 1956 and did not want to lose control of its offspring), *security* (the U.S. depended upon the Shah regime to counter rising revolutionary movements and increasing Soviet activities in the region and had supplied it with some of the most sophisticated military hardware in the U.S. arsenal), and *economy* (vast oil reserves essential for transportation, heating, and industry in the United States and billions of American dollars invested in and loaned to Iranian business and industry).[59] For example, a flier entitled "Bloodbath in Iran" claimed:

> The U.S. government and establishment are deeply concerned about the fate of the Shah and monarchy in Iran. Should the regime be toppled, the U.S. huge economic, political, and military interests would be in clear jeopardy. That is why the U.S. government is trying its utmost, though at the cost of massive bloodshed and all-out repression, to keep the puppet Shah in power.[60]

Mark Lane, in his book *Rush to Judgment*, claimed to reveal the true story behind President Kennedy's assassination. The CIA, according to Lane, orchestrated Kennedy's assassination because Kennedy had planned to withdraw U.S. troops from Vietnam and to dissolve the CIA because it had refused to take orders from him and was out of control.[61]

In each of the examples above, persuaders identified important motives that were sufficient enough to lead organizations, leaders, agencies, and governments to enter into deadly conspiracies. Too much was at stake for them not to take decisive and deadly action through a conspiracy.

Evilness

One essential question remains: Were the elements that entered into the alleged conspiracy capable of unspeakable evil? If audiences do not believe that an alleged conspirator was willing to carry out evil plots and deeds, they are unlikely to accept the conspiracy argument. A critical link is missing.

Some persuaders portray the evilness of the conspiracy without regard to specific events. For example, Robert Welch launched the John Birch Society by describing the communist conspiracy as devious, brutal, bloodthirsty, and inhumane. Its leaders were "determined, cunning, and utterly ruthless gangsters" who had used "brutality, the countless tentacles of treason, and murder on a scale never before dreamed of in the world."[62] Iranian students reported that the Shah and Savak had executed more than 109 intellectuals while antiriot squads, Iran's version of the Green Berets, had massacred 28 students. In the meantime, the Nixon administration had sold three billion dollars worth of sophisticated war equipment to the Shah.[63] Was it farfetched, then, to believe that Savak and the U.S. would conspire with Iran to harass, beat, and arrest Iranian student dissidents studying in the United States?

Other persuaders tie the conspiracy to historical events and associate it with evil groups to establish the evil nature of the conspiracy. Tony Alamo, President and Pastor of the Alamo Christian Church in Alma, Arkansas, claims that the Communist party, the Nazi party in Germany, Neo-Nazis, and many other terrorist groups are or were secret divisions of the Vatican. The Vatican has used these divisions as well as the FBI, the CIA, and all military and police agencies to destroy Christians, Jews, and other non-Catholics in the United States and around the world. It should come as little surprise to Alamo's readers, then, when he tells them that the Vatican was behind the Holocaust. Alamo writes:

> Remember, as I told you in my literature *The Pope's Secrets*, the Vatican and her agents always cover themselves to her advantage, especially when someone starts exposing her. For instance, she slaughtered six million Jews in WWII; then, when she saw that she was losing the war, she hid 1,000 Jews in Catholic convents and some in the Vatican. Then she said, "See how we love the Jews!!" And, of course, the Vatican media only showed the part about their hypocritically hidden 1,000 and shifted the blame from the Vatican to a nation of people (the Germans) knowing that no one would exterminate all Germans for such a crime.[64]

If readers believe these associations are the real cause and force behind the Holocaust, they are likely to believe the Vatican is capable of any evil, including a "smear campaign" against Rev. Alamo and efforts to stir up violence against Christians and Jews.

Other persuaders tie the conspiracy to specific events to establish its evilness. For instance, Kidwell acknowledged that "Some, perhaps, find it beyond belief that the Soviets would actually resort to such 'dirty tricks'" as sabotaging the *Challenger,* and then asked "But, given the opportunity, would the same Kremlin leaders who ordered the destruction of a civilian airliner with 269 innocent human beings on it [a reference to the shooting down of KAL Flight 007 by Soviet fighter planes in 1983] fail to order the sabotage of the U.S. space program?"[65] Congressman Larry McDonald, head of the John Birch Society, was aboard that plane.

In a similar vein, Norman Olson of the Michigan Militia chided those who question "how terrible it would be to even consider that the Federal Government had anything to do with killing Americans" in Oklahoma City. "I submit to you sir," he replied angrily to Senator Specter of the Senate Judiciary Committee, "that the Central Intelligence Agency has been in the business of killing Americans and killing people in the United States and around the world since 1946. I submit to you sir that the Central Intelligence Agency is probably the grandest conspirator behind all of this government," including the U.S. Senate.[66] John Trochman, representing the Militia of Montana at the same hearings, explained why American citizens were angry and did not consider it far-fetched to suspect the government of involvement in the Oklahoma City bombing. It is a government, Trochman stated (barely constraining himself), that allows "our military to label caring patriots as the enemy then turn their tanks loose on U.S. citizens to murder and destroy [an allusion to the Branch Davidian disaster in Waco, Texas] or directs a sniper to shoot a mother in the face while holding her infant in her arms" [an allusion to the infamous Ruby Ridge incident].[67]

When defiant Moslem protestors took to the streets on December 1, the first day of Moharram, to commemorate the martyrdom of Mohammad's grandson in 682, Iranian troops were allegedly ordered to "shoot to kill." Handouts on U.S. campuses claimed the resulting bloodshed throughout Iran was so brutal from hours of continuous shooting at protestors that "troops prevented people from watching from windows and rooftops."[68] This bloodbath was possible because of the conspiracy between the Shah and the United States:

> The U.S. government, which has been fully backing the Shah over the past 26 years, has thrown its all-out support behind the Shah. While endorsing the imposition of military rule in Iran, the U.S. government, and Jimmy Carter himself personally, have openly encouraged the Shah to take any steps necessary and to use whatever means possible to "restore authority and stability."

The persuaders in each of these illustrations claimed that the alleged conspirators were, without doubt, ruthless enough to commit the evils for which they were being accused. In Hofstadter's words, the enemy "is the perfect model of malice, a kind of amoral superman: sinister, ubiquitous, powerful, cruel, sensual, and luxury-loving."[69] Thus, the conspiracy had both motive and capability to do unspeakable harm.

Conclusions

Conspiracy argument in protest rhetoric is common, interesting, complex, varied, and often outrageous. Many have seemingly withstood the test of time—the communist conspiracy, the secular humanist conspiracy, the Vatican or Papal conspiracy, international bankers, the illuminati. A growing number of scholars have attempted to understand conspiracy argument, reveal its complexities and weaknesses, and develop standards for judging its rationality or validity.

Though understanding the argumentative forms conspiracy argument takes provides important insights, conspiracy argument may be understood best when it is viewed as a process in relation to competing argument. Conspiracy argument usually appears after an official or institutional explanation of a phenomenon has been widely disseminated in the media and has attained an aura of credibility and legitimacy. Some societal elements find the official explanation unsatisfactory and determine to set the record straight by revealing a sinister conspiracy as the driving force behind the phenomenon. In challenging an institutional or official explanation, the conspiracy persuader is at a distinct disadvantage, not only starting out after a competing argument has been disseminated but also rarely having the credibility, legitimacy, and resources readily available to institutional story tellers.

Persuaders, in their efforts to make conspiracy arguments palatable to audiences beyond small numbers of true believers, need to fulfill three essential persuasive functions. First, they must undermine trust in an institution to locate and tell the truth. Second, they must challenge the believability of the official explanation or story. Third, they must offer a more believable explanation that establishes both motive and evilness of the conspiracy.

Conspiracy persuaders may undermine trust by capitalizing upon a sense of distrust that permeates societal interactions or by associating the institutional explanation with distrusted institutional agents or agencies and societal groups. Even if there is an aura of distrust in society or distrust of agencies and groups, persuaders may find it necessary to create distrust of the explanation by claiming that the institution is attempting to stifle the search for truth rather than encourage it. They label events and institutional acts as mysterious, curious, or suspicious; they cite secrecy and silence as signs or a cover up or manipulation of the truth.

Conspiracy persuaders challenge the believability of an official explanation by making explanatory labels such as accident, mishap, or coincidence appear ridiculous or deceptive. They express surprise and dismay that the institution has failed to follow up on obvious explanations and evidence. And they attack the extreme simplicity of the official explanation, the same tactic institutions use to debunk conspiracy arguments.

Conspiracy theorists cannot succeed by merely attacking official explanations; they must offer more believable explanations. Thus, conspiracy arguments tend to be carefully crafted and coherent patterns or mosaics of facts, examples, signs, causes, associations, and claims. The accumulation of large bodies of evidence meets the counterarguer's burden of proof and attempts to overwhelm the competing institutional argument. Coherent pattern and an abundance of evidence accompany and help to establish motive and evilness of the alleged conspiracy. The persuader attempts to establish that the conspiracy had both substantial reason for and the capability of committing unspeakable evil.

Conspiracy argument, then, is more process than form. It counters an explanation or argument found wanting in significant ways with one constructed and supported by those who, supposedly, have no motive other than locating and telling the truth. It is an effort to offer a more believable explanation and to overwhelm competing argument with an abundance of "proof." Without an argument to compete with, the conspiracy persuader has no evil target to discredit, no explanation to debunk, and little evidence from which to draw different premises and conclusions. In many ways, the institutional storyteller and narrative enhance the likelihood of a competing conspiracy argument. The institution's efforts to maintain control of the story enhance the conspiracy weaver's credibility and the believability of the conspiracy argument itself. Each effort to maintain secrecy, each revision of the original story, each admission of error or withholding of vital information, each denial, and each attack against the conspiracy theory and its proponents may create doubts about the institution's version of the story and its commitment to locating and telling the truth.

Endnotes

[1] David Zarefsky, "Conspiracy Arguments in the Lincoln–Douglas Debates," *Journal of the American Forensic Association* 21 (Fall 1984): 72.

[2] Steven R. Goldzwig, "Theo–Political Conspiracy Rhetoric in The Wanderer," The *Journal of Communication and Religion* 14 (September 1991): 27.

[3] Charles J. Stewart, "The Master Conspiracy of the John Birch Society," unpublished paper delivered at the 1998 convention of the National Communication Association.

[4] Kenneth Burke, *The Rhetoric of Motives* (Berkeley, CA: University of California Press, 1969): 166

[5] Marilyn Young and Michael K. Launer, "Evaluative Criteria for Conspiracy Arguments: The Case of KAL 007," in Edward Schiappa, Ed. *Warranting Assent: Case Studies in Argument Evaluation* (Albany, NY: State University of New York Press, 1995): 23; Richard Hofstadter, *The Paranoid Style in American Politics and Other Essays.* (New York: Alfred Knopf, 1954): 32 and 36; Dan Nimmo and James E. Combs, "Devils and Demons: The Group Mediation of Conspiracy," *Mediated Political Realities* (New York: Longman, 1983): 211.

[6] Hofstadter, 32 and 36.

[7] Nimmo and Combs, 211.

[8] Stephen H. Browne, *Edmund Burke and the Discourse of Virtue* (Tuscaloosa, AL: University of Alabama Press, 1993): 19; Goldzwig, 16; G. Thomas Goodnight, and John Poulakos, "Conspiracy Rhetoric: From Pragmatism to Fantasy in Public Discourse," *Western Journal of Speech Communication* 45 (Fall 1981): 306; Hans Toch, *The Social Psychology of Social Movements* (New York: Bobbs-Merrill, 1965): 52; Marilyn J. Young, Michael K. Launer, and Curtis C. Austin, "The Need for Evaluative Criteria: Conspiracy Argument Revisited," *Argumentation and Advocacy* 26 (Winter 1990): 97; Zarefsky, 66.

[9] Young, Launer, and Austin, 100 and 103.

10 Justin D. Fulton, *Lincoln's Assassination* (Minneapolis: Osterhus, n.d.); *How the Conservative Revolution Crowd Plans to Destroy America* (Leesburg, VA: The New Federalist, 1995); Tony Alamo, *Genocide Treaty, FBI and the Neo-Nazis* (Alma, AR: Alamo Christian Church, n.d.).

11 *Elements of Conspiracy Investigation* (Washington, D.C.: Department of Treasury and BATF, 1993): 5.

12 Zarefsky, 72

13 Zarefsky, 72.

14 Goodnight and Poulakos, 301.

15 Young and Launer, 8; Goodnight and Poulakos, 309.

16 Toch, 61.

17 Toch, 62.

18 Dale G. Leathers, "Fundamentalism of the Radical Right," *Southern Speech Journal* 33 (Winter 1968): 248 and 255.

19 Charles J. G. Griffin, "Jedidiah Morse and the Bavarian Illuminati: An Essay in the Rhetoric of Conspiracy," *Central States Speech Journal* 39 (Fall/Winter 1988): 299.

20 Garry Wills, *A Necessary Evil: A History of American Distrust of Government.* (New York: Simon & Schuster, 1999): 16.

21 Young and Launer, 22.

22 Bernard K. Duffy, "The Anti-Humanist Rhetoric of the New Religious Right," *Southern Speech Communication Journal* 49 (Summer 1984): 359.

23 "U.S. Militia Movement," Senate Judiciary Committee, 16 June 1995, recorded by C-SPAN.

24 George Lincoln Rockwell, "Speech at the University of Kansas," 20 February 1964, from a tape recording.

25 Goodnight and Poulakos, 303.

26 Stephen Jones and Peter Israel, *Others Unknown: The Oklahoma City Bombing Case and Conspiracy* (New York: Public Affairs, 1998): XII–XIII.

27 Jones and Israel, 313.

28 *American Patriot Network* (http://www.civil-liberties.com/home.html) http://www.civil-liberties.com/home.html) 1 September 1999.

29 Ralph de Toledano, "Was *Challenger* Sabotaged?" *The New American*, 10 March, 1986, 19.

30 Kirk Kidwell, "What a Coincidence! The *Challenger* Fits a Pattern of 'Accidents,'" *The New American*, 29 September 1986, 17.

31 Zarefsky, 66.

32 Goldzwig, 22.

33 Leathers, 254; Craig Allen Smith, "The Hofstadter Hypothesis Revisited: The Nature of Evidence in Politically 'Paranoid' Discourse," *Southern Speech Communication Journal* 42 (Spring 1977): 287.

34 Smith, 287.

35 Griffin, 300.

36 Smith, 287; Leathers, 254; Barbara Warnick, "The Narrative Paradigm: Another Story," *Quarterly Journal of Speech* 73 (May 1987): 176.

37 *A Cross Section of the Truth* (Belmont, MA: The Review of the News, 1968).

38 Kidwell, 17.

39 Kidwell, 17.

40 De Toledano, 19.

41 "U.S. Militia Movement."

42 Jones and Israel, 160.

43 "The Jonestown Massacre: CIA Mind Control Run Amock?" excerpted on the Internet from Jonathan Vankin and John Whalen, *50 Greatest Conspiracies of All Time*, 1995.

44 Jones and Israel, XII.

45 "U.S. Militia Movement."

46 "U.S. Militia Movement."

47 Toch, 52.

48 Browne, 19.

[49]   Young, Launer, and Austin, 106.

[50]   Ralph de Toledano, "The Question Persists: Was Shuttle Sabotaged?" *The New American*, 30 June 1986, 24.

[51]   Zarefsky, 73; Goldzwig, 17; Browne, 19.

[52]   Jones and Israel, 117–165.

[53]   *Why Don't You Believe What We Tell You?* (Torrance, CA: The Noontide Press, 1982).

[54]   Hofstadter, 65.

[55]   Smith, 281 and 282.

[56]   Zarefsky, 74.

[57]   Kidwell, 17.

[58]   De Toledano, "The Question Persists," 24.

[59]   *Expose the Reactionary Shah – U.S. Conspiracy,* pamphlet of the Iranian Students Association in the United States, n.d.; "U.S. Police, Savak Collaboration," flier of the Iranian Students Association at Purdue University, n.d.; "Expose the CIA—Lex. Court Plot Against the 11," leaflet of the Organization of Iranian Moslem Students, 1 October 1978; *Defend the 41*, pamphlet of the Iranian Students Association in the U.S., January 1973.

[60]   "Bloodbath in Iran," flier of the Organization of Iranian Moslem Students, n.d.

[61]   Mark Lane, *Rush to Judgment* (Greenwich, CT: Fawcett, 1966): IX.

[62]   Robert Welch, *The Blue Book of the John Birch Society* (Boston: Western Islands, 1961): 21 and 3.

[63]   *Expose the Reactionary Shah—U.S. Conspiracy.*

[64]   Alamo.

[65]   Kidwell, 17.

[66]   "U.S. Militia Movement."

[67]   "U.S. Militia Movement."

[68]   "Bloodbath in Iran." Moharram is a highly respected Islamic month during which Moslems in Iran commemorate the 682 A.D. Martyrdom of Imam Hussein, grandson of Mohammad.

[69]   Hofstadter, 31–32.

14

RESISTING SOCIAL MOVEMENTS

As noted in previous chapters, efforts to initiate or stifle change challenge established institutions (governments, religious denominations, corporations, industries, educational systems) and generate resistance from, or in the name of, the threatened institutions. The specific sources, forms, and types of response to social movements are varied, complex, and often situation-driven. This chapter investigates the nature of resistance to social movements by focusing on the philosophical bases of response and the strategies and tactics institutions and their surrogates utilize to counter protest.

Institutions and Social Order

Every organization has a set of explicit or implicit purposes that include self-preservation, perpetuation, value maintenance, policy making, and enforcement.[1] All are protective of territorial boundaries, cultural norms, and values because of real and imagined enemies both within and without. Leaders, elected officials, and rulers must concern themselves with authority, legitimacy, and power. Emblems of authority and rituals such as civic holidays, religious holy days, days of thanksgiving, days of honoring founders and military heroes, inaugurations, college commencements, flags, memorials, insignia, uniforms, and limousines readily reinforce the status quo and the current allocation of influence.

Power is a concept relevant to individuals and groups. In chapter 3, for instance, we noted that when society confers legitimacy upon institutions, it confers powers to perpetuate this grant. Bowers, Ochs, and Jensen discuss how French and Raven's "five social powers" (legitimate, coercive, reward, referent, and expert) are distributed between institutions and social movements. They maintain that an institution always controls legitimate power (is perceived to have a charter, social contract,

319

or assigned position through which it can exert influence) and normally is capable of exerting coercive power (is perceived as able to influence by threat of punishment). Institutions and social movements share reward power because each is capable of conferring some rewards. While both share referent power (ability to identify with groups and individuals) and expert power (the image of having superior knowledge or skill in a particular area), social movements "depend almost completely on referent power and expert power."[2] See figure 14.1 for the ways these powers are controlled and shared in society.

Andrew King argues, from a group perspective, that power is derived from three bases: material resource base, psychosocial base, and organizational/syntactic base.[3] In feudal times, the *material resource* base was primarily land. The material resource in modern times has been money, but we are in an age when information and access to it may replace money. The *psychosocial* base provides a sense of identity for group members who are bound together by common interests, habits, culture, and values. *Organizational/syntactic* bases of power are legislative rules, regulations, and norms of behavior. Power, then, is a multidimensional offensive and defensive weapon of institutions and social movements. We will discuss later how institutions and their surrogates use the forms of power to resist change.

According to Hugh Dalziel Duncan, social order is always expressed in some kind of hierarchy.[4] Hierarchy differentiates people into ranks based on variables such as age, sex, race, skills, knowledge, and wealth, and these ranks function as societal structures that allow institutions to maintain control. Forms of social drama help to create national symbols that unify and transcend local, isolated concerns. Drama, as enacted within situations that provide legitimacy and continuation of regimes, ultimately results in social order and control.

Legitimacy is the most vulnerable point of attack for social movements. Regimes must actively demonstrate that they are competent, fair,

Figure 14.1

	Institution	Social Movement
Legitimate Power	Constitution Elected Officials	
Coercive Power	Courts IRS, FBI, ATF	
Reward Power	Contracts Tax incentives	Leadership Ego enhancement
Referent Power	Churches Founding Fathers	Organizations Heroes and martyrs
Expert Power	Universities Scientists	Authors Personal experience

just, and reasonable in order to maintain public support. Social control is usually viewed as the result of institutional influences such as laws or the police, but social order is not totally dependent upon agencies of control. No institution can long survive solely on the threat of force. Public communication is a vital tool, and through it institutions create and control images that legitimize their authority. The growing influence of the mass media and the Internet has made it increasingly difficult for institutions to create and control images and sustain authority.

Situations are never neutral. People experience them through language, and throughout society people describe similar situations in a wide variety of ways. Events do not simply exist. They are interpreted by those affected by them. Consequently, the *definitions of situations* are a valuable commodity that both leaders of institutions and social movements compete to control and own. Public perceptions and impressions are influenced by significant myths and symbols that are emotional, intense, and cultural in nature, including freedom, justice, and equality. Society, therefore, is a dynamic, interacting entity consisting of many levels acting and competing simultaneously. The fight for legitimacy is a fight for public perceptions, and patriotic, religious, and social myths and symbols are important weapons in this struggle. Sherry Shepler and Anne Mattina note "Cultural myths, especially those engendered by a patriarchal structure, may inhibit and/or repress groups who try to challenge a long-standing myth, while championing other groups."[5]

Institutions and their supporters are accustomed to defining and interpreting situations in their own terms and may find it difficult to counteract opposing definitions. How, for instance, should institutions respond to challenging definitions of *situations* such as "the corporation or the police provoked the confrontation with workers or demonstrators," *symbols* such as "our legal system is prejudiced against black and Hispanic Americans" or "the flag is a symbol of imperialism," and *acts of violence* such as "the police gassed us because of our appearance" or "the FBI shot an unarmed mother?" The philosophy of democracy and the Bill of Rights makes institutional responses to social movement challenges and activities troublesome. The Constitution denies the right of institutions to abridge the freedom of speech, the freedom of the press, and the "right of the people peaceably to assemble," while granting rights to the people to "petition the Government for a redress of grievances" and "to keep and bear arms."

Democracy and Resistance to Social Movements

There is probably no concept more important to the theory of democratic government than free speech. Historically, however, institutions have attempted to limit, control, or suppress freedom of expression by the press and individuals for the "good of the nation" or "national security." For instance, the Sedition Law of 1798 attempted to suppress newspapers that attacked the U.S. government for remaining neutral when the Republic of France declared war upon England. This law forbade the publication of matter intended to defame the government or to bring its officers into disrepute. The Sherman Antitrust Act of 1890 was used to stifle the organizing activities of labor unions rather than the monopolistic power and actions of industrial trusts. The Espionage Acts of 1917 forbade anyone to cause or to attempt to cause insubordination, disloyalty, mutiny, or refusal of duty in the armed forces. These acts made it unlawful to write or speak against U.S. involvement in World War I. Eugene V. Debs, leader of the socialist movement, was arrested in Canton, Ohio in 1918 shortly after giving a speech that opposed America's involvement in a "European war." He was tried under the Espionage Act and received a ten-year sentence, entering a federal prison four months after the war had ended. During World War II, Congress established the U.S. Office of Censorship to monitor all actions and written materials that challenged the wisdom of a United States presence in Europe and Asia. Colleges and universities routinely restricted the speaking activities of politicians, activists, and unapproved student groups on their campuses.

During the 1960s and 1970s demonstrators brought numerous challenges to laws restricting free expression and assemblage. The civil rights, students' rights, and anti–Vietnam War movements stimulated the consideration of free speech issues such as limits of expression, limits of criticism of public officials, citizen surveillance, the right to privacy, and the right to wear emblems such as peace symbols, flags, and black armbands. Court challenges led to some important victories for protestors. For example, the Supreme Court broadened the definition of speech to include the wearing of symbols such as armbands and symbolic acts. Other decisions supported the right to speak against the government and talk about its overthrow (as long as no action to overthrow is proposed), to resort to a rhetoric of the streets if other channels of redress are blocked, to carry a foreign or "enemy" flag as long as the carrier is not advocating the overthrow of the government, and to burn the American flag as a symbolic act.

In response to the broadening of civil rights and rights of expression, institutions have sought to control access and dissemination of information as the principal means of shaping and guiding public understanding of social policy. The war over the freedom of expression has become the war over the freedom of information. Beginning with President Lyndon Johnson, the press has had less access to government leaders and information. Official information from many government agencies has become secret, classified, or selective, so it is increasingly difficult to distinguish fact from fiction, truth from propaganda. "Good" reporters get interviews and important news leaks while others get little of either. Some presidents and vice presidents have tended to view the press as an enemy rather than as a partner in the democratic process; they attack the "liberal," "eastern establishment," and "biased" press. In his famous Des Moines, Iowa address to the Midwest Regional Republican Committee meeting in 1969, then Vice President Spiro Agnew declared, "The purpose of my remarks tonight is to focus your attention on this little group of men [television news directors and anchors] who not only enjoy a right of instant rebuttal to every presidential address but, more importantly, wield a free hand in selecting, presenting, and interpreting the great issues of our nation."[6] Agnew warned that this "tiny and closed fraternity of privileged men, elected by no one, and enjoying a monopoly" wielded immense power. For instance, "A raised eyebrow, an inflection of the voice, a caustic remark dropped in the middle of a broadcast can raise doubts in a million minds about the veracity of a public official or the wisdom of a government policy." Political institutions and agents are not alone in efforts to control information and free speech. During the 1990s, the University of Wisconsin and other educational institutions created policies to guarantee "politically correct" speech and to eliminate "hate speech" such as racial, ethnic, and gender name-calling on their campuses. The courts have ruled against many of these policies as infringements on freedom of expression.

In resisting social movements, how much free expression should institutions tolerate? Are all opinions equal? What differences between the form and content of expression are sufficient to limit some expressions rather than others? These are difficult and important issues to ponder, especially for residents of a democracy. For instance, many groups who want to display nativity scenes on courthouse lawns or in public schools would be outraged if atheistic groups or devil worshipers were allowed to erect their symbols in the same places. Ethnic and religious groups who have fought for the rights to protest, to hold demonstrations, and to present their cases without interruption want to deny the same rights to "hate groups" such as the American Nazi Party, the Ku Klux Klan, and the Aryan Nation.

A balance between rights is difficult for institutions to maintain. For example, communication scholars generally agree that speakers who appeal only to the emotions of audiences impede logical and critical thinking. Thus, many scholars have concluded that such appeals are unethical and undemocratic because they undermine the free, full, and rational discussion of issues. Wayne Flynt argues that during the 1963 civil rights disturbances in Birmingham, Alabama, prominent leaders took undemocratic stances, employed faulty logic, and appealed to white fear, frustration, and anger. A former mayor of Birmingham publicly charged that he was "Kicked out of the city hall by niggers" and that the new mayor would probably make the African violet the city's official flower.[7] Is such rhetoric more unethical, however, than protestors shouting insults and obscenities at clergy, public officials, and police officers?

Another troublesome area for institutions is the level of response. The national government may be most concerned with issues, policy, and movement leaders, while the local government may focus primarily on property, events, maintenance of order, and citizens' rights. Local police, for example, believe they are charged with maintaining law and order. A *good* officer is one who strictly enforces the law. A *bad* officer is one who uses discretion and overlooks certain offenses. Police often view protestors as disruptors of peace, using tactics that lead to anarchy. Of course, protestors often view police as brutish "pigs" and mindless enforcers of suppression.[8] Law enforcement officers are usually reactors to rather than initiators of either protest or institutional counteractions. Police, for example, respond to individual demonstrators and their actions rather than to or from an ideological view of gay rights, pro-life, or the environment. Protestors' actions tend to be contrary to the basic values and upbringing of police officers. While local responses to social movements are sometimes counter to national policy, they are symbolic of national attitudes and responses.

This discussion suggests problems inherent in institutional bureaucracies. First, there is little agreement on whether negotiations with social movements should rest with the executive, legislative, or judicial branch of government. Second, institutions are comprised of individuals with their own beliefs, attitudes, and values. Third, consensus and policy implementation are not merely matters of issuing directives because there are differences between theory and practice, issues and policy implementation. And fourth, democracy is not an entity but a process of regulating human behavior. This process is often slow and insensitive with contradictory principles.

How does an institution balance the rights of society against individuals, the majority against the minority, or the popular against the unpopular? For most social movements, the cause is supreme, the resources are few, and the time to act is now. The urgency expressed in social movement rhetoric encounters a rhetoric of democratic government based on the premise that policies enacted are the will of the majority and policies rejected are favored by small minorities with special interests.

Thus, the philosophical principles as well as the operational structure of a democracy dictate not only the strategies and tactics of social movements but also the forms and types of institutional responses. Democracy makes resistance to social movements varied and complex. According to Theodore Windt, "administrative" rhetoric is characterized by a defensive posture that views all questions of policy as attacks on the authority and credibility of the institution.[9] In the same vein, Bowers, Ochs, and Jensen write that the principle that governs the rhetorical stance of decision makers is the assumption that the worst will happen in any instance of outside agitation.[10] Institutional leaders, to maintain their power, credibility, and legitimacy within the hierarchy, must continually provide evidence of superiority, control, and willingness to respond quickly and decisively to all threats or attacks upon the institution. It is mandatory, then, for institutional leaders to confront the opposition to maintain support among institutional members and sympathizers.

In summary, institutions seem to maintain a universal perspective toward outside threats and attacks. All challenges are viewed as questioning established authority, doctrines, myths, and symbols. For most protestors, however, their challenges are questions of legitimacy, such as how good are certain policies or actions? Obviously, these divergent views toward challenges influence the nature and types of responses to social movements. The remainder of this chapter focuses on six strategies institutions and their supporters employ in response to outside challenges: evasion, counterpersuasion, coercive persuasion, coercion, adjustment, and capitulation.[11]

The Strategy of Evasion

The strategy of evasion is usually the first strategy employed. Institutions attempt to ignore a social movement, either pretending that it does not exist or seeing it as unworthy of response. The media devote little time or space to coverage of the new or continuing social movement, so most Americans are unaware, for example, that a United Students Against Sweatshops, the Rainforest Action Network, the Earth Liberation Front, and anarchist groups exist or that the temperance and Native-American movements are continuing their struggles. When violent protests erupted in Seattle in December 1999 during the World Trade Organization (WTO) meetings, reports noted that the city had not taken the situation seriously even though many groups had been planning protests for months and had consulted regularly with city officials. There were warning signs that the protests could be violent.[12]

"Invisible" social movements and organizations are not consulted or represented on task forces dealing with their concerns, do not appear on election ballots, and are denied meeting places or parade permits because they are not recognized as legitimate student, religious, social, political, or civic groups. For example, during the Democratic Convention in Chicago in 1968, Chicago Mayor Richard Daly denied permits for the Yippies to use Soldier Field and members of the National Mobilization Committee to use Lincoln Park after curfew hours. Organizers of the annual Saint Patrick's Day parade in New York have attempted to deny permission for gay and lesbian Irish to take part.

Institutional leaders avoid meeting with representatives of social movements. Such a meeting may be interpreted as symbolizing that the movement is worthy of serious consideration. Bureaucratic procedures allow institutions to delay official responses to social movements. Institutional bureaucracies are adept at passing-the-buck, being unavailable for comment, and giving the runaround. Institutions maintain the appearance of addressing issues by referring them to committees, special commissions, or task forces, often populated with those who support the institutions. Postponement tactics slow or delay the decision-making process regarding a social movement's charges and demands. Some issues, such as civil rights and women's rights, are tied up in the courts or Congress for years while little or no change takes place. Members of civil rights movements throughout most of the twentieth century faced jury trials with all-white juries and were afraid to call law enforcement officers who were likely to be members of the KKK or white citizens councils.

When laws or decisions are made, some are so ambiguous or full of loopholes that offenders can easily circumvent them. For instance, when the Supreme Court handed down a decision on abortion in the late 1990s, newspaper headlines exemplified the ambiguity of what the Court had decided:[13]

The Miami Herald: "Court Affirms Abortion Rights"

The Orlando Sentinel: "Court Weakens Abortion Rights"

The Oakland Tribune: "Roe Reaffirmed"

USA Today: "High Court Reins in Roe"

San Francisco Chronicle: "Court Upholds Right to Abortion"

Chicago Tribune: "Ruling Weakens Abortion Right"

Some laws lack enforcement mechanisms or teeth to make them effective. In other instances, institutions unsympathetic to social movement demands simply do not enforce existing laws. The hope is that protestors will become discouraged and go away or that the issue will disappear.

During the civil rights movement's efforts to integrate public schools, a common strategy for white citizens was to close public schools or to create their own schools to avoid integration. In 1963 Reverend George Fisher, pastor of the Edgewater Baptist Church in Birmingham, Alabama, obtained 75,000 signatures on petitions endorsing the closing of schools rather than acquiescing to enforced integration.[14] Even in more progressive states such as Virginia, there was massive resistance to integrating schools in the late 1950s. Opposition came from governors, legislatures, and members of congress. For example, Governor Thomas Stanley of Virginia urged that "consideration be given to the repeal of Section 129 of the state constitution, which mandated that the state maintain free public schools."[15] Many school districts delayed opening public schools, and Norfolk closed its public schools from September 1958 to February 1959.

The Strategy of Counterpersuasion

Institutions employ a strategy of counterpersuasion when they can no longer avoid problems or encounters with social movements. If an encounter quickly turns violent, such as the W.T.O. protest in Seattle, institutions may resort to coercion to maintain order. In most situations, however, institutions employ counterpersuasion strategies that challenge a social movement's version of reality and discredits its leaders, members, and demands. The secret to success is usually not to overreact but to characterize the social movement, its leaders, and its ideas as ill-advised and lacking merit.

By manipulating the social context, an institution or resistance movement can expand, narrow, or selectively alter arguments and definitions of the situation.[16] It may appeal to fundamental *fears*. Thus, institutional agents and agencies argue that environmentalists are endangering the U.S. economy and threatening factory workers, loggers, and fish workers with the loss of their livelihoods; that antiwar or antimilitary groups are unpatriotic and a threat to national security; that gay rights advocates are immoral and grievous threats to the family and traditional way of life; or that protestors are a threat to democracy because they are socialists or communists. During the woman's rights movement in the nineteenth century, the media warned Americans that terrible things would happen if women gained the right to vote. Cartoonists portrayed female army officers reviewing all-female military units; women at political rallies while husbands were at home taking care of the children; and women smoking and drinking in saloons while husbands were doing the laundry. The alleged stripping of soldiers, workers, husbands, and fathers of their manhood has remained a rhetorical staple of those opposing women's rights and supporting the military for more than a century.[17]

An institution or its surrogates may challenge the *nature and motives* of persuasive efforts. In 1983, when ABC-TV was about to air its famous nuclear holocaust video entitled *The Day After*, Phyllis Schlafly (President of the Eagle Forum) sent leaflets to schools throughout the nation denouncing the video in advance as "virulently anti-American," "dishonest," and a "vicious smear of America" because it suggested that the United States might have started the war. To Schlafly *The Day After* was a thinly veiled "political" video created to support the pro-pacifist and antinuclear movements and "offensive to President Reagan and to religious people."[18]

Institutions and agents may challenge the *accuracy or veracity* of movement persuasion. Following the demonstrations in 1999 during the WTO meetings in Seattle, Fareed Zakaria wrote a column in *Newsweek* challenging the "plea for the downtrodden of the world" common in much of the protest rhetoric. He argued:

> There's just one problem: the downtrodden beg to differ. Representatives of the developing nations at the meeting angrily pointed out that the demonstrators were seeking to protect the jobs and benefits of *Western* workers, who are rich and privileged by any standard. In fact, if the demonstrators' demands were met, the effect would be to crush the hopes of much poorer Third World workers—the original indigenous people."[19]

Cries of anarchy have often united the "silent majority" of Americans by identifying protestors as dangerous criminals and degenerates. Ralph Smith and Russell Windes note that antigay persuaders who identify themselves as "agents of the majority" describe their pro-gay antagonists as a "small but vocal minority" that "is about to impose its will on the silent and inactive majority" and as "a loud, militant, and overinfluential minority."[20] Opponents of social movements throughout U.S. history have found it easy to generate feelings of suspicion toward those who are "different" or "foreign" and to create fears about social movement motives and objectives. Local officials during the racial confrontation in Birmingham, Alabama in 1963 identified integration with despised external movements and threats such as communism. Thus, integration became a tool of the communist conspiracy that was a grave threat to Christian and democratic principles and values. Movement leaders must spend a great amount of rhetoric and time explaining and justifying actions and ideology to sympathizers as well as the public. Although the violent actions of the true anarchists in Seattle during the WTO meeting resulted in thousands of dollars in damage and greatly embarrassed the city and the United States government, the anarchists' actions and threatening rhetoric enabled authorities to crack down on all protestors, violent and nonviolent, and to identify all as dangerous to society.

Moral outrage and righteous indignation justify counterattacks that nearly always employ labeling and name-calling. Lawrence Rosenfeld defines coercive semantics as attempts "to discourage real discussion of alternatives, and to render counterarguments meaningless by labeling the opponents as evil."[21] A common epithet hurled by and at social movements is "Nazi." For example, Rush Limbaugh throughout the 1990s labeled all women's rights leaders as "feminazis" on his radio and television shows. Henry Gonzalez, elected to Congress in 1961 from Texas, led an aggressive counterattack against militant Chicanos. His charges followed three themes: (1) militants practiced reverse racism and preached hate based upon race; (2) militants displayed bad qualities and harmed the Mexican-American community; and (3) militant attacks on him were personal and unfair. Gonzalez's perspective was that the militants "have adopted the same positions, the same attitudes, the same tactics as those who have so long offended them."[22] Nearly identical charges were made in the 1980s and 1990s against Louis Farrakhan (leader of the Nation of Islam) for allegedly making anti-Semitic statements and against the Black Panthers in Indianapolis for urging African Americans to boycott stores owned by Korean Americans in their neighborhoods. S. I. Hayakawa, President of San Francisco State University in 1968, claimed that rebellious students were attempting to overthrow the government and were all drug addicts. He referred to students as "cowards who resort to violence, lies, and deceit."[23]

Martha Solomon, in examining the rhetorical strategies of the Stop ERA (Equal Rights Amendment) campaign, found that opponents of the women's movement ridiculed members as unattractive and lesbian. She concluded that "with sharp satire the group paints an unappealing picture of the feminists' physical appearance and nature, emphasizing their disregard for traditional standards of feminine attractiveness and sexuality."[24] Men were not alone in stereotyping pro-ERA women. Phyllis Schlafly proclaimed, "if man is targeted as the enemy, and the ultimate goal of women's liberation is independence from men and the avoidance of pregnancy and its consequences, then lesbianism is the highest form in the ritual of women's liberation."[25] Ridicule may weaken the self-confidence and self-esteem of protestors and challenge their efforts to attain legitimacy among potential sympathizers and members.

Counterpersuasion deals primarily with social movement leaders and members rather than the movement's issues and demands. Name-calling, labeling, and ridicule attack individuals directly. Perhaps the easiest way to discredit a movement is to discredit its leaders and most fervent followers. If the leaders and true believers are evil, then the motives, goals, and objectives of the movement must be evil. For instance, political cartoonists of the 1990s portrayed militia movement leaders and members as ignorant, uneducated, marginally employed, paranoid trailer-trash whose motives and goals were laced with anti-Semitic and racist slurs. Sherry Shepler and Anne Mattina claim that when Jane Addams spoke out against entry by the United States into World War I, resistance forces framed "Addams as a less than credible source" to marginalize her concerns and make "them undeserving of response."[26]

The Strategy of Coercive Persuasion

The strategy of coercive persuasion involves tactics ranging from threats to general harassment. These tactics tend to evolve when avoidance and counterpersuasion fail to stifle a social movement and an institution commits itself to direct action and sustained conflict.

Institutions have a war chest of potentially lethal threats at their disposal and have exhibited little reluctance to use them. They may threaten to fire workers, expel students, deport the foreign born, excommunicate the true believer, or discharge members of the military. Employers fought the labor movement for years with threats to blacklist union members by publicizing their names throughout the country so no one would hire them. Governments exile or deport social movement leaders. Schools suspend or expel students. The military discharges gay members who dare to testify for gay rights or to reveal that they are gay under the "don't ask, don't tell" rule. Female members of the armed forces who have made claims of sexual harassment have been demoted or discharged. Religious organizations excommunicate members or deny them important rites or sacraments. The Roman Catholic Church, for example, barred an eleven-year-old child from a Catholic school because she would not renounce her mother's pro-choice activism; denied sacraments to members of NOW in California because the organization was pro-choice; threatened to expel pro-choice nuns from their religious orders; and denied the sacraments to elected officials who espoused pro-choice views.[27]

During the red scare following World War I and the cold war that followed World War II, concern for national security led many states to require anyone who would teach at a state college or university to sign a loyalty oath in front of a notary public who then affixed his or her seal to the document. The oath in Indiana read:

> I solemnly swear (or affirm) that I will support the Constitution of the United States of America, the Constitution of the State of Indiana, and the laws of the United States and the State of Indiana, and will, by precept and example, promote respect for the flag and the institutions of the United States and the State of Indiana, reverence for law and order and undivided allegiance to the Government of the United States of America.

Any professor, instructor, or teacher who, in the judgment of the college or university, exhibited behavior inimical to this oath could be fired. Persons wishing to join the Armed Forces had to read a list of some three hundred organizations deemed by the Attorney General of the United States to pose a danger to national security and fill out the Armed Forces Security Questionnaire swearing that they had never been members of or associated with members of any of the organizations listed. If they refused to answer the questions and sign their names, they could be denied admittance to any of the armed forces. If they answered falsely, they could be fined up to $10,000, imprisoned for up to five years, or both.

University administrators and police photographed student demonstrators in the 1960s and 1970s to identify students for possible expulsion and reporting to parents or draft boards. Anti–environmental groups such as the Wise Use Movement and the Sahara Club have not only telephoned threats and warnings to environmental activists but have recorded license plate numbers and videotaped activists as a signal of future retaliation.[28] The signal is clear—we know who you are and where we can find you.

Some institutions have tried to replace social movement organizations with more cooperative ones. Corporations played the CIO and AFL against one another during the 1930s and 1940s. Grape growers in California signed contracts with the Teamsters union to counteract the United Farm Workers Organizing Committee's efforts to unionize grape workers. Nine growers and right-wing organizations created, financed, and handpicked the leaders for a counterorganization called the AWFWA (Agricultural Workers Freedom to Work Association), allegedly a farm workers' organization. The courts eventually outlawed the AWFWA organization as a flagrant violation of fair employment laws.

Harassment tactics may be covert. During the Johnson and Nixon Administrations, agencies of the federal government such as the FBI, the CIA, Army Intelligence, and the Treasury Department investigated anti-war demonstrators and student leaders for communist connections or sympathies upon which the government might base administrative actions. The FBI launched its counterintelligence operation (COINTEL-PRO) in May 1968 to counteract the New Left. Until it ceased operation on April 28, 1971, COINTELPRO secretly photographed college students, created files and lists of suspected communist sympathizers, and sent letters (many allegedly from parents and concerned citizens) to boards of trustees to get leftist students expelled.[29] It also sent letters to school boards and superintendents suggesting that certain teachers be fired for leftist activities. For instance, a Washington, DC teacher's only dangerous activity was participation in the Young Socialist Alliance, the youth affiliate of the Socialist Workers. The FBI reported activities of students to parents, encouraging them to protest to the college for allowing leftist organizations to operate on campus. President Clinton's secret file created while he was a college student and anti–Vietnam War protestor was used against him as he campaigned for the presidency in 1992. The file included details of a visit he made to the Soviet Union while a Rhodes scholar at Oxford University.

Government agents and sympathizers routinely infiltrate social movement organizations and protest groups in the United States with the primary purpose of gathering information to inhibit their activities. During the cold war, a standing joke was that the membership of communist groups in the United States included more undercover FBI agents than communists. Years after Malcolm X's assassination it became known that his chief bodyguard was an undercover New York police officer.

One purpose of infiltration is to instigate militant and violent acts that will discredit the social movement. Michael Stohl reports "regimes and their agent provocateurs (both official and self-identified) have both encouraged insurgent groups to plan and execute terrorist actions not only to provide grounds for arrest but also to alienate potential supporters within the population."[30] Labor movement leaders for more than a century have charged that corporations have routinely planted people within unions to instigate strikes and violent acts during strikes to discredit unions and justify repression. For example, Terence Powderly charged that during the long and disruptive strike of the car-drivers in St. Louis in 1886, "men who were employed by detective agencies" hired by employers "stood up on the floor of that Assembly, made inflammatory speeches urging the men to deeds of violence, and urged that the property of the streetcar companies be destroyed." Although "the good sense of the men" in the union prevented violent actions by Knights, "agents of a nefarious spy system induced some desperate men to blow up the cars on the streets."[31]

The Strategy of Coercion

Institutions often rely on surrogates to suppress social movements. Jerome Skolnick claims that counterdemonstrators have attacked many protestors with the knowledge and tacit approval of administrative and civil authorities. For example, the Ku Klux Klan and White Citizens Councils served as surrogates for southern state and community authorities during the civil rights struggles. In addition to videotaping environmental activists and taking down their license plate numbers, members of counterorganizations such as Wise Use and Sahara Club have picked fights with demonstrators, assaulted movement leaders, and set fire to homes.[32] Skolnick writes:

> By far the greater portion of physical harm has been done to demonstrators and movement workers, in the form of bombings of homes and offices, crowd-control measures used by police, physical attacks on demonstrators by American Nazi party members, Hell's Angels and others, and random harassment such as the Port Chicago Vigil has endured.[33]

Institutions employ harassment to intimidate and to show who has the real power in the confrontation. In an overt form of harassment during the Vietnam War, the head of the Selective Service System ordered the reclassification of leading student protestors. For example, Peter Wolff and Richard Shortt were classified II-S as full-time students at the University of Michigan. When they participated in a demonstration protesting U.S. involvement in Vietnam, the local Selective Service Board reclassified both as I-A, eligible for the draft. The Board argued that by participating in the antiwar demonstration, Wolff and Shorn became "delinquents" and thus were in violation of Section 12(a) of the Universal Military Training and Service Act. They further argued that a student deferment was not a "right" but a "legislative grace."[34] In a less obvious form of harassment, National Guardsmen were called out to "protect students" in a two-day march on the Pentagon in 1967. The large number of heavily armed troops restricted the movement of and access to the student marchers. It soon became clear that the troops were present to control rather than to protect the protestors; this institutional show of force cost the taxpayers more than one million dollars.[35]

The easiest method of coercion is the passage and implementation of restrictive legislation and policies. For example, the University of California at Berkeley in 1964 established a policy prohibiting individuals from the solicitation of funds and advocacy of political causes on campus. The administration had several students arrested for violating this policy. This undemocratic and unconstitutional policy suppressed student actions until protest organizations challenged it in court. Some cities used zoning laws during the 1960s and 1970s to eliminate underground presses in private homes, contending that such presses were businesses and could not be operated in homes zoned as family dwellings. Challenging restrictive policies and legislation through legal channels takes time and money, assets that favor institutions rather than social movements.

Some coercion is indirect and opportunistic. For instance, a student at the University of California at Berkeley was arrested for public obscenity because he carried a sign that read "Freedom Under Clark Kerr" (Kerr was president of the University). The first letter of each word was high-lighted.[36] This arrest was obviously aimed more at the protestor than at the "offending" obscenity. The institutional arsenal of laws, rules, and regulations is a vast and powerful tool of suppression.

Arrest is perhaps the most common form of coercion and has been used in recent years against antinuclear power, environmentalists, anti-apartheid policies of South Africa, pro-choice, pro-life, and gay rights activists. Some groups such as pro-life Operation Rescue want to be arrested; others do not. For instance, when students at Purdue University failed to remove their simulated South African shanty from the Memorial Mall by the university-appointed deadline, Purdue grounds personnel tore down the shanty and Purdue police arrested several demonstrators present at the scene.

Multiple charges can tie up movement leaders for years with court appearances, bad publicity, and drains on a movement's precarious finan-cial state. Bowers, Ochs, and Jensen write that the Black Panthers were involved in more than sixty criminal prosecutions requiring $300,000 in bail money in the first six months of 1967.[37]

While the courts have made many rulings in favor of protestors dur-ing the past quarter-century—most notably the expansion of freedom of speech (meanings words) to symbolic speech (including symbols and sym-bolic actions)—rulings still place severe limits on social movements. For instance, protestors may speak against the government, but they cannot advocate its overthrow, cannot put the American flag to "an ignoble use," cannot exceed the bounds of rational discourse, cannot invade the privacy of others, cannot place "undue strain" on a community's resources, and cannot "inconvenience" people not in the target audience. Institutions, of course, determine when protestors are advocating overthrow of the gov-ernment and what is ignoble, irrational, invasive or inconvenient.

The most severe form of coercion is assassination, when threats become brutal reality. Assassinations are often acts of individuals or mobs, such as the untold number of lynchings of blacks in the south for nearly a century after the Civil War, rather than of institutions and institu-tional policies. Nevertheless, many movement leaders and followers have been killed in the United States. Students at Jackson State and Kent State, members of the Black Panthers, Medgar Evers, Malcolm X, and Martin Luther King, Jr. are merely the best known. Very few people have ever come to trial or been convicted for killing movement activists. A growing number of physicians who have performed abortions and abortion clinic personnel have been shot or blown up during the past ten years by those attempting to end legalized abortion in the United States. Stohl writes that "disappearance" of leaders and followers "is one of the quiet terrors employed by many governments in the modern world."[38]

Coercion offers several advantages to institutions and their surrogates. First, coercive tactics generate fear among a social movement's leaders, followers, and sympathizers. Stohl notes "The violence of the terrorist act is not intended simply to destroy but also to be heard." "For regimes," he continues, "the terror is a message of strength, a warning designed to intimidate, to ensure compliance without the need to physically touch each citizen."[39] Thus, social movement leaders may become hesitant to act; members may become hesitant to take part in demonstrations; and sympathizers may withdraw moral and financial support. Second, coercion isolates leaders from followers. Third, coercion enables institutions to portray social movement leaders as common criminals and dangerous social deviants.

The Strategy of Adjustment

The strategy of adjustment involves making some concessions to a social movement while not accepting the movement's demands or goals. Adjustment tactics give the appearance of being responsive to movement concerns. Accommodation, according to Andrew King, is usually a short-term solution that, for the institution, buys time, saves face, and appears gracious.[40] This strategy, by design, addresses only superficial elements of conflict and seldom results in permanent solutions to social unrest and movement demands. For instance as discussed in chapter 1, newspapers reported in December 1999 that Julia "Butterfly" Hill had descended from the twenty-five-story-high redwood tree on top of which she had been sitting in protest since December 10, 1997. In an agreement filed at the Humboldt County Recorder's Office, "Hill and her supporters pledged to pay $50,000 to Pacific Lumber to make up for lost logging revenue. The company agreed to spare Hill's redwood and a 2.9 acre buffer zone around it."[41] Although Hill was out of the tree and the company agreed to a small, mainly symbolic, saving of one giant redwood tree, nothing was resolved. The struggle would continue because logging would continue.

Adjustment tactics range from symbolic gestures to concrete acts of concession. Symbolic tactics include issuing press releases that promise investigation of problems or the naming of special committees and commissions to study the issues the social movement has raised. Such gestures provide a visible response and show of concern while reducing the sense of urgency of social movement demands, which buys time for the institution. Presidents, governors, and political candidates address concerns such as equal rights, the environment, animal rights, ethics, and the needs of senior citizens and then go about business as usual. Although this adjustment strategy is similar to bureaucratic delays, it does involve a public acknowledgment of the movement's demands.

Sacrificing personnel is a common institutional tactic. University deans and presidents, police chiefs and officers, and mid-level executives often are dismissed or "resign" from their positions when they become targets of social movements, are portrayed as unresponsive to citizen or group needs, or become convenient and expendable symbols of institutional "responsiveness." This tactic is particularly effective when a social movement focuses its agitation and hatred upon a single individual or unit. Elimination of the individual or unit leaves the movement without a target. Public sympathy for an institution may increase when sacrificed individuals are seen as tragic victims of *radical* protestors.

A subtle adjustment tactic is cooperation with protestors and movement organizations by providing protection, access to facilities, or material support. Open and publicized cooperation frustrates social movements by making institutions less of an obvious enemy and target of outrage. Cooperation may defuse a movement's energy, momentum, and recruiting efforts, buy time for counterefforts, encourage attitudes of neutrality among citizens, and generate favorable press. It may lead to outright co-optation of the cause in which institutions seemingly take on the cause as their own. Congress, for example, seemed to take on the civil rights cause in the years following the assassination of John F. Kennedy by passing civil rights and voting laws and creating an equal employment opportunity commission. Many institutional groups, including corporations and the Advertising Council, literally took over the ecology or environmental movement in the 1970s. Few people of that period will forget the ads of the Advertising Council that featured a tearful Native American looking upon a trashed America from his canoe or a hilltop overlooking a freeway.

Incorporation of movement leaders and sympathizers within institutional bodies is a common adjustment tactic. During the 1960s and 1970s, students, blacks, and women became appointees, often as tokens, to committees, boards, and study commissions. Governmental agencies, schools, religious groups, and corporations began to hire a few minorities and to appoint them to serve in a variety of nonauthoritative—and therefore nonthreatening—positions. For example, U.S. colleges and universities appointed students to serve on boards of trustees, grievance committees, grade-appeal committees, and curriculum committees. Representation, however, did not mean power to influence policy decisions. At the start of the twenty-first century, the phrase "glass ceiling" still has significance for women and minorities who lag far behind white males in salaries and leadership positions.

The strategy of adjustment can be tricky for institutions because they must not appear to be deceptive, cynical, weak, or tyrannical. Nearly any concession may rejuvenate a social movement by renewing hope of immediate or ultimate victory. Adjustments are most often mere tokens to appease public questioning and social movement demands. There is the real danger, however, that social movements may replace moderate persons incorporated into institutional positions with more radical elements and become more of a threat to institutions. This happened in the civil rights movement when the Black Panthers and more radical leaders of SNCC (Stokely Carmichael and H. Rapp Brown) became highly visible and popular, particularly among young movement members. It happened in the antiwar and counterculture movements when the violence-prone Weathermen gained widespread attention and notoriety.

The Strategy of Capitulation

Total capitulation is the acceptance of a social movement's ideology: beliefs, goals, objectives, and solutions. This has rarely happened in U.S. history because (1) institutions control rewards, channels of communication, and regulatory agencies, and (2) as noted in previous chapters, Americans cherish the institutions they have created, adapted, and borrowed from other societies and are not inclined toward social-political instability or revolutionary change. Indeed, as Raymond Duvall and Michael Stohl write, Americans can hardly imagine their governments being evil:

> Particularly in the American political culture, the concept of the state as neutral conflict manager or arbiter of social conflict within society is so ingrained that many have difficulty emotionally accepting the idea of state terrorism. Terrorism is felt to be something done by revolutionaries against the state. How could a government—at least a legitimate government like that in the United States—be thought to engage in terrorism? Surely such talk must be revolutionary rhetoric![42]

While total capitulation short of violent civil war or revolution is rare, institutions do make tactical capitulations such as accepting portions of movement ideologies or some demands such as social security, voting rights, an eight-hour workday, and integration of public facilities. The effort is to make such changes appear to be the work of progressive institutions—Congress, the president, Supreme Court, corporations—rather than social movements who have pressed institutions into accepting change. President Franklin Roosevelt's New Deal was essentially a capitulation to Huey Long's Share the Wealth program, labor's demand for collective bargaining, and the Townsendites' demand for a national pension program. When the New Deal gave movement followers vested interests in institutions, movement leaders found themselves without the means to maintain interest in the cause.

Institutions may capitulate to end strikes and social movement campaigns they decide are too costly or difficult to oppose over time, particularly if their legitimacy appears threatened. Corporations may agree to union demands to end a strike because of profit or customer losses, often with the intention of nullifying these concessions (salary increases, benefits, job security) at a future date when the environment is more in their favor. Some universities in the 1990s agreed to eliminate investments in South African corporations in their endowments to end demonstrations on their campuses opposing the apartheid policies of the South African government. Others in 1999 and 2000 agreed to spend the few thousand dollars to join the Workers Rights Consortium (WRC) to satisfy students protesting the sweatshop conditions of workers producing apparel rather than suffer the public and well-reported embarrassment of pickets, sit-ins, and hunger strikes. Relatively minor capitulations ended major headaches.

Conclusions

Institutions must confront challenges and threats to their beings, even though complete annihilation of existing institutions seldom occurs in today's world. For an institution, any concession to dissenters may be costly. Even negotiations create strains within an order by creating an atmosphere of tension and risk in a win/lose situation. Thus, institutions and their surrogates tend to employ a combination of six strategies in meeting the threats posed by social movements: evasion, counterpersuasion, coercive persuasion, coercion, adjustment, and capitulation. The combination depends upon the relationship of institutions to their surrogates as well as the social movement, the environment within which it is operating, and acceptable evolutionary results.

When using the strategy of *evasion*, institutions attempt to ignore a social movement, pretending that it does not exist or is not worthy of response. They try to avoid direct contacts with movement leaders and to make the movement invisible. When an institution can no longer ignore a social movement, it may use *counterpersuasion* to challenge the movement's version of reality and to discredit it leaders, members, or demands. Institutional persuasion appeals to fundamental fears among the public. It warns of dire results, even anarchy, if the movement is successful. It may challenge the nature and motives of the movement and question the accuracy or veracity of the movement's persuasive efforts. Institutions use *coercive persuasion* when the strategies of evasion and counterpersuasion seem ineffective in stifling a movement. Coercive persuasion includes tactics ranging from threats to harassment. It may be overt through police actions, telephoned threats, and arrests or covert through secret files on protestors, sending letters under the guise of concerned parents or citizens, and infiltration of movement organizations.

Institutions often rely upon surrogates to employ a strategy of *coercion* to suppress social movements. Coercive tactics range from the passage of restrictive legislation and court decisions, to physical confrontations and arrests, to shootings, bombings, and arsons. Institutions use a strategy of *adjustment* to give the appearance of being responsive to "legitimate concerns" by pledging funds to address elements of a problem, create special study commissions, and sacrificing personnel the movement finds offensive. And an institution may use a strategy of *capitulation* to end strikes and other confrontations and to implement portions of a social movement's ideology that is not threatening to its powers and legitimacy.

Thus, over time bits and pieces of social movement ideologies find their way into institutional policies regardless of the strategies employed to stifle them. Social security, farm supports, unemployment benefits, the eight-hour day, civil rights, equal opportunity, voting rights, collective bargaining, and fair housing were social movement demands long before established political parties enacted them into law. The task for institutions is to allow (perhaps even to encourage) dissent without threatening social, political, economic, or religious orders. Institutions and their surrogates have many more resources than social movements, and responses may emanate from individuals, organized resistance groups, local leaders, statewide organizations, and national authorities that may include the whole federal government. The trick for an institution is to use the best strategy for the situation and to avoid the appearance of overreacting or abusing the powers granted to it by the people.

Endnotes

[1] See John W. Bowers, Donovan J. Ochs, and Richard J. Jensen, *The Rhetoric of Agitation and Control* (Prospect Heights, IL: Waveland Press, 1993): 11–12.

[2] Bowers, Ochs, and Jensen, 13–15.

[3] Andrew King, *Power and Communication* (Prospect Heights, IL: Waveland Press, 1987): 48–53.

[4] Hugh Dalziel Duncan, *Symbols in Reality* (New York: Oxford University Press, 1968): 78–92.

[5] Sherry R. Shepler and Anne F. Mattina, "'The Revolt Against War': Jane Addams' Rhetorical Challenge to the Patriarchy," *Communication Quarterly* 47 (Spring 1999): 152.

[6] Spiro T. Agnew, "Des Moines, Iowa Address to the Midwest Republican Committee," November 13, 1969, from a tape recording.

[7] Wayne Flynt, "The Ethics of Democratic Persuasion and the Birmingham Crisis," *Southern Speech Communication Journal* 35 (Fall 1969): 45.

[8] For a discussion of police response to protestors, see Irving Horowitz, *The Struggle Is the Message* (Berkeley, CA: The Glendessary Press, 1970): 48–58.

[9] Theodore Windt, "Administrative Rhetoric: An Undemocratic Response to Protest," *Communication Quarterly* 30 (Summer, 1982): 247.

[10] Bowers, Ochs, and Jensen, 47.

[11] See Bowers, Ochs, and Jensen, 48–64.

[12] "The Siege of Seattle," *Newsweek*, 13 December 1999, 30–35.

[13] These headlines were compiled by Al Neuharth, retired CEO of the Gannett Company and founder of *USA Today*.

[14] Flynt, 45–46.

[15] Alexander S. Leidholdt, *Standing Before the Shouting Mob: Lenoir Chambers and Virginia's Massive Resistance to Public-School Integration* (Tuscaloosa, AL: The University of Alabama Press, 1997): 67.

[16] King, 27.

[17] Shepler and Mattina, 159.

[18] ABC Film *The Day After*, Eagle Forum, November 1983.

[19] Fareed Zacharia, "After the Storm Passes," *Newsweek*, 13 December 1999, 40.

[20] Ralph R. Smith and Russell R. Windes, "The Pro-gay and Antigay Issue Culture: Interpretation, Influence and Dissent," *Quarterly Journal of Speech* 83 (February 1997): 31 and 38.

[21] Lawrence Rosenfeld, "The Confrontation Policies of S. I. Hayakawa: A Case Study in Coercive Semantics," *Today's Speech* 18 (Spring 1970): 18.

[22] John Hammerback, Richard Jensen, and Jose Gutierrer, *A War of Words* (Westport, CT: Greenwood Press, 1985): 104.

[23] Rosenfeld, 20.

[24] Martha Solomon, "The Rhetoric of Stop ERA: Fatalistic Reaffirmation," *Southern Speech Communication Journal* 44 (Fall 1978): 47.

[25] Solomon, 47.

[26] Shepler and Mattina, 163.

[27] Lafayette, Indiana *Journal and Courier*, 19 December 1984, A 13; Lafayette, Indiana *Journal and Courier*, 21 September 1986, A13; *Newsweek*, 14 January 1985, 29; Lafayette, Indiana *Journal and Courier*, 16 August 1986, C 1; Lafayette, Indiana *Journal and Courier*, 28 April 1975, A10.

[28] CBS, *60 Minutes*, 6 June 1993.

[29] "FBI Documents Show '60s Campus Capers," Lafayette, Indiana *Journal and Courier*, 25 June 1975, B–7.

[30] Michael Stohl, ed., *The Politics of Terrorism* (New York: Dekker, 1983): 5.

[31] "Report of the General Master Workman," *Proceedings of the General Assembly of the Knights of Labor*, 6 October 1886, 38.

[32] CBS, *60 Minutes*, 6 June 1993.

[33] Jerome Skolnick, "The Politics of Protest," *Dissent: Symbolic Behavior and Rhetorical Strategies*, Haig Bosmajian, ed. (Boston: Allyn and Bacon, 1972): 156.

[34] Harold Medina, "Students Have Rights Too," *Free Speech and Political Protest*, Marvin Summers, ed. (Lexington, MA: D. C. Heath, 1967): 102.

[35] Horowitz, 58.

[36] Windt, 246.

[37] Bowers, Ochs, and Jensen, 55.

[38] Stohl, 3.

[39] Stohl, 3.

[40] King, 27

[41] "Tree's Best Pal Returns to Earth," Lafayette, Indiana *Journal and Courier* 19 December 1999, A3.

[42] Raymond Duvall and Michael Stohl, "Governance by Terror," in Stohl, *The Politics of Terrorism*, 181.

SELECTED BIBLIOGRAPHY

Articles

"An Interview with Bert Carona," *Western Journal of Speech Communication* 44 (Summer 1980): 214–220.

"An Interview with Jose Angel Gutierrez," *Western Journal of Speech Communication* 44 (Summer 1980): 202–213.

Abbott, Don. "Ian Paisley: Evangelism and Confrontation in Northern Ireland," *Today's Speech* 21 (Fall 1973): 49–55.

Anderson, Judith. "Sexual Politics: Chauvinism and Backlash?" *Today's Speech* 21 (Fall 1973): 11–16.

Andrews, James R. "The Ethos of Pacifism: The Problem of Image in the Early British Peace Movement," *Quarterly Journal of Speech* 53 (February 1967): 28–33.

———. "Piety and Pragmatism: Rhetorical Aspects of the Early British Peace Movement," *Speech Monographs* 34 (November 1967): 423–436.

———. "Confrontation at Columbia: A Case Study in Coercive Rhetoric," *Quarterly Journal of Speech* 55 (February 1969): 9–16.

———. "The Rhetoric of Coercion and Persuasion: The Reform Bill of 1832," *Quarterly Journal of Speech* 56 (April 1970): 187–195.

———. "Reflections of the National Character in American Rhetoric," *Quarterly Journal of Speech* 57 (October, 1971): 316–324.

———. "The Passionate Negation: The Chartist Movement in Rhetorical Perspective," *Quarterly Journal of Speech* 59 (April 1973): 196–208.

———. "Spindles vs. Acres: Rhetorical Perceptions on the British Free Trade Movement," *Western Speech* 38 (Winter 1974): 41–52.

———. "History and Theory in the Study of the Rhetoric of Social Movements," *Central States Speech Journal* 31 (Winter 1980): 274–281.

———. "An Historical Perspective on the Study of Social Movements," *Central States Speech Journal* 34 (Spring 1983): 67–69.

Appel, Edward C. "The Rhetoric of Dr. Martin Luther King, Jr.: Comedy and Context in Tragic Collision," *Western Journal of Communication* 61 (Fall 1997): 376–402.

Armada, Bernard J. "Memorial Agon: An Interpretive Tour of the National Civil Rights Museum," *Southern Communication Journal* 63 (Spring 1998): 235–243.

Bacon, Jacqueline. "Taking Liberty, Taking Literacy: Signifying the Rhetoric of African-American Abolitionists," *Southern Communication Journal* 64 (Summer 1999): 271–287.

Banninga, Jerald L. "John Quincy Adams on the Right of a Slave to Petition Congress," *Southern Speech Communication Journal* (Winter 1972): 151–163.

Baskerville, Barnet. "The Cross and the Flag: Evangelists of the Far Right," *Western Speech* 27 (Fall 1963): 197–206.

Benson, Thomas W. "Rhetoric and Autobiography: The Case of Malcolm X," *Quarterly Journal of Speech* 60 (February 1974): 1–13.

Benson, Thomas W., and Bonnie Johnson. "The Rhetoric of Resistance: Confrontation with the Warmakers, Washington, DC, October 1967," *Today's Speech* 16 (September 1968): 35–42.

Betz, Brian R. "Eric Fromm and the Rhetoric of Prophecy," *Central States Speech Journal* 26 (Winter 1975): 310–315.

Bezayiff, David. "Legal Oratory of John Adams: An Early Instrument of Protest," *Western Journal of Speech Communication* 40 (Winter 1976): 63–71.

Black, Edwin. "Secrecy and Disclosure as Rhetorical Forms," *Quarterly Journal of Speech* 74 (May 1988): 133–150.

Bloodworth, John D. "Communication in the Youth Counter Culture: Music as Expression," *Central States Speech Journal* 26 (Winter 1975): 304–309.

Bormann, Ernest G. "Fantasy and Rhetorical Vision: The Rhetorical Criticism of Social Reality," *Quarterly Journal of Speech* 58 (December 1972): 396–407.

———. "Fetching Good Out of Evil: A Rhetorical Use of Calamity," *Quarterly Journal of Speech* 63 (April 1977): 130–139.

———. "Some Random Thoughts on the Unity or Diversity of the Rhetoric of Abolition," *Southern Communication Journal* 60 (Spring 1995): 266–274.

Bosmajian, Haig A. "The Nazi Speaker's Rhetoric," *Quarterly Journal of Speech* 46 (December 1960): 365–371.

———. "Nazi Meetings: The *Sprechabend*, the *Versaamlung*, the *Kundgebung*, the *Feierstunde*," *Southern Speech Journal* 31 (Summer 1966): 324–337.

———. "The Persuasiveness of Nazi Marching and *Der Kampf um Die Strasse*," *Today's Speech* 16 (November 1968): 17–22.

———. "'Speech' and the First Amendment," *Today's Speech* 18 (Fall 1970): 3–11.

———. "Obscenity and Protest," *Today's Speech* 18 (Winter 1970): 9–14.

———. "Freedom of Speech and the Heckler," *Western Speech* 36 (Fall 1972): 218–232.

———. "Defining the 'American Indian': A Case Study in the Language of Suppression," *Speech Teacher* 22 (March 1973): 89–99.

———. "The Abrogation of the Suffragists' First Amendment Rights," *Western Speech* 38 (Fall 1974): 218–232.

———. "The Sources and Nature of Adolf Hitler's Technique of Persuasion," *Central States Speech Journal* 25 (Winter 1974): 240–248.

———. "Freedom of Speech and the Language of Oppression," *Western Journal of Speech Communication* 42 (Fall 1978): 209–221.

Bowen, Harry W. "Does Non-Violence Persuade?" *Today's Speech* 11 (April 1963): 10–11, 31.

———. "The Future of Non-Violence," *Today's Speech* 11 (September 1963): 3–4.

———. "A Realistic View of Non-Violent Assumptions," *Today's Speech* 15 (September 1967): 9–10.

Branham, Robert James. "Speaking Itself: Susan Sontag's Town Hall Address," *Quarterly Journal of Speech* 75 (August 1989): 259–276.

———. "The Role of the Convert in *Eclipse of Reason* and *The Silent Scream*," *Quarterly Journal of Speech* 77 (November 1991): 407–426.

Brinson, Susan L. "The Myth of White Superiority in *Mississippi Burning*," *Southern Communication Journal* 60(Spring 1995): 211–221.

Brock, Bernard L. "A Special report on Social Movement Theory and Research: Editor's Commentary," *Central States Speech Journal* 34 (Spring 1983): 80–82.

Brock, Bernard L., and Sharon Howell, "The Evolution of the PLO: A Rhetoric of Terrorism," *Central States Speech Journal* 39 (Fall/Winter, 1988): 281–292.

Brockreide, Wayne E. and Robert L. Scott. "Stokely Carmichael: Two Speeches on Black Power," *Central States Speech Journal* 19 (Spring 1968): 3–13.

Brommel, Bernard J. "The Pacifist Speechmaking of Eugene V. Debs," *Quarterly Journal of Speech* 52 (April 1966): 146–154.

———. "Eugene V. Debs: The Agitator as Speaker," *Central States Speech Journal* 20 (Fall 1969): 202–214.

Brooks, Robert D. "Black Power: The Dimensions of a Slogan," *Western Speech* 34 (Spring 1970): 108–114.

Brown, William J. "The Persuasive Appeal of Mediated Terrorism: The Case of the TWA Flight 847 Hijacking," *Western Journal of Speech Communication* 54 (Spring 1990): 219–236.

Browne, Stephen H. "Encountering Angelina Grimke: Violence, Identity, and the Creation of Radical Community," *Quarterly Journal of Speech* 82 (February 1996): 55–73.

———. "Textual Style and Radical Critique in William Lloyd Garrison's *Thoughts on African Colonization*," *Communication Studies* 47 (Fall 1996): 177–190.

———. "Remembering Crispus Attucks: Race, Rhetoric, and the Politics of Commemoration," *Quarterly Journal of Speech* 85 (May 1999): 169–187.

Burgchardt, Carl R. "Two Faces of American Communism: Pamphlet Rhetoric of the Third Period and the Popular Front," *Quarterly Journal of Speech* 66 (December 1980): 375–391.

Burgess, Parke G. "The Rhetoric of Black Power: A Moral Demand," *Quarterly Journal of Speech* 54 (April 1968): 122–133.

———. "The Rhetoric of Moral Conflict: Two Critical Dimensions," *The Quarterly Journal of Speech* 56 (April 1970): 120–130.

———. "Crisis Rhetoric: Coercion vs. Force, *Quarterly Journal of Speech* 59 (February 1973): 61–73.

Burgoon, Michael. "A Factor-Analytic Examination of Messages Advocating Social Change," *Speech Monographs* 39 (November, 1972): 290–295.

Burkholder, Thomas R. "Kansas Populism, Woman Suffrage, and the Agrarian Myth: A Case Study in the Limits of Mythic Transcendence," *Communication Studies* 40 (Winter 1989): 292–307.

Bytwerk, Randall L. "Rhetorical Aspects of the Nazi Meeting: 1926-1933," *Quarterly Journal of Speech* 6l (October 1975): 307–318.

Campbell, Finley C. "Voices of Thunder, Voices of Rage: A Symbolic Analysis of a Selection from Malcolm X's Speech 'Message to the Grass Roots'," *Speech Teacher* 19 (March 1970): 101–110.

Campbell, Karlyn Kohrs. "The Rhetoric of Radical Black Nationalism: A Case Study in Self-Conscious Criticism," *Central States Speech Journal* 22 (Fall 1971): 151–160.

———. "The Rhetoric of Women's Liberation: An Oxymoron," *Quarterly Journal of Speech* 59 (February 1973): 74–86.

———. "Femininity and Feminism: To Be or Not To Be a Woman," *Communication Quarterly* 31 (Spring 1983): 101–108.

———. "Style and Content in the Rhetoric of Early Afro-American Feminists," *Quarterly Journal of Speech* 72 (November 1986): 434–445.

———. "'The Rhetoric of Women's Liberation: An Oxymoron' Revisited," *Communication Studies* 50 (Summer 1999): 138–142.

Carcasson, Martin and Mitchell F. Rice. "The Promise and Failure of President Clinton's Race Initiative of 1997–1998: A Rhetorical Perspective," *Rhetoric and Public Affairs* 2 (Summer 1999): 243–274.

Carlson, A. Cheree. "Gandhi and the Comic Frame: 'Ad Bellum Purificandum'," *Quarterly Journal of Speech* 72 (November 1986): 446–455.

———. "Albert J. Beveridge as Imperialist and Progressive: The Means Justify the End," *Western Journal of Speech Communication* 52 (Winter 1988): 46–62.

———. "The Rhetoric of the Know-Nothing Party: Nativism as a Response to the Rhetorical Situation," *Southern Communication Journal* 54 (Summer 1989): 364–383.

———. "Creative Casuistry and Feminist Consciousness: A Rhetoric of Moral Reform," *Quarterly Journal of Speech* 78 (February 1992): 16–32.

———. "Defining Womanhood: Lucretia Coffin Mott and the Transforming of Feminity," *Western Journal of Communication* 58 (Spring 1994): 85–97.

Carson, Herbert L. "An Eccentric Kinship: Henry David Thoreau's 'A Plea for Captain John Brown'," *Southern Speech Journal* 27 (Winter 1961): 151–166.

Carter, David A. "The Industrial Workers of the World and the Rhetoric of Song," *Quarterly Journal of Speech* 66 (December 1980): 365–374.

Cathcart, Robert S. "New Approaches to the Study of Movements: Defining Movements Rhetorically," *Western Speech* 36 (Spring 1972): 82–88.

———. "Movements: Confrontation as Rhetorical Form," *Southern Speech Communication Journal* 43 (Spring 1978): 233–247.

———. "Defining Social Movements by Their Rhetorical Form," *Central States Speech Journal* 31 (Winter 1980): 267–273.

———. "A Confrontation Perspective on the Study of Social Movements," *Central States Speech Journal* 34 (Spring 1983): 69–74.

Chapel, Cage William. "Christian Science and the Nineteenth Century Woman's Movement," *Central States Speech Journal* 26 (Summer 1975): 142–149.

Charland, Maurice. "Constitutive Rhetoric: The Case of the *Peuple Quebecois*," *Quarterly Journal of Speech* 73 (May 1987): 133–150.

Chesebro, James W. "Rhetorical Strategies of the Radical Revolutionary," *Today's Speech* 20 (Winter 1972): 37–48.

———. "Cultures in Conflict: A Generic and Axiological View," *Today's Speech* 21 (Spring 1973): 11–20.

Chesebro, James W., John F. Cragan, and Patricia McCullough. "The Small Group Technique of the Radical Revolutionary: A Synthetic Study of Consciousness Raising," *Speech Monographs* 40 (June 1973): 136–146.

Christiansen, Adrienne E. and Jeremy J. Hanson, "Comedy as Cure for Tragedy: ACT UP and the Rhetoric of AIDS," *Quarterly Journal of Speech* 82 (May 1996): 157–170.

Clark, Thomas D. "Rhetorical Image-Making: A Case Study of the Thomas Paine-William Smith Propaganda Debates," *Southern Speech Communication Journal* 40 (Spring 1975): 248–261.

———. "Rhetoric, Reality, and Rationalization: A Study of the Masking Function of Rhetoric in the London Theosophical Movement," *Communication Quarterly* 26 (Fall 1978): 24–30.

Cloud, Dana L. "The Null Persona: Race and the Rhetoric of Silence in the Uprising of '34," *Rhetoric and Public Affairs* 2 (Summer 1999): 177–210.

Condit, Celeste Michelle. "The Functions of Epideictic: The Boston Massacre Orations as Exemplar," *Communication Quarterly* 33 (Fall 1985): 284–299.

———. "Crafting Virtue: The Rhetorical Construction of Public Morality," *Quarterly Journal of Speech* 73 (February 1987): 79–97.

———. "Democracy and Civil Rights: The Universalizing Influence of Public Argumentation," *Communication Monographs* 54 (March 1987): 1–18.

Condit, Celeste Michelle, and John Louis Lucaites, "The Rhetoric of Equality and the Expatriation of African-Americans, 1776–1826," *Communication Studies* 42 (Spring 1991): 1–21.

Conrad, Charles. "The Transformation of the 'Old Feminist' Movement," *Quarterly Journal of Speech* 67 (August 1981): 284–297.

———. "The Rhetoric of the Moral Majority: An Analysis of Romantic Form," *Quarterly Journal of Speech* 69 (May 1983): 159–170.

Corbett, Edward P. J. "The Rhetoric of the Open Hand and the Rhetoric of the Closed Fist," *College Composition and Communication* 20 (December 1969): 288–296.

Coughlin, Elizabeth M., and Charles E. Coughlin. "Convention in Petticoats: The Seneca Falls Declaration of Women's Rights," *Today's Speech* 21 (Fall 1973): 17–23.

Cox, J. Robert. "The Rhetoric of Child Labor Reform: An Efficacy-Utility Analysis," *Quarterly Journal of Speech* 60 (October 1974): 359–370.

———. "Perspectives on Rhetorical Criticism of Movements: Antiwar Dissent, 1964–1970," *Western Speech* 38 (Fall 1974): 254–268.

Crandell, S. Judson. "The Beginnings of a Methodology for Social Control Studies in Public Address," *Quarterly Journal of Speech* 33 (February 1947): 36–39.

Crenshaw, Carrie and David R. Roskos-Ewoldsen, "Rhetoric, Racist Ideology, and Intellectual Leadership," *Rhetoric and Public Affairs* 2 (Summer 1999): 275–302.

Crocker, James W. "A Rhetoric of Encounter Following the May 4th, 1970, Disturbances at Kent State University," *Communication Quarterly* 25 (Fall 1977): 47–56.

Cuklanz, Lisa M. "'Shrill Squawk' or Strategic Innovation: A Rhetorical Reassessment of Margaret Sanger's *Woman Rebel*," *Communication Quarterly* 43 (Winter 1995): 1–19.

Cusella, Louis P. "Real-Fiction Versus Historical Reality: Rhetorical Purification in 'Kent State'—The Docudrama," *Communication Quarterly* 30 (Summer 1982): 159–164.

Darsey, James. "The Legend of Eugene V. Debs: Prophetic Ethos as Radical Argument," *Quarterly Journal of Speech* 74 (November 1988): 434–452.

———. "From 'Gay Is Good' to the Scourge of AIDS: The Evolution of Gay Liberation Rhetoric, 1977–1990," *Communication Studies* 42 (Spring 1991): 43–66.

Dees, Diane. "Bernadette Devlin's Maiden Speech: A Rhetoric of Sacrifice," *Southern Speech Communication Journal* 38 (Summer 1973): 326–339.

Delgado, Fernando Pedro, "Chicano Movement Rhetoric: An Ideological Interpretation," *Communication Quarterly* 43 (Fall 1995): 446–455.

———. "Chicano Ideology Revisited: Rap Music and the (Re)articulation of Chicanismo," *Western Journal of Communication* 62 (Spring 1998): 95–113.

———. "When the Silenced Speak: The Textualization and Complications of Latino Identity," *Western Journal of Communication* 62 (Fall 1998): 420–438.

Denton, Robert E. "The Rhetorical Functions of Slogans: Classifications and Characteristics," *Communication Quarterly* 28 (Spring 1980): 10–18.

Delia, Jesse G. "Rhetoric in the Nazi Mind: Hitler's Theory of Persuasion," *Southern Speech Communication Journal* 37 (Winter 1971): 136–149.

Dick, Robert C. "Negro Oratory in the Anti-Slavery Societies: 1830–1860," *Western Speech* 28 (Winter 1964): 5–14.

Dionisopoulos, George N.; Victoria J. Gallagher; Steven R. Goldzwig; and David Zarefsky. "Martin Luther King, the American Dream and Vietnam: A Collision of Rhetorical Trajectories," *Western Journal of Communication* 56 (Spring 1992): 91–107.

Doolittle, Robert J. "Riots as Symbolic: A Criticism and Approach," *Central States Speech Journal* 27 (Winter 1976): 310–317.

Dow, Bonnie J. "The 'Womanhood' Rationale in the Woman Suffrage Rhetoric of Frances E. Willard," *Southern Communication Journal* 56 (Summer 1991): 298

———. "AIDS, Perspective by Incongruity, and Gay Identity in Larry Kramer's '1112 and Counting'," *Communication Studies* 45 (Fall-Winter 1994): 225–240.

———. "Spectacle, Spectatorship, and Gender Anxiety in Television Coverage of the 1970 Women's Strike for Equality," *Communication Studies* 50 (Summer 1999): 143–157.

Duffy, Bernard K. "The Anti-Humanist Rhetoric of the New Religious Right," *Southern Speech Communication Journal* 49 (Summer 1984): 339–360.

Duncan, Rodger D. "Rhetoric of the Kidvid Movement: Ideology, Strategies, and Tactics," *Central States Speech Journal* 27 (Summer 1976): 129–135.

Edwards, Michael L. "A Resource Unit on Black Rhetoric," *Speech Teacher* 22 (September 1973): 183–188.

Eich, Ritch K. and Donald Goldmann. "Communication, Confrontation, and Coercion: Agitation at Michigan," *Central States Speech Journal* 27 (Summer 1976): 120–128.

Erickson, Keith V. "Black Messiah: The Father Divine Peace Mission Movement," *Quarterly Journal of Speech* 63 (December 1977): 428–438.

Erlich, Howard S. "Populist Rhetoric Reassessed: A Paradox," *Quarterly Journal of Speech* 63 (April 1977): 140–151.

Ferris, Maxine Schnitzer. "The Speaking of Roy Wilkins," *Central States Speech Journal* 16 (May 1965): 91–98.

Fishman, Donald. "Reform Judaism and the Anti-Zionist Persuasive Campaign, 1897–1915," *Communication Quarterly* (Fall 1998): 375–395.

Fletcher, Winona L. "Knight Errant or Screaming Eagle? E. L. Godkin's Criticism of Wendell Phillips," *Southern Speech Journal* 29 (Spring 1964): 214–223.

Flores, Lisa A. "Creative Discursive Space through a Rhetoric of Difference: Chicana Feminists Craft a Homeland," *Quarterly Journal of Speech* 82 (May 1996): 142–156.

Flynt, Wayne. "The Ethics of Democratic Persuasion and the Birmingham Crisis," *Southern Speech Journal* 35 (Fall 1969): 40–53.

Flynt, Wayne and William Warren Rogers. "Reform Oratory in Alabama, 1890–1896," *Southern Speech Journal* 29 (Winter 1963): 94–106.

Foss, Karen A. "Out from Underground: The Discourse of Emerging Fugitives," *Western Journal of Communication* 56 (Spring 1992): 125–142.

Frank, David A. "*Shalem Achschav* Rituals of the Israeli Peace Movement," *Communication Monographs* 48 (September 1981): 165–182.

Freeman, Sally A., Stephen Littlejohn, and W. Barnett Pearce. "Communication and Moral Conflict," *Western Journal of Communication* 56 (Fall 1992): 311–329.

Fulkerson, Gerald. "Exile as Emergence: Frederick Douglass in Great Britain, 1845–1847," *Quarterly Journal of Speech* 60 (February 1974): 69–82.

Fulkerson, Richard P. "The Public Letter as a Rhetorical Form: Structure, Logic, and Style in King's 'Letter from Birmingham Jail'," *Quarterly Journal of Speech* 65 (April 1979): 121–136.

Gallagher, Mary Brigid. "John L. Lewis: The Oratory of Pity and Indignation," *Today's Speech* 9 (September 1961): 15–16, 29.

Gallagher, Victoria J. "Memory and Reconciliation in the Birmingham Civil Rights Institute," *Rhetoric and Public Affairs* 2 (Summer 1999): 303–320.

Gilder, Eric. "The Process of Political *Praxis*: Efforts of the Gay Community to Transform the Social Significance of AIDS," *Communication Quarterly* 37 (Winter 1989): 27–38.

Gillespie, Patti P. "Feminist Theatre: A Rhetorical Phenomenon," *Quarterly Journal of Speech* 64 (October 1978): 284–294.

Glancy, Donald R. "Socialist with a Valet: Jack London's 'First, Last, and Only' Lecture Tour," *Quarterly Journal of Speech* 49 (February 1963): 31–39.

Goldzwig, Steven R. "A Rhetoric of Public Theology: The Religious Rhetor and Public Policy," *Southern Speech Communication Journal* 52 (Winter 1987): 128–150.

———. "A Social Movement Perspective on Demagoguery: Achieving Symbolic Realignment," *Communication Studies* 40 (Fall 1989): 202–228.

Goldzwig, Steven R., and Patricia A. Sullivan. "Narrative and Counternarrative in Print-mediated Coverage of Milwaukee Alderman Michael McGee," *Quarterly Journal of Speech* 86 (May 2000): 215-231.

Goodman, Richard J., and William I. Gorden. "The Rhetoric of Desecration," *Quarterly Journal of Speech* 57 (February 1971): 23–31.

Goodnight, G. Thomas and John Poluakos. "Conspiracy Rhetoric: From Pragmatism to Fantasy in Public Discourse," *Western Journal of Speech Communication* 45 (Fall 1981): 299–316.

Gravlee, G. Jack, and James R. Irvine. "Watts' Dissenting Rhetoric of Prayer," *Quarterly Journal of Speech* 59 (December 1973): 463–473.

Gregg, Richard B. "The Ego-Function of the Rhetoric of Protest, " *Philosophy and Rhetoric* 4 (Spring 1971): 71–91.

Gregg, Richard B., and A. Jackson McCormack. "'Whitey' Goes to the Ghetto: A Personal Chronicle of a Communication Experience with Black Youths," *Today's Speech* 16 (September 1968): 25–30.

Gregg, Richard B., A. Jackson McCormack; and Douglas J. Pederson. "The Rhetoric of Black Power: A Street-Level Interpretation," *Quarterly Journal of Speech* 55 (April 1969): 151–160.

Griffin, Charles J. G. "Jedidiah Morse and the Bavarian Illuminati: An Essay in the Rhetoric of Conspiracy," *Central States Speech Journal* 39 (Fall/Winter, 1988): 293–303.

———. "'Movement as Motive': Self Definition and Social Advocacy on Social Movement Autobiographies," *Western Journal of Communication* 64 (Spring 2000): 148–164.

Griffin, Cindy L. "A Web of Reasons: Mary Wollstonecraft's *A Vindication of the Rights of Woman* and the Re-Weaving of Form," *Communication Studies* 47 (Winter 1996): 272–288.

Griffin, Leland M. "The Rhetoric of Historical Movements," *Quarterly Journal of Speech* 38 (April 1951): 184–188.

———. "The Rhetorical Structure of the 'New Left' Movement: Part I," *Quarterly Journal of Speech* 50 (April 1964): 113–135.

———. "On Studying Social Movements," *Central States Speech Journal* 31 (Winter 1980): 225–232.

Gring-Pemble, Lisa M. "Writing Themselves into Consciousness: Creating a Rhetorical Bridge Between the Public and Private Spheres," *Quarterly Journal of Speech* 84 (February 1998): 44–61.

Gunter, Mary F. and James S. Taylor. "Loyalist Propaganda in the Sermons of Charles Inglis, 1717–780," *Western Speech* 37 (Winter 1973): 47–55.

Gustainis, J. Justin, and Dan F. Hahn, "While the Whole World Watched: Rhetorical Failures of Anti-War Protest," *Communication Quarterly* 36 (Summer 1988): 203–216.

Hagan, Martha. "The Antisuffragists' Rhetorical Dilemma: Reconciling the Private and Public Spheres," *Communication Reports* 5 (Summer 1992): 73–81.

Hagen, Michael R. "*Roe vs. Wade*: The Rhetoric of Fetal Life," *Central States Speech Journal* 27 (Fall 1976): 192–199.

Hahn, Dan F. "Social Movement Theory: A Dead End," *Communication Quarterly* 28 (Winter 1980): 60–64.

Hahn, Dan F., and Ruth M. Gonchar, "Studying Social Movements: A Rhetorical Methodology," *Speech Teacher* 20 (January 1971): 44–52.

Haiman, Franklyn S. "The Rhetoric of the Streets: Some Legal and Ethical Considerations," *Quarterly Journal of Speech* 53 (April 1967): 99–114.

———. "Nonverbal Communication and the First Amendment: The Rhetoric of the Streets Revisited," *Quarterly Journal of Speech* 68 (November 1982): 371–383.

Hammerback, John C. "The Rhetoric of Righteous Reform: George Washington Julian's 1852 Campaign against Slavery," *Central States Speech Journal* 22 (Summer 1971): 85–93.

———. "George W. Julian's Antislavery Campaign," *Western Speech* 37 (Summer 1973): 157–165.

———. "Jose Antonio's Rhetoric of Fascism," *Southern Communication Journal* 59 (Spring 1994): 181–195.

Hammerback, John C., and Richard J. Jensen. "The Rhetorical Worlds of Cesar Chavez and Reis Tijerina," *Western Journal of Speech Communication* 44 (Summer 1980): 166–176.

———. "Ethnic Heritage as Rhetorical Legacy: The Plan and Delano," *Quarterly Journal of Speech* 80 (February 1994): 53–70.

Hancock, Brenda Robinson. "Affirmation by Negation in the Women's Liberation Movement," *Quarterly Journal of Speech* 58 (October 1972): 264–271.

Hart, Roderick P. "The Rhetoric of the True Believer," *Speech Monographs* 38 (November 1971): 249–261.

Hasian, Marouf, Jr. "Understanding the Power of Conspiratorial Rhetoric: A Case Study of *The Protocols of the Elders of Zion*," *Communication Studies* 48 (Fall 1997): 195–214.

———. "Jurisprudence as Performance: John Brown's Enactment of Natural Law at Harper's Ferry," *Quarterly Journal of Speech* 86 (May 2000): 190–214.

Hayden, Sara. "Reversing the Discourse of Sexology: Margaret Higgins Sanger's *What Every Girl Should Know*," *Southern Communication Journal* 64 (Summer 1999): 288–306.

———. "Negotiating Feminity and Power in the Early Twentieth Century West: Domestic Ideology and Feminine Style in Jeannette Rankin's Suffrage Rhetoric," *Communication Studies* 50 (Summer 1999): 83–102.

Heath, Robert L. "Dialectical Confrontation: A Strategy of Black Radicalism," *Central States Speech Journal* 24 (Fall 1973): 168–177.

———. "Black Rhetoric: An Example of the Poverty of Values," *Southern Speech Communication Journal* 39 (Winter 1973): 145–160.

———. "Alexander Crummell and the Strategy of Challenge by Adaptation," *Central States Speech Journal* 26 (Fall 1975): 178–187.

Heisey, D. Ray, and J. David Trebing. "A Comparison of the Rhetorical Visions and Strategies of the Shah's White Revolution and the Ayatollah's Islamic Revolution," *Communication Monographs* 50 (June 1983): 158–174.

———. "Authority and Legitimacy: A Rhetorical Case Study of the Iranian Revolution," *Communication Monographs* 53 (December 1986): 295–310.

Henry, David. "Recalling the 1960s: The New Left and Social Movement Criticism," *Quarterly Journal of Speech* 75 (February 1989): 97–128.

Henry, David, and Richard J. Jensen. "Social Movement Criticism and the Renaissance of Public Address," *Communication Studies* 42 (Spring 1991): 83–93.

Hensley, Carl Wayne. "Rhetorical Vision and the Persuasion of a Historical Movement: The Disciples of Christ in Nineteenth Century American Culture, " *Quarterly Journal of Speech* 61 (October 1975): 250–264.

Hillbruner, Anthony. "Inequality, the Great Chain of Being, and Ante Bellum Southern Oratory," *Southern Speech Journal* 25 (Spring 1960): 172–189.

Hogan, J. Michael. "Wallace and the Wallacites: A Reexamination," *Southern Speech Communication Journal* 50 (Fall 1984): 24–48.

Hogan, J. Michael, and L. Glen Williams. "Defining 'the Enemy' in Revolutionary America: From the Rhetoric of Protest to the Rhetoric of War," *Southern Communication Journal* 61 (Summer 1996): 277–288.

———. "Republican Charisma and the American Revolution: The Textual Persona of Thomas Paine's *Common Sense*," *Quarterly Journal of Speech* 86 (February 2000): 1–18.

Hong, Nathaniel. "Constructing the Anarchist Beast in American Periodical Literature, 1880–1903," *Critical Studies of Mass Communication* 9 (March 1992): 110–130.

Hope, Diana Schaich. "Redefinition of Self: A Comparison of the Rhetoric of the Women's Liberation and the Black Liberation Movements," *Today's Speech* 23 (Winter 1975): 17–25.

Houck, Davis W. "'By Any Means Necessary': Re-Reading Malcolm X's Mecca Conversion," *Communication Studies* 44 (Fall 1993): 285–298.

Howe, Roger J. "The Rhetoric of the Death of God Theology," *Southern Speech Communication Journal* 37 (Winter 1971): 150–162.

Hunsaker, David M. "The Rhetoric of *Brown v. Board of Education*: Paradigm for Contemporary Social Protest," *Southern Speech Communication Journal* 43 (Winter 1978): 91–109.

Huxman, Susan Schultz. "Mary Wollstonecraft, Margaret Fuller, and Angelina Grimke: Symbolic Convergence and a Nascent Rhetorical Vision," *Communication Quarterly* 44 (Winter 1996): 16–28.

Hynes, Sandra S. "Dramatic Propaganda: Mercy Otis Warren's 'The Defeat,' 1773," *Today's Speech* 23 (Fall 1975): 21–27.

Ilkka, Richard J. "Rhetorical Dramatization in the Development of American Communism," *Quarterly Journal of Speech* 63 (December 1977): 413–427.

Jabusch, David M. "The Rhetoric of Civil Rights," *Western Speech* 30 (Summer 1966): 176–183.

Japp, Phyllis M. "Esther or Isaiah?: The Abolitionist-Feminist Rhetoric of Angelina Grimke," *Quarterly Journal of Speech* 71 (August 1985): 335–348.

Jefferson, Pat. "The Magnificent Barbarian in Nashville," *Southern Speech Journal* 33 (Winter 1967): 77–87.

———. "Stokely's 'Cool:' Style," *Today's Speech* 16 (September 1968): 19–24.

Jensen, J. Vernon. "British Voices on the Eve of the American Revolution: Trapped by the Family Metaphor," *Quarterly Journal of Speech* 63 (February 1977): 43–50.

Jensen, Richard J., and Cara J. Abeyta. "The Minority in the Middle: Asian-American Dissent in the 1960s and 1970s," *Western Journal of Speech Communication* 51 (Fall 1987): 402–416.

Jensen, Richard J., and John C. Hammerback. "'No Revolutions without Poets:' The Rhetoric of Rodolfo 'Corky' Gonzales," *Western Journal of Speech Communication* 46 (Winter 1982): 72–91.

———. "Radical Nationalism Among Chicanos: The Rhetoric of Jose Gutierrez," *Western Journal of Speech Communication* 44 (Summer 1980): 191–202.

———. "Feminists of Faith: Sonia Johnson and the Mormons for ERA," *Central States Speech Journal* 36 (Fall 1985): 123–137.

———. "From Muslim to Mormon: Eldridge Cleaver's Rhetorical Crusade," *Communication Quarterly* 34 (Winter 1986): 24–40.

———. "'Your Tools Are Really the People': The Rhetoric of Robert Parris Moses," *Communication Monographs* 65 (June 1998): 126–140.

Jensen, Richard J., and Allen Lichtenstein. "From Yippie to Yuppie: Jerry Rubin as Rhetorical Icon," *Southern Communication Journal* 60 (Summer 1995): 332–346.

Johannesen, Richard L. "The Ethics of Plagiarism Reconsidered: The Oratory of Martin Luther King, Jr.," *Southern Communication Journal* 60 (Spring 1995): 185–194.

Jorgensen-Earp, Cheryl R. "'Toys of Desperation': Suicide as Protest Rhetoric," The Southern Speech Communication Journal 53 (Fall 1987): 80-96.

Jurma, William E. "Moderate Movement Leadership and the Vietnam Moratorium Committee," *Quarterly Journal of Speech* 68 (August 1982): 262–272.

Kendall, Kathleen E., and Jeanne Y. Fisher. "Frances Wright on Women's Rights: Eloquence versus Ethos," *Quarterly Journal of Speech* 60 (February 1974): 58–68.

Kennicott, Patrick C. "Black Persuaders in the Antislavery Movement," *Speech Monographs* 37 (March 1970): 15–24.

Kennicott, Patrick C., and Wayne E. Page. "H. Rap Brown: The Cambridge Incident," *Quarterly Journal of Speech* 57 (October 1971): 325–334.

Killingsworth, M. Jimmie, and Jacqueline S. Palmer. "The Discourse of 'Environmentalist Hysteria," *Quarterly Journal of Speech* 81 (February 1995): 1–19.

King, Andrew A. "The Rhetorical Legacy of the Black Church," *Central States Speech Journal* 22 (Fall 1971): 179–185.

———. "The Rhetoric of Power Maintenance: Elites at the Precipice," *Quarterly Journal of Speech* 62 (April 1976): 127–134.

King, Andrew A., and Floyd D. Anderson. "Nixon, Agnew, and the 'Silent Majority': A Case Study in the Rhetoric of Polarization," *Western Speech* 35 (Fall 1971): 243–255.

King, Andrew A., and Kenneth Petress. "Universal Public Argument and the Failure of Nuclear Freeze," *Southern Communication Journal* 55 (Winter 1990): 162–174.

Klumpp, James F. "Challenge of Radical Rhetoric: Radicalism at Columbia," *Western Speech* 37 (Summer 1973): 146–156.

Knupp, Ralph E. "A Time for Every Purpose Under Heaven: Rhetorical Dimensions of Protest Music," *Southern Speech Communication Journal* 46 (Summer 1981): 377–389.

Kosokoff, Stephen, and Carl W. Carmichael. "The Rhetoric of Protest: Song, Speech, and Attitude Change," *Southern Speech Journal* 35 (Summer 1970): 295–302.

Kroll, Becky Swanson. "From Small Group to Public View: Mainstreaming the Women's Movement," *Communication Quarterly* 31 (Spring 1983): 139–147.

Kuypers, Jim A. "From Science, Moral-Poetics: Dr. James Dobson's Response to the Fetal Tissue Research Initiative," *Quarterly Journal of Speech* 86 (May 2000): 146–167.

Lake, Randall A. "Enacting Red Power: The Consummatory Function in Native American Protest Rhetoric," *Quarterly Journal of Speech* 69 (May 1983): 127–142.

———. "Order and Disorder in Anti-Abortion Rhetoric: A Logological View," *Quarterly Journal of Speech* 70 (November 1984): 425–443.

Lange, Jonathan I. "Refusal to Compromise: The Case of Earth First!" *Western Journal of Speech Communication* 54 (Fall 1990): 473–494.

———. "The Logic of Competing Information Campaigns: Conflict Over Old Growth and the Spotted Owl," *Communication Monographs* 60 (September 1993): 239–257.

Larson, Barbara A. "Samuel Davies and the Rhetoric of the New Light," *Speech Monographs* 38 (August 1971): 207–216.

Larson, Charles U. "The Trust Establishing Function of the Rhetoric of Black Power," *Central States Speech Journal* 21 (Spring 1970): 52–56.

Lawton, Cynthia Whalen. "Thoreau and the Rhetoric of Dissent," *Today's Speech* 16 (April 1968): 23–25.

Leathers, Dale G. "Fundamentalism of the Radical Right," *Southern Speech Journal* 33 (Summer 1968): 245–258.

Lee, Ronald E. "Moralizing and Ideologizing: An Analysis of Political Illocutions," *Western Journal of Speech Communication* 52 (Fall 1988): 291–307.

———. "The Rhetorical Construction of Time in Martin Luther King, Jr.'s 'Letter from Birmingham Jail'," *Southern Speech Communication Journal* 56 (Summer 1991): 279–288.

Lee, Ronald E., and James R. Andrews. "A Story of Rhetorical-Ideological Transformation: Eugene V. Debs as Liberal Hero," *Quarterly Journal of Speech* 77 (February 1991): 20–37.

Linkugel, Wil A. "The Speech Style of Anna Howard Shaw," *Central States Speech Journal* 13 (Spring 1962): 171–178.

———. "The Woman Suffrage Argument of Anna Howard Shaw," *Quarterly Journal of Speech* 49 (April 1963): 165–174.

———. "The Rhetoric of American Feminism: A Social Movement Course," *Speech Teacher* 23 (March 1974): 121–130.

Lippman, Monroe. "Uncle Tom and His Poor Relations: American Slavery Plays," *Southern Speech Journal* 28 (Spring 1963): 183–197.

Logue, Cal M., and Eugene E. Miller. "Communicative Interaction and Rhetorical Status in Harriet Ann Jacobs' Slave Narrative," *Southern Communication Journal* 63 (Spring 1998): 182–198.

Lomas, Charles W. "The Agitator in American Society," *Western Speech* 24 (Spring 1960): 76–83.

———. "Kearney and George: The Demagogue and the Prophet," *Speech Monographs* 28 (March 1961): 50–59.

———. "Agitator in a Cassock," *Western Speech* 27 (Winter 1963): 16–24.

Lucaites, John Louis, and Celeste Michelle Condit. "Reconstructing Equality: Culturetypal and Counter-Cultural Rhetorics in the Martyred Black Vision," *Communication Monographs* 57 (March 1990): 4–24.

Lucas, Stephen E. "Coming to Terms with Movement Studies," *Central States Speech Journal* 31 (Winter 1981): 255–266.

Makay, John J. "George C. Wallace: Southern Spokesman with a Northern Audience," *Central States Speech Journal* 19 (Fall 1968): 202–208.

Makay, John J., and Alberto Gonzalez. "Dylan's Biographical Rhetoric and the Myth of the Outlaw Hero," *Southern Speech Communication Journal* 52 (Winter 1987): 165–180.

Mann, Kenneth Eugene. "Nineteenth Century Black Militant: Henry Highland Garnet's Address to the Slaves," *Southern Speech Journal* 36 (Fall 1970): 11–21.

Mansfield, Dorothy M. "Abigail S. Duniway: Suffragette with Not-so-common Sense," *Western Speech* 35 (Winter 1971): 24–29.

Martin, Howard H. "The Rhetoric of Academic Protest," *Central States Speech Journal* 17 (November 1966): 244–250.

Martin, Kathryn. "The Relationship of Theatre of Revolution and Theology of Revolution to the Black Experience," *Today's Speech* 19 (Spring 1971): 35–41.

Mattina, Anna F. "'Rights as Well as Duties': The Rhetoric of Leonora O'Reilly," *Communication Quarterly* 42 (Spring 1994): 196–205.

McClearey, Kevin E. "'A Tremendous Awakening': Margaret H. Sanger's Speech at Fabian Hall," *Western Journal of Communication* 58 (Summer 1994): 182–200.

McDorman, Todd F. "Challenging Constitutional Authority: African American Responses to *Scott v. Sandford*," *Quarterly Journal of Speech* 83 (May 1997): 192–209.

McEdwards, Mary G. "Agitative Rhetoric: Its Nature and Effect," *Western Speech* 32 (Winter 1968): 36–43.

McGaffey, Ruth. "Group Libel Revised," *Quarterly Journal of Speech* 65 (April 1979): 157–170.

McGee, Brian R. "Speaking About the Other: W.E.B. DuBois Responds to the Klan," *Southern Communication Journal* 63 (Spring 1998): 208–219.

———. "Thomas Dixon's The Clansman: Radicals, Reactionaries, and the Anticipated Utopia," *Southern Communication Journal* 65 (Summer 2000): 300–317.

McGee, Michael C. "In Search of 'The People': A Rhetorical Alternative," *Quarterly Journal of Speech* 61 (October 1975): 235–249.

———. "'Social Movement': Phenomenon or Meaning," *Central States Speech Journal* 31 (Winter 1980): 233–244.

———. "Social Movement as Meaning," *Central States Speech Journal* 34 (Spring 1983): 74–77.

McGee, Michael C., and Martha A. Martin. "Public Knowledge and Ideological Argumentation," *Communication Monographs* 50 (March 1983): 45–65.

McGuire, Michael. "Mythic Rhetoric in Mein Kampf. A Structuralist Critique," *Quarterly Journal of Speech* 63 (February 1977): 1–13.

McKerrow, Raymie E. "Antimasonic Rhetoric: The Strategy of Excommunication," *Communication Quarterly* 37 (Fall 1989): 276–290.

McPhail, Mark Lawrence. "Passionate Intensity: Louis Farrakhan and the Fallacies of Racial Reasoning," *Quarterly Journal of Speech* 84 (November 1998): 416–429.

McPherson, Louise. "Communication Techniques of the Women's Liberation Front," *Today's Speech* 21 (Spring 1973): 33–38.

Mechling, Elizabeth W., and Gale Auletta. "Beyond War: A Socio-Rhetorical Analysis of a New Class Revitalization Movement," *Western Journal of Speech Communication* 50 (Fall 1986): 388–404.

Mechling, Elizabeth W., and Jay Mechling. "Hot Pacifism and Cold War: The American Friends Service Committee's Witness for Peace in 1950s America," *Quarterly Journal of Speech* 78 (May 1992): 173–196.

———. "The Jung and the Restless: The Mythopoetic Men's Movement," *Southern Communication Journal* 59 (Winter 1994): 97–111.

Medhurst, Martin J. "The Sword of Division: A Reply to Brummett and Warnick," *Western Journal of Speech Communication* 46 (Fall 1982): 383–390.

———. "The First Amendment vs. Human Rights: A Case Study in Human Sentiment and Argument from Definition," *Western Journal of Speech Communication* 46 (Winter 1982): 1–19.

———. "Resistance, Conservatism, and Theory Building: A Cautionary Note," *Western Journal of Speech Communication* 49 (Spring 1985): 103–115.

Mele, Joseph C. "Edward Douglas White's Influence on the Louisiana Anti-Lottery Movement," *Southern Speech Journal* 28 (Fall 1962): 36–43.

Merriam, Allen H. "Symbolic Action in India: Gandhi's Nonverbal Persuasion," *Quarterly Journal of Speech* 61 (October 1975): 290–306.

Miller, Jackson B. "'Indians,' 'Braves,' and 'Redskins': A Performative Struggle for Control of an Image," *Quarterly Journal of Speech* 85 (May 1999): 188–202.

Miller, Keith D., and Kevin Quashie. "Slave Mutiny as Argument, Argument as Fiction, Fiction as America: The Case of Frederick Douglass's *The Hero Slave*," *Southern Communication Journal* 63 (Spring 1998): 199–207.

Mixon, Harold D. "Boston's Artillery Election Sermons and the American Revolution," *Speech Monographs* 34 (March 1967): 43–50.

Monsma, John W., Jr. "John Brown: The Two Edged Sword of Abolition," *Central States Speech Journal* 13 (Autumn 1961): 22–29.

Morris, Richard. "Educating Savages," *Quarterly Journal of Speech* 83 (May 1997): 152–171.

Morris, Richard, and Philip Wander. "Native American Rhetoric: Dancing in the Shadows of the Ghost Dance," *Quarterly Journal of Speech* 76 (May 1990): 164–191.

Murphy, John M. "Domesticating Dissent: The Kennedys and the Freedom Rides," *Communication Monographs* 59 (March 1992): 61–78.

———. "Epideictic and Deliberative Strategies in Opposition to War: The Paradox of Honor and Expediency," *Communication Studies* 43 (Summer 1992): 65–78.

Nelson, Elizabeth, Jean. "'Nothing Ever Goes Well Enough': Mussolini and the Rhetoric of Perpetual Struggle,' *Communication Studies* 42 (Spring, 1991): 22–42.

Nelson, Jeffrey, and Mary Ann Flannery. "The Sanctuary Movement: A Study in Religious Confrontation," *Southern Communication Journal* 55 (Summer 1990): 372–387.

Newsom, Lionel, and William Gorden. "A Stormy Rally in Atlanta," *Today's Speech* 11 (April 1963): 18–21.

O'Brien, Harold J. "Slavery Sentiments that Led to War," *Today's Speech* 9 (November 1961): 5–7.

Olson, Kathryn M., and G. Thomas Goodnight. "Entanglements of Consumption, Cruelty, Privacy, and Fashion: The Social Controversy Over Fur," *Quarterly Journal of Speech* 80 (August 1994): 249–276.

Orban, Donald K. "Billy James Hargis: Auctioneer of Political Evangelism," *Central States Speech Journal* 20 (Summer 1969): 83–91.

Osborn, Michael, and John Bakke. "The Melodrama of Memphis: Contending Narratives During the Sanitation Strike of 1968," *Southern Communication Journal* 63 (Spring 1998): 220–234.

Panetta, Edward M., and Marouf Hasian, Jr. "Anti-Rhetoric as Rhetoric: The Law and Economics Movement," *Communication Quarterly* 42 (Winter 1994): 57–74.

Patton, John H. "Rhetoric at Catonsville: Daniel Berrigan, Conscience and Image Alteration," *Today's Speech* 23 (Winter 1975): 3–12.

Pauley, Garth E. "John Lewis's 'Serious Revolution': Rhetoric, Resistance, and Revision at the March on Washington," *Quarterly Journal of Speech* 84 (August 1998): 320–340.

———. "Harry Truman and the NAACP: A Case Study in Presidential Persuasion on Civil Rights," *Rhetoric and Public Affairs* 2 (Summer 1999): 211–242.

Pearce, Kimber Charles. "The Radical Feminist Manifesto as Generic Appropriation: Gender, Genre, and the Second Wave Resistance," *Southern Communication Journal* 64 (Summer 1999): 307–315.

Pearce, W. Barnett, Stephen W. Littlejohn, and Alison Alexander. "The New Christian Right and the Humanist Response: Reciprocated Diatribe," *Communication Quarterly* 35 (Spring 1987): 171–192.

Pearson, Kyra. "Mapping Rhetorical Interventions in 'National' Feminist Histories: Second Wave Feminism and *Ain't I a Woman*," *Communication Studies* 50 (Summer 1999): 158–173.

Perkins, Sally J. "The Rhetoric of Androgyny as Revealed in *The Feminine Mystique*," *Communication Studies* 40 (Summer 1989): 69–80.

Perse, Elizabeth M., Douglas M. McLeod, Nancy Signorielli, and Juliet Dee. "News Coverage of Abortion Between *Roe* and *Webster*: Public Opinion and Real World Events," *Communication Research Reports* 14 (Winter 1997): 97–105.

Phifer, Elizabeth F., and Dencil R. Taylor. "Carmichael in Tallahassee," *Southern Speech Journal* 33 (Winter 1967): 88–92.

Pollock, Arthur. "Stokely Carmichael's New Black Rhetoric," *Southern Speech Journal* 37 (Fall 1971): 92–94.

Powell, Kimberly A. "The Association of Southern Women for Prevention of Lynching: Strategies of a Movement in the Comic Frame," *Communication Quarterly* 43 (Winter 1995): 86–99.

Powers, Lloyd D. "Chicano Rhetoric: Some Basic Concepts," *Southern Speech Journal* 38 (Summer 1973): 340–346.

Press, Andrea L. "The Impact of Television on Modes of Reasoning about Abortion," *Critical Studies of Mass Communication* 8 (December 1991): 421–441.

Railsback, Celeste Condit. "The Contemporary American Abortion Controversy: Stages in the Argument," *Quarterly Journal of Speech* 70 (November 1984): 410–424.

Ramsey, E. Michele. "Inventing Citizens During World War I: Suffrage Cartoons in The *Woman Citizen*," *Western Journal of Communication* 64 (Spring 2000): 113–147.

Reed, Robert Michael. "The Case of Missionary Smith: A Crucial Incident in the Rhetoric of the British Anti-Slavery Movement," *Central States Speech Journal* 29 (Spring 1978): 61–71.

Reynolds, Beatrice K. "Mao Tse-Tung: Rhetoric of a Revolutionary," *Central States Speech Journal* 27 (Fall 1976): 212–217.

Riach, W. A. D. "'Telling It Like It Is': An Examination of Black Theatre as Rhetoric," *Quarterly Journal of Speech* 56 (April 1970): 179–186.

Rice, George P., Jr. "Freedom of Speech and the 'New Left'," *Central States Speech Journal* 21 (Fall 1970): 139–145.

Richardson, Larry S. "Stokely Carmichael: Jazz Artist," *Western Speech* 34 (Summer 1970): 212–218.

Riches, Suzanne V., and Malcolm O. Sillars. "The Status of Movement Criticism," *Western Journal of Speech Communication* 44 (Fall 1980): 275–287.

Rigsby, Enrique D. "African American Rhetoric and the 'Profession'," *Western Journal of Communication* 57 (Spring 1993): 191–199.

Ritchie, Gladys. "The Sit-In: A Rhetoric of Human Action," *Today's Speech* 18 (Winter 1970): 22–25.

Ritter, Ellen M. "Elizabeth Morgan: Pioneer Female Labor Agitator," *Central States Speech Journal* 22 (Winter 1971): 242–251.

Ritter, Kurt W. "Confrontation as Moral Drama: The Boston Massacre in Rhetorical Perspective," *Southern Speech Communication Journal* 42 (Winter 1977): 114–136.

Rogers, Richard S. "The Rhetoric of Militant Deism," *Quarterly Journal of Speech* 54 (October 1968): 247–251.

Rosenfeld, Lawrence B. "The Confrontation Politics of S. I. Hayakawa: A Case Study in Coercive Semantics," *Today's Speech* 18 (Spring 1970): 18–22.

Rosenwasser, Marie J. "Rhetoric and the Progress of the Women's Liberation Movement," *Today's Speech* 20 (Summer 1972): 45–56.

Rossiter, Charles M. and Ruth McGaffey. "Freedom of Speech and the 'New Left': A Response," *Central States Speech Journal* 22 (Spring 1971): 5–10.

Rosteck, Thomas. "Irony, Argument, and Reportage in Television Documentary: *See It Now* Versus Senator McCarthy," *Quarterly Journal of Speech* 75 (August 1989): 277–298.

———. Narrative in Martin Luther King's *I've Been to the Mountain Top*," *Southern Communication Journal* 58 (Fall 1992): 22–31.

Rothman, Richard. "On the Speaking of John L. Lewis," *Central States Speech Journal* 14 (August 1963): 177–185.

Rothwell, J. Dan. "Verbal Obscenity: Time for Second Thoughts," *Western Speech* 35 (Fall 1971): 231–242.

Rude, Leslie G. "The Rhetoric of Farmer Labor Agitators," *Central States Speech Journal* 20 (Winter 1969): 280–285.

Salvador, Michael. "The Rhetorical Subversion of Cultural Boundaries: The National Consumer's League," *Southern Communication Journal* 59 (Summer 1994): 318–332.

Sanchez, John, and Mary E. Stuckey. "Communicating Culture Through Leadership: One View from Indian Country," *Communication Studies* 50 (Summer 1999): 103–115.

Sanger, Kerran L. "Slave Resistance and Rhetorical Self-Definition: Spirituals as a Strategy," *Western Journal of Communication* 59 (Summer 1995): 177–192.

Scott, Robert L. "Justifying Violence—The Rhetoric of Militant Black Power," *Central States Speech Journal* 19 (Summer 1968): 96–104.

———. "The Conservative Voice in Radical Rhetoric: A Common Response to Division," *Speech Monographs* 40 (June 1973): 123–135.

Scott, Robert L., and Donald K. Smith. "The Rhetoric of Confrontation," *Quarterly Journal of Speech* 55 (February 1969): 1–8.

Sedano, Michael Victor. "Chicanismo: A Rhetorical Analysis of Themes and Images of Selected Poetry from the Chicano Movement," *Western Journal of Speech Communication* 44 (Summer 1980): 177–190.

Seibold, David. "Jewish Defense League: The Rhetoric of Resistance," *Today's Speech* 21 (Fall 1973): 39–48.

Shafer, George. "The Dramaturgy of Fact: The Treatment of History in Two Anti-War Plays," *Central States Speech Journal* 29 (Spring 1978): 25–35.

Shepler, Sherry R., and Anne F. Mattina, "'The Revolt Against War': Jane Adams' Rhetorical Challenge to the Patriarchy," *Communication Quarterly* 47 (Spring 1999): 151–165.

Short, Brant. "Earth First! and the Rhetoric of Moral Confrontation," *Communication Studies* 42 (Summer 1991): 172–188.

Sillars, Malcolm O. "The Rhetoric of the Petition in Boots," *Speech Monographs* 39 (June 1972): 92–104.

———. "Defining Movement Rhetorically: Casting the Widest Net," *Southern Speech Communication Journal* 46 (Fall 1980): 17–32.

Silvestri, Vito N. "Emma Goldman, Enduring Voice of Anarchism," *Today's Speech* 17 (September 1969): 20–25.

Simons, Herbert W. "Patterns of Persuasion in the Civil Rights Movement," *Today's Speech* 15 (February 1967): 25–27.

———. "Confrontation as a Pattern of Persuasion in University Settings," *Central States Speech Journal* 20 (Fall 1969): 163–169.

———. "Requirements, Problems, and Strategies: A Theory of Persuasion for Social Movements," *Quarterly Journal of Speech* 56 (February 1970): 1–11.

———. "Persuasion in Social Conflicts: A Critique of Prevailing Conceptions and a Framework for Future Research," *Speech Monographs* 39 (November 1972): 227–247.

———. "Changing Notions about Social Movements," *Quarterly Journal of Speech* 62 (December 1976), 425–430.

———. "On Terms, Definitions and Theoretical Distinctiveness: Comments on Papers by McGee and Zarefsky," *Central States Speech Journal* 31 (Winter 1980): 306–315.

———. "Genres, Rules, and Collective Rhetorics: Applying the Requirements-Problems Strategies Approach," *Communication Quarterly* 30 (Summer 1982): 181–188.

———. "On the Rhetoric of Social Movements, Historical Movements, and 'Top Down' Movements: A Commentary," *Communication Studies* 42 (Spring 1991): 94–101.

Simons, Herbert W., James W. Chesebro, and C. Jack Orr, "A Movement Perspective on the 1972 Presidential Campaign, " *Quarterly Journal of Speech* 59 (April 1973): 168–179.

Simpson, Tessa, and Stephen King. "The Sanctuary Movement: Criminal Trials and Religious Dissent," *Journal of Communication and Religion* 15 (March 1992): 15–28.

Sklar, Alissa. "Contested Collectives: The Struggle to Find the 'We' in the 1995 Quebec Referendum," *Southern Communication Journal* 64 (Winter 1999): 106–122.

Smiley, Sam. "Peace on Earth: Four Anti-War Dramas of the Thirties," *Central States Speech Journal* 21 (Spring 1970): 30–39.

Smith, Arthur L. "Henry Highland Garnet: Black Revolutionary in Sheep's Vestments," *Central States Speech Journal* 21 (Summer 1970): 93–98.

Smith, Craig Allen. "The Hofstadter Hypothesis Revisited: The Nature of Evidence in Politically 'Paranoid' Discourse," *Southern Speech Communication Journal* 42 (Spring 1977): 274–289.

———. "An Organic Systems Analysis of Persuasion and Social Movement: The John Birch Society, 1958–1966," *Southern Speech Communication Journal* 59 (Winter 1984): 155–176.

Smith, Donald H. "Social Protest . . . and the Oratory of Human Rights," *Today's Speech* 15 (September 1967): 2–8.

———. "Martin Luther King, Jr.: In the Beginning at Montgomery," *Southern Speech Journal* 34 (Fall 1968): 8–17.

Smith, Ralph R. "The Historical Criticism of Social Movements," *Central States Speech Journal* 31 (Winter 1980): 290–297.

Smith, Ralph R., and Russell Windes. "The Innovational Movement: A Rhetorical Theory," *Quarterly Journal of Speech* 61 (April 1975): 140–153.

———. "The Rhetoric of Mobilization: Implications for the Study of Movements," *Southern Speech Communication Journal* 42 (Fall 1976): 1–19.

———. "Collective Action and the Single Text," *Southern Speech Journal* 43 (Winter 1978): 110–128.

———. "Symbolic Convergence and Abolitionism: A Terministic Reinterpretation," *Southern Communication Journal* 59 (Fall 1993): 45–59.

———. "The Interpretation of Abolitionist Rhetoric: Historiography, Rhetorical Method, and History," *Southern Communication Journal* 60 (Summer 1995): 303–311.

———. "The Progay and Antigay Issue Culture: Interpretation, Influence and Dissent," *Quarterly Journal of Speech* 83 (February 1997): 28–48.

Snow, Malinda. "Martin Luther King's 'Letter from Birmingham Jail' as Pauline Epistle," *Quarterly Journal of Speech* 71 (August 1985): 318–334.

Solomon, Martha. "The Rhetoric of STOP ERA: Fatalistic Reaffirmation," *Southern Speech Communication Journal* 44 (Fall 1978): 42–59.

———. "Stopping ERA: A Pyrrhic Victory," *Communication Quarterly* 31 (Spring 983): 109–117.

———. "Ideology as Rhetorical Constraint: The Anarchist Agitation of 'Red Emma' Goldman," *Quarterly Journal of Speech* 74 (May 1988): 184–200.

———. "Autobiographies as Rhetorical Narratives: Elizabeth Cady Stanton and Anna Howard Shaw as 'New Women'," *Communication Studies* 42 (Winter 1991): 354–370.

Sproule, J. Michael. "An Emerging Rationale for Revolution: Argument from Circumstance and Definition in Polemics Against the Stamp Act, 1765-1766," *Today's Speech* 23 (Spring 1975): 17–23.

Stephens, Gregory. "Frederick Douglass' Multiracial Abolitionism: 'Antagonistic Cooperation' and 'Redeemable Ideals' in the July 5 Speech," *Communication Studies* 48 (Fall 1997): 175–194.

Stewart, Charles J. "A Functional Approach to the Rhetoric of Social Movements," *Central States Speech Journal* 31 (Winter 1980): 298–305.

———. "A Functional Perspective on the Study of Social Movements," *Central States Speech Journal* 34 (Spring 1983): 77–80.

———. "The Internal Rhetoric of the Knights of Labor," *Communication Studies* 42 (Spring 1991): 67–82.

———. "The Ego Function of Protest Songs: An Application of Gregg's Theory of Protest Rhetoric," *Communication Studies* 42 (Fall 1991): 240–253.

———. "The Evolution of a Revolution: Stokely Carmichael and the Rhetoric of Black Power," *Quarterly Journal of Speech* 83 (November 1997): 429–446.

———. "Championing the Rights of Others and Challenging Evil: The Ego Function in the Rhetoric of Other-Directed Social Movements," *Southern Communication Journal* 64 (Winter 1999): 91–105.

Stitzel, James A. "Inflammatory Speaking in the Victor, Colorado, Mass Meeting, June 6, 1904," *Western Speech* 32 (Winter 1968): 11–18.

Strother, David B. "Polemics and the Reversal of the 'Separate but Equal' Doctrine," *Quarterly Journal of Speech* 49 (February 1963): 50–56.

Tedesco, John L. "The White Character in Black Drama, 1955-1970: Description and Rhetorical Function," *Communication Monographs* 45 (March 1978): 64–74.

Terrill, Robert E. "Colonizing the Borderlands: Shifting Circumference in the Rhetoric of Malcolm X," *Quarterly Journal of Speech* 86 (February 2000): 67–85.

Thomas, Cheryl Irwin. "'Look What They've Done to My Song, Ma': The Persuasiveness of Song," *Southern Speech Communication Journal* 39 (Spring 1974): 260–268.

Thomas, Gordon L. "John Brown's Courtroom Speech," *Quarterly Journal of Speech* 48 (October 1962): 291–296.

Thurber, John H., and John L. Petelle. "The Negro Pulpit and Civil Rights," *Central States Speech Journal* 19 (Winter 1968): 273–278.

Tonn, Marie Boor. "Militant Motherhood: Labor's Mary Harris 'Mother' Jones," *Quarterly Journal of Speech* 82 (February 1996): 1–21.

———. "Donning Sackcloth and Ashes: *Webster v. Productive Health Services* and Moral Agony in Abortion Rights Rhetoric," *Communication Quarterly* 44 (Summer 1996): 265–279.

Veenstra, Charles. "The House Un-American Activities Committee's Restriction of Free Speech," *Today's Speech* 22 (Winter 1974): 15–22.

Vonnegut, Kristin S. "Poison or Panacea?" Sarah Moore Grimke's Use of the Public Letter," *Communication Studies* 46 (Spring 1995): 73–88.

Wagner, Gerard A. "Sojourner Truth: God's Appointed Apostle of Reform," *Southern Speech Journal* 28 (Winter 1962): 123–130.

James F. Walsh, Jr. "An Approach to Dyadic Communication in Historical Social Movements: Dyadic Communication in Maoist Insurgent Mobilization," *Communication Monographs* 53 (March 1986): 1–15.

———. "An Approach to Group Communication in Historical Social Movements: Group Communication in Maoist Insurgent Mobilization," *Southern Speech Communication Journal* 51 (Spring 1986): 229–255.

———. "Paying Attention to Channels: Differential Images of Recruitment in Students for a Democratic Society, 1960–1965," *Communication Studies* 44 (Spring 1993): 71–86.

Wander, Philip C. "Salvation Through Separation: The Image of the Negro in the American Colonization Society," *Quarterly Journal of Speech* 57 (February 1971): 57–67.

———. "The John Birch and Martin Luther King Symbols in the Radical Right," *Western Speech* 35 (Winter 1971): 4–14.

———. "The Savage Child: The Image of the Negro in the Pro-Slavery Movement," *Southern Speech Communication Journal* 37 (Summer 1972): 335–360.

Ware, B. L., and Wil A. Linkugel. "The Rhetorical *Persona*: Marcus Garvey as Black Moses," *Communication Monographs* 49 (March 1982): 50–62.

Warnick, Barbara. "The Rhetoric of Conservative Resistance," *Southern Speech Communication Journal* 42 (Spring 1977): 256–273.

———. "Conservative Resistance Revisited," *Western Journal of Speech Communication* 46 (Fall 1982): 373–378.

Weatherly, Michael. "Propaganda and the Rhetoric of the American Revolution," *Southern Speech Journal* 36 (Summer 1971): 352–363.

Weaver, Richard L., II. "The Negro Issue: Agitation in the Michigan Lyceum," *Central States Speech Journal* 22 (Fall 1971): 196–201.

Weisman, Martha. "Ambivalence Toward War in Anti-War Plays," *Today's Speech* 17 (September 1969): 9–14.

Weithoff, William E. "Rhetorical Strategy in the Birmingham Political Union, 1830–1832," *Central States Speech Journal* 29 (Spring 1978): 53–60.

Weitzel, Al. "King's 'I Have a Dream' Speech: A Case Study of Incorporating Orality in Rhetorical Criticism," *Communication Reports* 7 (Winter 1994): 50–56.

Whitfield, George. "Frederick Douglass: Negro Abolitionist," *Today's Speech* 11 (February 1963): 6–8, 24.

Wilkie, Richard W. "The Self-Taught Agitator: Hitler 1907–1920," *Quarterly Journal of Speech* 52 (December 1966): 371–377.

———. "The Marxian Rhetoric of Angelica Balabanoff," *Quarterly Journal of Speech* 60 (December 1974): 450–458.

Wilkinson, Charles A. "A Rhetorical Definition of Movements," *Central States Speech Journal* 27 (Summer 1976): 88–94.

Williams, David E. "The Drive for Prohibition: A Transition from Social Reform to Legislative Reform," *Southern Communication Journal* 61 (Spring 1996): 185–197.

Williams, Donald E. "Protest Under the Cross: The Ku Klux Klan Presents Its Case to the People," *Southern Speech Journal* 27 (Fall 1961): 43–55.

Wilson, Kirt H. "The Contested Space of Prudence in the 1874-1875 Civil Rights Debate," *Quarterly Journal of Speech* 84 (May 1998): 131–149.

Windt, Theodore O. "The Diatribe: Last Resort for Protest," *Quarterly Journal of Speech* 58 (February 1972): 1–14.

———. "Administrative Rhetoric: An Undemocratic Response to Protest," *Communication Quarterly* 30 (Summer 1982): 245–250.

Woodward, Gary C. "Mystifications in the Rhetoric of Cultural Dominance and Colonial Control," *Central States Speech Journal* 26 (Winter 1975): 298–303.

Wurthman, Leonard B. "The Militant-Moderate Agitator: Daniel O'Connell and Catholic Emancipation in Ireland," *Communication Quarterly* 30 (Summer 1982): 225–231.

Yoder, Jess. "The Protest of the American Clergy in Opposition to the War in Vietnam," *Today's Speech* 17 (September 1969): 51–59.

———. "Communication Between Catholics and Protestants in Northern Ireland," *Religious Communication Today* 4 (September 1981): 15–20.

Zacharis, John C. "Emmeline Pankhurst: An English Suffragette Influences America," *Speech Monographs* 38 (August 1971): 198–206.

Zaeske, Susan. "The 'Promiscuous Audience' Controversy and the Emergence of the Early Woman's Rights Movement," *Quarterly Journal of Speech* 81 (May 1995): 191–207.

Zarefsky, David. "President Johnson's War on Poverty: The Rhetoric of Three 'Establishment' Movements," *Communication Monographs* 44 (November 1977), 352–373.

———. "A Skeptical View of Movement Studies," *Central States Speech Journal* 31 (Winter 1980): 245–254.

Book Chapters

Griffin, Leland M. "The Rhetorical Structure of the Antimasonic Movement," *The Rhetorical Idiom*, Donald Bryant, ed. Ithaca, NY: Cornell University Press, 1958.

———. "A Dramatistic Theory of the Rhetoric of Movements," *Critical Responses to Kenneth Burke*, William Rueckert, ed. Minneapolis: University of Minnesota Press, 1969.

Gronbeck, Bruce E. "The Rhetoric of Social-Institutional Change: Black Action at Michigan," *Explorations in Rhetorical Criticism*, Gerald Mohrmann, Charles Stewart, and Donovan Ochs, eds. University Park, PA: Pennsylvania State University Press, 1973.

Leathers, Dale G. "Belief-Disbelief Systems: The Communicative Vacuum of the Radical Right," *Explorations in Rhetorical Criticism*, Gerald Mohrmann, Charles Stewart, Donovan Ochs, eds. University Park, PA: Pennsylvania State University Press, 1973.

Nimmo, Dan, and James E. Combs. "Devils and Demons: The Group Mediation of Conspiracy," *Mediated Political Realities*. New York: Longman, 1983.

Simons, Herbert W., and Elizabeth W. Mechling. "The Rhetoric of Political Movements," *Handbook of Political Communication*, Dan Nimmo and Keith Sanders, eds. Beverly Hills, CA: Sage, 1981.

Simons, Herbert W., Elizabeth Mechling, and Howard Schreier. "Functions of Communication in Mobilizing for Action from the Bottom Up: The Rhetoric of Social Movements, Handbook on Rhetorical and Communication Theory, Carroll C. Arnold and John W. Bowers, eds. Boston: Allyn and Bacon, 1984.

Stewart, Charles J. "Labor Agitation in America: 1865–1915," *America in Controversy: History of American Public Address*, DeWitte T. Holland, ed. Dubuque, IA: Brown, 1973.

Van Graber, Marilyn. "Functional Criticism: A Rhetoric of Black Power," *Explorations in Rhetorical Criticism*, Gerald Mohrmann, Charles Stewart, and Donovan Ochs, eds. University Park, PA: Pennsylvania State University Press, 1973.

Books

Albert, Judith, and Stewart Albert. *The Sixties Papers: Documents of a Rebellious Decade*. New York: Praeger, 1984.

Alinsky, Saul D. *Rules for Radicals: A Practical Primer for Realistic Radicals*. New York: Vintage, 1972.

Anderson, Wait, ed. *The Age of Protest*. Pacific Palisades, CA: Goodyear Publishing, 1969.

Andrain, Charles F., and David E. Apter. *Political Protest and Social Change: Analyzing Politics*. New York: New York University Press, 1996.

Armstrong, Gregory. *Protest: Man Against Society*. New York: Bantam Books, 1969.

Auer, J. Jeffrey, ed. *Antislavery and Disunion: 1858–1861*. New York: Harper and Row, 1963.

———. *The Rhetoric of Our Times*. New York: Appleton-Century-Crofts, 1969.

Barbrook, Alee, and Christine Bolt. *Power and Protest in American Life*. New York: St. Martin's Press, 1980.

Barkan, Steven E. *Protestors on Trial: Criminal Justice in the Southern Civil Rights and Vietnam Antiwar Movements*. New Brunswick, NJ: Rutgers University Press, 1986.

Blaustein, Albert P., and Robert Zangrando, eds. *Civil Rights and the American Negro*. New York: Trident Press, 1968.

Blee, Kathleen M., ed. *No Middle Ground: Women and Radical Protest*. New York: New York University Press, 1998.

Blocker, Jack S. *"Give to the Minds Thy Fears": The Women's Christian Temperance Crusade: 1873–1874*. Westport, CT: 1985.

Boase, Paul H. *The Rhetoric of Christian Socialism*. New York: Random House, 1969.

———., ed. *The Rhetoric of Protest and Reform: 1878–1898*. Athens, OH: Ohio University Press, 1980.

Bormann, Ernest G. *Forerunners of Black Power: The Rhetoric of Abolition*. Englewood Cliffs, NJ: Prentice-Hall, 1971.

Bosmajian, Haig A., ed. *Dissent: Symbolic Behavior and Rhetorical Strategies*. Boston: Allyn and Bacon, 1972.

Bosmajian, Haig A., and Hamida Bosmajian. *The Rhetoric of the Civil Rights Movement*. New York: Random House, 1969.

Bowers, John W., Donovan J. Ochs, and Richard J. Jensen. *The Rhetoric of Agitation and Control*. Prospect Heights, IL: Waveland Press, 1993.

Branch, Taylor. *Parting the Waters: America in the King Years*. New York: Simon and Schuster, 1988.

Brandes, Paul D. *The Rhetoric of Revolt*. Englewood Cliffs, NJ: Prentice-Hall, 1971.

Breitman, George. *Malcolm X Speaks*. New York: Grove, 1966

Brinkley, Alan. *Voices of Protest: Huey Long, Father Coughlin, and the Great Depression*. New York: Random House, 1983.

Brockriede, Wayne C., and Robert L. Scott. *Moments in the Rhetoric of the Cold War*. New York: Random House, 1970.

Brooks, Thomas R. *Walls Came Tumbling Down: A History of the Civil Rights Movement*. Englewood Cliffs, NJ: Prentice-Hall, 1974.

Browne, Stephen H. *Angelina Grimke: Rhetoric, Identity, and the Radical Imagination*. East Lansing, MI: Michigan State University Press, 1999.

Burns, W. Haywood. *The Voices of Negro Protest in America*. New York: Oxford Press, 1963.

Bytwerk, Randall L. *Julius Streicher: The Man Who Persuaded a Nation to Hate Jews*. Briarcliff Manor, NY: Stein and Day, 1982.

Cable, Sherry, and Charles Cable. *Environmental Problems, Grassroots Solutions: The Politics of Grassroots Environmental Conflict*. New York: St. Martin's Press, 1995.

Campbell, Karlyn Kohrs. *Critiques of Contemporary Rhetoric*. Belmont, CA: Wadsworth, 1972.

———. *Man Cannot Speak for Her: A Critical Study of Early Feminist Rhetoric*. New York: Greenwood Press, 1989.

Carawan, Guy, and Candie Carawan. *We Shall Overcome*. New York: Oak, 1963.

Carmichael, Stokely, and Charles V. Hamilton. *Black Power: The Politics of Liberation in America*. New York: Random House, 1967.

Carpenter, Ronald H. *Father Charles E. Coughlin: Surrogate Spokesman for the Disaffected*. Westport, CT: Greenwood, 1998.

Chatfield, Charles. *American Peace Movement: Ideal and Activism*. New York: Twayne, 1992.

Chesebro, James W., ed. *Gayspeak: Gay Male and Lesbian Communication*. New York: Pilgrim Press, 1981.

Chesebrough, David B. *Frederick Douglass: Oratory from Slavery*. Westport, CT: Greenwood, 1998.

Clabaugh, Gary. *Thunder on the Right*. Chicago: Nelson-Hall, 1980.

Cleaver, Eldridge. *Soul on Ice*. New York: Dell, 1968.

———. *Post-Prison Writings and Speeches*, Robert Scheer, ed. New York: Random House, 1969.

———. *Soul on Fire*. Waco, TX: World Books, 1978.

Coleman, William E., Jr., and William E. Coleman, Sr. *A Rhetoric of the People: The German Greens and the New Politics*. Westport, CT: Greenwood Press, 1993.

Condit, Celeste Michelle. *Decoding Abortion Rhetoric: Communicating Social Change*. Urbana: University of Illinois Press, 1990.

Crawford, Alan. *Thunder on the Right*. New York: Pantheon, 1980.

Darsey, James. *The Prophetic Tradition and Radical Rhetoric in America*. New York: New York University Press 1997.

Davis, Flora. *Moving the Mountain: The Women's Movement in America Since 1960*. New York: Simon and Schuster, 1991.

DeFrancisco, Victoria L. ed. *Women's Voices in Our Times: Statements by American Leaders*. Prospect Heights, IL: Waveland Press, 1994.

Denisoff, R. Serge. *Great Day Coming: Folk Music and the American Left*. Urbana: University of Illinois Press, 1972.

———. *Sing a Song of Social Significance*. Bowling Green, OH: Bowling Green University Popular Press, 1972.

Denisoff, R., and Richard A. Peterson. *The Sounds of Social Change*. Chicago: Rand McNally, 1972.

Dixon-Mueller, Ruth. *Population Policy and Women's Rights: Transforming Reproductive Choice*. Westport, CT: Greenwood Press, 1993.

Dow, Bonnie J. *Prime-Time Feminism: Television, Media, Culture, and the Women's Movement Since 1970*. Philadelphia: University of Pennsylvania Press, 1996.

Duffy, Bernard K., and Halford Ryan, eds. *American Orators Before 1900: Critical Studies and Sources*. Westport, CT: Greenwood Press, 1987.

———, eds. *American Orators of the Twentieth Century: Critical Studies and Sources*. Westport, CT: Greenwood Press, 1987.

Dunne, John Gregory. *Delano: The Story of the California Grape Strike*. New York: Farrar, Straus, and Giroux, 1967.

Edelman, Murray. *Politics as Symbolic Action: Mass Arousal and Quiescence*. San Diego, CA: Academic Press, 1971.

------. *The Symbolic Uses of Politics*. Urbana: University of Illinois Press, 1985.

------. *Constructing the Political Spectacle*. Chicago: University of Chicago Press, 1988.

Fabrizio, Ray, Edith Karas, and Ruth Menmuir. *The Rhetoric of NO*. New York: Holt, Rinehart, and Winston, 1970.

Fairclough, Adam. *To Redeem the Soul of America: The Southern Christian Leadership Conference and Martin Luther King, Jr.* Athens: University of Georgia Press, 1987.

Ferriss, Susan, and Ricardo Sandoval. *The Fight in the Fields: Cesar Chavez and the Farmworkers Movement*. New York: Harcourt Brace, 1997.

Feuer, Lewis S. *The Conflict of Generations: The Character and Significance of Student Movements*. New York: Basic Books, 1969.

Fisher, Randall M. *Rhetoric and American Democracy: Black Protest Through Vietnam Dissent*. Lanham, MD: University Press of America, 1985.

Foner, Philip S. *American Labor Songs of the Nineteenth Century*. Urbana: University of Illinois Press, 1975.

Fortas, Abe. *Concerning Dissent and Civil Disobedience*. New York: American Library, 1968.

Gallen, David., ed. *Malcolm X Reader*. New York: Carroll & Graf, 1994.

Gamson, William A. *Power and Discontent*. Homewood, IL: Dorsey Press, 1969.

------. *The Strategy of Social Protest*. Homewood, IL: Dorsey Press, 1975.

Glazer, Tom. *Songs of Peace, Freedom and Protest*. Philadelphia: University of Pennsylvania Press, 1953.

Goldsmith, Barbara. *Other Powers: The Age of Suffragism, Spiritualism, and the Scandalous Victoria Woodhull*. New York: Knopf, 1998.

Gusfield, Joseph R., ed. *Protest, Reform, and Revolt: A Reader in Social Movements*. New York: John Wiley, 1970.

Haiman, Franklyn S. *Freedom of Speech: Issues and Cases*. New York: Random House, 1965.

Hamilton, Neil A. *Militias in America: A Reference Handbook*. Santa Barbara: ABC-CLIO, 1996.

Hammerback, John C., R. J. Jensen, and J. A. Gutierrez. *A War of Words: Protest in the 1960s and 1970s*. Westport, CT: Greenwood, 1985.

Hammerback, John, and Richard J. Jensen. *The Rhetorical Career of Cesar Chavez*. College Station, TX: Texas A & M University Press, 1998.

Hampton, Wayne. *Guerrilla Minstrels: John Lennon, Joe Hill, Woody Guthrie, and Bob Dylan*. Knoxville, TN: University of Tennessee Press, 1986.

Harre, Rom, Jens Brockmeier, and Peter Muhlhausler. *Greenspeak: A Study of Environmental Discourse*. Thousand Oaks, CA: Sage, 1998.

Herman, Didi. *Antigay Agenda: Orthodox Vision and the Christian Right*. Chicago: University of Chicago Press, 1997.

Heyman, Steven, ed. *Hate Speech and the Constitution*. New York: Garland, 1996.

Hill, Roy L. *The Rhetoric of Radical Revolt*. Denver: Bell Press, 1964.

Hille, Waldemar. *The People's Song Book*. New York: Sing Out, 1960.

Hoffer, Eric. *The True Believer*. New York: Mentor, 1951.

Hoffman, Abbie. *Revolution for the Hell of It*. New York: Dial, 1968.

Holland, DeWitte T., ed. *Preaching in American History*. Nashville, TN: Abingdon Press, 1969.

------. *America In Controversy: A History of American Public Address*. Dubuque, IA: Brown, 1973.

Hribar, Paul A. *The Social Fasts of Cesar Chavez: Critical Study of Nonverbal Communication, Nonviolence, and Public Opinion*. Los Angeles: University of Southern California, 1978.

Huey, Gary. *Rebel with a Cause: P.D. East, Southern Liberalism, and the Civil Rights Movement, 1953–1972*. Wilmington, DL: Scholarly Resources, 1985.

Huls, Mary Ellen. *United States Government Documents on Women, 1800-1900*. Westport, CT: Greenwood Press, 1993.

Jacobs, Donald Trent. *Bum's Rush: The Selling of Environmental Backlash: Phrases and Fallacies of Rush Limbaugh*. Boise, ID: Legendary Publications, 1994.

Jaggar, Alison, and Paula Rothenberg. *Feminist Frameworks*. New York: McGraw Hill, 1984.

Jay, Karla and Allen Young, eds. *Out of the Closet: Voices of Gay Liberation*. New York: Douglas/Links, 1972.

Jameson, J. Franklin. *The American Revolution Considered as a Social Movement*. Boston: Beacon, 1956.

Jeansonne, Glen. *Women of the Far Right: The Mothers' Movement and World War II*. Chicago: University of Chicago Press, 1996.

Jeffreys-Jones, Rhodri. *Violence and Reform in American History*. New York: New Viewpoints, 1978.

Johnston, Kenneth R. *Rhetoric of Conflict*. New York: Bobbs-Merrill, 1969.

Jorgensen-Earp, Cheryl R. *"The Transfiguring Sword": The Just War of the Women's Social and Political Union*. Tuscaloosa, AL: University of Alabama Press, 1997.

Katope, Christopher George, and Paul Zolbrod. *The Rhetoric of Revolution*. New York: Macmillan, 1970.

Kriesi, Hanspeter, Ruud Koopmans, Jan Willem Duyvendak, and Marco G. Giugni. *New Social Movements in Western Europe: A Comparative Analysis*. Minneapolis: University of Minnesota Press, 1995.

Lampe, Gregory P. *Frederick Douglass: Freedom's Voice, 1818–1845*. East Lansing, MI: Michigan State University Press, 1998.

Lamy, Philip. *Millennium Rage: Survivalists, White Supremacists, and the Doomsday Prophecy*. New York: Plenum Press, 1996.

Leeman, Richard W. *The Rhetoric of Terrorism and Counterterrorism*. Westport, CT: Greenwood Press, 1991.

———, (ed). *African-American Orators: A Bio-Critical Sourcebook*. Westport, CT: Greenwood, 1996.

Linkugel, Wil A., and Martha Solomon. *Anna Howard Shaw: Suffrage Orator and Social Reformer*. Westport, CT: Greenwood Press, 1991.

Lipset, Seymour, and Sheldon S. Wolin, eds. *The Berkeley Student Revolt: Facts and Interpretations*. Garden City, NY: Anchor Books, 1965.

Lomas, Charles W. *The Agitator in American Society*. Englewood Cliffs, NJ: Prentice-Hall, 1968.

Malcolm X. *The Autobiography of Malcolm X*. New York: Grove, 1966.

———. *The Movement 1964–1970*. Westport, CT: Greenwood Press, 1993.

Marable, Manning. *Black American Politics from the Washington Marches to Jesse Jackson*. London: Verso, 1985.

Marcus, Eric. *Making History: The Struggle for Gay and Lesbian Rights, 1945-1990: An Oral History*. New York: Harper Collins, 1992.

Marilley, Suzanne M. *Woman Suffrage and the Origins of Liberal Feminism in the United States, 1820–1920*. Cambridge, MA: Harvard University Press, 1996.

Maybee, Carleton. *Sojourner Truth—Slave, Prophet, Legend*. New York: New York Union Press, 1993.

Meier, August, Elliot Rudwick, and Francis L. Broderick, eds. *Black Protest Thought in the Twentieth Century*. Indianapolis: Bobbs-Merrill, 1971.

Michener, James. *Kent State: What Happened and Why*. New York: Random House, 1971.

Miller, Gerald R., and Herbert W. Simons, eds. *Perspectives on Communication in Social Conflicts*. Englewood Cliffs, NJ: Prentice-Hall, 1974.

Miller, James. *"Democracy Is in the Streets": From Port Huron to the Siege of Chicago*. New York: Simon and Schuster, 1987.

Mills, Nicolaus. *Like a Holy Crusade: Mississippi, The Turning of the Civil Rights Movement in America*. Chicago: I. R. Dee, 1992.

Morris, Aldon D., and Carol McClurg Mueller, eds. *Frontiers in Social Movement Theory*. New Haven, CT: Yale University Press, 1992.

Moses, Greg. *Revolution of Conscience: Martin Luther King, Jr., and the Philosophy of Nonviolence*. New York: Guildford, 1997.

Neuzil, Mark, and William Kovarik. *Mass Media and Environmental Conflict*. Thousand Oaks, CA: Sage, 1996.

Oberschall, Anthony. *Social Conflicts and Social Movements*. Englewood Cliffs, NJ: Prentice-Hall 1973.

Olasky, Marvin. *The Press and Abortion, 1838–1988*. Hillsdale, NJ: Lawrence Erlbaum, 1988.

Payne, Gregory. *Mayday: Kent State*. Dubuque, IA: Kendall/Hunt, 1981.

Pearce, W. Barnett, and Stephen W. Littlejohn. *Moral Conflict: When Social Worlds Collide*. Thousand Oaks, CA: Sage, 1997.

Phillips, Donald E. *Student Protest, 1960–1970: An Analysis the Speeches and Issue*. Lanham, MD: University Press of America, 1985.

Powledge, Fred. *Free at Last? The Civil Rights Movement and the People Who Made It*. Boston: Little, Brown and Company, 1991.

Price, Jerome B. *The Antinuclear Movement*. Boston: Twayne, 1982.

Raboy, Marc. *Movements and Messages: Media and Radical Politics in Quebec*. David Homel, ed. Bridgewater, NJ: Baker and Taylor, 1984.

Rice, Donald E. *The Rhetorical Uses of the Authorizing Figure: Fidel Castro and Jose Marti*. Westport, CT: Praeger, 1992.

Rinzer, Alan. *Manifesto: Addressed to the President of the United States from the Youth of America*. New York: Collier Books, 1970.

Rochon, Thomas R., and David S. Meyer, eds. *Coalition and Political Movements: The Lessons of the Nuclear Freeze*. Boulder, CO: Lynne Rienner Publishers, 1997.

Rosen, David M. *Protest Songs in America*. Westlake Village, CA: Aware Press, 1972.

Rudy, Kathy. *Beyond Pro-Life and Pro-Choice: Moral Diversity in the Abortion Debate*. Boston: Beacon Press, 1996.

Ryan, Barbara. *Women's Movement: References and Resources*. New York: G. K. Hall, 1996.

Sale, Kirkpatrick. *SDS*. New York: Vintage, 1974.

Salisbury, Harrison E. *The Eloquence of Protest: Voices of the 70s*. Boston: Houghton Mifflin, 1972.

Schaeffer, Robert K. *Power to the People: Democratization Around the World*. Boulder, CO: Westview Press, 1997.

Schmid, Alex, and Janny de Graaf. *Violence as Communication: Insurgent Terrorism and the Western News*. Beverly Hills: Sage, 1982.

..

Scott, Robert L., and Wayne E. Brockriede. *The Rhetoric of Black Power.* New York: Harper and Row, 1969.

Seeger, Pete. *American Favorite Ballads.* New York: Oak Publications, 1961.

Sherry, Clifford J. *Animal Rights: A Reference Handbook.* Santa Barbara: ABC-CLIO, 1994.

Shupe, Anson D., and David G. Bromley. *The New Vigilantes: Deprogrammers, Anti-Cultists, and the New Religions.* Beverly Hills, CA: Sage, 1980.

Smith, Arthur L. *Rhetoric of Black Revolution.* Boston: Allyn and Bacon, 1969.

———. *Language, Communication, and Rhetoric in Black America.* New York: Harper and Row, 1972.

Smith, Arthur L., and Stephen Robb. *The Voice of Black Rhetoric.* Boston: Allyn and Bacon, 1971.

Smith, Ralph R., and Russell R. Windes. *Progay/Antigay: The Rhetorical War over Sexuality.* Thousand Oaks, CA: Sage Publications, 2000.

Smith, Robert C. *We Have No Leaders: African Americans in the Post-Civil Rights Era.* Albany, NY: State University of New York Press, 1996.

Stern, Robert N., and Daniel B. Cornfield. *U.S. Labor Movement: References and Resources.* New York: G. K. Hall, 1996.

Stohl, Michael, ed. *The Politics of Terrorism.* New York: Dekker, 1983.

Stohl, Michael, and George Lopez, eds. *The State as Terrorist: The Dynamics of Governmental Violence and Repression.* Westport, CT: Greenwood, 1984.

Taylor, Michael, and Charles Lomas. *The Rhetoric of the British Peace Movement.* New York: Random House, 1976.

Terborg-Penn, Rosalyn. *African American Women in the Struggle for the Vote, 1850–1920.* Bloomington, IN: Indiana University Press, 1998.

Tilly, Charles. *Popular Contention in Great Britain, 1758–1834.* Cambridge, MA: Harvard University Press, 1995.

Tobias, Sheila. *Faces of Feminism: An Activist's Reflections on the Women's Movement.* Boulder, CO: Westview Press, 1997.

Touraine, Alain. *The Voice and the Eye: An Analysis of Social Movements,* Alan Duff, trans. Cambridge: Cambridge University Press, 1981.

Towns, W. Stuart. *Oratory and Rhetoric in the Nineteenth-Century South: A Rhetoric of Defense.* Westport, CT: Greenwood, 1998.

———. *Public Address in the Twentieth Century South: The Evolution of a Region.* Westport, CT: Greenwood, 1999.

Turner, Kathleen J. *Lyndon Johnson's Dual War: Vietnam and the Press.* Chicago: University of Chicago Press, 1985.

Turner, Victor. *The Ritual Process.* Chicago: Aldine, 1969.

———. *Dramas, Fields, and Metaphors.* Ithaca, NY: Cornell University Press, 1974.

Viorst, Milton. *Fire in the Streets: America in the 1960s.* New York: Simon and Schuster, 1979.

Waddell, Carid, ed. *Landmark Essays on Rhetoric and the Environment.* Mahwah, NJ: Lawrence Erlbaum, 1997.

Walker, Daniel. *Rights in Conflict: The Walker Report to the National Commission on the Causes and Prevention of Violence.* New York: Bantam, 1968.

Waller, Douglas. *Congress and the Nuclear Freeze: An Inside Look at the Politics of a Mass Movement.* Amherst, MA: University of Massachusetts Press, 1987.

Wardlaw, Grant. *Political Terrorism.* Cambridge: Cambridge University Press, 1982.

Waskow, Arthur. *From Race Riot to Sit-In.* Garden City, NY: Doubleday, 1966.

Watters, Pat. *Down to Now: Reflections on the Southern Civil Rights Movement.* New York: Pantheon Books, 1971.

Westin, Alan. *Freedom Now.* New York: Basic Books, 1964.

Weston, Mary Ann. *Native Americans in the News: Images of Indians in the Twentieth Century Press.* Westport, CT: Greenwood, 1996.

Wheeler, Marjorie Spruill, ed. *One Woman, One Vote: Rediscovering the Woman Suffrage Movement.* Troutdale, OR: New Sage Press, 1995.

Whillock, Rita Kirk, and David Slayden, eds. *Hate Speech.* Thousand Oaks, CA: Sage, 1995.

White, James W. *Ikki: Social Conflict and Political Protest in Early Modern Japan.* Ithaca NY: Cornell University Press, 1995.

Windt, Theodore Otto. *Presidents and Protestors: Political Rhetoric in the 1960s.* Tuscaloosa: University of Alabama Press, 1990.

Witt, Stephanie L., and Suzanne McCorkle, eds. *Anti-Gay Rights: Assessing Voter Initiatives.* Westport, CT: Greenwood, 1997.

Zaretsky, Irving I., and Mark P. Leone, eds. *Religious Movements in Contemporary America.* Princeton, NJ: Princeton University Press, 1974.

Zingo, Martha T. *Hate Speech, and Freedom of Expression.* Westport, CT: Greenwood, 1998.

INDEX